GEOGRAPHY AND HISTORY

Bridging the Divide

Geography and History is the first book for over a century to examine comprehensively the interdependence of the two disciplines. Alan Baker, an internationally honoured historical geographer, focuses upon the work of North American, British and French historians and geographers but takes a global and interdisciplinary perspective upon the theory and practice of historical geography and geographical history. He analyses the views of historians on the relationship of their discipline to geography, and of geographers on the relationship of theirs to history. He considers in turn locational geographies and spatial histories, environmental geographies and histories, landscape geographies and histories, and regional geographies and histories. Seeking to bridge the 'Great Divide' between history and geography, Dr Baker identifies some basic principles relating historical geography not only to history but also to geography, a reworking which signifies a 'new beginning' for this scholarly hybrid.

ALAN BAKER is an internationally renowned historical geographer who in 1998 was honoured by France as a *Chevalier dans l'Ordre des Palmes Académiques* for his contribution to the field.

Cambridge Studies in Historical Geography 36

Series editors
ALAN R. H. BAKER, RICHARD DENNIS, DERYCK HOLDSWORTH

Cambridge Studies in Historical Geography encourages exploration of the philosophies, methodologies and techniques of historical geography and publishes the results of new research within all branches of the subject. It endeavours to secure the marriage of traditional scholarship with innovative approaches to problems and to sources, aiming in this way to provide a focus for the discipline and to contribute towards its development. The series is an international forum for publication in historical geography which also promotes contact with workers in cognate disciplines.

For a full list of titles in the series, please see end of book.

GEOGRAPHY AND HISTORY

Bridging the Divide

ALAN R. H. BAKER
Emmanuel College, Cambridge

CAMBRIDGE
UNIVERSITY PRESS

PUBLISHED BY THE PRESS SYNDICATE OF THE UNIVERSITY OF CAMBRIDGE
The Pitt Building, Trumpington Street, Cambridge, United Kingdom

CAMBRIDGE UNIVERSITY PRESS
The Edinburgh Building, Cambridge, CB2 2RU, UK
40 West 20th Street, New York, NY 10011–4211, USA
477 Williamstown Road, Port Melbourne, VIC 3207, Australia
Ruiz de Alarcón 13, 28014 Madrid, Spain
Dock House, The Waterfront, Cape Town 8001, South Africa

http://www.cambridge.org

First published 2003

Printed in the United Kingdom at the University Press, Cambridge

Typeface Times 10/12 pt.   *System* LATEX 2$_\varepsilon$ [TB]

A catalogue record for this book is available from the British Library

Library of Congress Cataloguing in Publication data
Baker, Alan R. H.
Geography and history : bridging the divide / Alan R. H. Baker.
   p.   cm. – (Cambridge studies in historical geography ; 36)
Includes bibliographical references and index.
ISBN 0 521 24683 0 – ISBN 0 521 28885 1 (pbk.)
1. Historical geography.   I. Title.   II. Series.

G141.B29   2003
911 – dc21   2003046037

ISBN 0 521 24683 0 hardback
ISBN 0 521 28885 1 paperback

'Dwellers all in time and space'
Praise my soul, the King of Heaven   H. F. Lyte (1793–1847)

For Sandra, Jeremy, Andrew, Bethan, Jack and Sarah

Contents

Figures

Preface

More than a century ago, H. B. George wrote a book addressing *The Relations of Geography and History* (Oxford 1901). He was writing as a historian working with the basic premise, stated in his opening sentence, that 'history is not intelligible without geography'. I start as a geographer from the complementary premise that geography is not intelligible without history. My aim in this book is to explore the interdependence of geography and history, doing so as a geographer. Although much has been written on the relations of geography and history since 1901, there has not been another book-length treatment of the topic in English. Lucien Febvre's *La terre et l'évolution humaine: introduction géographique à l'histoire* (1922), translated as *A Geographical Introduction to History* (1925), came close to being so. A more recent approximation, the posthumous editing of some lectures by H. C. Darby, published almost forty years after they were written, is more concerned with the nature of historical geography than with 'the relations of history and geography', despite using the latter theme as the book's title (Darby 2002). The absence of a successor to George's book may be because its topic is so vast, but it may also be because its theme has been so contentious, with the persistence of what one place-sensitive historian has described as 'the Great Divide' between history and geography (Marshall 1985: 22). My book explores the nature of that divide and ways of bridging it.

I am writing mainly for a senior undergraduate and graduate student audience, both in history and in geography. The base from which I conduct these historiographical forays is my own doctoral research on the agricultural and settlement geography of medieval England and my later work on the social geography of rural France during the nineteenth century. Underpinning those substantive research projects has been a deepening curiosity about the theory and practice of both geography and history, coupled with a growing awareness of the diversity of the practice of historical geography both from time to time and from place to place. I have attempted to make sense of this heterogeneity while joyfully celebrating the different perspectives and practices of geography and history.

This book is not a manual of historical geography: it is not an instruction book for those wishing to become one of its practitioners. Nor is it a kind of Michelin Guide to historical geography: it is not my intention to list and appraise all, or even any, of the specific problems and sources, methods and techniques, in the realm of historical geography. My more general objective is to survey the historiography of the relations of geography and history, and to explore the territories of historical geography and geographical history. My dual aim is to deepen the historical awareness of geographers and to widen the geographical consciousness of historians. I am not seeking primarily either to reflect current trends in historical geography or to set an agenda for its future development, although both of these issues will be touched upon. Research interests wax and wane, but my concern is to identify some of the basic continuities of historical geography and of the relations between geography and history.

The idea of writing this book originated some years ago. Its completion has been my academic priority since retiring from my lectureship at Cambridge. I have benefited from discussions on its theme with many colleagues throughout the world over many years. H. C. Darby initially awakened my interest in the methodology of historical geography when I was a student at University College London and I owe Clifford an enormous debt. My own ideas developed independently, however, while I was fortunate enough to be a colleague of his at Cambridge and I began to question some of his views, much to his thinly disguised disapproval for he did not bear criticism lightly. None the less, Clifford remained the basic inspiration for my interest in the methodology of historical geography. As Friedrich Nietzsche observed in his *Also sprach Zarathustra* (1883), 'one repays a teacher badly if one remains only a pupil'.

Other colleagues have shared readily my enthusiasm for debate. I am especially grateful to Hugh Prince, who has been willing to engage in argument with me ever since he was my tutor and then colleague at University College London. I am also heavily indebted to many colleagues in historical geography at Cambridge who over many years have participated in lively discussions with me about the natures of geography and history. They have included Tim Bayliss-Smith, Mark Billinge, Jim Duncan, Harold Fox, Robin Glasscock, Derek Gregory, Philip Howell, Gerry Kearns, Jack Langton, Ron Martin, Jean Mitchell, John Patten, Clifford Smith, Richard Smith and Tony Wrigley. In addition, I have learned a great deal from my graduate students, especially from those who have subsequently become distinguished historical geographers or geographical historians: Michael Barkham, Sarah Bendall, Iain Black, Laura Cameron, Bruce Campbell, Mark Cleary, Michael Heffernan and Mark Overton.

As my interest in the methodology of historical geography deepened, so I developed productive contacts with a widening band of its practitioners. Members of the Historical Geography Research Group of the Institute of British Geographers have provided intellectual stimulation over many years, most especially Robin Butlin, Hugh Clout, Richard Dennis, Felix Driver, Roger Kain, Richard Lawton,

Paul Laxton, Chris Philo, Michael Williams and Charles Withers – and, of course, the late Brian Harley. Furthermore, this book would not have been the same without the international contacts I have enjoyed, for example, with many North American historical geographers, including Serge Courville, Jock Galloway, Peter Goheen, Leonard Guelke, Cole Harris, Deryck Holdsworth, Donald Meinig, Brian Osborne, David Robinson and Graeme Wynn. In addition, I have made a deliberate attempt over the years to bridge linguistic and cultural barriers, cultivating links with historical geographers throughout the world. I have especially benefited from those made with, and through, Yehoshua Ben-Arieh (Israel), Paul Claval (France), Dietrich Denecke (Germany), Leos Jelecek (Czech Republic), Jianxiong Ge (China), Akihiro Kinda (Japan), Jean-Robert Pitte (France), Joe Powell (Australia), Ulf Sporrong (Sweden) and Weimin Que (China).

I have also benefited enormously from personal contacts with many historians, although my encounters with each of them have been more casual than have those with geographers. Especially influential have been Maurice Beresford, Régis Bouis, Peter Burke, Alain Corbin, W. G. Hoskins, John Merriman, Joan Thirsk and Robert Tombs, and I am grateful to them for their stimulus and encouragement.

Some of the ideas presented in this book I have tested at seminars and conferences, especially those organised by the Historical Geography Research Group of the Institute of British Geographers and by the Association of American Geographers, at the series of International Conferences of Historical Geographers, at meetings of the Permanent European Conference for the Study of the European Landscape, and in the Cambridge series of Occasional Discussions in Historical Geography. Such exposure has always been beneficial and I am grateful to the many participants at those gatherings for their constructive comments.

In addition, of course, this book rests upon my knowledge and understanding of the writings of many geographers, historians and other scholars with whom I am not acquainted personally. My debt to them is beyond measure. Some of that obligation is explicitly acknowledged in the references. Given the scope of this book, however, my citations embrace only a small part of the relevant literature and relatively few of the scholars cultivating the two fields of geography and history. The references cited are those which are familiar to me and which seem to me to serve well in illustrating particular points I wish to make. Although extensive, the references are specific to this book and do not comprise a general or comprehensive list of works on, and in, geography and history. The relative merits of studies included and of those omitted are not in question. I confess to many sins of omission; I plea by way of mitigation that in a book of this kind such sins are unavoidable. All readers of my book will know of other case studies that I might have used to illustrate its general points.

Let me spell out two of my stylistic conventions. First, in the text I use the past tense when referring to publications prior to 1994 and the present tense when citing works published in that year or later (my working assumption being that the half-life of historico-geographical literature – the time during which one-half of all the currently active literature was published – is about eight years). Second, when mentioning an author in the text for the first time, I include her/his initials or forename; subsequent mentions normally use only the surname.

Material for this book has been garnered in many institutions and I am grateful to their libraries and staffs without whose expert assistance this project could not have been achieved. I am grateful especially to the many supportive staff of the University Library at Cambridge and to Jane Robinson and Colin MacLennan of the Library of the Department of Geography at the University of Cambridge. I owe thanks to Phil Stickler and James Youlden of that department for help with preparing the illustrations. I am also literally indebted to various institutions which have funded my explorations. I thank especially the University of Cambridge, Emmanuel College, Cambridge, the British Academy, the British Council, the Canada Council, the Chinese Academy of Sciences, and the Leverhulme Trust. In addition, I am grateful to the many universities in North America, Europe, Israel, Japan, and China which have invited me to present papers and to engage in discussions with their staffs and students. I am also considerably beholden to Cambridge University Press, and especially to Richard Fisher, its Director in Humanities and Social Sciences, for the opportunity to write this book and for patiently awaiting its completion. Similarly, I am immensely grateful to Richard Dennis and Deryck Holdsworth who made very constructive comments on my drafts. For any errors that persist, I remain responsible – as I am, of course, for the opinions expressed.

The final stages of the book have benefited enormously from the care of Jackie Warren, Production Editor (Humanities and Social Sciences) at Cambridge University Press, and from the attention to detail given to the copy and proofs by Carol Fellingham Webb. The index has been compiled by Simon Cross. I am very appreciative of the contribution each of them has made to the end product.

I also thank the following for permission to use copyright material: Cambridge University Press for figures 2.1, 2.2, 2.3, 2.4, 3.1, and 4.2; Blackwell Publishing for figures 2.5 and 2.6; Elsevier Science Ltd for figure 3.2; The Yale Center for British Art for figure 4.1; and Yale University Press for figure 5.1.

Finally, I am deeply grateful to Sandra, my wife, for her unbounded confidence and support. I am dedicating this book to her and to our sons, Andrew and Jeremy, and to our daughter-in-law, Bethan, and our two grandchildren, Jack and Sarah. While this book is about researching and writing the past, what matters most to me are their futures.

Emmanuel College, Cambridge
St Cecilia's Day, 2002

1

On the relations of geography and history

Intentions

Richard Evans, in his powerful '*defence*' of history against its attack by postmodernism, claims that the 1960s saw 'the *invasion* of the social sciences into history in Britain' and that in the post-war years in France the *Annales* historians aimed to make history far more objective and scientific than ever before by 'incorporating the methods of economics, sociology and especially *geography* into their approach to the past' (Evans 1997: 38–9). The writing of regional histories and of histories which addressed geographical concerns became such a distinctive characteristic of the *Annales* school that some observers claimed that its historians had '*annexed*' geography (Harsgor 1978; Huppert 1978). A geographer, Etienne Juillard (1956), had written earlier of the '*frontiers*' between history and geography. Use of these military and territorial metaphors (in all cases, the italics are mine) is indicative of the tensions which have long existed between historians and geographers, tensions which cannot be made to disappear simply by counter-citing pleas made for greater collaboration between the two 'rival' camps. We need to engage with the relations of geography and history in a more sustained fashion. How can that objective be achieved?

Let me initially approach the question negatively. It is not my aim to provide a history of historical geography, although I will employ a historiographical approach to the problem of the relations of geography and history. I have provided a brief history of historical geography elsewhere (Baker 1996a; see also Butlin 1993: 1–72). Nor am I setting out to present a critical appraisal of the sources and techniques available for researching and writing historical geography: some such already exist (for example: Morgan 1979; Hooke and Kain 1982; Courville 1995; Baker 1997; Grim et al. 2001). Nor is it my purpose to review recent progress in historical geography: such reviews are published regularly in an international journal, *Progress in Human Geography*. Nor is it my aim either to police the boundaries between geography and history or to promote the autonomy of historical geography as an academic discipline. When I identify categories of geography and of history I will not be doing so in order to fence them off from each other, providing each with its own demarcated intellectual territory. On the contrary, my purpose in labelling different kinds of geography and history is simply to promote a common language in which their practitioners can conduct meaningful dialogues. I am seeking connection not closure.

Now to expand my aims positively. I am writing mainly for a senior undergraduate and graduate student audience, both in geography and in history, but what I have to say will also be of interest more generally both to historians seeking more knowledge and understanding of the ideas and practices of geographers and to geographers wishing to improve their knowledge and understanding of the ideas and practices of historians. My central aim is to contribute to the long-standing discourse on the relations of geography and history, doing so through a critique of the practices of their two intellectual hybrids, historical geography and geographical history, but primarily that of the former and only to a lesser extent that of the latter. I seek to identify both the potential for, and the achievements of, close relations between geography and history. I want to bridge what one place-sensitive historian has described as 'the Great Divide' between geography and history (Marshall 1985: 22).

Indeed I see contact rather than separation between the aims and methods of geographers and historians. That contact will be demonstrated sometimes in terms of common interests and at other times in terms of collaborative projects. Beneath the passions of individuals and even the enthusiasms of each generation of historical geographers, there lie some basic characteristics of historical geography and of its relations with history. My concern is primarily with those fundamental characteristics. I maintain that the changing subject matter of historical geography does not of itself matter: that beneath the changes there can be detected structural continuities. Moreover, as the baton is handed on to a new generation of historical geographers, I want to make it clear that there is not one, monolithic, prior tradition of historical geography to be replaced. Historical geography is better viewed as a dynamic discursive formation. New interests and new directions being taken up by a new generation of practitioners are to be both welcomed and expected, and they are also needed if historical geography is to continue to flourish.

So, to outline my basic argument. History, historical geography and geographical history have a shared experience over a wide range of matters. They address very similar, and often the same, problems and sources; they employ very similar, and often the same, research and presentational techniques; they straddle, not always without difficulty and sometimes with great discomfort, knowledges and understandings from both the natural sciences and the social sciences while they themselves are part of the broad spectrum of humanities or historical sciences. But, given the different epistemological positions of geography and history, they provide distinctive perspectives upon the past. Every object, phenomenon or idea – such as sugar, singing and sorcery – has its own geography and its own history as well as its own structural forms and associated functions. To consider this

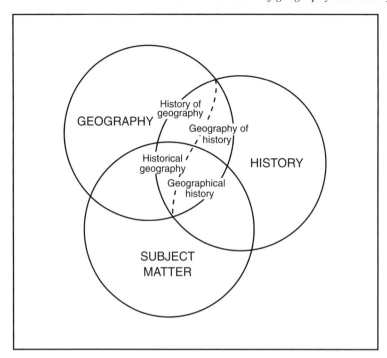

Figure 1.1 Venn diagram of the relations of geography, history and their subject matter

trilogy – of subject matter, geography and history – as three sets, overlapping in Venn diagrammatic form, is to appreciate the central roles of historical geography and geographical history, poised at the intersection of all three. In this light, historical geography may be viewed as being concerned with the historical dimension in geography and geographical history with the geographical dimension in history (Fig. 1.1).

Geography and history are different ways of looking at the world but they are so closely related that neither one can afford to ignore or even neglect the other. Moreover, each of them offers not just one perspective upon the world but multiple perspectives upon the characters of peoples, places and periods. It is sometimes argued that historians focus upon people in past periods and historical geographers upon places in past periods (Mitchell 1954: 12). But contrasting history and geography as being concerned respectively with people and with places is a distorted representation of their concerns. The fundamental difference between them is better expressed in terms of history's focus upon periods and geography's focus upon places, fully recognising that both periods and places were (and are) peopled and were (and are) constructed and experienced by people. Historical geographers tell us stories about how *places* have been created in the past by people in their own image, while historians tell us different stories about how *periods* have been created in the past by people in their own image.

While the difference between the perspective of the historian and that of the geographer is significant, it can too easily be exaggerated. There is a substantial overlapping of interests between history and geography. If period, place and people are represented as overlapping concerns, then where all three intersect may be described as both historical geography and geographical history: any difference in practice between those two will reflect the specific intellectual origins, distinctive cultural baggages and personal preferences which individual researchers bring to their enquiries. We do not all – and do not all need to – ask exactly the same questions: there are many ways of journeying to even one destination and there are also multiple historical and geographical destinations.

Geographers and historians have expanded enormously the range of subjects they study. They embrace not only almost every conceivable aspect of human activity but also many features of the natural world: for example, not only canals and criminality but also cotton and climate, not only mining and music but also marshlands and malaria, not only factories and fears and but also forests and furs. Moreover, histories and geographies embrace both the actions and the attitudes of individuals and of groups, and they do so taking into account the shaping and experiencing of histories and geographies by people who differ, for example, in terms of their class, ethnicity, gender, age, wealth or education. In addition, histories and geographies are drawing upon a widening spectrum of social, cultural and literary theories and so are adopting increasingly diverse perspectives upon historical geographies.

To take just one example, the emergence of a feminist historical geography and of a historically informed feminist geography. Mona Domosh (1990) and Gillian Rose (1993), drawing upon feminist theory, highlighted critically the foregrounding of white males in historiographies of geographical knowledge and thus the gendered nature of that knowledge. They argued for greater recognition of the roles of formerly marginalised groups, especially women. Similarly, Jeanne Kay (1990: 619) argued that 'the US historical geography literature is unintentionally yet largely racist and sexist' and pleaded for 'more rounded and diversified presentations of our heritage'. The challenge of establishing closer links between feminism and historical geography (Rose and Ogborn 1988; Domosh 1997) is being taken up in a variety of ways, as exemplified in a set of geographical essays on gender and the city in historical perspective (Mattingly 1998). For some it means focusing more sharply on the gendered use of space, on the spatial and material expression of gender relations and power struggles between women and men; for others it embraces the role of women in the making and in the observing of past geographies; and for yet others it involves trying to understand those geographies from a feminine perspective and listening to the voices of women in the past. For example, Kay (1991, 1997) specifically explores attitudes to nature revealed in the writings of nineteenth-century Mormon women and she has argued more generally that historical geographers of rural Canada and the United States are to some extent limited by their frequent use of one narrative form, the national epic, that cannot readily portray women as important actors unless its essential plot line is reinterpreted in ways less familiar to geographers. Taking examples of three western frontier women, Kay discussed how their narratives indicate ways of providing a more balanced impression of both women and men in studies of regional economies and landscape modification.

A particularly fruitful avenue in feminist historical geography leads to the ways in which places and their landscapes have been experienced and represented by women. For example, K. M. Morin (1999) examines English women's 'heroic adventures' in the nineteenth-century American West while Mary Kingsley's travels in West Africa at the end of that century have been given differently nuanced, gendered, readings by Mary Louise Pratt (1992), Alison Blunt (1994) and Gerry Kearns (1997). That men and women saw things differently has been forcefully argued in relation to landscape painting in the Western world where, in the eighteenth century, it was a product of a 'male gaze' upon a landscape considered to be a natural and feminine body, a subject unsuitable for women to paint. But in the colonies white women were freer to paint landscapes because they assumed the colonial authority of white men, the advantaged position of their ethnicity counting for more than the disadvantages of their gender (Blunt and Rose 1994). While feminist historical geography emphasises the gendering of spaces, environments, landscapes and places, it also stresses the importance of acknowledging the diversity of women and of not treating the category 'woman' as unitary. Alongside this feminist discourse within historical geography one could lay the colonial and post-colonial discourses which address the geographical practices, experiences and imaginations of both the colonisers and the colonised (Lester 2000; Ploszajska 2000; Yeoh 2000).

This increasing attention to the multiple voices in the past and to multiple perspectives upon the past could be a cause for celebration or grounds for gloom. While some might find the new pluralism and interdisciplinary perspectives challenging, others might deplore what they see as the intradisciplinary fragmentation and even disintegration of history and of geography into more and more divisive specialisms. Can we find a balance between these two extreme positions? I believe we can.

I will try to do so – as an aspirant *Annaliste* – by identifying some of the *événements, conjonctures* and *structures* in historical geography and then listening for resonances within history. Each individual historical researcher pursues his or her own interest, each of us becomes personally involved with the period, place and people we choose to study in the past, often doing so to an extent and with a passion that others find difficult to comprehend. Thus one nineteenth-century historical geographer might be excited by covered bridges in one American county, a second by marriage fields in a few French communes, and a third by Owenism in a handful of English parishes. It is certainly the case that individual historical geographers have been animated by some very specific topics, as H. C. Darby – one of the founding fathers of historical geography – was by the architectural geography of south Britain, the birds of the undrained English Fenland, the geographical ideas of the Venerable Bede and the regional geography of Thomas Hardy's Wessex (Darby 1928, 1934, 1935, 1948). Such 'one-off' and essentially autarchic studies conducted by individual researchers giving rein to their own interests and enthusiasms are examples of *événements* in the practice of historical geography. Such individual work stands on its own merits and undoubtedly possesses intrinsic interest and value. It may, but does not necessarily, provide a stimulus for similar research by others. Its contribution to knowledge and understanding could be considered to be more additive than cumulative, making advances arithmetically rather than geometrically.

When the product of historical researchers is viewed collectively, then it becomes possible to identify patterns of research interests in both the medium and the long term. The research foci of one generation are often abandoned or at least neglected by the next, which prefers setting out its own agenda to inheriting that of its elders (who are, rightly, not deemed always to be their betters). As Aidan McQuillan (1995) points out in his progress report on historical geography, research interests – what he terms 'research clusters' – wax and wane over time as the intellectual climate changes. All historical and geographical research (like all research) reflects the ideas and techniques of its own time: each generation seeks answers to questions which are framed in terms of the concerns of its own 'present day'. Like McQuillan, Deryck Holdsworth (2002) sees generational vitality in the emergence of 'new directions' in historical geography which respect rather than reject 'old ways'. The considerable current interest in historical geographies of modernisation and modernity may be seen in this light as also connecting with intellectual trends in contemporary human geography and in the social and historical sciences generally (Dunford 1998; Ogborn 1999; Graham and Nash 2000). New ideas and interests and the use of new sources or the reinterpretation of familiar sources made possible by the use of new techniques combine with an understandable desire on the part of a new generation to prosecute a 'new' history or a 'new' geography to produce a different – if not always entirely 'new' – kind of history and geography.

Conjonctures of research in history and in historical geography can be identified and used to impose a pattern on the work of scholars as an academy. This assumption underpins the designation of 'schools' of history and of geography, which wax and wane to varying degrees and which are often grounded in clusters of influential individuals. But it also relates to specific research agenda. For example, in the 1960s and 1970s, many historical geographers in Britain were working on field systems and on urban systems, and many were exploiting the Tithe Surveys and the manuscript enumerators' returns of the Population Census; by the 1980s and 1990s, many were more concerned with issues flowing from debates about modernity and postmodernism and excited by exploiting a wider range of literary and pictorial sources. But I would not expect researchers even in the near future – in the 2010s and 2020s – to be enthused by the same problems and to be restricted to using the same sources and techniques as those currently attracting attention – and if some are, I would not expect them to be addressing 'our' problems and sources in the way we are now doing. Innovations come in waves that break, and of course (as physical geographers know well) waves can be both destructive of existing features and creative of new ones. Historical geography is constantly seeking and finding new research realms, it is constantly renewing itself, constantly moving on to new periods, new places and new topics. Thus Richard Schein, as editor of a set of methodological essays on practising historical geography, argues that the topics embraced in his collection 'represent new directions in, and perhaps even a break in tradition for, historical geography', because 'they signal a certain engagement with contemporary critical and reflexive scholarly practice across the social sciences and the humanities'. Schein's edited essays are presented as reflecting the post-positivist turn in historical geography. He sees them as 'a re-placing of historical geography', with the double meaning of bringing to historical geography both the theoretical and methodological debates of post-positivist scholarship and a new generation of scholars prosecuting a non-traditional form of historical geography. But even Schein admits that many of the ideas presented in these essays – such as the problematic nature both of archives and of geographical description – 'are at least foreshadowed in the annals of historical geography' (Schein 2001: 8–10).

While I will from time to time refer to the *événements* and *conjonctures* of historical geography, they are not my main focus. I am not concerned here principally with ephemeral enthusiasms. I employ instead what might be considered to be the *structures* of geography, because they give coherence to the increasingly diverse and expanding output of historical geography. While it is appropriate to acknowledge the exceptionalist position of those who are fascinated by *événements* and to celebrate the changing character of historical geography's *conjonctures*, I will argue for the fundamental significance of some of its underlying *structures*. Here I concur with D. W. Meinig (1997: 8) that while every generation rewrites its history, this is 'not to say that everything in history is mutable'. While the interests of individual historical geographers and of generations of historical geographers change, there are some basic continuities in the theory and practice of historical geography. Fundamentally, and perhaps surprisingly, the subject matter of historical geography does not matter. Viewing the intersections of *événements* and *conjonctures* – of individual historical geographers and of successive generations of historical geographers – within the wider intellectual *structures* in which they have been and are situated moves towards a structurationist approach, with its emphasis on both the human agents and the social and intellectual systems and structures in which they are necessarily imbricated (Giddens 1984). I will use these *structures* as a platform from which to explore the relations of geography and history. My argument is grounded in the major discourses of geography. The three 'deviant' or peripheral discourses – of location, environment, and landscape – can

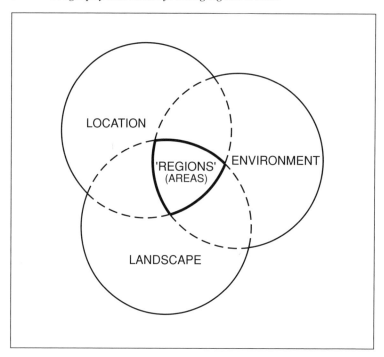

Figure 1.2 Venn diagram of the four principal discourses of geography

be overlapped in Venn diagrammatic form to create a central discourse of regional geography at the intersection of all of those three (Fig. 1.2). These four discourses are interconnected: there are no impermeable boundaries between any of them. Individual geographers and their writings are unlikely to be situated exclusively within just one of these discourses. They serve, none the less, as a useful framework for discussion of the nature of historical geography and of the relations of geography and history.

I shall illustrate my argument with reference to selected examples of 'best practice' in historical geography, those examples being drawn not only from burgeoning recent work but also from historical geography's bulging library of classical studies. It would be easy, but in my view misleading, to draw just upon work published during the past dozen or so years. Easy, because there has been a great flowering of new work in historical geography during this period, with new problems, new sources and new analytical techniques enriching the quality of the increasing quantity of studies being undertaken. Misleading, because even the most original and novel of recent works have been constructed – knowingly or otherwise – on foundations laid by earlier generations of scholars. I am reminded of Julian Barnes' comments on developments in French cinema and cuisine:

The *nouvelle vague* was a revolt against *le cinéma de papa*, but it was less a matter of mass patricide than of selective culling. The wisest innovators know – or at least find out – that the history of art may appear linear and progressive but it is in fact circular, cross-referential and backtracking. The practitioners of the *nouvelle vague* were immersed (some, like Truffaut, as critics) in what had preceded them . . . Like the *nouvelle vague,* twentieth-century *nouvelle cuisine* was a noisy, useful, publicity-driven revolt: one against *le cinéma de papa*, the other against *la cuisine de maman*. Both resulted in temporary forgetting of just exactly what Maman and Papa did; and of how ineluctable genetic inheritance is. (Barnes 2002: 38–9 and 56)

There are lessons here for advocates of any 'new' departure. Accordingly, before entering into my main discussion of the relations of geography and history, I want briefly to consider both specific possible forerunners to this present book and the general intellectual context within which it is situated. How has historical geography been conceptualised? How have historians regarded geography and how have geographers viewed history?

Legacies

There have been very few book-length treatments of historical geography as a field of study as opposed to books on the historical geographies of particular places, periods, and topics. Books bearing the title 'historical geography' have been published since at least the early seventeenth century, such as those by Edward Wells on the historical geography of the New and Old Testaments (Butlin 1992, 1993: 1–72) and many such works were published in the closing decades of the twentieth century, too numerous even to exemplify judiciously. But there have been remarkably few endeavours to write at length about 'historical geography' *per se*. It might, therefore, be instructive to consider those works briefly but individually, to ponder the approach which each adopted to its subject matter.

In 1954, Jean Mitchell published her *Historical Geography* in a series of books under the general title 'Teach Yourself Geography'. The bulk of the work comprised essays on important themes (such as 'the peopling of the land' and 'the evolution of villages and farms') in 'the changing geography' of Britain from prehistoric times to the early twentieth century, but it also included a chapter on the data of the historical geographer and two others on general issues. In her introductory chapter, Mitchell posed the question: 'What is historical geography?' She considered that both geography and history were difficult to define and concluded that historical geography was 'a still greater mystery'. She continued:

few go further than a belief that it is about 'old' maps, and perhaps concerns itself too much with tales of ancient mariners, medieval travellers and merchant adventurers. Some feel that it is an unsound attempt by geographers to explain history, and think that the historical geographer is most certainly trespassing and probably should be prosecuted. That is not so, the historical geographer is a geographer first, last and all the time . . . (Mitchell 1954: 1–2)

But the object of geographical study was, for Mitchell, no mystery: it was the study of places, both in their individuality and in their generality, of places as products of interactions between peoples and their physical environments. The central geographical question for Mitchell was to describe and explain the distribution, the location, of phenomena. Accordingly, for Mitchell, 'historical geography is, simply stated, a geographical study of any period in the past for which a more or less ordered and dated sequence is established in human affairs'. To Mitchell, historical geography was the geography of the past, but the historical geographer was always a geographer and never a historian. She argued that just as a historian could write a history of France without becoming a geographer, so a geographer could write a geography of some place in the nineteenth century or the ninth century and remain a geographer. Mitchell was absolutely clear that historians and geographers have different perspectives:

There is much in common between the historian and the geographer, both are attempting to see the pattern in a multitude of facts in order to appreciate the world about them, but there is a fundamental difference in outlook between them. The 'world' to the historian means civilisation; the 'world' to the geographer means the surface of the earth. (Mitchell 1954: 12)

Thus Mitchell argued that many books with the title 'historical geography' would be better titled 'geographical history', 'for they are concerned essentially not with the place but with the civilisation . . . It would seem that the attempt to examine historical events in relation to their geographical setting is best left to the historian' (Mitchell 1954: 11).

For Mitchell, history and geography had different objectives, they occupied separate intellectual territories. That exclusive stance was reinforced by her view that the historical geographer is concerned mainly with the geography of an area at some past time: 'the historical geographer is not concerned with the survival of geographical patterns [into the present] or with the evolution of geographical patterns in time, but with the establishment and study of their design at any one particular time [in the past]' (Mitchell 1954: 14). Here Mitchell was not only exclusive but also confused, because much of her book was in practice a consideration of changing geographical patterns, of their evolution through time. But, as Mitchell made clear in her final chapter, she had no doubt that the analytical work of a historical geographer should ultimately be seen as contributing to a geographical synthesis, to a study of place in both its physical and human aspects. 'If every historical geographer must be versed in all parts of geography, every geographer must be to some extent a historical geographer' (Mitchell 1954: 328). She argued for the necessity of a historical approach in all geographical work; for her, historical geography was not an ornamental coping to geographical study, it was instead with physical and biological geography the foundation upon which the geography of the modern world rested (Mitchell 1954: 332).

For thirty years, Mitchell's survey remained the only book-length, English-language treatment of the nature of historical geography. It was a remarkable achievement, justifiably claimed in its Preface to be a pioneering effort. But the book's substantive focus upon the changing geography of Britain meant that its impact was more limited than its general discussion of the nature of historical geography merited. The next such general survey of historical geography to be published, William Norton's *Historical Analysis in Geography* (1984), has also had a relatively constrained impact but for a different reason: it aligned itself primarily with a particular and limited view of geography.

Norton initially acknowledged three major concerns of geography (and thus of historical geography) – those of geographical change through time, the development of landscape, and the evolution of spatial form. But it was the last of these which attracted most of his attention. In the first chapter of his book, Norton examined developments in history and economic history, surveying debates about the relative merits of positivist and idealist modes of explanation. He focused upon methods adopted by the 'new' economic history, on the blinkered grounds that 'social, rural and political history . . . are generally of less relevance to historical geography' (Norton 1984: 15). Norton was especially attracted to the quantitative, theoretical and counterfactual methods of the 'new' economic history, to the 'scientific' approach to historical explanation. In his second chapter, Norton explored the problem of temporal explanation in geography, examining briefly solutions to it offered by cultural analyses, by diffusion studies, and by time geographies, but reserving most of his attention to, and approval for, analyses of process-form relationships through time. In the following two chapters, Norton reviewed developments in historical geography. He argued that the main concerns of historical geography during the 1960s and 1970s could be listed as being the study of past geographies, of changing geographies, and of relict features in present-day landscapes. He argued that the ideas and methods of spatial analysis then being increasingly adopted within geography generally had as yet made little impact upon historical geography specifically. He recognised that there were indeed lively debates among historical geographers, for example, about problems posed by available data, about the role of theory and quantification in historical research, and about alternatives to positivism (such as phenomenology, idealism, and structuralism). But Norton's main advocacy was of a 'temporally oriented spatial analysis', focused upon studies of the evolution of spatial forms and employing, for example, simulation techniques and counterfactual methods.

In six succeeding chapters Norton reviewed what he identified as some major themes in historical geography: regional studies; frontier studies; analyses of the evolution of settlements and of agricultural, transportation, industrial and urban landscapes; and population studies. In each of these, wherever appropriate, he highlighted studies of process-form relationships. Then, in his final chapter, Norton argued that developments in historical geography might benefit from those taking place within the 'new' economic history (especially in relation to regional growth and staple theory). While suggesting that advances might be made by making greater use of simulation modelling, of the idea of progress, and of the attitudes of historical actors, Norton reserved his main sign-post to the way ahead for his advocacy of studies of 'spatial form evolution'.

While acknowledging the diversity of historical geography, both Jean Mitchell and William Norton could not avoid lending their support to one approach (but different in each case) above others. Surprisingly, each backed an approach just at the time when it was coming increasingly to be questioned. Mitchell's view of historical geography as being concerned exclusively with geographies of past times and not with changing geographies through time reflected the traditional view of the subject inherited from the 1930s which was already by the 1950s, when she was writing, being challenged by Darby's (1951a, 1953a) rethinking of historical geography, with his additional emphasis upon historical geography as the study of changing landscapes. Norton's view of historical geography as the evolution of spatial form, outlined in a paper in 1982 and then elaborated in his book in 1984, reflected the view of geography as spatial analysis which was developed during the 1960s and 1970s but which was coming under attack by the 1970s and early 1980s (Harris 1971, 1978a; Baker 1981). There are lessons to be learned here, and pitfalls to be avoided, in relation to the argument I will develop in this book.

Such hazards were, for the most part, successfully negotiated in Robin Butlin's *Historical Geography: Through the Gates of Space and Time* (1993), perhaps because he adopted a historical perspective which highlighted the changing character of historical geography itself. Of the book's eleven chapters, the first three examined the history of historical geography as practised in many parts of the world from the early eighteenth century to the late twentieth century. This consideration led Butlin to organise the bulk of his book thematically. After an essay on sources of evidence and data in historical geography, he presented chapters which treated in turn, systematically, some major topics: the reconstruction of physical environments; historical geographies of landscapes; historical geographies of social power and control; rural transformations; historical geographies of urbanisation; and historical geographies of industrialisation. Writing his book mainly during the 1980s, Butlin did none the less catch the incoming tide of postmodernism and dealt at various points throughout his book with issues such as representation, identity and power which feature so prominently in today's 'new' cultural and historical geography (Graham and Nash 2000). Butlin's book was very ambitious: it was offered as 'a celebration, critique, and demonstration of historical geography', and was constructed as a historiography of the subject and a review of its major research domains, stretching from prehistory to the present and encompassing the whole world. As a general overview, Butlin's book has expectedly – but not always reasonably or fairly – been criticised for omitting specific problems, periods and places, but its range was extensive and its astonishing breadth meant that Butlin could not achieve the comprehensive coverage which was his declared aim.

None the less, having defined historical geography straightforwardly as 'the study of the geographies of past time' (Butlin 1993: ix), Butlin went on to demonstrate the complexity, diversity and vitality of the subject. On the relations between geography and history, Butlin was brief but instructive. In what he described as the 'proto-modern' form of historical geography before the early twentieth century, historical geography 'evolved as a branch of history, that is as an ancillary subject, providing in essence background or environmental information to the study of the chronology and major political and social experiences of peoples, states, empires, frontiers, and civilisations' (Butlin 1993: ix). From the 1920s and 1930s, a 'modern' form of historical geography began to emerge within the growing discipline of geography, to some extent distanced from that of history as historical geographers attempted to construct a separate existence for their sub-discipline. Such an endeavour created a gap between geography and history which was compounded by the retention by historians of an outmoded view of the nature of geography: many historians continued to think geographically only in terms of the influences of the physical environment upon the course of historical events. Then the move within geography in the 1960s and 1970s away from historical and towards functionalist modes of explanation widened the gap between geographers and historians, and so also that between contemporary geographers and historical geographers. Butlin concluded that 'there is still much scope for detailed examination of the relationships, past and present, between historical geography and history' (Butlin 1993: 47). I want to take up that challenge.

None of the three book-length accounts of historical geography considered so far – by Mitchell, by Norton and by Butlin – consistently addressed the nature of the relation between its two parent disciplines. As far as I am aware, the same is true of such accounts in other languages. Jean-René Trochet's broadly titled *Géographie historique* (1998) is not a general prospectus but a focused discussion of expressions of territoriality in traditional, pre-modern communities and societies. Helmut Jäger's *Historische Geographie* (1969) examined the history and methodologies of historical geography, and reviewed work specifically on the historical (physical and cultural) geography of Germany and on historical landscapes. Toshio Kikuchi's *Method in Historical Geography* (1977, 2nd edn 1987), drawing upon both Japanese and (especially for the second edition) Western literatures, examined the concepts, methods and techniques employed in historical geography. Ren-Zhi Hou's *Theory and Practice in Historical Geography* (1979) was a set of essays which monitored the history of historical geography in China, demonstrating that an earlier concern with changing political boundaries and place-names was replaced, after the establishment of the People's Republic, with an emphasis on applied historical geography, in relation to both physical and human environments. Zhang Butian's *An Introduction to Historical Geography* (1993) provided not only an account of the changing character of historical geography in China (showing that it has become both more systematically comprehensive and more explicitly responsive to developments in the field elsewhere in the world), but also an examination of the practice of historical geography in Asia, Europe, North America, Russia, Egypt and Australia. Xiaofeng Tang's *From Dynastic Geography to Historical Geography* (2000), while addressing not so much the relations between geography and history in general but the practice of historical geography in China, does identify a significant change in the studies of the geographical past of China, with work on the historical geography of China coming to be influenced increasingly by its theory and practice in the West. Similarly, Weimin Que's *Ideas of Historical Geography* (2000) reviews recent work in historical geography in the English-speaking world and broadcasts it to the Chinese academy. The books by Kikuchi and Zhang drew upon both Asian and Western literatures and they are probably the most wide-ranging discussions so far published of the nature of historical geography. Even so, neither includes much consideration of the relations of geography and history and, to the extent that they do so, they rely mainly upon discussions of them in papers by Western scholars.

It is, therefore, to those papers that I will turn shortly, but before doing so there is one further book and a few other issues to consider. Serge Courville's *Introduction à la géographie historique* (1995) is essentially a very useful manual for the subject, a guide to the practice of historical geography: it considers the formulation of research problems, the need for a critical approach to historical sources, the use of qualitative, quantitative and cartographical analyses of data, and the problems of generalisation and synthesis. But Courville's manual is also prefaced by a lengthy review of the history of historical geography and a discussion of its character. Courville makes the point – although not in these words – that historical geography was born to history and adopted by geography before achieving a large measure of independence from both sets of intellectual parents while maintaining positive relationships with both of them. For Courville, historical geography is neither a discipline nor a sub-discipline but an interdisciplinary field of enquiry nourished by the ideas, languages and methods of both history and geography. He sees historical geography as a way of resolving the traditional tensions between history and geography. This is a perspective which deserves closer attention than Courville is able to give it, because his principal concern is with the practice, not with the theory, of historical geography.

Of course, the suggestion that historical geography should be seen not as a discipline or sub-discipline is not itself new. Similar suggestions have been made before. For example, Norton concluded that historical geography should be viewed not as a sub-discipline of geography but as 'a set of approaches' and Darby, claiming that he was not seeking to establish the frontier between history and geography, argued that it would be 'more true' to say that there are problems demanding investigation than academic subjects to be pursued (Norton 1984: 61; Darby 1962a: 156). It none the less remains the case that 'modern' historical geography, to use Butlin's term, has been institutionalised and developed largely within the disciplinary frameworks provided by university structures inherited from the nineteenth century. Moreover, Darby himself – unarguably the founding father of 'modern' historical geography in Britain but whose influence went far beyond its shores – set out deliberately to rethink the nature of historical geography, to promote historical geography as a sub-discipline within geography: he laboured with a missionary zeal to establish historical geography as a self-conscious, distinctive subject, distinguishable from contemporary human geography and different from other historical disciplines (Darby 1979, 2002).

The practice of historical geography and its vigorous pursuit as a discipline or sub-discipline has largely shaded-out serious consideration not only of its epistemological status but also of its potential for making significant interdisciplinary contributions to knowledge and understanding. As has already been noted, the contributions of historical geography have changed in character through time. But they have also varied from place to place. A collection of essays published thirty years ago brought sharply into focus the contrasting characteristics of historical geography as practised in selected countries and continents of the world (Baker 1972). Since then, many further reviews of the practice of historical geography in particular places have been published and have emphasised the diversity of the problems being investigated and of approaches being adopted. Each continent, country or locality has its own historical and geographical questions, its own sources, and its own intellectual and scholarly traditions. For example, within North America have been identified different 'schools' of historical geography associated respectively with Carl Sauer and the University of California at Berkeley and with Andrew Clark and the University of Wisconsin (Conzen 1993), while the practice of historical geography in Canada developed its own distinctive character (Wynn 1993). Similarly, but not exactly in parallel, within Britain a distinction has been made between the 'school' of historical geography associated with Clifford Darby at University College London and Cambridge, and that linked with H. J. Fleure and Emrys Bowen at Aberystwyth (Langton 1988a). Again, the practice of historical geography has a different character in Germany (Kleefeld and Burggraaff 1997) from that in France (Pitte 1994, 1995), in capitalist countries from that to be found in socialist (or until recently socialist) countries (Baker 1986). Critical reviews of the practice of historical geography in particular places can be both informative and instructive, despite the inevitability of their becoming dated. I have in mind, as excellent examples in this genre, reviews of relatively recent work in historical geography in America (Earle et al. 1989; Conzen 1993; Wynn 1993; Colten et al. forthcoming), Australia (Jeans 1988), China (Weimin Que 1995) and Japan (Kinda 1997). My own encounters with the literatures of historical geography in different countries and continents (to the extent that my knowledge of the necessary languages allows them), coupled with meetings and discussions with historical geographers in different countries and continents during the past thirty years or so (if necessary, facilitated by interpreters), have led me to celebrate the diversity of studies being conducted under the single banner of historical geography (Baker 1996a).

That diversity can be – and has been – seen not only as a strength but also as a weakness. For example, Xavier de Planhol (1972) has argued that the ambiguous status of French historical geography in the schools both of history and of geography meant that it appeared, paradoxically, 'both everywhere and nowhere', whereas Lucien Gaillabaud (1999) contends that the lack of a precise definition of historical geography in France, in effect its heterogeneous character, reflects a fertile interdisciplinarity. Far from suggesting that the scope and purpose of historical geography should be narrowed, I argue that it should be enlarged. It is not my intention to refine a purist definition of historical geography as a discipline or sub-discipline. I will instead argue the merits of historical geography as an interdisciplinary project, offering a number of distinctive perspectives upon peoples, places and periods in the past. In order to move towards that goal, I will now consider more closely views expressed by historians and geographers about the relations between their own subjects. I will not be conducting an overall review of progress in historical geography. Such assessments exist both as one-off 'snapshots' (Baker 1972; Pacione 1987) and as a series of on-going reports published periodically in the journal *Progress in Human Geography*. Such reviews tend to focus on the *événements* and *conjonctures* of historical geography. But what are its underlying *structures*?

Historians and geography

As the topics of interest to historians have changed, at least in emphasis, so also have their attitudes towards geography and to the relations of history and geography. From a restricted view of geography either as the physical stage upon which the drama of history is enacted or as the framework of physical frontiers and political boundaries within which history is to some extent contained, historians have developed a very much broader perspective upon geography which embraces concepts of environment, of space and of place.

In the late nineteenth century, historians viewed geography generally as the handmaiden to history and 'geography' itself was understood by them primarily as physical geography, necessarily providing the context for historical studies and also possibly providing evidence for historians to draw upon. For example, in J. R. Green's *The Making of England* (1881), it was claimed that 'the ground itself, where we can read the information it affords, is, whether in the account of the Conquest or in that of the Settlement of Britain, the fullest and most certain of documents. Physical geography has still its part to play in the written record of that human history to which it gives so much of its shape and form' (Green 1881: vii). For Green, 'History strikes its roots in Geography, for without a clear and vivid realisation of the physical structure of a country the incidents of the life which men [*sic*] have lived in it can have no interest or meaning' (Green 1881: xi). The view of geography as crucial to historical understanding was widely held a century or so ago. James Bryce, for example, saw geography as 'the key to history' (Bryce 1902: 54). Bryce's introduction to an eight-volume survey of world history argued that 'Geography determines History' and that 'in all countries and at all times Geography is the necessary foundation of History, so that neither the course of a nation's growth nor its relations with other nations can be grasped by one who has not come to understand the climate, surface and products of the country wherein that nation dwells'. Bryce saw the relationship of Man to Nature (the physical environment) changing through time: from being its servant, Man became its master. Bryce's conception of geography embraced not only the characteristics of the physical environment but also locational and spatial relationships and what he termed 'the diffusion of European Civilisation' throughout the world (Bryce 1901: xxv, xxxix and liii).

Similar ideas permeated H. B. George's (1901) sustained examination of the relations between geography and history, in which he argued:

> History is not intelligible without geography. This is obviously true in the sense that the reader of history must learn where are the frontiers of states, where wars were fought, whither colonies were dispatched. It is equally, if less obviously, true that geographical facts largely influence the course of history. Even the constitutional and social developments within a settled nation are scarcely independent of them, since the geographical position affects the nature and extent of geographical intercourse with other nations, and therefore of the influence exerted by foreign ideas. All external relations, hostile and peaceful are based largely on geography, while industrial progress depends primarily, though not exclusively, on matters described in every geography book – the natural products of a country, and the facilities which its structure affords for trade, both domestic and foreign. (George 1901: 1)

In his survey of 'the general nature of geographical influences', George ventured towards the position of an environmental determinist:

> No one will deny, however firmly he insists on believing in free will, that the destinies of men [*sic*] are very largely determined by their environment . . . Climate determines what men's food shall be, at any rate before extensive commerce has been developed, and whether or not they need work hard for a living. The physical features of the earth, sea, mountains &c., go far to fix their occupations, and to decide whether they are to live within easy reach of intercourse with their neighbours. The aspect of nature about them colours, and to a certain extent suggests, their ideas and beliefs. (George 1901: 7)

But there were also factors other than the physical environment which George recognised as shaping history, such as race, so that 'in setting forth the geographical influences which have guided or modified history, it is necessary to guard against overstating their force' (George 1901: 8). In his book of more than 300 pages, George went on to explore the influence of geography – by which he meant mainly physical resources and position – upon the development of frontiers, of towns and of wars, before undertaking a remarkable survey of the relations of geography and history in some of the world's major countries, regions and continents. George's views on geography probably shaped the ideas of generations of British – and quite possibly other – historians during the first half of the twentieth century.

Similar ideas were to the fore at about the same time in the work of Frederick Jackson Turner, an American historian, when he was developing and elaborating his thesis about the significance of the frontier in American history. In his early study of the frontier in Wisconsin, Turner (1891) stressed the importance of physical conditions, especially river courses, in shaping the pattern of settlement. When reflecting more generally upon some of the major problems of American history, Turner (1894) advocated careful consideration of 'the part played by the environment in determining the lines of [American] development' and emphasised 'the need for thorough study of the physiographic basis of [American] history'. Turner's report on the American Historical Association's conference in 1907 suggested that the relations between geography and history should be close, with study of the interactions between people and their environment being one of the most important fields of enquiry in America at that time. But it also showed that geography was then generally conceived by historians passively as physiography and as location, while history was seen as being concerned with people actively evaluating their geographical environment and situation (Turner 1908).

Such ideas about geographical 'influences' on history were discussed by many American historians (Sparks 1909; Turner 1914), but only a few, like James C. Malin (1955) and Walter Prescott Webb (1960), seem to have considered them critically or at length, at least not until recently. That task was, however, undertaken by historians in France and I will turn to their work in a moment, after lingering briefly with Webb's classic study *The Great Plains* (1931). When addressing a plenary session at the 1960 Annual Meeting of the Association of American Geographers, Webb took as his theme 'geographical-historical concepts in American history'. He explained the thinking which underpinned his account of the encounter between 'environment and civilisation' on the Great Plains of the American West. Webb described himself as 'a geographic historian', by which he meant one who elected 'to approach history, civilisation, if you please, through geography, by way of the physical environment'. He was pleased to admit that practically all of the history he had written, and certainly the best of it, was 'based solidly and consciously on geography, on the character of the land where the action described took place' (Webb 1960: 85–6). Webb saw the physical (geographical) environment as a structure, as a stage, upon which the drama of history was enacted, but because different groups of actors came with different ideas and used the stage in different ways, the precise unfolding of the drama depended upon them. Although Webb's conception of geography, like that of many American historians of his generation, was remarkably narrow, it none the less productively shaped much scholarly and valuable work.

Many French historians embraced a wider conception of geography. In France during the nineteenth century, studies of the history of changing political and administrative boundaries were often designated as 'historical geographies': such boundaries defined the geographical territories within which historical events and processes were researched. These studies had strong links both with the geographical dictionaries which had preceded them and with the historical atlases which often succeeded them. In all of them geography was seen as playing a very subordinate role to that of history. That was also to be the case in the second form which the relationship between history and geography took in France during the nineteenth century, as enunciated by Jules Michelet and adopted by many historians. In his nineteen-volume *Histoire de France* (1833–44; 1855), Michelet argued that 'the true starting-point of our history is a political division of France founded on its natural and physical divisions. At first, history is entirely geography' (Michelet 1833: 2). Michelet accordingly presented a 'Tableau de la France', a geographical description of its regions. This approach to history through geography was one which came to be emulated by many French-speaking historians: it is an approach which emphasised the physical geographical settings for historical dramas. For example, Jean Brunhes and Camille Vallaux (1921) wrote a book on *La géographie de l'histoire* which examined the geographical (physical and locational) underpinnings of war and peace on land and sea. Earlier, Emile Miller, a French Canadian, in his 1915 essay on 'La géographie au service de l'histoire', had endorsed Victor Cousin's famous claim: 'Donnez-moi la géographie d'un pays et je vous trouverai son histoire.' But Miller also went beyond that limited conception of the relations of history and geography, for he embraced other writings of Jean Brunhes, with their emphasis upon the landscape as a product of the interaction of people with their physical environments.

Indeed, with the development of a new school of geography, especially of human geography, in France during the late nineteenth and early twentieth century, the conception of geography held by historians had itself to be reworked. Particularly under the influence of Paul Vidal de la Blache, French geographers came increasingly to be concerned with the reciprocal relations between culture and nature, with the complex character of interactions between peoples and their environments, and with regions and places as products of such relations and interactions over long periods of time. With geographers rethinking such issues, French historians in turn had to reject any residual geographical determinism from their own works and embrace the new notions of possibilism and probabilism (Sanguin 1993). The most thorough endeavour to do so was that provided by Lucien Febvre ([1922] 1925) in his (now classic) 'geographical introduction to history'.

Febvre was an active participant in the broadly based reaction which spread in France during the early twentieth century against the positivist methods of nineteenth-century historical scholarship. A desire to go beyond the documents themselves and to conquer the distrust of historical generalisation had characterised both Henri Berr's journal, *Revue de synthèse historique*, founded in 1900, and his edited book series, *L'évolution de l'humanité*, launched in 1913 as a synthetic history animated, as William Keylor put it, by 'a passion for recapturing the complexity of past epochs through the broad sweep of historical narrative' (Keylor 1975: 211). Febvre had written articles and reviews on geographical topics for Berr's journal and then contributed to his book series an extended treatment of the interactions between environments and peoples, his *La terre et l'évolution humaine: introduction géographique à l'histoire* (1922). Febvre started from the assumption that 'in reality' little or nothing was as yet known of the influence of geographical environment on human societies, because, as he put it, the geography which would explain that influence had scarcely been born at the time he was writing (Febvre [1922] 1925: 28–9). But Febvre then drew upon the concepts of the new Vidalian school of human geography to produce a powerful rejection of geographical determinism in history and to set out instead a strong case for possibilism. 'There are', he concluded, 'no necessities, but everywhere possibilities; and man [*sic*], as master of the possibilities, is the judge of their use. This, by the reversal which it involves, puts man in first place – man, and no longer the earth, nor the influence of climate, nor the determinate conditions of localities.' Again, 'men can never entirely rid themselves, whatever they do, of the hold their environment has on them. Taking this into consideration, they utilise their geographical circumstances, more or less, according to what they are, and take advantage more or less completely of their geographical possibilities. But here, as elsewhere, there is no action of necessity.' Just as importantly, Febvre argued against searching for geographical 'influences' upon history, preferring instead to advocate a concern with the reciprocal relations between environments and societies through time (Febvre [1922] 1925: 236, 315 and 363).

In his reworking of the relations between history and geography, Febvre explicitly challenged both the view of that relationship as being one concerned with changing administrative boundaries and the view of it as a study of geographical 'influences' upon history. He offered instead a much broader prospectus: 'What', he asked, 'are the relations of human societies of bygone times, at different epochs in the various countries of the world, with the geographical environment of their day, so far as we are able to reconstruct it?' And to Febvre it mattered 'little whether those who undertake such research be labelled at the outset geographers, historians, or even sociologists' (Febvre [1922] 1925: 394). Berr, in his 'Foreword' to Febvre's book, expressed himself slightly differently: 'The problem of the influence of environment is not the domain of a geographer pure and simple. The purely "geographical geographer" does not trouble himself about history, or is even disposed to absorb it in geography. The treatment of this complex problem needs a geographical historian, or an historical geographer, who is also more or less a sociologist' (Berr 1925: v).

Febvre's magisterial treatment of the relations between geography and history, combined with the conclusions which he reached, licensed 'historians' to practise 'geography' – and, of course, 'geographers' to practise 'history'. Such licence was certainly to be one of the tenets upon which Lucien Febvre and Marc Bloch, in 1929, founded the *Annales d'histoire économique et sociale* and also of the distinctive school of history which evolved from, and revolved around, that journal. French historians had no hesitation in drawing deeply from the well of geographical concepts to nourish their changing discipline (Friedman 1996). Febvre was to make explicit his own recognition of the very considerable intellectual debt owed by the practice of history in France to geography: 'In fact, one might say that, to a certain extent, it is Vidalian geography which has sired the history of the *Annales* [school]' (Febvre 1953: 374). For Febvre, the close relations between history and geography were clear but had constantly to be emphasised to others. In 1950 he commented on Roger Dion's 1948 inaugural lecture on taking the Chair of the Historical Geography of France at the Collège de France, endorsing Dion's claim that the human geography of France must necessarily be a historical geography. Febvre stressed that such apparently obvious assertions had to be reiterated in order to correct short-sighted geographers and shallow-minded historians who both, to his dismay, still existed then – just as they do today (Febvre 1950: 87).

French history has been imbued with geography (Ozouf-Marignier 1995). One classic regional study was Fernand Braudel's panoramic reconstruction of the Mediterranean world during the sixteenth century. For Braudel, geography was not simply a stage, a physical environmental space upon which historical dramas were enacted, and it was also more than a framework of administrative boundaries. His study involved an awareness of the changing ecological components of the physical environment, of the role of environmental perception and of natural resources (including time and space) as cultural appraisals, and of the significant interplay of human and non-human forces in the making and the changing of the history of the Mediterranean world (Braudel 1949). Such regional historical syntheses became a distinctive characteristic of the *Annales* school of history. Braudel's kind of history not only borrowed heavily from geography; it also reworked some concepts about time and space. One key idea was that historical changes proceed at different rates. In his study on the Mediterranean, Braudel distinguished three such rates, devoting to each a separate section of his book. Before considering the short time-spans of individuals and events (*histoire événementielle*) and the slow but perceptible rhythms (*histoire conjoncturelle*) of economies and societies over periods of, say, ten to fifty years, Braudel initially considered long-term, hardly perceptible changes in the physical environment and in the relations between people and their environment. This third category of change was described by Braudel in his book both as 'geographical time' and as 'structural history' (*histoire structurelle*), and the idea of slow but fundamental change, whether in the physical (geographical) or the cultural (social) domains, he elaborated later into that of '*la longue durée*', a concept which has itself left an enduring impression upon the study of history as practised by the *Annalistes*. For example, recognising the role of multiple time-scales within societies, Jean-Luc Piveteau in his book *Temps du territoire* (1995) portrays the social organisation of space at a moment in time as a horizontal cut made through the vertical arrow of time within which are embedded processes operating in short-term, medium-term and long-term time-scales. But for Braudel, historical processes operated not only at different time-scales but also at different spatial scales. It was this emphasis in Braudel's work, together with his recognition of the roles of the physical environment and of distance and location in the making of regional histories, which led Yves Lacoste (1986) to refer to Braudel as a 'geographer' after Pierre Chaunu had referred to Braudel more transitionally as 'the master of historical geography' (Chaunu 1969: 70).

A related key concept outlined by Braudel was that of 'geohistory' (*géohistoire*). For Braudel, geography was the study of society in space and in his monograph on the Mediterranean world during the sixteenth century he described what for him would be a project in geohistory. It would seek a historical understanding of the spatial and environmental contexts of human activities and would, if at all possible, involve mapping them. For Braudel, geohistory was explicitly a way of making historians more geographically aware and geographers more historically sensitive (Braudel 1949, 2nd edn 1966: t. II, 295). It must be admitted that Braudel's monograph on the Mediterranean world was not universally acclaimed. One especially critical reviewer, B. Bailyn (1951), claimed that the book was neither focused nor problem-orientated: it had no central problem because Braudel had set out to do the impossible, to find out everything there is to know about the Mediterranean world in the sixteenth century. Nor did its organising principles, including that of geohistory, permit in practice the construction of an integrated view of that world. But another and much later critique of Braudel's work concluded that the conceptual novelty of his work on the Mediterranean world lay precisely in its geohistory. S. Kinser (1981) argued that, before Braudel's exposition of geohistory, historians who had acknowledged aspects of physical geography had not successfully connected the effects of environmental considerations with social activity in temporally specific ways, instead treating an area's physical geography just as a stage for the historical drama. But since that exposition, historians have had to seek to interweave geography and history much more continuously and much more subtly, recognising that people and their environments interact to produce a distinctive *milieu*.

Although geohistory has become embedded within the practice of French history as a concept, as a term it has not been much used by historians, perhaps because some thought it a 'barbarous' connotation, possibly because some confusion arose when it was employed to refer to the history of geography and of geology (Dunbar 1980) and when it was used interchangeably with 'historical geography' by the historian Pierre Chaunu (1969). A sustained discussion and elaboration of geohistory as a concept was provided by Charles Higounet (1961), who saw it both as an approach which emphasised the importance of locating historical events and as a method which prioritised mapping historical data as a way of exploring problems. He cited two examples from his own work: first, his mapping of 'new towns' (*bastides*) in south-western France suggested the existence there in the thirteenth century of frontier zones between differently administered or owned territories; and secondly, his comparison of a map of the distribution of Romanesque churches in the Gironde region in the twelfth and thirteenth centuries with one of medieval woodland clearance enabled Higounet to suggest that the church-building movement was probably associated with the growth of the viticultural economy of the Bordeaux region. Geohistory in this limited sense, as 'the cartographic method in history', has come to be widely adopted in practice if not in name. But Braudel had given the term much broader meaning, embracing both the spatial and environmental contexts of human activities. Although few historians have used the term *géohistoire*, it has recently been the explicit organising principle of two books by geographers. Christian Grataloup's *Lieux d'histoire: essai de géohistoire systématique* (1996) addresses the spatial organisation of societies on a global scale through time. Examining spatial relations and the roles of location and distance in the changing fortunes of empires, continents, countries and cities from the Neolithic to the Industrial Revolution, Grataloup sees space as a significant 'actor' in world history. Peter Taylor's (1999a, 1999b) 'geohistorical interpretation' of the modern world's development since the sixteenth century is an approach which 'focuses on the embeddedness of social practices within specific space-time locations' and which interprets 'the concrete face of modernity as a single inter-connected story and map'.

Surveying the relations of history and the social sciences, Braudel argued the need to refer each society to the space, place or region in which it exists, to its broad geographical context. For Braudel, writing in 1958, not only history but all the social sciences would have 'to make room for an increasingly geographical conception of humanity' – and here he was explicitly repeating the claim made in 1903 by Paul Vidal de la Blache, the founder of modern geography in France (Braudel 1958: 753). Braudel's reiterated plea for what might be called the 'geographicisation' of history and the social sciences took a long time to be heard but has come to be highly significant. In 1971 an American historian, Edward Fox, published a book on *History in Geographic Perspective*, in which he regretted the fact that 'history and geography were once assumed to be sister sciences so close in method and focus as to verge on representing two aspects of a single subject' but that 'today they share nothing' (Fox 1971: 19). Fox's exploration of 'the geographic dimension of history' argued for historically specific studies of the limits on human action imposed by geography, and the opportunities offered by it. For Fox, the 'geographic dimension' embraced both environmental and spatial components, while his interest in geography sprang from his concern to understand regional variations in the social and economic history of France. In 1989, Eugene Genovese and Leonard Hochberg, in their editorial preface to a collection of essays in honour of Fox, claimed that it was only during the previous decade or so that 'the long and debilitating separation of geography from history and, more broadly, the social sciences [had] begun to be overcome' (Genovese and Hochberg 1989: vi). History and the social sciences have in recent years become increasingly aware that geography matters in all of its guises and they have become especially attentive to the spatiality of social activity (Lepetit 1986a; Benko and Strohmayer 1995). Edward W. Soja (1989) has provided a general examination of the reassertion of space – the 'spatial turn' – in critical social theory. Soja's critique of historicism's prioritising of time over space and his critical examination of the role of space in the ideas of, *inter alia*, Michel Foucault, Anthony Giddens and Henri Lefebvre, led him to argue for a historical and *geographical* materialism.

The inclusion of geographical concepts within the 'total history' project of the *Annales* school led some to argue that geography in France itself suffered as a consequence, with geography as a subject having been annexed by history (Harsgor 1978; Huppert 1978; Ozouf-Marignier 1995). From its beginnings, the *Annales* school of history argued the merits of academic hybridity rather than purity and its founders contested the drawing of boundaries between disciplines (Baker 1984). For example, in reviewing Daniel Faucher's regional monograph on the middle Rhône valley, Bloch took Faucher to task for his insistence that geographers should never forget that their proper concern was to write geography, not history. Bloch saw no value in such a distinction between two disciplines whose combined purpose was to construct a science of man in society (Bloch 1929). Precisely the same view was to be expressed in the *Annales* almost thirty years later when a historian, Robert Mandrou (1957), admonished geographers for recognising the existence of a frontier between history and geography and for placing boundaries around categories of historical geography.

But this inclusive view of the relation between history and geography by *Annaliste* historians could be seen as having limited further discussion, for it appeared to have rendered the relation unproblematic – at least for historians, who readily incorporated geographical perspectives into their historical analyses and syntheses, as well as into their epistemologies. Geography has come to be seen by historians in France as being *a part of* history, *not apart from* history. Marie-Vic Ozouf-Marignier (1995) portrays that relationship as an appropriation by historians of the geographical concepts of environmental change and of spatial variation. Bernard Lepetit (1986a), in his prefatory remarks to a set of essays on *espace et temps* in honour of Braudel, chose to emphasise Braudel's privileging of space in historical studies, his highlighting of the role of spatial variations and of spatial relations in the making of histories. But in claiming this to be 'geographical history', Lepetit imposed – no doubt unintentionally – a limit on the relation between history and geography. That relation, I will argue, has to be seen not only in terms of 'geographical history' but also in terms of 'historical geography'. The translation of geography by French historians from broad environmental considerations into narrow spatial variations (and the consequent construction of spatial histories) impoverishes unnecessarily the nature of the connections between history and geography. There is more to geography than spatial relationships – and indeed more even than spatial relationships and environmental conditions. Fortunately, this is now coming again to be recognised by some French historians, for example by Jean-Pierre Poussou (1997) in his recent discussion of what he sees as a renaissance of the relation between geography and history in France, reflecting a revival there of historical geography itself (Pitte 1989; Claval 1995). So it is now necessary to turn the coin over and to ask: 'How have geographers viewed history?'

Geographers and history

Generally speaking, while historians have been able to put geography in its place, geographers have been perplexed about how best to make time for history. While there have been few, but substantial, considerations by historians of the relations of geography and history, there have been many, but slighter, discussions of that issue by geographers. There is no need to consider all of the latter. After considering the historical context of the debate, I will focus upon recent discussions of the relations of geography and history.

In Europe during the late nineteenth and early twentieth centuries, 'historical geography' was a term used by geographers principally to describe studies of changing political boundaries and entities, but it came to be given a much broader meaning. Charles Pergameni, an Italian geographer who worked for some time in Belgium, argued in 1942 in an article written in French that historical geography (*la géographie historique*) should move away from its traditional, *sensu stricto*, limited concern with identifying and explaining changing political boundaries to a new, *sensu lato*, broad study of the human geography of the past – and, to distinguish this new approach from the old, Pergameni referred to it conveniently but confusingly as the 'geography of history' or geographical history (*la géographie de l'histoire*). Drawing especially upon the ideas of the German geographer Carl Ritter and of French geographers like Paul Vidal de la Blache and Jean Brunhes, Pergameni advocated a new historical geography or geographical history which embraced the relations between people and their environments in the past: for Pergameni, his new 'geography of history' was nothing less than a study of the human geography of the past (*la géographie humaine du passé*), in effect, of past geographies (Pergameni 1942: 25). Roger Dion expressed similar but differently nuanced and more influential ideas in his 1948 inauguration of his course on historical geography at the Collège de France in Paris. In his exposition on retrospective human geography (*la géographie humaine rétrospective*), Dion argued forcefully for a new historical geography which would move away from studies of changing political boundaries and from studies which allocated a primary role to physical geographical influences. He proposed a wider scope for studies in historical geography, while paradoxically restricting them to historical studies of 'present-day' geographies. Dion advocated a greater emphasis on human agency and argued that all cultural landscapes should be seen as historical constructions: 'Tout paysage humanisé est le reflet d'une histoire.' For Dion, full understandings of today's human geographies could only be achieved by looking back into their histories. Historical geography was properly geography and not history because its objective was to explain the 'present-day' human geography of an area (Dion 1949, 1957). In practice, Dion's own work was to become on his own terms decreasingly geographical and increasingly historical, focused less on the present and more on the past (Planhol 1972). A slightly different twist was given to this argument by Lucien Gachon (1955), who insisted that, because the impress of the past is never completely erased, geographical accounts of the present-day must be thickened by historical explanation; moreover, the geography of any place is continually changing, it is never static, which means that a historical perspective is necessary in order to capture its dynamic character.

In North America during the late nineteenth and early twentieth centuries, geographers engaged with historians in debate about the nature and extent of geographical influences on historical developments and in so doing established what Michael Conzen (1993) considered to be the first school of American historical geography. Albert P. Brigham's *Geographic Influences in American History* and Ellen Churchill Semple's *American History and its Geographic Conditions* were both published in 1903, and Brigham and Semple both published papers which considered the relations of geography and history (Brigham 1904; Semple 1909). In their different ways – Brigham's work was the more regional, Semple's the more thematic – these books examined the role of the physical environment, of 'geographical influences' and 'geographical controls', on historical events and developments. These issues were also pursued in general discussions of the relations of geography and history by Ellsworth Huntington (1914, 1937) and Harry E. Barnes (1921). Such studies brought the work of geographers to the attention of historians, confirming for most of them their view that 'geography' could be treated as the physical environment, as what Semple ([1903] 1933: v) herself termed 'the stage on which history unfolds'. They also stimulated numerous studies in similar vein, both by historians and by geographers. As Conzen has pointed out, many such studies were flawed by over-generalisation and special pleading and at worst they became outright arguments for environmental determinism, ascribing only a passive role to people. Unsurprisingly, some historians immediately – and some geographers eventually – were unwilling to accord 'geographical influences' such primacy over historical agents (Conzen 1993: 15–19).

Unfortunately, discussion by Anglo-American geographers of the relation between history and geography came to be constrained for decades by Richard Hartshorne's argument, set out in his massive examination of *The Nature of Geography* (1939), that geography and history were distinct and different disciplines, the former concerned with chorography and the latter with chronology, the former with differences from place to place and the latter with changes from time to time. Defining geography as 'areal differentiation', Hartshorne explicitly excluded considerations of changes through time from geographical studies. For Hartshorne, geography's purpose was to provide understanding of the present and that of history to provide understanding of the past. For him, the boundary between geography and history was both well defined and not to be transgressed. With hindsight, it is extraordinary that this view was expounded so forcefully and so influentially, given the very positive views then being expressed in France – and indeed elsewhere outside America, as well as by some of Hartshorne's geographical colleagues in America – about the intimate relations of history and geography. Hartshorne's extremist position was eroded gradually by the ideas and researches of cultural and historical geographers like Carl Sauer, Clifford Darby and Andrew Clark. But even when Hartshorne modified his view some twenty years later, in his *Perspective on the Nature of Geography* (1959), he persisted in arguing that geographers could incorporate 'time and genesis' in their studies only to the extent that they 'facilitate comprehension of the present' (1959: 106). For Hartshorne, 'historical studies of changing integrations are essentially geography rather than history as long as the focus of attention is maintained on the character of areas, changing in consequence of certain processes, in contrast to the historical interest in the processes themselves' (1959: 107).

Acceptance of the need to study the contribution of history to the making of a present-day geography was only a limited renegotiation of the relations between history and geography. Interpretations of present-day geographical phenomena, both physical and cultural, were widely accepted as necessitating an understanding of their evolution, of their historical development. For example, Derwent Whittlesey's (1929) concept of 'sequent occupance' – the portrayal of a chronological succession of cross-sections of an area – had been elaborated as a partial answer to the fundamental question which he would famously pose in 1945: 'Is there a solution for the puzzle of writing incontestable geography that also incorporates the chains of event necessary to understand fully the geography of the present day?' (Whittlesey 1945: 32). Recognition of the significance of what A. G. Ogilvie (1952) termed 'the time-element in geography' and of what both Whittlesey (1945) and Sauer (1974) called 'the fourth dimension of geography' demonstrated beyond doubt that all geographical studies should take cognisance of the factor of time. In his explicit consideration of 'the relation of geography to history', J. M. Houston argued that many of the problems which are considered by the geographer can best be resolved by viewing them in their historical contexts; but while acknowledging that geography needs a genetic conception of the problems it meets and studies, he insisted that geography must not become history (Houston 1953: 39–46).

Hartshorne's massive treatise, published in 1939, certainly and most unfortunately overshadowed a smaller but significant exploration of the relations between geography and history published in the previous year. W. Gordon East, in his consideration of *The Geography behind History* (1938), developed the line of argument which had been pursued by many historians, viewing geography initially as providing a study of the physical setting to history. Admittedly, East explicitly objected that the often-repeated analogy between geography and history as the stage and the drama was misleading in several respects: 'for whereas a play can be acted on any stage regardless of its particular features, the course of history can never be entirely unaffected by the varieties and changes of its setting'. East preferred another metaphor: for him, geographers 'assert that the physical environment, like the wicket in cricket, owing to its particularities from place to place and from time to time, has some bearing on the course of history' (East 1938, revised edn 1965: 2–3). His central concern was to discover in what ways and to what extent the geographical 'cricket pitch' affected the historical 'game'. But East's prospectus for the geography behind history went beyond geography as mere physical setting to include also study of the interactions between people and their physical environments and their resultant distinctive regions and landscapes, as well as an assessment of the significance of geographical position and location on the course of history. East's concern was to demonstrate how geographical concepts and enquiries could enhance historical understanding and he did so in a series of exemplary case studies.

There had been other dissenting voices, but they were either more softly spoken or not heard with the same authority as Hartshorne's. Some were muffled because they seemed to resonate with environmental determinism, providing echoes from studies such as those by Semple (1903) on the geographical 'influences' and 'controls' upon American history. But there were significant exceptions to Hartshorne's disciplinary *apartheid*. For example, in 1941 Jan Broek – who in 1932 had published a study of the changing landscape of the Santa Clara valley in California which has come to be seen as a classic work in historical geography, a model methodologically – argued that history and geography 'are closely interwoven', that no matter how geography is defined it contains a strong historic element, and that both historians and geographers are concerned with the processes and products of cultural change (Broek 1941: 321). Sauer's studies of changing cultures and their landscapes led him to state in 1941: 'I wish to reckon historical geography as part of culture history' (Sauer 1941a: 9). J. K. Wright (1943) argued that in the zone where history and geography met were to be found two types of study: histories of geographical discovery and reconstructions of the 'geographic actuality of a particular region as it was in the past', in both instances drawing largely upon the records of explorers, travellers and contemporary maps. In due course, Wright's ideas on the geographical imagination were to promote significant studies in historical geosophy – study of the geographical ideas, 'true' or 'false', which people had about places in the past (Wright 1947).

But undoubtedly the most forceful and influential consideration of the relations of geography and history provided by a geographer was that by Darby (1953b), who identified four themes within what he described as the 'intellectual borderland' between geography and history. The first, 'geography behind history', involved considerations of the geographical influences – in effect, the physical geographical influences – upon history. The second, 'past geographies', reconstructions of the geographies of past times, were produced by both historians and geographers, but with somewhat different emphases. The third, 'the history behind geography', comprised portrayals of changing landscapes which were simultaneously historical and geographical studies. The fourth, 'the historical element in geography', was concerned with how to solve Whittlesey's riddle, with how to provide 'a historical approach in geographical description'. More generally, Darby claimed that he found it 'difficult to delimit the frontier' between history and geography, both because 'the geography of the present-day is but a thin layer that even at this moment is becoming history' and because 'art as well as nature has gone into the making of most landscapes'. Arguing that 'to set tariff frontiers [between history and geography], and so hinder the flow of ideas, is as unnecessary as it is unprofitable', Darby claimed that the extent to which geographical enquiry needed to call upon historical analysis would depend upon the nature of the particular problem being investigated. Notwithstanding these liberal attitudes, Darby explicitly stated that forays into 'the geography behind history' were 'not studies in geography'. During the 1950s and early 1960s Darby was developing his ideas about the distinctiveness of historical geography and in so doing deliberately distanced his kind of geography from history – as well as his kind of historical geography from geography itself (Darby 1962a). Darby's explorations of the relations between history and geography were transmitted directly but somewhat critically into the French-speaking world by Etienne Juillard (1956): while acknowledging the artificiality of any frontiers between history and geography, Juillard none the less accepted the practical necessity for selecting among research topics and recognised that social historians and human geographers do ask different questions about the same phenomena. Darby's ideas were also diffused, less critically, into the Spanish-speaking, Latin American world by Patricio Randle (1966).

In addition to these attempts by geographers to examine the general relations of history and geography, there were two notable endeavours to consider those relations more precisely. Andrew H. Clark (1960) addressed specifically the concept of geographical change as a theme for economic history. He pleaded for more emphasis on the geographical structure of change, on the changing patterns of phenomena and relationships in and through an area – in effect, for more regional studies of economic change and for more regional economic histories which took account of the locational aspects of change. John A. Jakle (1971), arguing that during the 1960s geographers like David Harvey (1967, 1969) had come to focus increasingly on spatial changes through time, sought to define common interdisciplinary grounds for history and geography within the debate about how temporal and spatial parameters could be effectively related, how change through time and across space should be measured and analysed. The broadcasting of Jakle's views on historical geography in the *American Historical Review* in 1971 coincided with a direct and fruitful conversation between American historical geographers and historians (and archivists) at a conference held that year on the USA's national archives and research in historical geography. This was a direct attempt to bridge the 'Great Divide', led by Clark (Clark 1975a; Ehrenberg 1975). It echoes a much earlier highlighting by a French geographer, Albert Demangeon (1905a, 1907), of the geographical potential of national archives.

In relation to French historiography, André Blanc (1967) examined the relations between social history and human geography. He argued that today's geography becomes tomorrow's history, that geography is a victim of history. Pierre George (1992) took up this point, arguing that with the accelerating pace of cultural change today's geography is ever more rapidly becoming contemporary history. For Blanc, human geography in France took two forms: either it was retrospective, concerned with the historical evolution of the (transient) present, or it was prospective, focused upon the future development of present-day geographies. For George, with history and geography converging, the specificity of geography lies in its emphasis on examining each phenomenon in its place, in its location. Blanc also made the point that, while much lip service was paid to the idea of co-operation between historians and geographers, to the principle of interdisciplinary encounters, not much was being achieved in practice. Since Blanc's essay, there have been two further reviews by French scholars of the relations of history and geography. Alain Reynaud (1981) identified three different uses of history by geographers: first, the past studied for its own sake, often in the form of *géohistoires* and always addressing geographical questions in historical circumstances; secondly, history studied for its contribution to the making of the 'present', with change viewed as being either progressively linear (evolutionary) or structurally discontinuous (revolutionary); and thirdly, history reduced to being time, to the time-dimension in geography, and to temporal (especially short-term) variations in phenomena. For Reynaud, personally, geography begins and ends with the present day even if in between it is necessary to make a detour via history: if the focus is on the past, then the study is fundamentally history even if it is posing geographical questions. François Gay (1982), examining the role of time in geography, argued that geographers focused on the 'present day' must of necessity also consider both the past and the future: both impress themselves on the 'present', the former as inherited legacies and the latter as prospective aspirations. But Gay saw time as constituting the primary concern of the historian and space that of the geographer, and this is a debatable issue to which I will return shortly.

For the moment, I want to look at more recent but still direct contributions by geographers to this long-standing debate about the relations of geography and history. In two reviews of history, geography and historical geography, Richard Dennis (1991, 1994) provides an account of developments in the practice of Anglo-American historical geography for an audience of social science historians. He emphasises the diversity of the topics researched by historical geographers as well as the renewed, wide acceptance of the need for historical perspectives throughout human geography. But he also notes that such diversity can be read as a lack of intellectual coherence and that recognition of the historicity of human geography had led some to question whether historical geography will, or should, survive as a distinctive part of the discipline of geography. Dennis touches upon important issues which I want to address in this book: he raises significant questions but shies away from exploring possible answers to them. R. Marconis (1996), in his review of the relations between history and geography in France since 1918, rightly insists that they have to be interpreted not just intellectually but also institutionally: while there is an affinity between the two subjects, there is often alienation between their sets of practitioners, as noted previously by Paul Claval (1984). But what Marconis observes is a growing reconciliation, a rethinking of the relations between history and geography, reflecting a number of trends: a growing awareness of the fallibility of macro-economic models of change; a turn towards locality studies; and increased attention to problems relating to protection of the cultural heritage and of the physical environment.

Signs of the reconciliation between historians and geographers in France had been noted earlier by Marcel Roncayolo (1989), a *rapprochement* which he interpreted as reflecting the fundamental complementarity of their disciplines and in particular of their common interest in the relations between culture and nature and in questions of territoriality. For Roncayolo, the specificity of history and geography could not be defined by associating the former with time and the latter with space: it could only be identified by their practices and by their perspectives upon common problems. Confirmation of that process of reconciliation between history and geography is provided by Jean Bastié (1997, 1999) who, as President of the Société de Géographie of Paris, scripts one of the most positive and thorough reviews by a French geographer of the relations between history and geography. For Bastié, the study of geography encourages us to compare places, that of history to compare periods, in both cases highlighting both similarities and differences between the places and periods observed. At its most simplistic, everything which can be dated or which changes is historical; everything which can be located or mapped and which varies spatially is geographical. Thus the two approaches are complementary; they are two lights illuminating a single 'reality'. Both history and geography can be cut horizontally into periods or places and vertically into systematic studies such as economic history or social geography. For Bastié, there are not any limiting boundaries between history and geography, nor between them and cognate disciplines: history and geography, and *a fortiori* historical geography, are interdisciplinary perspectives. Moreover, Bastié recognises the existence of three processes in both history and geography: those of continuity (inertia), of change and of chance. He finally argues – much less convincingly – that, while history and geography are on common ground in not being exact sciences, they are differentiated in part because chance plays a greater role in the former and continuity a greater role in the latter.

Clearly, history is about much more than dating, and geography is about much more than locating, phenomena. So, too, historical geography is about much more than dating and locating. The reduction of 'history' to 'time' and of 'geography' to 'space' would be to over-simplify and even to misrepresent the nature of these two complex disciplines. Far fewer historians have claimed their subject to be concerned with 'temporal analysis' than geographers have claimed theirs to be with 'spatial analysis', but those scholars who have done so have offered a limiting view of their disciplines. While 'spatial analysis' is indeed part of the 'truth' of historical geography, it is far from being 'the whole truth and nothing but the truth'. I will pursue this further in due course, but I simply claim at this stage that it would be mistaken to confuse the complex, multi-dimensional relations of history and geography with those of time and space, and even more mistaken to reduce 'historical geography' to 'time geography'. 'Time' is clearly important within geographical studies in a variety of ways, not least in providing parameters and scales but also in itself constituting a resource which is culturally appraised and evaluated (Carlstein et al. 1978; Parkes and Thrift 1980; Kellerman 1987,

1989; May and Thrift 2001). But endeavours to elevate such approaches into a new sub-discipline of 'time geography' or 'chrono-geography' are founded on weak intellectual footings. For geographers to attempt to appropriate 'time' is as absurd as historians attempting to appropriate 'space'. Both 'time' and 'space' are properties shared by the entire community of scholars and disciplines across the natural sciences, social sciences and humanities (or historical sciences). Moreover, space is inherently temporal, and time is inherently spatial. While both time and space need to be measured and evaluated, neither can logically either form the distinguishing core of an individual discipline or serve to integrate sub-disciplines. For this reason, Doreen Massey's (1999) project to reconcile along such lines the divisions which she identifies within geography (and especially between physical and human geography) is unlikely to be successful. A common interest in 'space-time' is a weak foundation upon which to rebuild the links between physical and human geography: much stronger would be their shared interest in environmental problems and processes and in the interactions of nature and culture.

While there is much to be said for a pragmatic approach to historical and ge-ographical enquiry, it does lay its practitioners open to the charge that they have not given enough consideration to the philosophy of either history or geography, to the *idea* of history or the *idea* of geography. This charge has long been levelled against 'traditional' historical geographers by Leonard Guelke (1974, 1982). He restates it both in an article explicitly 'reconsidering' the relations between ge-ography and history, and in a jointly authored essay which is a modification of his full-blown advocacy of idealist historical geography into a less controversial (but for Guelke still 'radical') claim that ideas and ideologies underpin human landscapes (Guelke 1997; Guelke and Katz 1999). In 1959, G. R. Lowther had initially explored the relations between idealist history and historical geography, but subsequently Guelke's persistent advocacy of a Collingwoodian idealist ap-proach (Collingwood 1946) to historical understanding in geography has found little support, for many reasons. Guelke's long-standing charge that 'traditional' historical geographers like Sauer, Darby, Clark and Meinig ignored or neglected the ideas and beliefs of people in the past can readily be contested; so too can his refusal to recognise the challenge and legitimacy of writing history (and his-torical geography) not only from the viewpoint of the contemporary 'actors' but also, with hindsight, as a historical 'observer'; so too can his absolute rejection of other modes of historical understanding and his total reliance on Anglo-American literature, his total neglect of other schools of history and geography; and so also can his recently expressed view that history and geography each has a clearly de-fined subject matter focus, the former upon people–people relations and the latter upon people–environment relations (Guelke 1997). Guelke's attempt to establish a special relationship between history and geography while trying to avoid defining precisely any boundary between them in practice fails with this final, unambiguous identification for each of them of different subject matters. In this respect, Guelke himself can be regarded as a 'traditional' historical geographer, following in the footsteps of those who have sought to establish the autonomy of historical geography. That trail now needs to be retraced – but in the hope and intention that by doing so a new way can be found out of the impasse into which so many discussions of the relations between geography and history seem to have led. While agreeing with Robin Donkin's (1997) claim that a historical geographer is a 'servant of two masters', I want to argue that position as being a source of joy and not, as it ultimately seems to have been for Donkin, one of disillusionment.

On 'Historical Geography'

In early 1932 there was held in London a joint meeting of the (British) Historical Association and the (British) Geographical Association – professional societies of history and geography teachers and lecturers – to discuss the question: 'What is Historical Geography?' No entirely satisfactory answer was given to that question then and many attempts to seek one have been essayed subsequently.

In the most extended response given at that meeting to that basic question, E. W. Gilbert (1932) sought 'to distinguish between the different subjects which are at present included within the scope of historical geography, and to attempt a definition of the real subject'. He claimed that at least five different meanings could be given to the term 'Historical Geography' but that only one of them 'properly' described the subject. The four earlier conceptions of historical geography which Gilbert considered no longer to be appropriate in the 1930s were historical geography as the history of changing political frontiers; as the history of geographical discovery and exploration; as the history of geographical ideas and methods; and as the study of the influence of the geographical environment on the course of history. For Gilbert, the 'real function' of historical geography was 'to reconstruct the regional geography of the past'. Gilbert's view, that 'historical geography should confine itself to a descriptive geographical account of a region at some past period, and should not endeavour to make an explanation of historical events its main objective', was simultaneously a way of differentiating geography from history and historical geography from geography. It was, like most such definitions, intentionally divisive rather than integrative. It was, of course, founded on Halford Mackinder's (1930) depiction of historical geography as study of the 'historic present' and upon J. F. Unstead's (1907) portrayal of historical geography as the cutting of 'horizontal sections through time'.

Although this view of historical geography as study of the geography of a past period (or periods) was widely accepted by a generation of historians and geographers from the 1930s, it was being questioned even then by some of the new generation, notably in Britain by Darby, who sought both to broaden the meaning of the term 'historical geography' and to achieve recognition for it as a new academic sub-discipline. Setting out deliberately to rethink the then orthodox view of historical geography as a reconstruction of past geographies, Darby gradually established a new tradition concerned as much with changing landscapes and regions as with the cross-sectional study of places at critical periods in their past. Historical geography under his influence came to be increasingly identified with an approach in which the data are historical but in which the problems and methods are geographical. Darby promoted historical geography as a sub-discipline: he laboured with a missionary zeal to establish historical geography as a self-conscious, distinctive subject, distinguishable from contemporary human geography and different from other historical disciplines (Darby 1979, 1987).

Darby's (1953b, 1962a) codification of historical geography came to be widely accepted as defining it for a new generation. He identified four approaches in historical geography but, it seems to me, he was himself fully at ease with only two of them. To traditional studies of 'geographies of the past' he confidently added studies of 'changing landscapes': both of these were *geographical* in their subject matter and *historical* in their focus, so that for Darby they were unambiguously *historical geography*. By contrast, studies of what Darby variously called 'the historical element in geography' or 'the past in the present' were geographical in their subject matter but focused upon historical survivals and influences into the *present day* (and could thus be seen, somewhat disconcertingly, as being both contemporary geography and historical geography). Again, studies of what Darby termed either 'the geography behind history' or 'geographical history', studies of the influence of geographical conditions upon the course of history, he regarded as being essentially studies in *history* rather than in geography, although obviously of interest to historical geographers. Darby's anatomy of historical geography was an integral part of his explicit endeavour to create a separate existence for the 'discipline'. But he himself adopted a somewhat ambivalent stance in relation to two of his four categories. While studies of 'the past in the present' enabled him to claim that 'all geography is historical geography', their focus upon the present rather than upon the past, their selective use of the past in order to understand the present, meant that they might well be much more geographical than historical in their emphasis and in the process be studies in contemporary geography rather than in historical geography.

Darby's definition and classification of historical geography has been very influential. It provided a range of opportunities for researchers to grasp. It was the basis for the promotion of historical geography as a separate sub-discipline. It was to be an important component in the globalisation of historical geography. There have, of course, been many other discussions of the nature of historical geography, but none of them, in my view, has had the enduring influence of Darby's set of methodological essays – indeed, his lectures to undergraduates on the methodology of historical geography have recently been published posthumously, some forty years after they were written (Darby 2002). Even so, it needs to be recognised that from its initial appearance in 1953 and subsequent revision in 1962, Darby's framework for historical geography was questioned by some, and that recently others have talked up an aspect of it which Darby himself played down. Let me explore this point further. A particularly significant, early reservation about Darby's taxonomy of historical geography was expressed by Clark (1972) in his review of progress in historical geography in North America. He argued that 'most attempts at classification tend to become procrustean operations' and headings of the kind used by Darby (1953b, 1962a), Jäger (1969), Hugh Prince (1969) and Clifford Smith (1965) were in his view 'insupportably so' in relation to the historical geography of North America. Clark used instead the sub-headings of 'regional historical geography', 'urban interests', 'general topical studies', 'current fashions in methods and models', 'changing geographies and geographical change', 'cultural geography', 'morphological interests' and 'environment and perception', and he added a separate section on 'historical geography in Canada'. Clark's categories lacked – indeed were not intended to possess – intellectual coherence, reflecting instead the pragmatic notion that 'historical geography' is 'what historical geographers do'.

While Darby claimed that he had no wish to establish boundaries between academic subjects, arguing that 'there are problems not subjects' (Darby 1962a: 156), in practice he did precisely that by identifying four differentiating forms of historical geography as part of a self-confessed mission to establish historical geography's own intellectual credentials and indeed its independence both from history and from geography (Darby 1979, 1987). While proclaiming the importance of interdisciplinary co-operation, Darby sought to practise a kind of intradisciplinary hegemony with his claim that 'all geography is historical geography, either actual or potential' (Darby 1953b: 6). This was, admittedly, repeating similar claims made earlier by Derwent Whittlesey (1945: 33) and Rodwell Jones (1925: 250). More importantly, Darby's methodological writings on historical geography were not founded on a coherent set of criteria. The four-fold classification of the relations between history and geography which Darby elaborated in 1953 (the geography behind history, past geographies, the history behind geography, the historical element in geography) he replaced in 1962 by a different quartet (geographies of the past, changing landscapes, the past in the present, geographical history). Although Darby presumably considered his 1962 version to be an improvement on his earlier taxonomy, he none the less retained the 1953 framework for his lectures at Cambridge from 1966 until his retirement in 1976 (Darby 2002). In the revised (1962) taxonomy, two of the categories of historical geography were identified principally by their time perspectives ('past geographies' and 'the past in the present') and two by their focus upon problems ('changing landscapes' and 'geographical history'). But the category 'past geographies' could be theorised as subsuming all forms of geographical enquiry related to the past rather than the present, in which case it stands alone as a general definition of historical geography rather than being a specific description of just one of its forms. Darby even marginalised one of his own categories of historical geography – that of 'geographical histories' – by arguing that such studies were really histories rather than geographies. Finally, Darby's direct claim that all geography is historical geography was also making the point indirectly that all historical geography is geography and not history. Darby sought to make historical geography identifiably different both from economic history and from contemporary human geography (and he never really envisioned the possibility of a pre-historical geography).

I will make here a different case. There is no necessity for historical geography to stake out its own 'territory' nor any logical justification for doing so. There are no themes or areas of study which are exclusive to historical geography; rather, it shares its methods of enquiry with historical (and pre-historical) studies while sharing its problems of enquiry with geographical studies. Consequently, any codification – or even discussion – of historical geography should be grounded in the discourses of geography generally. Geography and history are perspectives; they are different ways of looking at the world. Geography and history do not have different subject matters, so that any distinction between them cannot be made on those grounds.

On the contrary, they provide complementary approaches to shared problems and themes. The closeness of the relationship between them is being recognised once again by geographers (Pitte 1989; Bastié 1997; Entrikin 1998) and I want in this book to bind the two ever more tightly. In order to do so, I will work within the main intellectual discourses of geography. Each of these will be discussed in terms of the contributions of historical geography to those discourses and of the benefits which have already been realised, and might in future be realised, from blending both historical perspectives into geographical enquiries and geographical perspectives into historical enquiries. There is neither the space nor the need in this brief volume to undertake a detailed reconstruction of the main discourses of geography. Fortunately, there exists a wealth of literature on the history of geographical ideas and practices upon which I am able to draw. Of course, that literature provides multiple readings of the history of geography, for the subject is by no means uncontested (see, for example, Pinchemel and Pinchemel 1981; Livingstone 1992). None the less, following Peter Haggett (1965) and Richard Hartshorne (1939), I accept that it is possible to identify one 'central' discourse of geography, its concern with places, areas and regions, and three 'peripheral' discourses, its concerns with distributions, with environments and with landscapes.

While such an approach cannot claim necessarily to have caught all of geography within its frame, I consider that it captures enough of geography's diversity to justify its use as the structure for my argument. Given that the regional discourse is broadly based upon synthesis and the three others upon analysis, I will consider in turn each discourse in the latter group before turning to the regional discourse. How, then, and to what extent, can historical geography within these discourses offer a means of bridging the divide between geography and history? That is the key question.

2

Locational geographies and histories

The locational discourse in geography

Edmund Bentley's well-known claim that 'Geography is about maps, but biography is about chaps' is, of course, incorrect both epistemologically and politically: geography is about much more than maps and biography (employed here as a surrogate for history) is about much more than chaps. But this claim's endurance as an aphorism rests in its capturing, while caricaturing, at least part of a truth: one essential trait of geography has been its concern with mapping distributions. Describing and explaining the specific location and general distribution of both 'natural' and 'cultural' phenomena has long been and remains a major theme of much geographical writing. Indeed, for some of its practitioners, geography is the science of location and distribution; it is the art of describing the spatial or geographical patterns of phenomena in particular places. All phenomena may be seen as having their own geographies at a moment in time and also geographies which change over time. But while location and distribution may be viewed as geographical concepts, they cannot be claimed to be exclusively so. A German geographer, Alfred Hettner, recognised almost a century ago that 'distribution by place forms a characteristic of objects . . . and must necessarily be included in the compass of their research and presentation' (Hettner 1905: cited in Haggett 1965: 13). Thus 'objects' studied by historians – such as art and alcoholism, boundaries and battles, and cultures and consciousness – each have their own geographical (spatial) distributions. None the less, although distribution is not exclusively a geographical concept, it is quintessentially so. It has certainly been the foundation of one of the major discourses within geography as a whole and within historical geography in particular. 'Where?' and 'Why there?' are basic geographical questions, just as 'When?' and 'Why then?' are basic historical questions.

The centrality to geography of the problem of spatial distribution was claimed by Sauer in his Presidential Address to the 1940 Meeting of the Association of American Geographers:

The ideal geographic description is the map. Anything that has unequal distribution over the earth at any given time may be expressed by the map as a pattern of units in spatial occurrence. In this sense geographic description may be applied to an unlimited number of phenomena. Thus there is a geography of every disease, of dialects and idioms, of bank failures, perhaps of genius. That such a form of description is used for so many things indicates that it provides a distinctive means of inspection. The spacing of phenomena over the earth expresses the general geographic problem of distribution, which leads us to ask about the meaning of presence or absence, massing or thinning of any thing or group of things variable as to areal extension. In this most inclusive sense, the geographic method is concerned with examining the localisation on the earth of any phenomenon. (Sauer 1941a; citation from Leighly 1963: 357–8)

The tasks involved in such geographical analysis are multiple, for it requires first identifying the location of particular phenomena, secondly mapping them at appropriate geographical scales using appropriate cartographic techniques, and thirdly describing verbally or mathematically the distribution pattern which has been depicted (carto)graphically. But whatever pattern is identified and however it is described, there then remains the task of explaining and understanding its configuration. The search for explanation and understanding might involve comparing one distribution pattern with another one, while bearing in mind that two different phenomena with identical or very similar geographical distributions might not necessarily be causally related. Moreover, any such search for the processes underlying a specific pattern has also to bear in mind the principles of equifinality and of indeterminacy: different processes can operate to produce very similar geographical patterns in different places, while the same or very similar processes operating in different places can result in different patterns.

Given that mapping distributions of phenomena in the present day is a major concern of geography, it follows logically that mapping distributions in the past is a major concern of historical geography. Indeed, Camille Vallaux (1925), in a chapter on historical geography within his broad survey of the geographical sciences, went so far as to argue that historical geography is primarily concerned with mapping the past. While I reject such an unnecessary and illogical limitation on the scope of historical geography, I accept fully mapping and interpreting distributions both as one legitimate end for historical geography and as a significant means towards its other objectives. I will, therefore, now consider in turn the related questions of geographical distribution at specific times in the past and of spatial diffusion through periods in the past.

Geographical distributions

The problems of making and interpreting maps of historical data are intrinsically serious but they are often neglected, sometimes ignored. The geographical interpretation of historical sources is a skill which can provide a distinctive insight into some aspect of the past (Baker et al. 1970). But such interpretation has to be conducted with circumspection. Very often, the historical sources themselves are not explicitly geographical, having been compiled for non-geographical purposes. It thus becomes necessary to build from and into such source materials the required locational or spatial dimension. In order to do so, a historical geographer has to contextualise the source material being employed: this involves understanding the purposes for which, and the manner in which, the material was compiled. It is not unusual for the survival of historical data to be incomplete, or indeed for the original collection of the data to have employed non-standard measures and also not to have covered the whole time period, geographical area or range of topics under examination. Apparently negative areas in a mapped distribution pattern might well be explicable in terms of the manner in which the source was originally compiled, not necessarily in terms of the absence of the phenomenon being studied. Again, a further complication is that the areal units to which a historical source refers might long since have disappeared and their location and size – or some surrogates for them – have to be reconstructed before the data can be mapped.

Mapping historical data, often the next stage of an investigation after that of laboriously harvesting data in archives or from published sources, is a surprisingly difficult and demanding task, not one to be undertaken lightly or regarded as being uncomplicated. Furthermore, it needs to be recognised that, as with almost all historical investigations, the process involves selection and thus subjectivity on the part of a researcher. Brian Harley (1989a) showed how the cartographic representation of historical sources has remained a largely unexamined aspect of discourse in historical geography. He suggested that maps constructed by historical geographers – and this would equally apply to those drawn by historians and others – should themselves be treated as texts rather than as mirrors of reality. Like any other source material, geographers' maps need to be deconstructed.

Mapping historical sources both legitimates and is itself legitimated by the view of historical geography as the reconstruction of geographies of the past, as 'horizontal cross-sections'. Individual years or periods of years selected for cross-sections tend to be those for which either a 'thick' single source (such as a taxation assessment or a census of population) or a cluster of different sources is available. Such reconstructions are impracticable without either the former or the latter, while the very existence of such sources tends to promote the reconstruction of cross-sections based on them, 'just because they are there'. An individual cross-section can be justified for its own intrinsic interest, in providing a snapshot of the geography (or of aspects of the geography) of a particular place at a specific moment in time. A series of cross-sections can be employed to provide an indication of the changes that have taken place during the intervening periods, focusing on the additions to and the subtractions from the geography of an area between one date and another. This method – comparative statics – focuses on changes in the distribution patterns, leaving to be inferred the processes behind the changes. It thus contains, rather than resolves, the problem of studying geographical change as process, itself a very difficult task because of the paucity of historical records of change as a continuous process, as a moving film rather than as a collection of snapshots. Of course, more precise measurement of geographical change is often possible by comparing a given situation at a later date in terms of some proportional increase or decrease of the situation at an earlier date.

But whether the comparison between two (or more) cross-sections is undertaken by casual inspection or by statistical calculation, a fundamental problem remains if it is attempted not just in terms of one or more components of the geography of an area but also in terms of its total geography. On purely theoretical grounds, cross-sections of the past may legitimately be drawn only for periods of historical and geographical stability. The cross-sectional method assumes that the geography of a place can be stable, unchanging for a given time or period in the past; it assumes a balance, an order, among the components of an area's geography at a particular moment or period in time. Such an assumption is questionable, both theoretically and empirically: any place is continuously changing, although not necessarily at a steady rate. These limitations of the cross-sectional methodology certainly constrain and possibly prohibit its application to the reconstruction of an area's total geography. But they do not thereby undermine the continuing relevance and legitimacy of mapping the distributions of individual components, or even of related sets of components, of an area's geography. Such mappings need to be seen, however, as contributions as much to the study of geographical change as to the study of past geographies.

The classic case of a cross-section of the past presented primarily as a set of distribution maps is that of the geography of England reconstructed from Domesday Book (Fig. 2.1). In a monumental work comprising seven books containing some 800 maps, Darby and his collaborators have constructed a remarkable picture of the geography of England in the late eleventh century, or more specifically, in 1086, or, more accurately, as evidenced in Domesday Book. They have been able to do so in part because of the relatively short time in which Domesday Book was compiled (in this sense it approaches a camera taking a snapshot), and in part because of the vast amount of detailed information which it contains. The Domesday Geographies of England have come to be seen as model historical geographies of distributions (Darby 1952, 1977; Darby and Maxwell 1952; Darby and Terrett 1954; Darby and Campbell 1962; Darby and Finn 1967; Darby and Versey 1975). The methodology which the Domesday Geographies employ, of mapping distributions teased out from a major source of data compiled within a very short period of time, has come to be emulated and might even be seen as constituting a significant and particular historico-geographical perspective.

It is an approach which has been applied to other major data sets, such as taxation returns, land use surveys and population censuses. For example, the geographical distribution of wealth in England in the early fourteenth century has been reconstructed by R. E. Glasscock (1975), principally from a taxation assessment of 1334. A similar geography of wealth in England in the early sixteenth century has been produced by J. Sheail (1972) from taxation assessments of 1524–5. Darby,

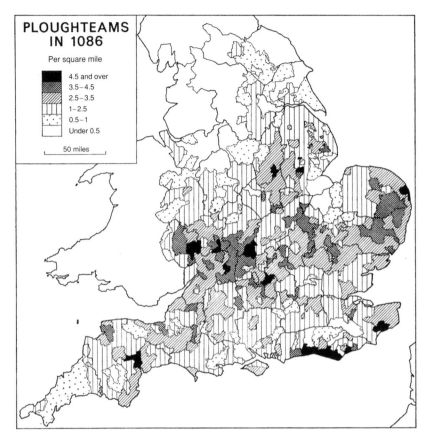

PLOUGHTEAMS IN 1086

Per square mile

- 4.5 and over
- 3.5–4.5
- 2.5–3.5
- 1–2.5
- 0.5–1
- Under 0.5

50 miles

Figure 2.1   The distribution of ploughteams in England in 1086, as recorded in Domesday Book
Source: Darby (1997: 127)

Glasscock and Sheail were all geographers but historians had previously ventured into this field. E. J. Buckatzsch (1950), in an explicitly 'experimental study', had reconstructed from a wide range of tax assessments a broad picture of the changing geographical distribution of wealth in England between 1086 and 1843, and R. S. Schofield (1965) had traced geographical changes in taxable wealth in England from 1334 to 1649. Both Buckatzsch and Schofield had used the county as their basic unit of comparison, but it was clear to geographers that each county could contain within it significant differences in the geographical distribution of wealth. Accordingly, four collaborated to produce a detailed mapping of the changing distribution of wealth in England 1086–1334–1525, employing 610 areal units standardised over the three dates in order to obtain a finer-grained and controlled comparative picture (Darby et al. 1979). The resulting maps, the products of years of meticulous data collection and analysis, constitute a wonderful set of windows upon medieval England, providing new perspectives on significant temporal and spatial (historical and geographical) changes and differences.

Reflecting his belief that 'cartographic representation of economic and social conditions in times past is central to historical geography', Hugh Clout is among those many historical geographers who 'would argue that spatial representation of available information not only adds a valuable new dimension to complement national average figures, computed by historians and economists, but also permits the results of more localised enquiries to be placed in context' (Clout 1980: 8). Clout undertook two major such exercises in relation to the agricultural geography of France. The first mapped, for the whole of the country and using the *arrondisse-ments* as the areal mapping units, a very wide array of agricultural data culled from statistics collected in the 1830s, thereby providing an astonishingly detailed picture of the agricultural geography of France on the eve of the railway age (Clout 1980). The second mapped, again for the whole country but using the broader-brush *départements* as plotting units, aspects of the agricultural geography of France at a number of dates between 1815 and 1914, using data excavated from a number of statistical and cadastral surveys. Clout recognised the limitations of his method: 'Considerable reliance must of necessity be placed on the comparison of evidence of cross sections and the inference of intervening change . . . [P]rocesses at work between successive cross sections may have been infinitely more complex than direct comparison might suggest.' But he took the view that in the absence of explicit evidence on process *per se* there was really no alternative to this approach and that the sheer volume of statistical data to be analysed necessitated the use of summarising devices to depict directions and average rates of inferred change over specified periods. Clout placed heavy reliance on what he termed 'quantitative cartography as a synthesising mechanism' (Clout 1983: 11). French historians have long been fascinated by the broad cultural contrast between an 'enlightened' France to the north and east of a line joining St Malo and Geneva and a 'dark' France to the south and west of that line. That idea was first represented cartographically in 1826 by Charles Dupin, who drew attention to significantly different levels of school attendance on either side of that frontier. Computer-based cartographical analysis of nineteenth-century data has brought that image into a much sharper focus, for example, in B. Lepetit's (1986b) examination of the geographical distribution of a range of key economic variables throughout France in the 1830s.

Advances in data-management and in cartography, the application of computerised data-processing and mapping, have enhanced enormously studies of past geographical distributions. For example, J. Palmer (1986, 2000) is undertaking a major computerised-mapping analysis of Domesday Book; R. Kain (1986) has used computer-produced maps in his ground-breaking atlas of statistical data on land use in England and Wales culled from the tithe files of the mid-nineteenth century; M. Overton (1977, 1985, 1996) has conducted a highly original computerised analysis of probate inventories in early-modern East Anglia, throwing new light on the changing geography of the Agricultural Revolution in England; and B. M. S. Campbell and J. P. Power (Campbell and Power 1989; Campbell 2000) have produced equally remarkable results from computer mapping of the agricultural geography of medieval England. Mapping distributions has become a sophisticated analytical technique in historical geography.

Computer-based mapping is especially likely to produce some of the most striking results in relation to large data sets, mainly but not exclusively from the nineteenth and twentieth centuries. Humphrey Southall is directing a major project whose objective is to construct a massive historical geographical information system (GIS) for Great Britain (Gregory and Southall 1998, 2000; Southall 2002). The project addresses the fact that, although over the past two centuries a vast amount of spatially based data about Britain has been gathered by public authorities, it is difficult to analyse the information geographically unless we know to which areas it relates. Systematic spatial frameworks for the census of population date only from 1981 and the system of reporting units has been subject both to complete transformations (in 1911, the mid-1930s and 1974) and to continuous revision of individual boundaries. Southall's historical GIS project aims to cut through this complexity in order to reveal underlying geographical trends from the mid-nineteenth century to the present. Its GIS contains the changing boundaries of more than six hundred Registration Districts *c.* 1840–1911, of almost two thousand Local Registration Districts 1911–74, and of about fifteen thousand Civil Parishes 1876–1974. The GIS is linked to a data-base which includes data from every population census since 1801 and mortality statistics since 1840, as well as many other sources. Constructing such a historical GIS is a very labour-intensive enterprise, but the potential of such a system for depicting geographical changes over long time periods is enormous. Results from this massive project are keenly awaited, as are those from other large GIS projects, such as those of Richard Healey and Anne Knowles on nineteenth-century industrial development in the north-eastern United States (Healey 2000). But the merits of such an approach to mapping are clearly demonstrated in a recent paper which analyses geographical trends in poverty in England and Wales between 1891 and 1991 by comparing significant quantitative indicators, such as infant mortality and housing overcrowding, from key dates. The comparison is made possible by a GIS which interpolates all the data sets on to standardised geographical units for mapping purposes (Gregory et al. 2001). Mapping poverty has a long history but the advent of GIS, releasing cartography from some of its traditional constraints, provides a significantly new range of visualisation techniques (Dorling 1992, 1998).

That the construction and use of historical GIS is increasingly attracting the attention not only of geographers but also of historians is demonstrated in a recent set of papers presented by geographers to a conference of social science historians. They covered diverse topics: a GIS-based approach to longitudinal analysis of age- and gender-specific population migration in England and Wales (Gregory 2000), historical GIS as a foundation for the analysis of regional economic growth

(Healey and Stamp 2000), and using GIS to visualise and interpret Tokyo's spatial history (Siebert 2000). An exciting and sustained attempt to address the use of GIS for history is to be found in a collection of essays edited by Anne Knowles (2002). Using historical GIS to explore such diverse topics as the Salem witch trials in seventeenth-century Massachusetts and race and ethnicity in twentieth-century New York, they demonstrate how this powerful tool is both enhancing co-operation between geographers and historians (and indeed other scholars) and leading to new ways of representing past geographies and of contesting long-standing historical interpretations. For example, Geoff Cunfer (2002) uses GIS to test systematically the extent to which detailed case studies apply to broader regions: his use of new analytical methods as well as of new data allows him to study the Dust Bowl of the American Great Plains at a regional scale during the 1930s. Employing data on soil type, land use and weather for all 280 counties in the Dust Bowl region enables Cunfer to challenge Donald Worster's (1979) long-accepted account of this phenomenon – an account based on intensive case studies of just two counties.

Historical GIS is an exciting and challenging development. It makes possible the spatial integration of large sets of both quantitative and qualitative data and permits standardised spatial comparisons over long time periods. Historical GIS is thus an analytical tool which is encouraging a renewed convergence of history and geography, promoting communication among those who have a shared interest in patterns of cultural change through time and over space. The collection of essays edited by Knowles signals a very important development both for the mapping and understanding of changing geographical distributions and of spatially referenced data, and for improving the relations of history and geography. The potential of historical GIS will be increasingly exploited as researchers rise to the challenge of mastering the necessary technical knowledge and as guides to their use, such as that by Ian Gregory (2002), become increasingly accessible. Historical GIS enables us, as Knowles puts it, 'to tell an enriched story about the past' (Knowles 2002: viii).

The mapping of distributions either in traditional or in new ways can make a crucial contribution to our understanding of the geographies of places in the past. Moreover, it can do so at a variety of scales from the local through to the global. This has long been recognised in the making of historical atlases, whether they are systematic or place-based in their organisation. I will consider historical atlases again in more detail later (in chapter 5) because in many ways they can be seen as potentially representing the closest possible integration of geography and history: they present for specific places graphical syntheses of changing geographical distributions.

Mapping historical data, then, has an important role to play in furthering our geographical and historical knowledges and understandings. It requires significant data-processing and cartographical skills, and it can take a long time to execute successfully and thoroughly. Such mapping is fundamentally descriptive and provocative, rather than necessarily being interpretative and productive. While it might answer the question 'Where?', it does not of itself also answer the question 'Why there?' Indeed, far from answering this latter question, mapping distributions itself raises that very question. A distribution map becomes, as soon as it is drawn, not an end product but a research tool: it identifies and describes, but it also poses new questions to which answers will have to be sought by further research. Maps tell us more about geographical patterns than they do about historical processes, which is not to deny that maps might be suggestive of those processes. But to consider the latter it becomes necessary to address the more historical question of how geographical distributions are generated and changed.

Spatial diffusions

'When?' and 'Why then?' are basic historical questions to be asked in relation to what might otherwise be considered as geographical phenomena. Alongside maps of geographical distributions we need graphs of historical events, each serving as another building block in the construction of a more complete historico-geographical synthesis. Such maps and graphs may be used as bricks of knowledge with which, working with a mortar of theory, we can build new understandings of past geographies. Graphs portray the temporal/historical distribution of a phenomenon, potentially adding considerable value to pictures of its spatial/geographical distribution. Such an approach moves us closer to an understanding not only of the patterns of historical and geographical change but also of the processes which underpinned them. Comparison of the two sets of patterns, of graphs and maps, a consideration of the extent to which they might be related, can in turn raise new questions and suggest new lines of research.

These are the premises on which I base my own study of sociability and voluntary associations in the Loire Valley during the nineteenth century. I examine the timing (or historical development) and the spacing (or geographical distribution) of distinctive sets of associations, including livestock insurance societies, mutual aid societies, fire brigades and agricultural syndicates, between 1815 and 1914. Deceptively simple graphs of their 'histories' and maps of their 'geographies' (Figs. 2.2, 2.3 and 2.4) serve as the foundation for more complex investigations and interpretations of the historical geography of these voluntary associations, of their economic, social and political significance, all set within the contexts of the nineteenth-century discourse of fraternity in France and of the modern theorisation of voluntary associations (Baker 1999a). Such graphs and maps are by no means as 'simple' as they seem to be at first sight. They are problematic both to construct and to interpret.

Just as in the case of geographical distributions, so also in that of historical trends, the surviving records may be incomplete and any graphs constructed from them have to be treated with utmost circumspection. Rarely have changes in the past been monitored continuously, recorded as and when they happened. Much of

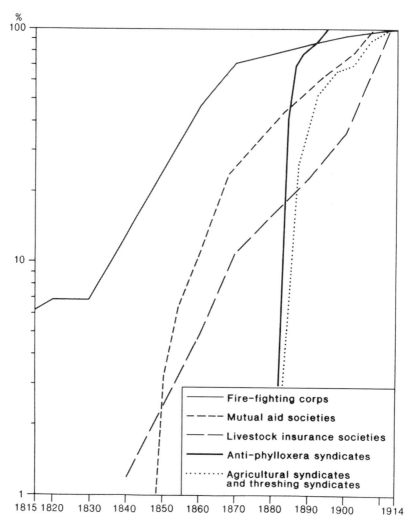

Figure 2.2   The 'timing' of some voluntary associations in Loir-et-Cher, France, 1815–1914
Source: Baker (1999a: 285)

our understanding of change has, of necessity, to be gleaned through comparative statics or through theoretically informed interpretations of non-standard sources. To the extent that geographical changes may be seen as resulting from transfers of energy, we ideally need to have as much information as possible about flows of people, commodities, capital and ideas, but it is unusual for such movements to have been recorded continuously. More usually records have been made at particular times for specific reasons, using different methods or criteria, so that constructing a coherent and comparable picture of changes through time is at worst impossible and at best a difficult exercise demanding judgements which must themselves expect to be challenged on either empirical or theoretical grounds, or even possibly on both counts.

Probably some of the records which best monitored events 'as they happened' relate to people and to property. In the former case, records of births or baptisms, of marriages, and of deaths or burials provide massive data sets from which impressive reconstructions have been compiled of demographic changes. In the latter case, land registers provide records of property transactions from which have been reconstructed changing profiles of land ownership and use. For England from 1538, parish registers recorded baptisms, marriages and burials 'as they happened' for three hundred years before the civil registration of these events occurred from 1837 onwards. The registers have by no means survived for the whole of that period for all of the parishes of England and they are not complete in their coverage of the data (for example, because some babies had died before they could be baptised and so are recorded only as burials; and the registers relate only to the established Church). None the less, they comprise a remarkable data source from which a range of time series of demographic characteristics can be produced. An outstanding study by Tony Wrigley and Roger Schofield (1981) analysed data from the ecclesiastical and civil registers of more than four hundred parishes in England between 1541 and 1871. The mass of data which they skilfully managed, using ingenious techniques (including that of retrodiction), was summarised primarily as time series (graphs) but also, to a lesser extent, as spatial series (maps).

Somewhat similar data sets exist for many European and other countries, but England does not have any land register to compare with that which has been compiled and maintained as a continuing record in France since the early nineteenth century. The cadastral survey initiated by Napoleon generated large-scale plans and registers encompassing every plot of land, private and communal, in each of the more than 30,000 communes of France. It recorded the ownership, use, quality and fiscal evaluation of each parcel when the survey was first completed (mainly during the 1830s and 1840s), providing a massive data-base for the reconstruction of cross-sections of individual communes, of departments and regions, and even of the country as whole at particular dates (Clout and Sutton 1969; Clout 1983). Remarkably, and just as importantly, these cadastral registers have been maintained as an up-to-date record through to the present day. Each time that a parcel of land has changed ownership, the transfer has been recorded, so that the registers were in effect monitoring the history of land parcels, recording changes of ownership 'as they happened'. Such a source is potentially invaluable for historico-geographical research, but its sheer bulk makes it difficult to use: computerised data-management techniques can be very sophisticated and speedy, but they depend often upon initially constructing a secondary data-base from a primary source, a task which can be very labour-demanding, prolonged and expensive. But also very rewarding. For example, a study of the property structures

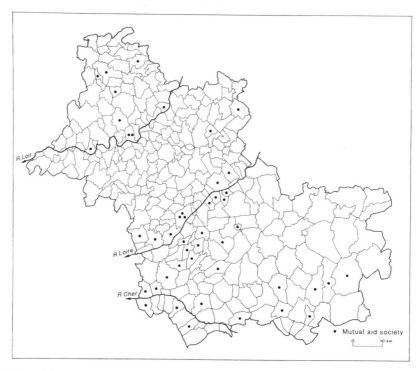

Figure 2.3   The 'spacing' of mutual aid societies in Loir-et-Cher, France, in 1868
Source: Baker (1999a: 156)

of five *départements* in the French Alps during the nineteenth century, based upon a detailed analysis of the cadastral registers of almost 700 communes and more than 500,000 parcels of land, showed *inter alia* the slow disintegration of the larger properties between 1820 and 1870, with parcels of land being purchased by owners of smaller properties: a frenetic market in land and a growing fragmentation of properties was reflected in the revelation that the number of parcels in those *départements* increased by more than 50 per cent during that fifty-year period (Vigier 1963).

Reconstructing time series of data – graphs, for example, of fertility and migration rates, of exports and imports, of prices and productivity, of the foundation and membership of learned societies, and of borrowing and investments – enriches our historical understandings by itself but geographical value is added when it is used in combination with reconstructions of spatial series, with distribution maps. The relations between history and geography are especially close in studies of the development of a phenomenon through time and of its diffusion over space. Such studies have a very long pedigree in both history and geography, and in both qualitative and quantitative forms.

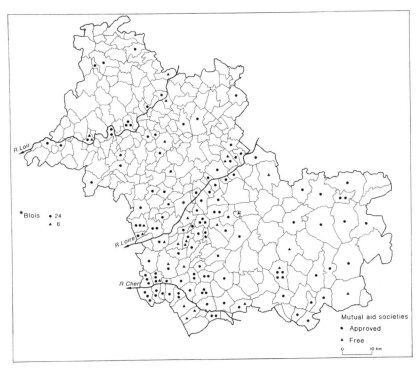

Figure 2.4 The 'spacing' of mutual aid societies in Loir-et-Cher, France, in 1907
Source: Baker (1999a: 159)

Diffusion studies in their varied forms have constituted a substantial and signif-icant component of geographical research during the past fifty years or so and they continue to hold an important position. Qualitative studies of diffusion owe much to the work of Sauer and the so-called Berkeley school. Sauer himself published an ambitious and inspirational study of the diffusion of agriculture throughout the world: his *Agricultural Origins and Dispersals* (1952) has come to be recognised as one of the major classic works in geography published during the twentieth century, as a bold synthesis on a grand scale (Conzen 1993: 29). The concept of spatial diffusion, of the historical development and geographical spread of phe-nomena, became the organising principle in much geographical work, especially but not exclusively in North America. The distribution and diffusion of plants and animals remains a central focus of work whose own origins can be traced back to Sauer's influence. It was seen, for example, in the study by Clark – one of Sauer's students – of the 'invasion' of the South Island of New Zealand by people, plants and animals (Clark 1949) and in the studies by Donkin – one of Sauer's British dis-ciples – of the distribution and diffusion of a number of (what some might consider esoteric) plants and animals (such as the opuntia cactus and the peccary) (Donkin

1977, 1985). But the concept has also been extended well beyond Sauer's own principal concerns to embrace features of the modern urban-industrial landscape, such as the grid-pattern town in the Americas and the skyscraper (Stanislawski 1946; Ford 1973).

Within history, one of the most influential interpretations of the colonisation of the United States has been the frontier thesis of Turner (1894). The diffusion of Europeans and of east coast Americans westwards through the Appalachians and across the Great Plains of the United States was presented by Turner as having had the greatest formative influence upon American history. The frontier was envisaged as both a place and a process: it was a thinly settled place, where 'civilisation' ended and migrants encountered a 'wilderness'; and it was a process of continuous adaptation to new physical and cultural environments, a melting-pot in which migrants with very different geographical and social origins were transformed into individualistic, democratic, Americans. The diffusion process was one of cultural transformation. But for Turner there was not just one frontier but a succession of frontiers, as wave after wave of migrants moved westwards:

stand at the Cumberland Gap [in the Appalachians] and watch the procession of civilisation, marching single file – the buffalo following the trail to the salt springs, the Indian, the fur trader and hunter, the cattle raiser, the pioneer farmer – and the frontier has passed by. Stand at the South Pass in the Rockies a century later and see the same procession with wider intervals in between. (Turner 1894, 1920 reprint: 12)

Turner's frontier thesis became deeply embedded not only within the historiography of American history but also within the populist 'American dream' – and it has arguably had a more enduring influence on the latter than on the former, for while it has been seriously challenged as a historical interpretation it has endured as part of popular myth about the development of American society. Turner's diffusionist interpretation of American history also appealed to historians of other countries and continents, and his ideas came to be applied to areas and circumstances well beyond those of the nineteenth-century United States – the thesis has itself diffused throughout the academic world, a process which ultimately served to emphasise not only its strengths but also its limitations (Gulley 1959). Turner's thesis was profoundly geographical as well as historical: for that reason Meinig (1960) acclaimed Turner as the lineal forebear, if not the father, of historical geography in the United States, while Robert Block saw Turner as a co-founder, with Semple and Brigham, 'of a subdiscipline in American geography that is concerned with the spatial consequences of the interface between geography and history' (Block 1980: 31). Turner's thesis engendered a host of studies by both historians and geographers on the fact of colonisation and questions of cultural transformation and transfer (Gulley 1959; Mikesell 1960; Block 1980). While the answers which Turner provided to questions about society on the frontier are not wholly acceptable today, some attempts continue to be made to address the questions which he posed: for example, by Cole Harris in his studies of what he has termed 'the simplification of Europe overseas', of the impact upon European migrants of their colonisation of New France, New England and the Cape Colony of South Africa (Harris 1977).

So far I have been considering essentially qualitative studies of diffusion and I now want to move on to more quantitative approaches. Whether qualitative or quantitative diffusion studies are undertaken – reflecting the character of the problem being studied, the limitations of the surviving sources and the preferences of individual researchers – matters very little if they are imaginatively conceived and rigorously conducted. In addressing qualitative and quantitative studies separately and sequentially, I do not mean to imply that the former are in any sense inferior to the latter. Indeed, many diffusion studies are the better for being a combination of the two approaches.

Especially important work in human geography on innovation waves as a spatial process was initiated by the Swedish geographer Torsten Hägerstrand (1952, 1953 translated 1967). From an intensive study of the adoption of a wide range of innovations in the Asby district of south-central Sweden, embracing agricultural innovations like bovine tuberculosis controls and grazing improvement subsidies as well as industrial innovations like telephones and cars, Hägerstrand derived inductively a model for the passing of what he termed 'innovation waves'. He observed that when he plotted against time the cumulative number of adopters of a given innovation, or the number adopting as a percentage of those who could potentially adopt an innovation, the result was an S-shaped or 'logistic' growth curve which could be divided into three phases: first, an early phase of slow but accelerating adoption of the innovation; secondly, an intermediate phase of rapid adoption; and thirdly, a late period of slower, decelerating, adoption. What was particularly important was Hägerstrand's observation that these S-shaped curves varied in slope not only from one innovation to another but also from one place to another. The temporal pattern of diffusion was shown to have significant spatial expression. Hägerstrand suggested that the spatial pattern of diffusion of an innovation could be characterised as having four temporal stages: the first or *primary* stage exhibited a marked contrast between the innovating centres and the areas distant from them; the second or *diffusion* stage was marked by a strong centrifugal effect, by considerable spread of the innovation and by the creation of new centres of innovation in the remote areas and a diminution of the strong spatial contrasts of the primary stage; the third or *condensing* phase saw the innovation being adopted at more or less the same rate throughout the area; and the fourth or *saturation* phase saw a slowing down of adoption, the innovation having become generally adopted throughout the area. The diffusion of innovations was thus demonstrated by Hägerstrand to be a fundamental process in the production of spatial or regional differences, in the understanding of 'leading' and 'lagging' regions. Some regional differences mapped from historical records were shown to have been products of the spatial diffusion process.

The aim of Hägerstrand's initial inductive model was to provide a generalised account of many specific examples of diffusion, to identify the general process underlying individual patterns of geographical change. He then advanced his work into the field of stochastic modelling, developing dynamic simulation methods which enable historical researchers to experiment theoretically with ideas about situations for which there is limited empirical evidence. Theories and techniques are here being employed imaginatively to bridge gaps in the available historical record. This deductive approach can be very stimulating and could even be seen as giving rise to a sub-discipline of 'theoretical history/historical geography'. Such model building came to characterise much historical geography in Scandinavia (Helmfrid 1972). But most historical research, it must be said, remains fundamentally empirical, concerned with 'real' situations illuminated by theoretical insights; it is unlikely to become primarily concerned with the construction of formal theoretical histories/historical geographies which are then tested against historical data. Few historians/historical geographers view the pasts which they study as experimental laboratories in which theories can be tested – but there are, as we shall see, important exceptions.

This is not to deny that most historical research involves testing hypotheses against the available evidence (and, reciprocally, allowing the evidence to suggest new hypotheses). Nor is it to say that most historians/historical geographers are reluctant to employ generalised concepts. On the contrary, most do so when they think that it can enhance understanding. I have, for example, so far only been considering *contagious* diffusion, which is dependent upon direct contact and is thus strongly influenced by the frictional effect of distance or by what has been termed the 'neighbourhood effect'. The closer a non-adopter is to an adopter, the higher the probability that s/he will in turn become an adopter. Within a school community, measles spreads in this way but so too do 'crazes' like skateboarding and mobile phone ownership. Within a locality, the adoption of such innovations as digital television also exhibits the neighbourhood effect. And it has already been emphasised that this process can also be seen at a regional scale, contributing to the production of significant areal differentiation. But physical distance and proximity are not always the strongest influence in a diffusion process, for some innovations leapfrog over intervening areas and peoples. This process is termed *hierarchical diffusion*, in which information – the *sine qua non* of innovation adoption – flows initially between larger, better-connected, settlements or between more influential, better-connected individuals, whence the information and hence the innovation trickles through the settlement or social hierarchy. Hierarchical diffusion takes place because some settlements, individuals or institutions remote physically from each other none the less have closer links with each other than they do with settlements, individuals or institutions which are located closer to them. The intervening spaces are passed over in the diffusion process. The distinction between contagious and hierarchical diffusion processes is not as important in practice as it might seem to be theoretically. For in many instances both processes can be seen to be operating simultaneously. The important point is that these general concepts, of contagious and hierarchical diffusion, can be employed productively, both conceptually and statistically, to illuminate specific histories and historical geographies.

Within historical geography, some of the most sophisticated studies of spatial diffusion have been conducted in the field of historical medical geography, in part because of the existence of continuous or near-continuous historical records of the outbreak and spread of specific diseases. An outstanding example is the study by Andrew Cliff et al. (1981) of the historical geography of epidemics in an island community. For these authors, Iceland in the period 1896–1975 was a laboratory within which to test their ideas about diffusion processes: they progressed from the general to the particular and then returned to the general. They began with an overview of some of the phenomena that have been analysed within a diffusion framework, such as agricultural innovations and colonisation. The main part of their work examined the spatial regularities observable in the recurrent epidemic waves formed by a specific infectious disease – measles – in Iceland. They collected detailed information on sixteen major measles epidemic waves which passed through the island in eighty years. Iceland was selected in part because data were available for some fifty medical districts on a monthly basis for that entire period: its medical records are of exceptional quality in terms of their reliability, historical length and spatial detail. But Iceland was also selected because it is an island and thus an isolated community in which waves of measles were discrete rather than overlapping. With each wave having a distinct starting point in both time and space, and running its course before the next wave began, the chance of learning more about its generating process was greatly increased. Detailed spatial and time series analyses were conducted and various models of the patterns thus identified were proposed and tested. Finally, Cliff and his co-workers moved back to the general by considering the implications of their work for spatial diffusion studies as a field, its demographic and public-health implications, and some possible future research trends. This was a remarkable study, a superb example of the use of the past as a historical laboratory in which to develop and test some general ideas.

Others have used aspects of spatial diffusion theory to throw light on specific historical problems, employing it in part to bridge gaps in the surviving data. One of the best examples of such work in historical geography is that by Overton (1979, 1985, 1996) on the diffusion of agricultural innovations in early-modern England. His own pioneering work on the diffusion of turnips and clover in Norfolk and Suffolk between 1580 and 1740 was a computer-based analysis of thousands of unpublished probate inventories, which listed the possessions of farmers when they died. From these sources, Overton constructed not only time series of the adoption of the new crops during almost 150 years but also maps of their spatial diffusion throughout the two counties (Figs. 2.5 and 2.6). Even more remarkably, Overton

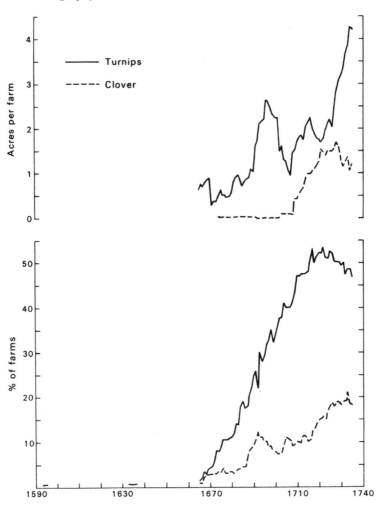

Figure 2.5   The adoption of turnips and clover in Norfolk and Suffolk, England, as recorded in probate inventories, 1590–1740

Source: reprinted from *Transactions of the Institute of British Geographers*, 10, M. Overton, 'The diffusion of agricultural innovations in early modern England: turnips and clover in Norfolk and Suffolk 1580–1740', 205–21. Copyright (1985), with permission from Blackwell Publishing.

(1977) used the probate inventories with great ingenuity to calculate changes in agricultural productivity. The result was a much more sharply focused picture than had hitherto been available of the transformation of the agrarian economy in England during what has impressionistically been termed the Agricultural Revolution. Overton's work was a fundamental contribution to a long-standing debate by

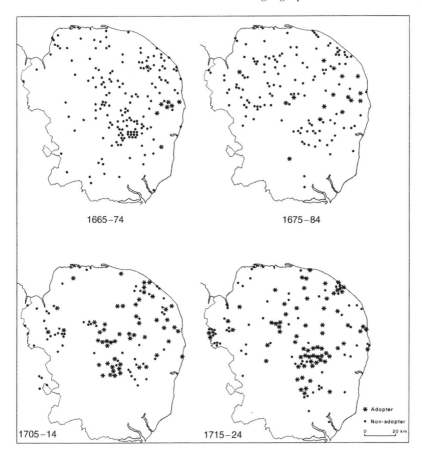

Figure 2.6   The distribution of adopters and non-adopters of root crops in Norfolk and
Suffolk, England, as recorded in probate inventories, 1665–1724
Source: reprinted from *Transactions of the Institute of British Geographers*, 10, M. Overton,
'The diffusion of agricultural innovations in early modern England: turnips and clover
in Norfolk and Suffolk 1580–1740', 205–21. Copyright (1985), with permission from
Blackwell Publishing.

historians and geographers: its quantitative approach, grounded in spatial diffusion
theory, scythed through acres of qualitative arguments.

The operation of both hierarchical and contagious processes simultaneously
in an urban context was clearly demonstrated in Brian Robson's (1973) study of
innovations and urban growth in England and Wales during the nineteenth century.
Robson argued that theoretically the spread of innovations within a system of
towns might be expected to follow both the size-hierarchy and a distance-spread
simultaneously. Logic for the hierarchical spread would have been in terms of

lessening the economic risks in a larger potential market, while the logic for the neighbourhood spread would have been in terms of imitation of the innovation by nearby places which would have had a higher probability of exposure to it. This was shown to have been the case with the spread of some very different kinds of innovation: building societies, gas works and urban street lighting, and telephone exchanges. In the case of telephone exchanges, for example, by 1892 not only was London linked to the relatively dense networks of the industrial regions, but also many of the originally separate networks in other parts of England and Wales had been joined into the evolving national system. Robson stressed both the novelty of such a national network by 1892 and the fact that, throughout the greater part of the 1880s, the development of this net had been in disconnected sub-networks. The effects of this trunk-line development were to reinforce or provide a stronger economic rationale for the essentially local diffusion of the telephone. Its diffusion was thus demonstrated both in terms of an over-riding control being exerted by the town-size, especially in the early years of development, and in terms of a local outward spread – either by imitation or through the effects of the development of the trunk network – to smaller places in the vicinity of the larger, early-adopting, towns. A similar stress on the hierarchical structuring of the diffusion of innovations within an urban system and of the circular and cumulative impact of innovations upon that system was seen in Allan Pred's (1966) theoretically informed study of the urban and industrial growth of the United States during the nineteenth century.

Studies of the development of innovations through time and of their spread across space tend inevitably to emphasise the time-space frameworks within which human activities take place. But other studies have even more overtly viewed time and space as resources appraised differently by different cultures and even dynamically within a single culture. While there are clear benefits to be derived from such perspectives, there are also some less obvious costs involved. I will now consider these specific approaches before considering some more general geographical perspectives upon history.

Historical geography, time geography and geographies of temporality

Hägerstrand's work on diffusion was founded on the premise that a pattern of diffusion is the product of a process of decision-making by myriad individual agents. One thread of his work on the historical population geography – what he called the 'population archaeology' – of the Asby district of central-southern Sweden thus involved endeavouring to trace the biographies of individuals as paths in time and space. Hägerstrand and his colleagues at the University of Lund established what has come to be termed the Lund school of 'time geography', an approach which argues that time and space are resources upon which individuals have to draw in order to realise their projects. Some stimulating, general, ideas have undoubtedly emerged from studies couched in time-geographical terms. Hägerstrand's time-space structuring of human activities suggests that they are subject to three sets of constraints: first, capability constraints, which limit the activities of individuals through their own capabilities and/or the facilities which they can command (and they derive essentially from an individual's livelihood position); secondly, coupling constraints, which define where, when and for how long an individual must join with other individuals, tools and materials in order to produce, transact or consume; and thirdly, authority or 'steering' constraints, which impose certain conditions of access to, and the modes of conduct within, particular space-time domains. These constraints are seen as delineating a series of boundary possibilities which mark out the paths available for individuals in pursuit of their projects. Those boundaries provide a structure within which competition among different projects for 'free paths' and 'open space-times' is identified by Hägerstrand as the 'central problem for analysis', with that competition between projects being mediated by specific institutions aiming to maintain as large a degree as possible of space-time coherence (Hägerstrand 1970, 1973, 1975).

Such ideas have certainly been productive within geography, as will shortly be seen, but the attempt to inflate them into a 'new' sub-field, that of 'time geography' (Carlstein et al. 1978; Parkes and Thrift 1980; Thrift and Pred 1981), can be questioned. Some very specific but fundamental criticisms have been made of time geography. For example, that it tends to regard human agents as unthinking and unimaginative elemental particles; that it is far too structuralist, minimising the role of human agency; that most empirical work executed within its framework has been fundamentally descriptive, essentially illustrative, and most frequently confined to local-scale and short-term situations affecting a limited number of individuals; that a focus upon constraints to the exclusion of opportunities is unwarranted; and finally, that time geography has only a weakly developed theory of power (Gregory 1985, 1986; Giddens 1984: 116–19). A much more general criticism is that an emphasis on time geography *per se* compounds the logical error of equating spatial organisation with geography (Baker 1981). Geography is no more the science of *space* than history is the science of *time*: both space and time are as much the concerns of other social and historical scientists as they are of geographers and historians. Concepts of spatial organisation and of temporal organisation are essentially interdisciplinary rather than quintessentially geographical or historical. Furthermore, ideologies structure space and time which must in turn be seen as reflecting power struggles. Thus we should focus on the social organisation of time and space, not the temporal and spatial organisation of society. Underlying this argument is the more general one that historical geography is fundamentally concerned not with time and space but with period and place. Aharon Kellerman's (1987, 1989) critique of the time-space homology concluded that time and space are best interpreted as both passive and active elements of societal life, with individuals and societies using them as resources and simultaneously expanding into them. But the use and expansion processes, Kellerman argued, do not necessarily have the same pace and duration in space and time at a given period: they both reflect the on-going relationship between human agency and social structure. There is therefore no need to throw out the baby with the bathwater. Nigel Thrift (1983) has stressed that time and space are central to the construction of all social interaction and therefore to the constitution of social theory. This does not mean, he argued, just that social theory must necessarily be both historically and geographically specific but also that social theory must be about the time-space constitution of social structure. Jon May and Thrift (2001) move beyond a narrow time geography because of its apparent separation from space to advocacy of a new conception of what they term 'TimeSpace' which examines the multiplicity and heterogeneity of social time. They emphasise the need to recognise not a singular or uniform social time stretching over a uniform space, but various and uneven networks of time stretching in different and divergent directions across an uneven social field, creating 'TimeSpace' or 'geographies of temporality'. May and Thrift engage a team of authors to deploy this notion of multi-dimensional networks of TimeSpace to rework traditional, historico-geographical, accounts of time-space convergence, time-space compression and time consciousness. It is the explicit recognition of different cultural practices of time and space and of a multi-dimensional, partial and uneven 'TimeSpace' that leads May and Thrift to their conception of 'geographies of temporality'.

As one way of viewing the world, even traditional time geography does provide a focused perspective and it has enabled some of those employing it to offer new insights into past geographies. Two studies of geographical change in Sweden, but not undertaken exclusively by Swedish geographers, demonstrate this very clearly. Pred's (1986) examination of the social and spatial transformation of southern Sweden between 1750 and 1850 explored the connections between time geography and structuration theory. Detailed empirical but theoretically informed research into the economic and social life of rural communities emphasised the shaping and reshaping of the structural features of those communities by the activities of individuals following their daily life-paths. Pred argued for the primary importance of household-based local interactions and projects and the secondary importance of kin-based social interaction with nearby villages. This emphasis on the local processes underpinning differences in the organisation and execution of agricultural projects enabled Pred to argue that such local processes were also given geographically distinctive expression in other cultural and social forms, such as dress, hair- and beard-style, diet, handicrafts, and church-bell-ringing practices as well as superstitions and beliefs.

Göran Hoppe and John Langton's (1994) study of the transformation from peasantry to capitalism in western Östergötland during the nineteenth century similarly conceptualises regional change within a time-geographical framework. Their remarkable study does, however, serve to highlight the complexities involved in applying the theory of time geography to real-world situations. As its authors point out:

It is undoubtedly true that the conceptualisation of change in a region in terms of the longitudinal progress of the livelihood positions [of individual agents], production structures and projects at all constituent stations [such as places of work and dwellings], and of changes in the patterns of flows between the component livelihood positions at those stations, would provide us with a rich and coherent depiction of the historical processes operating within it. But a moment's reflection demonstrates the utter impracticability of such a task. (Hoppe and Langton 1994: 48)

Their area of study, comprising twenty-five parishes or parts of parishes, contained 21,300 inhabitants in 1860. Their period of study, selected to capture the transition from peasantry to capitalism, spans fifty years, from 1810 to 1860. Hoppe and Langton calculate that there must have been over 400 million daily activity networks in the region over the period, and as many daily specifications of complete sets of livelihood positions. Unsurprisingly, rather than reconstructing continuous series of annual data on the resources, projects and livelihood positions of all stations, Hoppe and Langton choose to assemble only six sets of data, one for each decadal year from 1810 to 1860. Those cross-sections are connected through complex linkage procedures to acquire some semblance of properly longitudinal study, and a number of peasant farms and agricultural estates are traced through each of the cross-sections to provide more detailed longitudinal material. Compromises of this sort are necessary, as Hoppe and Langton admit, if researchers are not to drown in floods of data. Their intention is to use some of the ideas but not all of the techniques from time geography in order to study systematically the processes of economic transformation in a region. They use notions from time geography to guide them in the abstraction of data from impossibly copious sources of information towards a coherent statement which might help to answer unresolved questions about the nature of peasantry and the process of transformation from peasantry to capitalism.

Viewing time and space as resources has the merit of emphasising their relative rather than absolute characteristics. Time and space are social constructs and recognising them as such has resulted in some important studies of the ways in which time has been appraised and used in widely differing cultures. David Harvey (1990) emphasised how concepts of time and space are contested as part and parcel of the process of social change. His study of the historical geography of the concepts of time and space led him to conclude that the roots of their social construction lay in the mode of production and its characteristic social relations. In particular, he argued that the revolutionary qualities of a capitalistic mode of production, marked by strong currents of technological change and rapid economic growth and development, have been associated with powerful revolutions in the social conceptions of space and time, with what has come to be seen as the annihilation of space by time. A somewhat different stance was adopted by Thrift (1988) in his attempt to produce a historical geography of time consciousness. He identified three approaches to the subject: an ecological approach, a Marxist approach and an approach which understands time consciousness as an ideology of everyday time practice which, in particular, stresses the importance of language. Thrift then applied the insights gained from his appreciation of these three approaches to a study of time consciousness in medieval England. He examined the role and social significance, for example, of temporal rhythms and time discipline, and of documents and devices (especially church bells) that marked out time. Thrift's excursion into this field calls to mind work by French historians on both time and space consciousness, notably the study of medieval Montaillou by Emmanuel Le Roy Ladurie (1975) and of the sound and the meaning of village bells in the nineteenth-century French countryside by Alain Corbin (1994).

As resources, time and space have been culturally appraised and reappraised as part of a process which has involved the expansion of social interactions over space and their contraction over time. The significance of improvements in communications for the reshaping of temporal and spatial relationships among places was first elaborated within geography by D. Janelle (1968), who defined the convergence rate between two places as the average rate at which the time needed to travel between them decreased over time as a result of innovations in transport technology. Janelle's study of the lessening times taken to travel between Edinburgh and London between the mid-seventeenth century and the mid-twentieth century – from about 20,000 minutes by stage-coach in the 1650s to about 200 minutes by aeroplane in the 1950s – demonstrated that time-space convergence is itself usually discontinuous in time (with inflexions in the curve associated with major transportation innovations) and uneven over space (with places being linked differentially into speedier transportation networks). Janelle saw time-space convergence operating within a central place structure, arguing that any transportation improvement would tend to be of greater advantage to the higher-order centres that it connects. Later work by Harvey (1989, 1990) has distinguished between time-space convergence and time-space compression: the former refers to the accelerated circulation of goods, people, information and capital, and the consequential reduction in relative distances between places; the latter depicts the cultural shocks and disorientation produced by such changes.

The notion that over time the friction of distance tends to be significantly reduced has both underpinned some specific empirical studies and become integrated into the general account of society provided by structuration theory. Excellent examples of the former have been provided by studies of marriage patterns and population mobility in France during the nineteenth and twentieth centuries. Philip Ogden (1973) studied the distances separating the domiciles of marriage partners in a sample of 9,000 marriages in 70 communes of the Massif Central between 1870 and 1970. At the earlier date, 45 per cent of marriages were endogamous (that is, of partners domiciled in the same commune) and only 6 per cent were of partners whose domiciles were more than 50 km apart; at the later date, the comparable percentages were respectively 18 and 35. There had been between those two dates a gradual but complete rupture of the social system consequent upon a significant reduction in the friction of distance. But, having also examined data for some intervening dates in the early 1900s and in the 1930s, Ogden concluded that the progression from a relatively open system of social contact was not necessarily a simple or a uniform transition: it did not involve a gradual spatial extension of the marriage field over adjacent areas but rather an increase of direct contact with urban areas. Peter Perry (1977) came to a similar conclusion in his study of marriage fields in Lozère (France) between 1811–20 and 1891–1900. In the earlier period, when movement was essentially pedestrian or equestrian, marriages were contracted over relatively short distances and marriage fields were moulded by local topography; in the later period, marriages were contracted over much larger distances and marriage fields were structured much more by the settlement system, by the network of central places. By the later date much greater movement had been made possible not only by better roads but also by improved means of transport, including bicycles, cars and buses but most importantly railways, whose structures of tunnels and embankments significantly reduced topographical constraints. Empirical studies such as these on the erosion of rural isolation and what some see as the modernisation of the French peasantry (Weber 1977) have served to emphasise how the notion of time-space convergence can illuminate specific situations. But the concept has also been incorporated into the general theory of structuration developed by Anthony Giddens (1984).

In his sweeping endeavour to reveal the constitution of society, Giddens has shown particular concern about the modes in which social systems are constituted across time-space and he has, therefore, explicitly addressed work in time geography. Although, as already noted, Giddens expressed reservations about time geography, he none the less fully acknowledged the importance of analysing the social organisation of time-space and developed the concept of time-space distanciation. Following and extending Durkheim, Giddens emphasised that 'societal totalities not only pre-exist and post-date the lives of the individuals who reproduce them in their activities; they also stretch across space and time away from any particular agent considered singly'. An individual interacts with others who are not present in, who are distanced from, his/her own time or space. And time-space convergence compounds the role of time-space distanciation, while the greater the time-space distanciation of social systems the more resistant they are to manipulation or change by any individual agent (Giddens 1984: 170–1). Studies in time-space compression thus become more appropriate and necessary as local geographies become increasingly integrated into global geographies (Harvey 1989: 260–307; Gregory 1994: 406–14).

Moreover, social systems which stretch across time and space as envisaged by Giddens cannot be expected to have easily defined, clear-cut, boundaries (Gregory 1984). But geographers have long recognised both the artificiality and the necessity of the concept of the 'region', with the notion of 'place' being central to their studies (see chapter 5). A similar point could be made about historians and their concept of the historical 'period' and the notion of 'age' or 'era'. Such concepts are working tools, not completed projects. Giddens criticised Hägerstrand for using the terms 'place' and 'location' in a 'relatively unexamined fashion', without subjecting them 'to a close conceptual scrutiny'. He accordingly substituted his own concept of 'locales', by which he meant the use of space to provide the settings of interactions. Giddens' theorising allowed him to envisage locales as ranging 'from a room in a house, a street corner, the shop floor of a factory, towns and cities, to the territorially demarcated areas occupied by nation-states' (Giddens 1984: 118). But the geographical concept of place and even that of region, like that of locale, is not tied to any specific geographical scale. I will return to consider this further in later chapters. For now, I want to consider the concepts of space and location, which have been so fundamental to much geographical work and which some now argue should be the key organising principle in a reformulated historical geography, in a new 'geographical history'.

Spatial histories, locational histories and geographical history

Study of the influence of geographical conditions upon the course of history – what was called 'the geography behind history' – has a long and in many ways distinguished pedigree. While studies couched in that framework had many merits, they also had their faults, notably their tendency to equate 'geographical influences' with 'physical geographical influences' and their associated tendency to lean towards environmental determinism as a form of geographical explanation. But geographical perspectives upon history were considerably broadened and enriched under Fernand Braudel's influence to include the concepts of space and location (Lepetit 1986a). Increasingly, historians have been adopting a wider range of geographical concepts and they have been doing so when, paradoxically, some geographers have been arguing for a narrowing of the conception of historical geography, limiting it to what they call 'geographical history'. I will consider each of these stances in turn.

In the 1950s, Braudel was pleading that history and the social sciences should make room for an increasingly geographical conception of humanity, a conception which would embrace not only the influences of the physical environment but also those of space and location (Braudel 1958). He was doing so on the eve of a great surge of interest by geographers in the 1960s and 1970s in spatial and locational analysis. That wave, powered largely by the modernising forces of quantification and by the seekers of order in (and scientific respectability for) geography, was to engulf much of the field of human geography in those decades, leaving only islands of humanistic geography from which alarm calls could be sounded and preparations made for the recovery that would be needed after that flood had receded (Harris 1971, 1978a). Damage was done to human geography by the excesses of the so-called 'quantitative revolution' and by unjustifiable claims to geography's 'ownership' of space as a concept, but I am very willing none the less to concede that both the project and the methods of geography as spatial analysis have enriched the practice of a historical geography focused on the processes of the social organisation of space through time, as Jakle (1971) had suggested they might.

Not only geography but also history has been – and might still further be – a beneficiary of even closer attention to spatial and locational concepts. Let me illustrate this point at both continental and global scales. As a historian, Edward Cook (1980) has undertaken a critical review of the kinds of insights which historians can gain from geography and emphasised the ways in which they might profit from 'a heightened sense of the spatial dimensions of their studies'. His review was specifically of 'spatial approaches to early American history'. For Cook, 'a first step in the application of geographical thought to history is the simple but unfamiliar one of approaching problems with spatial influences as clearly in mind as those of time and cultural institutions' and he noted that 'a key part of the geographer's procedure involves asking each source how its data would look imposed on a map of the area in question'. Cook cites and praises work on colonial America by geographers like Carville Earle, Roy Merrens, Cole Harris and James Lemon, noting the emphasis which they all placed on areal differences and on spatial relations in their understandings of the periods and places they were studying. More specifically, Cook considered critically the extent to which early American history had been illuminated by the application of locational theory in general and of central place theory in particular, referring to work by geographers such as James Vance Jr, Michael Conzen, Robert Mitchell and Allan Pred. For Cook, 'implicit in the view of geography as a strategy for thinking in spatial terms is its usefulness in a wide range of historical situations' (Cook 1980: 20, 23). He could have added 'and at a wide range of geographical scales', because spatial and locational principles may also be insightful in different geographical contexts.

They can, for example, be applied at the global scale, as they have been so effectively by a French historian, Chaunu (1974), in his broad-brush portrayal of the history and geography of the world. Chaunu presented his work in three parts. The first part, *La durée*, examined the history of history, the relations between history and the social sciences, the concept of discontinuity in history, and the succession of civilisations; the second part, *L'espace*, considered what Chaunu termed 'the rules of space', examined the global distribution of food production and traced the transformation of essentially discrete 'worlds' into an integrated global economy; and the third part, *L'homme*, moved towards a historical demography of the world and of its different civilisations. This ambitious, stimulating work drew upon a range of geographical concepts, especially those of distribution, difference and distance, and of spatial relations and interactions. It made frequent and effective use of maps (for example, a world map of civilisations, cultures and primitive peoples *c*. 1500) as well as of graphs (for example, of literacy levels in Scotland, England and France, 1600–1900). While Chaunu made no distinction between 'geohistory' and 'historical geography', using the terms interchangeably, it is noticeable that he drew his inspiration explicitly from the geohistory of Braudel, with only passing references to the work of geographers (and then to members of the founding generation of French geographers, Paul Vidal de la Blache and Albert Demangeon, rather than to any of his own contemporaries).

Similarly broad and explicitly geographical approaches to world history are exhibited in Grataloup's (1996) *Lieux d'histoire: essai de géohistoire systématique* and in Trochet's (1998) *La géographie historique de la France*, which again indicates how the terms 'geohistory' and 'historical geography' are being used interchangeably by some French historical geographers as well as by some historians. Grataloup provides an examination of the roles of space, location and distance in the histories of societies at global, continental, national and city scales from the Neolithic to the Industrial Revolution. He even offers some simplified, graphical, geohistorical models of specific societies. Trochet addresses the organisation of space as territories in traditional societies. He deals first with the use of space as territory by various social groups, such as families and local communities, and tribes and peoples, and then he considers the territorial and spatial aspects of city-states, empires and nation-states. Chaunu's work on what he terms 'the geohistory of wheat' and of other crops and Grataloup's work on 'the geohistory of sugared-tea' both have considerable affinity with the kind of work associated in the English-speaking world with the Berkeley school of cultural geography. But, inspired by Braudel, Chaunu and Grataloup have dared to produce global-scale historical geographies of the world, whereas the work of the Berkeley school has – as it seems to me – disappointingly not been much greater than the sum of its parts.

Within the English-speaking world, the most provocative ideas about the historical processes of economic globalisation have been provided by Immanuel Wallerstein's world-system theory (Wallerstein 1974, 1980). Again, like Chaunu's geohistorical work, Wallerstein's geographical perspective upon the history of capitalism was inspired by Braudel. World-system theory is a spatial and temporal model which identifies three components, those of core, semi-periphery and periphery, and which envisages individual countries moving in and out of these three categories in a non-evolutionary manner. Wallerstein saw the capitalist world-system first emerging in Europe during the fifteenth and sixteenth centuries. It was a system based upon unequal exchange, with core areas exchanging high-value manufactured goods for low-value primary products, raw materials and food from peripheral areas. The initial European core embraced nations competing amongst each other for global economic hegemony, but it was subsequently to pass to European-settled colonies, notably the USA, and to countries like Japan which adopted European economic and technological ideas and systems. While some countries formed the core of the system and others the periphery, still others could move between the two sets and were accordingly themselves part of the semi-periphery. It is not my purpose here to appraise world-system theory. I want merely to stress the extent to which it draws on spatial – and so, in that limited sense, geographical – concepts.

Some geographers have in turn picked up world-system theory and incorporated it into their own perspectives upon the historical and geographical development of capitalism (Taylor 1985; Nitz 1987; Kearns 1988). Some significant 'big-picture' perspectives upon the development of the modern, capitalist world during the past five hundred or so years are now being provided by geographers. For example, Peter

Hugill (1993, 1997, 1999) provides major surveys of world trade since 1431 and of communications since 1844, emphasising the role of technology in his account of the historical geopolitics of the development of global capitalism. Similarly, Peter Taylor (1999a, 1999b) offers a broadly based 'geohistorical interpretation' of the modern world, focusing upon Dutch mercantile modernity in the seventeenth century, British industrial modernity in the late eighteenth and nineteenth centuries, and American consumer modernity in the twentieth century. More briefly but very astutely, Miles Ogborn (2000) summarises historical geographies of globalisation between *c.* 1500 and 1800. These broad studies employ geographical concepts – those related to the cultural organisation of space, to the cultural construction of location and distance. I suggest that they might most appropriately be termed 'spatial histories', given their concern with changing spatial relations among and within places. They could helpfully be distinguished from historical studies which focus on the social construction and use of spaces, which might best be termed 'histories of spaces'.

Historians are coming increasingly to acknowledge the spatial dimension in history at geographical scales ranging from the global to the local (see, for examples, Miller 1990 and MacDonald 1998). They are producing both more spatial histories and more histories of spaces. To a long-standing interest in macrospaces (such as continents and countries) has been added a lively interest in microspaces (such as house interiors) (Burke n.d.). Studies of the histories of spaces have been boosted by the writing of the French poststructuralist, Michel Foucault. His emphasis on historical discontinuities and contingencies led him in turn to focus on the significance of local and specific spaces. Foucault was convinced that analysis of power in society could be achieved through an analysis of control over space. Foucault saw power as being inscribed in space: accordingly, he stated, 'geography must necessarily lie at the heart of my concerns' (Foucault 1980: 77). For Foucault, history – the exercise of power – is embedded in specific spaces, such as churches, theatres, prisons, hospitals, schools and factories. He thus mapped spatial considerations on to the agenda of cultural history. But if Foucault drew upon some geographical concepts, then historical geographers have in turn been inspired by his conception of social power and of the role of knowledge in society. For example, Felix Driver and Chris Philo have both assessed Foucault's ideas in general terms and also incorporated them critically into their own geographical analyses of, respectively, workhouses and asylums in Victorian England (Driver 1992a, 1993, 1994a, 1994b; Philo 1992a, 1992b, 1995). Harris (1991) extended the debate on the geographical configuration of power, knowledge and modernity in a critique of the ideas not only of Foucault but also of Jürgen Habermas, Anthony Giddens and Michael Mann, emphasising the reciprocal significance of social theory to historical geography and of historical geography to social theory.

Another inspiration for some historical geographers has been the French philosopher Henri Lefebvre's (1974) work on 'the production of space' and on the connections between what he termed 'representations of space' (which included planning strategies, surveillance systems and the creation of spectacle) and 'spaces of representation' (which concerned the ways in which space was contested and reclaimed) in everyday life. Harvey (1985) employed this concept very effectively in his reinterpretation of the physical rebuilding and social restructuring of Paris between 1850 and 1870, laying bare all of the many financial, political and cultural tensions which underpinned the production and contestation of new Parisian spaces. More specifically, Harvey has shown how the building of the monumental Basilica of the Sacred Heart in Paris was intentionally charged with meaning and unintentionally with myth; and more generally, he examines how a variety of utopian projects have underpinned the construction and use of spaces (Harvey 1979, 2000). Derek Gregory (1994) juxtaposes Lefebvre's big ideas about the history of space with Harvey's (1989) grand project on historico-geographical materialism: the historical geography of capitalism and the passage from modernity to postmodernity in contemporary culture.

Historical geographers and historians today share common ground in their interest in the social construction and use of spaces such as streets, domestic interiors and ceremonial centres. They distinguish, for example, between private and public spaces, sacred and profane spaces, commercial and ceremonial spaces, shared and divided spaces, male and female spaces, and individual and institutional spaces. Spaces are contested resources which individuals and groups seek to control as demonstrations of their own power. Good recent examples are Teresa Ploszajska's (1994) analysis of the roles of gender and class in the manipulation of spaces in Victorian reformatory schools and Mark Billinge's (2001) 'natural history' of the cultural relations expressed both in the physical form of nineteenth-century Italian and Parisian opera houses, as a container of many different spaces, and in their interior social worlds. Philip Howell's (2001) discussion of the cultural production and significance of prostitutional space in the nineteenth-century European city is a very direct, worked example of Lefebvre's understanding of the production of space, a theoretically informed reconstruction of the historical geography of prostitutional space. Howell goes well beyond a traditional mapping of the geographies of prostitutional activity and its policing to show that prostitutional space was produced in the service of an interventionist and disciplinary state and he links these geographies of commercial sexuality to the mechanics of power in the modern city. By contrast, good examples of how specific social groups very explicitly asserted their claims to public space are provided by Peter Goheen's (1992, 1994) studies of different kinds of street parades (such as funeral processions, trade union demonstrations, cultural group parades) in nineteenth-century Canadian cities, revealing the social significance of the routes followed and of the order in which individuals and groups paraded.

A different spin has been given to this thread of thinking with the growing interest in spatial configurations of knowledge. A significant impetus to this work came from Edward Said's (1978) work on Orientalism, which demonstrated that the ideas of the 'Orient' had been produced politically, culturally, militarily, ideologically, scientifically and imaginatively by Westerners after the Enlightenment. The concept of the Orient was an amalgam of 'fact and fiction' which resulted in an imaginative geography of Europe's 'Other'. Crucial to Said's thesis was his insistence that ideas and theories are initially specific to particular places in which they are produced and that they then travel from person to person, from place to place, and from one period to another. The significance of place and space in the development and diffusion of scientific knowledges is an important theme addressed by historians of science (Ophir and Shapin 1991). Such studies have identified what have come to be called 'historical geographies of knowledge'. This concept is giving rise to some exciting work by geographers. For example, David Livingstone's (1994, 1995) work on the historical geography of science examines such issues as the regionalisation of science, the social and material spaces of laboratories and scientific societies, and the spatial diffusion of scientific knowledges, and he has also probed into the historical geography of the encounter between science and religion, while Charles Withers (2001) reconstructs the historical geography of geographical knowledge and its role in the development of national identity in Scotland since 1520 and David Smith (2000) explores 'the historical geography of morality and ethics', looking at the extent to which moral beliefs and practices differ in time and space and how those differences have arisen. Michael Heffernan (1996) shows how cartographic knowledges were placed, not unproblematically, in the service of European states during the Great War, and Simon Rycroft and Denis Cosgrove (1995) show in their study of Dudley Stamp's Land Utilisation Survey that this particular construction of geographical knowledge also fed into a politics of citizenship. The spatial turn witnessed within a variety of academic discourses today is productively reinvigorating work even in geography itself.

Unfortunately, some confusion and conflation of space with place was evident in Felix Driver and Raphael Samuel's (1995) note on 'spatial history: rethinking the idea of place'. Their remarks are about the changing character of places, about 'place histories', rather than about the changing spatial relations among and within places or even about changing cultural appraisals of spaces. Furthermore, I think that this issue has been clouded rather than clarified by the (as far as I am aware) only book-length study which explicitly claims to be 'an essay in spatial history'. Objecting – rightly so – to the limited view formerly taken by many historians of 'space' as the stage upon which a historical drama is enacted, P. Carter (1987) focused instead on 'the process of transforming space into place' and upon the role of language and specifically of place-naming in the settlement of Botany Bay in Australia. For Carter, spatial history is an examination of the social construction of places. I would not wish to argue with Carter's identification of a significant cultural process, but I do contend that terming his approach 'spatial history' is misleading: it would be better described as 'place history'. I suggest that the term 'spatial histories' would best be reserved for those studies which are concerned directly with spatial concepts, with the significance of spatial and locational relations at a time in the past or through periods in the past at particular places. 'Space' and 'place' are not interchangeable concepts and terms. I shall consider 'place histories' in my final chapter, but I want to conclude this one by trying to clarify two other aspects of historical geography as spatial history.

In 1996, Hester Parr and Chris Philo – the former a medical geographer and the latter a historical geographer – published a short monograph on what they termed the 'locational history' of mental health care in Nottingham (England) during the nineteenth and twentieth centuries. The term is employed because Philo wants to show how the precise locations adopted for lunatic asylums (for example, in different parts of the city, retreating into the countryside and relative to centres of population) reflected shifts in the prevailing understandings of 'madness' and its possible treatment – the location of asylums was not simply a question of where suitable buildings and/or building sites were available. Philo (private communication, 26 June 2000) encountered the term 'locational history' in an undergraduate thesis produced by an Emmanuel College student of mine, Duncan Rose (1986), entitled 'From Babbacombe to Wardour Street: a locational history of the film studios of Great Britain'. Clearly, many historical geographies – those concerned with changing distributions of phenomena – could have been called locational histories and, with hindsight, it is surprising that none seems to have been before Rose's study, given the appearance in 1965 of Haggett's highly influential *Locational Analysis in Human Geography*. Philo's (unpublished) book, '*The space reserved for insanity*: a historical geography of the mad-business in England and Wales to the 1860s', extends beyond matters of location to those of spatial relations. Philo explicitly terms his approach a historical geography and describes it as spatial history.

Such locational-spatial histories fall clearly within the traditions of geographical enquiry. The designation makes clear the approach being adopted and appropriate use of this new term could be helpful. But I do have a problem with a different suggestion, that traditional 'historical geography' should be supplanted by a new 'geographical history'. Carville Earle is a powerful advocate of the virtues of a 'geographical perspective' upon history (in his case, American history). The aim of a collection of his essays, *Geographical Inquiry and American Historical Problems* (1992), was to 're-examine a handful of perennial problems in American history from a geographical point of view', to consider the 'processes that defined the American experience . . . and the geographical factors that shaped them', and to offer 'an interpretation of the rhythms of American macrohistory and geography's role therein'. Earle wants to 'offer a fresh angle of vision on the [American] past, a varied series of locational and ecological reinterpretations of familiar historical problems'. Here Earle made it clear that he was drawing upon just two of the discourses of geography, rather than its full panoply. He ascribed a key role to locational analysis, to mapping, to spatial methods and interpretations, in his advocacy of the adoption of a geographical perspective upon history. Importantly, that advocacy led Earle quite explicitly, but I think mistakenly, to argue for the practice of 'geographical history' instead of historical geography. Even while quoting Sauer on the sterility of trying to police disciplinary boundaries, Earle entreated a number of named North American and British historical geographers to 'confer upon themselves the title of "geographical historians"'. He did so because he wished, quite explicitly, to put geography in the service of historical interpretation – hence his decision to write what he called 'geographical history' (Earle 1992: 1–23). But in taking this exclusive position Earle was insensitive to the predilections of others to put history in the service of geographical interpretation – and hence to write what they consider to be 'historical geography'. Historical geography and geographical history provide related but different perspectives upon the world; to collapse them into a single perspective or to argue for the retention of one and the elimination of the other is to impoverish an otherwise rich intellectual diversity. As previously noted, Earle's 'geographical history' is situated selectively within just two geographical discourses, those of location and of environment (or ecology). As conceived by Earle, 'geographical history' thus has much less of a purchase on past geographies than does historical geography as addressed in this book. Few have shared Earle's preference for a 'geographical history' as he envisaged it, although John Hudson's (1994) 'geographical history' of the American Corn Belt is an important exception.

Earle's position – a prioritising of 'geographical history' over 'historical geography' – has also been adopted recently by Philo (1994) in his essay on history, geography and what Jean Mitchell called the 'still greater mystery' of historical geography. Philo's argument does not, however, explicitly refer to that of Earle and, partly because of its independent but simultaneous advocacy of a new 'geographical history', I want to examine Philo's argument more closely. Its key point is 'that the importance of historical geography lies in bringing a geographical sensitivity to bear upon the study of all those past phenomena – economic, social, political or whatever – that are the very "stuff" of history' (Philo 1994: 253). Philo is here asking us to be 'alert to the role of geography in history': as with Earle, his focus is upon a geographical interpretation of history and the reservations which I have about Earle's argument also stand in relation to Philo's. Both Earle and Philo object to the way in which Darby, in his 1953 paper on the relations of history and geography, appeared to them to dismiss studies of the role of geography in history. Reflecting upon 'the geography behind history', Darby stated that 'just because a geographical spirit ought to, and does, inspire certain studies, it does not follow that such studies should be incorporated within even the broad embrace of geography'. Notwithstanding that cautionary stance, however, Darby included 'geographical history' (which he defined as the investigation of the influence of geographical conditions upon the course of history) as one of the four categories of historical geography (after 'geographies of the past', 'changing landscapes' and 'the past in the present') which he identified in 1962 in his rethought and most programmatic statement about historical geography. Earle and Philo overlook that more mature statement by Darby, I surmise, because, while his project was primarily geographical, their projects are – as I read them – primarily historical.

The 'opposition' between historical geography and geographical history which Philo identifies is not, in practice, as great as he makes it out to be. He is, to my mind, merely expressing his personal preference to work within one – the locational – discourse of historical geography. But Philo takes his case further and, I think, even more mistakenly, for he sets up an illusory difference between what he sees as the two opposing perspectives of historical geography and geographical history. He argues that what he might well have termed the 'old historical geography' was concerned with material geographies, with tangible features such as deserted villages, churches, factories and ghettos, while what he does call 'the new geographical history' is concerned with immaterial events, entities and structures, such as the diffusion of innovations, the migration of peoples, the operations of state machineries and the artistic representations of land and labour. Such a binary opposition is, in my view, not just a poor caricature but a gross misrepresentation of historical geography both as it has been practised in the past and as it continues to be practised today. Philo seems to consider 'old historical geography' to have been concerned exclusively with the material world, with artefacts and objects in landscapes, whereas the historical geographical discourse has been much richer than that. Philo seems to be surprisingly unaware of the extent to which historical geographers in the past have embraced studies of what the French call *mentalités*. I need only to refer to the genres of studies in historical geosophy (which I consider in chapter 3) and of the meanings of landscapes (which I consider in chapter 4) to prove the point. It is simply not the case, as Philo believes, that studies in historical geography in the past have 'close[d] themselves around the arrangement of objects in the material world' (Philo 1994: 261). Similarly, Philo seems surprisingly unaware of, or at least unwilling to acknowledge, the extent to which studies of the material world are still contributing vigorously to geography's powerful landscape tradition. Think, for example, of Peter Ennals and Deryck Holdsworth's (1998) study of the making of Canadian houses and dwellings during the past three centuries and of Jean-Robert Pitte's (1983) study of specific and significant material structures (such as roads and railways, villages and vineyards) in the making of the French landscape, and of the numerous papers on landscape forms presented to the succession of conferences held during the past (almost) fifty years on the European rural landscape (Baker 1988). There has indeed been during the past decade or so an undeniable and very exciting shift in emphasis away from studies of the making of landscapes and towards studies of the meanings of landscapes. But to ignore – or, worse, to deny – the continuing significance of the former serves only to underscore the element of special (and spatial) pleading inherent in Philo's argument.

In short, the more explicit adoption of spatial and locational concepts in historical geography (and in history) does not require us, Mao-like, to reject our traditions and embrace a brave 'new' world of geographical history. The more energetic prosecution of a new geographical history in the guise of spatial and locational histories is to be welcomed, but it does not of necessity involve forsaking all other geographical perspectives upon history. Why should we deprive ourselves of the intellectual wealth of studies framed in the environmental and landscape discourses? It is to these two discourses that I now turn in the following chapters.

3

Environmental geographies and histories

The environmental discourse in geography

Studies of the earth as the home of humanity have for centuries been a major concern of geography. The differential encounters of peoples with their physical environments, of 'cultures' with 'nature' as well as with other 'cultures', have intrigued generations of geographers and underpinned legions of geographical studies.

Such enquiries have taken varied forms. First, there have been studies investigating the physical, 'natural', environment as an intrinsically interesting problem, whether those environments have been actual or merely potential places for human settlement. Geomorphologists, climatologists and biogeographers have focused their researches on specific aspects of physical environments while recognising that their chosen topics are but part of a general environmental system. To purist physical geographers, of course, human activity is but one of many processes at work shaping physical structures over time, merely one 'character' in their dramatic, narrative, historical physical geographies. Secondly, there have been studies focusing explicitly on the interactions between people and their physical environments, examining both the impact of physical environments upon human activities and attitudes, and the impress of those ideas and actions upon physical environments. Thirdly, there have been studies conducted under the flag of 'human ecology' which have played down the role of the physical environment, privileging instead the interactions between social groups but doing so using concepts borrowed from biogeography specifically and from ecology generally.

The first two of these approaches to the environment have for centuries been absorbed into the practices of physical and human geography, but 'human ecology' was more historically and geographically specific, being associated with Harlan Barrows and other scholars at the University of Chicago during the 1920s and 1930s. Barrows (1923), viewing geography as 'human ecology', argued that reference need only be made to physical geography when its elements impacted directly upon human activities. Thus geography was promulgated as a social science, rather than as a natural science, its concern being more with relationships within and among human societies than with their relationships to the physical environment. None the less, for Barrows an understanding of human societies was enhanced by employing ecological concepts, and urban sociologists like R. E. Park and E. W. Burgess at Chicago gained renown for applying ecological principles – such as invasion and succession – to conditions in cities (Bulmer 1984). The Chicago school of human ecology has been severely (and rightly) criticised for its use of naïve analogies, crude empiricism and functionalist inductivism (Ellen 1996), but ecological concepts (and especially that of ecosystems) came to be widely applied not only in geography (Stoddart 1965) but also in anthropology (Moran 1990).

The broader debate about the nature of the interaction between people and their physical environments is, of course, much older than the invention of 'human ecology'. That debate began in earnest, in the Western world at any rate, during the eighteenth century although its antecedents are deeply rooted in classical antiquity (Hartshorne 1939; Glacken 1967; Livingstone 1992). A major concern of geographical (and some other) writings between the mid-eighteenth century and the early twentieth century was the extent to which the physical environment influences human activity and development. From Baron de Montesquieu (1689–1755) and Thomas Malthus (1766–1834) through Carl Ritter (1779–1859) and Friedrich Ratzel (1844–1904) to Ellen Churchill Semple (1863–1932) and Ellsworth Huntington (1876–1947), among others, there developed the geographical thesis of 'environmental determinism', which argued that the physical environment controlled the course of human action and thus accounted for differences in the nature of societies from place to place (and also, by logical extension, from time to time). Such a stance enabled geography to converse with the natural sciences, but it left little, if any, room for a dialogue with the historical sciences, because it envisaged (human) history as a product of (physical) geography.

Fortunately, an alternative way of thinking about these issues developed during the nineteenth century in the French school of geography, especially under the intellectual leadership of Paul Vidal de la Blache (1845–1918). Approaching the people–environment issue from a classical and historical background, Vidal envisaged it as a dialectic between society and nature, with the physical environment offering opportunities or possibilities for human activity and development. His was a voluntaristic stance, one which saw people as agents making judgements and exercising choices within a range of possibilities provided by physical environments. But not only by physical environments: among the range of concepts which Vidal developed, one of the most important was that of *milieu*, which embraced not only the physical but also the cultural environment within which such judgements and choices are made. Each distinctive locality or *pays* was for Vidal the resultant of an interaction between a society and its *milieu*, the product of a process which involved change. The French school of geography drew upon specifically ecological concepts in its portrayal of localities as products of the flows (or energy transfers) of people, commodities, capital and ideas, but it also drew heavily upon historical concepts in its depiction of regions constructed and transformed by human action. Many classic French regional monographs are retrospective human geographies, demonstrating how the present-day geography of a region has been moulded by a centuries-long process of interaction, of society with nature and of societies with each other (Buttimer 1971; Claval and Sanguin 1996).

The overall theme of the interaction of peoples and physical environments was, unsurprisingly, nuanced in different ways in different schools of geography, reflecting to some extent the distinctive historical geographies of the periods and places with which they were mostly concerned. In Britain in the 1920s, a significant group of human geographers insisted that their subject as they saw it – the relationships between people and the environments in which they live – not only should be concerned with the present day but also had to incorporate a historical perspective. Thus P. M. Roxby (1930) argued that 'historical geography is essentially human geography in its evolutionary aspects. It is concerned with the evolution of the relations of human groups to their physical environment and with the development of inter-regional relations as conditioned by geographical circumstances.' John Langton (1988a) has emphasised the (as he sees it) neglected role of this environmental tradition within British geography as exemplified in the works of H. J. Fleure, P. M. Roxby, E. W. Gilbert, E. G. Bowen, Daryll Forde, Estyn Evans, Emrys Jones, Glanville Jones and Frank Emery. Employing ecological and synthetic, rather than explanatory and analytical, perspectives in their writings on the relations between 'society' and 'environment', such writers saw themselves as human geographers rather than as part of the co-existing drive to establish historical geography as a distinct sub-discipline.

In North America, George Perkins Marsh had provided an early signal of the often-deleterious impact of human activities upon physical environments in a wide-ranging book *Man and Nature, or Physical Geography as Modified by Human Action* (1864). Marsh, an American diplomat who had travelled widely beyond his native land, both recorded anthropogenic disturbances of physical environments (especially wooded, watery and sandy environments) and was himself disturbed by them. His concerns, both scholarly and conservationist, have permeated research on human impacts upon physical environments, especially – but not only – in America (Lowenthal 1958). In the 1920s and 1930s they were harnessed by Carl Sauer, a German-born Californian geographer, into what has come to be termed the Berkeley school of geography, distinguished by its emphasis upon the transformation of physical environments, upon human-induced ecological changes, and upon the fashioning of 'natural' landscapes into 'cultural' landscapes. The domestication of plants and animals and the diffusion of peoples, plants and animals were emphasised as the means whereby human activities transformed physical environments (Leighley 1963; Williams 1983, 1987).

These environmental threads were woven into a major international and interdisciplinary garment in 1955, when a symposium was held on *Man's Role in Changing the Face of the Earth* (Thomas 1956) and then updated and reworked into another symposium on *The Earth as Transformed by Human Action: Global and Regional Changes in the Biosphere over the last 300 Years* (Turner et al. 1990). The environmentalist movement since the 1950s and 1960s has, of course, involved many disciplines in addition to that of geography. But within the environmental discourse of geography itself a significant and distinctive contribution has been made by historical geographers and it continues to be made in the substantive work of distinguished scholars like Joe Powell and Michael Williams. This will become very clear when such contributions are considered in more detail in due course. For the moment, I want simply to emphasise that the environmental discourse in geography has of necessity involved a historical approach. But it has also required and demanded an interdisciplinary approach. Consequently, before exploring historical environmental geography more fully, I will adventure into some adjacent territories, those of historical ecology and of environmental history.

Historical geography, historical ecology and environmental history

Thinking ecologically, thinking about the relations of animals and plants with each other and with their non-living environment, has great antiquity but was only codified in the Western world in the nineteenth century and developed as a scientific principle and put into practice in the twentieth century. Conceptually, ecology is holistic and synthetic; pragmatically, because of the complexity of the systems with which it deals, it tends to be reductionist and analytical. Developed initially within the natural sciences, ecological concepts gradually came to be applied also within the social and historical sciences. A central concept within ecology has been that of the ecosystem, a term coined by A. G. Tansley in 1935 and redefined by E. P. Odum (1969) as follows: 'Any unit that includes all of the organisms in a given area interacting with the physical environment so that a flow of energy leads to . . . exchange of materials between living and non-living parts of the system . . . is an ecosystem.' The concept is scale-independent, both spatially and temporally, and its focus is upon the processes whereby living species (including people) function and adapt to their environments, and especially upon the energy transfers involved in those processes. The concept of ecology is astonishingly broad and it is not surprising that its practical application within analytical disciplines has been narrowed. I will consider briefly three such applications: ecological perspectives in anthropology; ecological approaches in history; and histories of ecosystems as historical ecology.

Within the human analytical sciences, ecological perspectives were probably most developed within anthropology. Reacting to some extent against the environmental determinism detectable within the more synthetical disciplines of history and geography during the early twentieth century and embracing instead the work of scholars from those disciplines who emphasised the (both positive and negative) interaction of nature and society (or culture), some anthropologists like

Clark Wissler and Alfred Kroebler from the 1920s onwards saw that interaction as producing distinctive 'culture areas'. Around the fundamental question of the nature–society interaction emerged studies in ecological anthropology, in cultural ecology and in cultural anthropology – in short, studies focused on the ecological foundations of cultures, on the extent to which and the ways in which a society's interaction with nature has involved its own structuring and restructuring, its transformation from one form to another (Worster 1984, 1985).

Ecological approaches were much more slowly developed within history. Although it is tempting to argue that classic American historians like Frederick Jackson Turner, Walter Prescott Webb and James Malin incorporated ecological perspectives into their studies of frontiers and the Great Plains, their approaches were more generally environmentalist than specifically ecological. Only during the past thirty or so years have historians' studies of frontiers and of contacts between cultures come to apply explicitly ecological concepts to their analyses. Donald Worster, in his review of history as natural history, has argued that there is room for more ecological histories not only of frontiers but also of measures to increase food production (and especially of the West's post-feudal Agricultural Revolution) and of ways to regulate exploitative behaviour (and especially of environmentally conserving functions). He pleaded that 'we need to understand not only the ecological origins of [a] mode of production, but also its impact on the land – both on specific ecosystems and on the planet as a whole – and on the land's inhabitants' (Worster 1984: 16–19). Here, Worster could have drawn very productively upon works by some ecologically aware historical geographers, but they lay beyond his disciplinary horizon. For example, Tim Bayliss-Smith (1982) examined the ecological constraints on agricultural systems in pre-industrial systems (in New Guinea recently and in England in the 1820s), in semi-industrial systems (a Polynesian atoll and the Green Revolution in South India), and in full industrial systems (a Russian collective farm in the 1960s and England in the 1970s); Earle (1992) employed ecological concepts in his analyses of a series of demographic, agricultural, social and urban crises and problems in America from the sixteenth century to the nineteenth century; and Overton's (1996) analysis of the Agricultural Revolution in England between 1500 and 1850 dissects its ecological underpinnings as well as its economic and social characteristics.

Histories of ecosystems, of components of ecosystems, and of ecological crises are becoming increasingly numerous and significant as 'historical ecologies'. Growing concerns about the global ecosystem have been addressed since the 1970s by the newly emergent discipline of historical ecology which draws upon the traditions of geography, anthropology and history as well as that of ecology. In 1980, Lester J. Bilsky's edited collection of essays, *Historical Ecology: Essays on Environment and Social Change*, was based on the premise that our understanding of current environmental problems can be enhanced through the study of similar problems in the past. It presented histories of specific ecological crises, of major imbalances between peoples and their environments, such as those witnessed in ancient China, in medieval Europe and nineteenth-century America. In addition, in A. S. Boughey's overview of environmental crises past and present, it offered a model of the significant developmental stages of social evolution based on the abilities of peoples to manage their environments, arguing that successful crisis management has usually involved population controls, expansion of the living area through migration to a new frontier or annexation of the territory of others, or technological innovations. Similar edited collections have followed, such as C. L. Crumley's (1994) *Historical Ecology: Cultural Knowledge and Changing Landscapes* and William Balée's (1998a) *Advances in Historical Ecology*. In his introduction, Balée modestly admits that he is

not alone in considering [historical ecology] to be the most important current intellectual advance in the study of human and environmental relationships. A rapidly growing number of scholars from diverse fields also perceive historical ecology as representing a new, powerful, and holistic framework for research and debate on one of the most fundamental problems of our time: the diverse and complex relationships between humans and their environments. (Balée 1998b: 2)

Most of the essays in Balée's volume are case studies, historical ecologies of anthropogenic 'natures', dealing with such issues as human-induced modification of soils, the origins and spread of infectious diseases, the deliberate use of fire in environmental management, and the introduction and spread of alien animals and plants into places where they had not been present before. In addition, Balée himself provides an overview of historical ecology and in particular sets out four 'postulates' which he says will help explicate historical ecology as a viewpoint, rather than as a field or method *per se*. His four 'postulates' are as follows:

1 Much, if not all, of the non-human biosphere has been affected by human activity.
2 Human activity does not necessarily lead to degradation of the non-human bio-sphere and the extinction of species, nor does it necessarily create a more habit-able biosphere for humans and other life forms and increase the abundance and speciosity of these.
3 Different kinds of socio-political and economic systems (or political economies) in particular regional contexts tend to result in qualitatively unlike effects on the biosphere, on the abundance and speciosity of non-human life forms, and on the historical trajectory of subsequent human socio-political and economic systems (or political economies) in the same regions.
4 Human communities and cultures together with the landscapes and regions with which they interact over time can be understood as total phenomena. (Balée 1998b: 14)

This search for 'postulates' in historical ecology is remarkably akin to the quest for 'principles of human geography' essayed by geographers, and especially French geographers, during the first half of the twentieth century – and indeed some of the former have an affinity with the latter (Brunhes 1910; Vidal de la Blache 1922; Sorre 1943–52; Buttimer 1971). But with few exceptions, the geographical literature of all periods has been at best neglected and at worst ignored by the emergent historical ecologists. Although environmentalists from all disciplines stress the necessity for interdisciplinary study, the indivisibility of their object of study makes that a Herculean task which few, if any, achieve to the full – but that is not to deny that the enterprise is worth undertaking. Crossing boundaries, not policing them, is above all else what this book on the relations of geography and history is all about. The fruits of such border crossings are to be seen in a recent double issue of the *Journal of Biogeography* (2002) themed on 'insights from historical geography to ecology and conservation'. This issue provides a clear demonstration of the strengths of a historically informed biogeography and of the reciprocal relations of historical geography and historical ecology.

Historical ecology makes explicit the rigorous use of ecological concepts. But there are two qualifying points to note. First, ecologists are busily rethinking their discipline, with revisionists questioning the fundamental concept of an ecosystem, with its emphasis upon natural regularities and an atemporal dynamic equilibrium; they are highlighting instead disturbances and instabilities which are often anthropogenic in origin. Ecology itself is not as concerned with broad, context-independent generalisations about nature as it was a generation ago. It is less concerned than it was with what were seen as orderly natural processes and it is more concerned, for example, with rapid, unpredictable changes. A new, genuinely 'historical historical ecology' has come to challenge an older evolutionary ecology (Botkin 1990; Balée 1998b; Whitehead 1998). Secondly, historical ecologists seem to me, as a geographer, not to be very rigorous in their use of the concept of 'landscape', which they often – even usually – employ as a synonym for 'environment'. The two concepts of ecology and landscape are indeed closely related and in some instances are conflated into 'landscape ecology', itself sometimes used as a synonym for historical ecology (Forman and Godron 1986; Naveh and Lieberman 1990; Gragson 1998). But ecology and landscape are not identical twins and the one should not be confused with the other. Many historical ecologists seem to be unaware of the vast literature on landscape in other disciplines and especially in geography.

I will be considering the landscape discourse within geography separately in due course (chapter 4). For the moment, I want simply to emphasise that I take the term 'landscape' to refer essentially to the form, to the structure, to the appearance, to the visible manifestation of the relationship between people and the space/land they occupy, their *milieu* (both human and physical), while I take the term 'environment' to mean that *milieu*, its functioning and its processes, unrelated to their visibility and material expression. The conflation of 'landscape' and 'environment' within current historical ecology is confusing, limiting our ability to enhance our knowledge and understanding of both. The voluminous literature on the concepts of 'landscape' and of 'environment' demonstrates that they embrace overlapping but none the less distinct sets of ideas (Demeritt 1994a, 1994b; Cosgrove 1996; O'Riordan 1996).

There is one further point to note. Some historical ecologists refer to their own work as being environmental history and all acknowledge their debt to 'environmental historians' from George Perkins Marsh onwards to William Cronon and Donald Worster. In effect, it is not the subject matter which differentiates their studies but their approaches to it: it is their point of origin and the cultural baggage which they carry with them which distinguish historical ecologists and environmental historians, rather than their remarkably similar destinations. Historical ecologists and environmental historians bring to their studies of the relationships between peoples and their environments different questions, different preconceptions, different knowledges and different skills, but together they advance our collective understanding of those relationships.

Environmental history as a self-conscious sub-discipline developed in America only from the 1960s but its antecedents reach back into the nineteenth century, in part because of that continent's own history of European colonisation of thinly settled environments which both the colonisers and their historians assumed, often mistakenly, to be pristine wilderness. Turner's Presidential Address to the American Historical Association in 1893 on 'The significance of the frontier in American history' is a classic work on the relationship between the physical environment and American society, with conditions on the frontier portrayed as promoting individualism and democracy (Turner 1894). Webb's (1931) *The Great Plains* similarly depicted social and cultural adaptation to that environment, focusing on the technological and material changes which settlers made to meet its specific conditions. Another significant study was Malin's (1947) *The Grassland of North America: Prolegomena to its History*. But the environmental determinism seen as being embedded in the works of Turner and Webb and the limited deployment of ecological theory by Malin meant that these otherwise pioneering studies were not as formative of a new environmental history as they might have been.

Instead, a new environmental history emerged in America only during the 1960s and 1970s. It did so as a by-product of intellectual and political histories of conservation, and also as part of the wider environmentalist movement which developed apace during that period. Two seminal works were Sam Hays' (1959) *Conservation and the Gospel of Efficiency* and Roderick Nash's (1967) *Wilderness and the American Mind*. But, from being concerned principally with attitudes towards nature and with ideas about nature, environmental history broadened significantly into a study of the impact of human actions upon the 'natural' world. Important bridges in that process were provided by Worster's (1977) *Nature's Economy*, a general history of ecological ideas, and his *Dust Bowl: the Southern Plains in the 1930s* (1979), a spatially and temporally specific study of the relationship between social change and physical environmental change, a model of regional environmental history.

As an emergent sub-discipline, environmental history was gradually institutionalised and its agenda crystallised. In 1972 the *Pacific Historical Review* devoted a whole issue to environmental history; then in 1975 the American Society for Environmental History was established, and shortly afterwards its own journal *Environmental Review* (which became, from 1990, the *Environmental History Review* and then, from 1996, *Environmental History*). Until recently there has been no European equivalent: *Environment and History* was first published in 1995, initiated by Richard Grove, a geographically trained environmental historian; and the Czech Internet journal *Klaudyan: a Journal for Historical Geography and Environmental History* first appeared in 2000, reflecting the considerable interest of historical geographer Leos Jelecek and his colleagues in those two related fields (Baker 1986; Jelecek 1999). But from the 1980s there were published a number of *tours d'horizon*. That by T. W. Tate (1981) focused on the problems of defining environmental history, given its reach across both social and natural worlds. Tate argued none the less that some limitation was pragmatically necessary and identified four key (but essentially personal) themes for environmental history: human perceptions of and attitudes to the natural world; the impacts of technological innovations upon the environment; an understanding of ecological processes; and public debate about and political regulation of the environment. Much broader and much more coherent reflections about environmental history have been provided in essays by Worster (1984, 1988a), Richard White (1985) and Alfred Crosby (1995). Perhaps the most programmatic has been Worster's essay on 'Doing environmental history' in which he defined environmental history as 'understanding how humans have been affected by their natural environment through time and, conversely, how they have affected that environment and with what results'. Worster identified three main themes of study for environmental history: first, reconstructing past natural environments; secondly, understanding the interplay between human modes of production or material cultures and the natural environment; and thirdly, discovering how whole cultures perceived, valued and dealt with nature, viewing ideas as ecological agents (Worster 1988a: 290–1, 294–305).

Environmental history as defined and practised by a new generation of historians has become very productive. Some major collections of essays have been published, encompassing the whole sub-discipline and exploring its issues and methods (Bailes 1985; Miller and Rothman 1997; Hays 1998). A growing maturity has also led to monographic environmental histories focused on particular places at a variety of spatial and temporal scales. I am thinking here of James Miller's (1998) environmental history of north-east Florida, Albert Cowdrey's (1983) of the American South, Philip Scarpino's (1985) of the Upper Mississippi river basin between 1890 and 1950, Donald Davis' (2000) study of the southern Appalachians, and Gordon Whitney's (1994) history of environmental change in temperate North America between 1500 and the present. Additionally, environmental histories are being increasingly produced for places beyond America, such as South Asia (Arnold and Guha 1995; Grove et al. 1998), Africa (McCann 1999), Brazil (Dean 1987), Australia (Dovers 1994) and even of Britain since the Industrial Revolution (Clapp 1994). Another focus of study has been the environmental history of colonialism, an examination of the impact of empire on ecosystems and environments (Crosby 1986; Grove 1997; Griffiths and Robin 1997; Barton 2002). Even more ambitious is John McNeill's (2000) environmental history of the world. But the study in environmental history which has made most impact upon historical geography during the past decade or so has undoubtedly been William Cronon's *Nature's Metropolis: Chicago and the Great West* (1991), a monumental study of the plundering impact of economic and urban development on the environment of the American West during the nineteenth century. For this inspiring historical study, Cronon himself drew inspiration from a wide range of geographical concepts, such as urban hinterlands and the interdependence of cities and their countrysides, von Thünen's land-use zones and Christaller's settlement hierarchies, time-space relations and the social organisation of space. Cronon's book was a marvellous product of the meeting of historical and geographical thinking. Moreover, it occasioned a very direct encounter between historians and geographers. Ten geographers and one historian critique the book in one geographical journal, collectively admiring its ambitious scope while individually expressing specific reservations (*Antipode* 26, 1994). Cronon's response to those critics is unsurprisingly ambivalent, but together this set of essays constitute a very direct encounter between historians and geographers – as such, it represents a significant narrowing of the 'Great Divide', although residual differences and perhaps misunderstandings meant that it was not entirely overcome.

Both the key themes of environmental history identified by Worster (1988a) and the concerns of Cronon (1991) and of the other case studies previously mentioned are music to the ears of historical geographers who have been playing similar tunes for more than fifty years. It is remarkable that, in the development of environmental history as a sub-discipline, the contribution of historical geography to studies of the relationships between peoples and environments has been at best partially recognised and at worst completely overlooked. White's fleeting reference to the works of historical geographers like Carl Sauer, Andrew Clark and Donald Meinig is only made as part of his expression of regret that the long absence of historians from studies of the relationship between social and environmental change 'had left such concerns firmly in the hands of historical geographers' (White 1985: 320). P. G. Terrie's (1989) review of work in environmental history paid scant attention to similar work by historical geographers. Crosby, surveying the past and present of environmental history, gives much more consideration to the work of geographers, but even he mentions only Paul Vidal de la Blache, Carl Sauer and Andrew Clark, and he sees their contributions only as one of 'a number of intellectual developments prerequisite to environmental history' rather than as components of an active, substantial and long-established field of historical environmental research (Crosby 1995: 1182–4).

Similarly, Worster, reviewing environmental history and its cognate disciplines in his 1982 Presidential Address to the American Society of Environmental History, made only passing reference to 'the geographic work of Ellsworth Huntington, Ellen Semple, Friedrich Ratzel, and Elisée Reclus, all of whom had stressed the importance of habitat and climate in developing cultural diversity' (Worster 1984: 6–7). A few years later, Worster acknowledged that environmental historians 'have leaned on many geographers for insight', and he cited Michael Williams and Donald Meinig among presently active 'geographers' and Carl Sauer, Clifford Darby and Lucien Febvre (*sic*) from the recent past. Arguing that a weakness of geographers (and, to be fair to Worster, also of traditional historians) was 'their recurring tendency to lose sight of the elemental human–nature connection', Worster none the less conceded that it has been pre-eminently geographers who have helped historians to see that 'our situation is no longer one of being shaped by environment; rather, it is increasingly we who are doing the shaping, and often disastrously so' (Worster 1988a: 306). The dual interest in both the effect of the environment on human activity and the effect of such activity on the environment had been noted long ago by Berr in his foreword to Febvre's *A Geographical Introduction to History*. Berr argued that the treatment of this complex issue lay not 'within the domain of a geographer pure and simple' and that it required 'a geographical historian or an historical geographer, who is also more or less a sociologist' (Berr 1925: v).

Notwithstanding Worster's recognition of the instructive work of geographers, environmental history developed largely independently from historical geography, despite the obviously overlapping character of their concerns. Some might argue that, at least in part, this was because historical geographers abandoned or at least neglected the environmental discourse with their studies and focused instead on other objectives. Thus in the early 1980s McQuillan, apparently alarmed by the advance of social theory in historical geography, pleaded for putting 'more physical geography back into historical geography' (McQuillan 1982: 136), not least because the environment could no longer be taken as a constant in human geography. That plea has been repeated recently by other North American historical geographers who have undervalued the contribution of their own academy to the study of people–environment relations, doing so in part because they have seen that territory increasingly occupied by a burgeoning army of environmental historians (Trimble 1988, 1992; Colten and Dilsaver 1992).

What, then, has historical geography contributed to what has come recently to be seen as environmental history? There have been some major discussions of this question and I will begin with them, as it may be instructive to see how they have structured their approaches to the topic. Craig Colten and Lary Dilsaver (1992) identified three organising themes in historical geographies of the environment: first, the creation of cultural landscapes (thus conflating environment and landscape); secondly, past understandings and evaluations of environments; and thirdly, past environmental resource use and management. Michael Williams (1994) focuses his review on the recent work in historical geography in particular, and in geography in general, directly addressing some of the issues raised in the debate on the nature and content of environmental history. He organises his argument around four themes: first, 'the transformation and modification of

Earth', human-induced environmental change; secondly, 'global expansion and the capitalist economy' and their impact upon the environment; thirdly, 'the place of humans in nature', human attitudes towards nature; and fourthly, 'the interrelationships among habitat, economy and society'. Joe Powell (1999), reviewing the Anglophone literature on historical geography, environmentalism and culture, identifies four convergences: between physical geography and ecology, between cultural ecology and landscape studies, among heritage, identity and conservation studies, and between geographical historiography and historical geography. He sees studies in historical environmental geography as providing opportunity for convergences which are not only interdisciplinary but also intradisciplinary. Another survey by Powell (2000) of the literature on historical geographies of the environment is presented in two parts: the first reviews work under the general heading of 'changing the face of the earth', while the second is a more discursive reflection upon the relations not only between historical geography and environmental history but also between historical geography and physical geography (with Powell arguing that environmental histories provide an important opportunity for the closer convergence of work by human and physical geographers). In addition to these general reviews of historical environmental geography, there have been some perceptive critiques of work on the historical environmental geographies of particular countries, such as those by Powell (1996) on Australia and Graeme Wynn (1998) on Canada, while one issue of the *Journal of Historical Geography* (23 no. 4, 1997) is devoted to the historical environmental geographies of Australia and New Zealand.

That the relationship between historical geography and environmental history is very close is clearly demonstrated by the fact that to date (December 2002), there has been to my knowledge only one introductory textbook on environmental history published in English and it was written by a geographer. It provided a survey of the field as seen by a historical biogeographer. After a concise world history of the environmental relations of human societies over the past 10,000 years, I. G. Simmons (1993) presented a more analytical account of how human societies brought about a metamorphosis of the ecological communities around them and of what he termed 'the humanisation of the wilderness'. Two case studies of the environmental histories of England and Wales and of Japan were followed by a consideration of some of the cultural attitudes to environment that have been prevalent during the past one thousand or so years, especially in the Western world. Elsewhere, Simmons sketches for the world as a whole the regional distribution of human-induced environmental alteration (Simmons 1996: 405–11).

The paths of historical geography and environmental history have, as Craig Colten remarks, become 'so intertwined in recent years that it is not unreasonable to ask whether any distinction remains beyond the disciplinary labels and their intellectual foundations' (Colten 1998: iii). Theoretically, that might indeed be so. But from a practical point of view, disciplinary boundaries continue to act as filters of scholarship, as barriers to interdisciplinary co-operation. Recently, an applied historical geographer has tried to overcome one such barrier by examining the challenge which environmental history presents for local historians (Sheail 1997). It is also important to make work in historical geography more accessible to environmental historians. So I will now consider work in historical geography which is closest in its objectives to those of environmental history. I will discuss three key concerns in historical environmental geography: first, past physical environments; secondly, the impact of human activities upon natural environments in the past; and thirdly, human perceptions of environments in the past.

Historical environmental geographies

Reconstructing past natural environments

In so far as geographers and historical geographers have been concerned with the cultural transformation of natural environments, a logical starting point for a 'total' geography would be the natural environment before human occupation, before its alteration by human activities.

Reconstructing natural and primitive physical environments has become fully integrated into geography. Physical geographers might pursue such studies for their intrinsic interest, as enquiries into the physical forms and processes themselves; human geographers might engage in them in order to establish a datum line against which to try to measure the impact of human activities on the environment. And in turn such reconstructions can be static, endeavouring to capture the character of the natural or primitive environment at a moment or period in time, or they can be dynamic, trying to follow its changing character over time. Whatever their objective, all such studies require the use of a wide range of specialist analytical techniques. Reconstructing past physical environments is a demanding task, needing expertise not only in both physical and historical geography but also in related disciplines like archaeology, botany and palaeoecology. Such reconstructions depend upon the analysis of documentary evidence, literary, graphical (and perhaps especially cartographical) and statistical sources, both published and unpublished, as do all historical studies. But they rely also to varying extents upon the analysis of field evidence, such as archaeological artefacts and the morphology of landforms. In addition, the analysis of field evidence often requires the deployment of specialist techniques, such as sediment analysis, dendrochronology, lichenometry, pollen analysis and radiometric dating. Historical environmental studies are quintessentially interdisciplinary ventures, given the range of knowledge, understanding and skills which engaging in them demands. I am not providing here a 'do-it-yourself' manual on how to undertake such investigations: some general guides already exist (Sheail 1980; Hooke and Kain 1982; Trimble and Cooke 1991; Butlin 1993: 104–117; Whitney 1994: 8–38). I will instead consider briefly some examples of historical environmental studies in order simply to demonstrate the range of such work.

Logically, each of the systematic sub-disciplines or divisions within physical geography (as also within human geography) has its historical component. Thus literatures exist on what might be termed, for example, historical biogeography, historical soil geography, historical hydrology, historical geomorphology and historical climatology (just as they do on, for example, historical agricultural geography and historical urban geography). There is clearly room here only to point to the existence of those literatures and not to critique them. Probably the best guide to the systematic branches of historical environmental geography is that of Andrew Goudie, whose admirable book on *The Human Impact on the Natural Environment* was first published in 1981 and is now in its fifth (2000) edition. Although a physical geographer, Goudie focuses on the impact of human activities upon the natural environment, a perspective which I will defer considering until later in this chapter. My emphasis for the moment is on the reconstruction of past natural environments, whether or not they have been impacted by human activities.

This approach is, of course, most readily demonstrated in studies of natural environments before they were significantly, if at all, disturbed by people – that is to say, studies of environments not settled by people or at least settled only thinly and then by people with a low level of technology. In relation to the former, work by historical environmental geographers has interfaced with that of other environmental scientists, and in relation to the latter with work by archaeologists and anthropologists. Such studies have tended to emphasise the dynamic character of past natural environments, quite independently of any transformations which may have been brought about by human activities.

Some of the best examples of studies of past natural environments *per se* are those concerned primarily with climatic change. In this field, Jean Grove (1988) both summarised and extended our knowledge and understanding of the so-called 'Little Ice Age', a global phenomenon which culminated between the mid-sixteenth century and the mid-nineteenth century and whose existence has been established in large measure from documentary evidence (including paintings, sketches and lithographs) about the advance of European glaciers during the sixteenth century. Grove was here extending the earlier broad work by C. E. P. Brooks (1926) on climate change though the ages and the more detailed study by Le Roy Ladurie (1967) of climate change in France during the past one thousand years.

Good examples of studies of past natural environments which were only thinly settled are those which reconstruct North America's environments before their colonisation by Europeans. Here the work of Karl Butzer has been outstanding and is very helpfully summarised and contextualised by him in an essay published in an edited volume on the historical geography of North America. Butzer (1990) emphasised especially the role of climate change in altering the natural environments of North America, notably transforming many of them from glacial to non-glacial environments, and thus in influencing the pattern and character of Palaeoindian settlement. Here Butzer's stress was upon the extent to which changes in the natural environment impacted upon human activity. A similar focus was provided by

Martin Parry (1978) in his study of the effects of climate change, of a cooling climate, on the abandonment of marginal land in upland Britain between about 1300 and 1600. Much more wide sweeping, Neil Roberts (1998) provides, as a geographer, what he terms 'an environmental history' of the Holocene, a history of the natural environment and of human culture during the past 10,000 years. Roberts' emphasis is on physical environmental change and on adaptations to physical environments by societies with mainly low levels of technology and thus with limited capabilities to change their environments.

Reconstructions of past natural environments have come to be incorporated into historical geographies in a way which is not entirely dissimilar from portrayals by historians of the physical geography of an area as the stage upon which the drama of history has been enacted. For example, Stanley Trimble's (1990) depiction of the climates and physiography of North America served as an introduction to an edited collection of essays on the making of the American landscape: the natural environment was presented as 'the grand stage upon which the drama of human settlement and resettlement has been enacted on the North American continent over the last millennium or so'. A more sophisticated treatment of past natural environments was included in the first volume of the three-volume *Historical Atlas of Canada* (Harris 1987). Two of its sets of maps, together with the accompanying text on Canada's prehistoric environments and cultures, are of particular note in this context: Plate 4, 'Environmental change after 9000 BC', depicted the vegetation 'provinces' of Canada in 5000 BC and 1500 BC, and at five intervening dates, and Plate 17, 'Ecological regions, *ca* AD 1500', mapped the main ecological 'provinces', 'domains' and 'divisions', as defined by their climate, soils and predominant vegetation.

Work in historical environmental geography in North America and in Britain is well exemplified in two recent sets of edited essays. But those volumes are also instructive about the still relatively limited character of such work. Craig Colten and Lary Dilsaver's (1992) collection was offered as interpretations of past American environments. It included, as I have already noted, a plea by Trimble for more historical physical geographies, for more historical geographies of environment, a plea echoed of course by the book's editors. But of the ten substantive essays, not one was concerned with past environments or environmental change *per se* and only one was primarily concerned with the impact of environmental change (in this case, coastal shoreline erosion) upon human activity. Robin Butlin and Neil Roberts' (1995) edited essays on ecological relations in historical times constitute a collection of fifteen case studies, spread widely in time and space and embracing such disparate topics and studies as the growing population of the Highland midge in Scotland since the mid-nineteenth century and the invasion and transformation of California's valley grassland by Mediterranean species since the mid-eighteenth century. Almost all of the essays in these two volumes examine the environmental impacts of human activities and attitudes, practices and policies – in effect, they are studies in environmental management and, of course, mis-management.

The human modification of natural environments

Studies of the human impact on the natural environment are, as I have previously indicated, admirably reviewed by Goudie (2000). He astutely avoids the common pitfall of eliding environment into landscape, largely because of his focus upon environmental processes rather than forms and partly because of his primary concern with human activity as an environmental process, as a historical means rather than as an end in itself. The range of material reviewed by Goudie is wide and his citation of the relevant literature is extensive. His book is organised topic by topic, considering in turn key components of the natural environment – vegetation, animals, soils, waters, landforms, climate and atmosphere. A different, fundamentally chronological approach to reviewing the human impact on the natural environment is adopted by Simmons (1996) in his book *Changing the Face of the Earth*. Although the ecosystem concept provides the intellectual glue for this work, its procession from primitive hunter-gatherer societies through to advanced industrialised economies results in a less sharply focused picture of the environmental impact of human activity than the one provided by Goudie's systematic study. Although Simmons' approach is more historical than is Goudie's, the latter's is arguably more geographical. For that reason, and because Goudie's book is so comprehensive, I can do no better than to draw upon his organisational framework and append to it some examples of classic environmental-impact studies conducted by historical geographers.

Humankind, Goudie argues, has possibly had a greater influence on *plant life* than on any of the other components of the environment. Anthropogenic fires, grazing and the clearance of forest and wood have dramatically changed vegetation both throughout history and across the globe. Sauer (1969) emphasised both the role of fire in environmental change and its cultural significance as a focal fireside. Fire was used, for example, to clear land for cultivation; to improve the quality of grazing land for domesticated animals and to attract wild game; and to drive hunted game from cover. In addition, wood was cut to make fires to provide not only heat (for example, for warmth, for cooking and for baking pottery and smelting ores) but also light and security. Not all fires are anthropogenic, many are natural, but the impact of the former on changing vegetation cover has been considerable. The grazing of grassland and scrubland by animals has been beneficial (light grazing encourages plant growth, aids seed dispersal and adds nitrogen to the land), but it has also been detrimental (heavy grazing kills off plants and accelerates soil deterioration and erosion). Grazing has also had a selective impact upon vegetation, allowing less palatable species to flourish.

But the clearance of forest, whether by firing or by felling, is probably the most significant way in which human activity has altered vegetation: both historically, from prehistoric times onwards but with about one-fifth of the world's forests of all kinds having been removed since 1700 (Richards 1990: 164); and geographically, throughout the world, with the destruction by the end of the twentieth century of about one-third of the world's temperate forests, about one-quarter of its sub-tropical woody savannahs and deciduous forests, and about one-fifth of its tropical forests (World Resources Institute 1992: 107, cited in Goudie 1993: 43; Williams 1989a). Forests have been cleared for agriculture but also to provide wood for fuel and for construction. Within central and eastern Europe, especially significant deforestation took place between the mid-eleventh and late thirteenth century when there was both major population growth and eastward colonisation (Darby 1956). In North America, there was deforestation on a grand scale – of about 660,000 km^2 – as a result of its westward colonisation by European settlers between the early seventeenth and early twentieth century (Williams 1989a). A magisterial historical geography of the Americans and their forests from about 1600 has been provided by Williams (1989b). Although fundamentally a cultural study which investigated the complex evaluation and multiple utilisation of America's forests over more than four centuries, Williams' study also encompassed ecological and environmental issues, albeit largely indirectly as part of his consideration of the social practices and policies affecting the character and even the very existence of forests. Studies of forest clearance have been a major theme in historical geography but their emphasis has been upon deforestation, on the removal of forests rather than upon their human use and ecological modification. There are, of course, significant exceptions to that generalisation, such as Graeme Wynn's (1981) study of New Brunswick as what he termed 'a timber colony' in the early nineteenth century, and M. M. Roche's (1987) historical geography of forest policy in New Zealand between 1840 and 1919.

That human activity has had a significant impact upon vegetation is beyond dispute, but there has been considerable debate about its precise nature in certain environments. For example, the impact of human activity upon forests has not always involved their total clearance for cultivation or timber exploitation. Sometimes the clearance or exploitation has been partial, permitting the regeneration of a secondary forest but with vegetational characteristics which were different from the primary forest it replaced. This has especially been the case in tropical forests. As for tropical savannahs, there has been a major debate about the factors responsible for their creation and maintenance but few now doubt that anthro-pogenic fires must be included among them. Similarly, large areas of the *maquis* of Mediterranean lands represent forest degeneration as a result of human activity, including excessive timber exploitation, over-grazing by goats and fires.

People have also been important in spreading plants from one environment to another, both deliberately and accidentally. Plants which have been introduced into new environments intentionally fall into two categories: those with an economic value (such as food plants) and those with only an ornamental or cultural value. P. J. Jarvis (1979) argued that most plants introduced to the British Isles before the sixteenth century had some economic worth but that most species introduced from then onwards had principally amenity and decorative value, reflecting changing cultural preferences. Jarvis noted a major increase in the importation of woody species from the North American Atlantic seaboard between 1625 and 1820, from the Far East and China from the mid-eighteenth century onwards, from Latin America between 1820 and 1870, and from the North American Pacific seaboard between 1825 and 1900. He calculated that there were 103 alien woody species in England by 1600, 239 by 1700, 733 by 1800, and 1,911 by 1900. While many such introduced plants are only able to survive in their alien environments as a result of considerable human care and attention, some domesticated plants have 'escaped' and naturalised themselves in their new surroundings. Many plants have been dispersed accidentally as a result of human activity, having been unintentionally transported by the movements of people and commodities from place to place.

As with plants, so often too with *animals*. The principal impacts of human activities upon animals may, for convenience and from an environmental point of view, be considered as having been their domestication, dispersal and destruction. Domestication, the selective breeding of animals (and plants) in order to enhance specific characteristics, has been practised by humans with varying intensity from the Late Pleistocene or Early Holocene to the present day. Corralling or herding animals was a much more controlled and efficient process than was hunting them. Moreover, the reared beasts could be used not only as sources of products (such as milk and meat, fertiliser and fuel) but also as sources of power (as transport and traction, and as tools made from animal products). The anthropogenic dispersal of animals, consciously or otherwise, has had a major impact upon the distribution of animal species throughout the world. For example, the rabbit was introduced into the British Isles by the Normans in the eleventh century (Sheail 1971) – a local (or at best regional) and relatively minor example of a global and absolutely major phenomenon. Animals have been intentionally introduced to new places for many reasons, such as for food, for sport and for entertainment and curiosity. But accidental dispersals have been just as important and, like deliberate introductions, increased very significantly with the growth in the size and number of ocean-going vessels from the eighteenth century. An aphid unknowingly imported into France in the mid-nineteenth century on vines brought by sea from North America was to be responsible for the devastation of most of France's (and, indeed, Europe's) vineyards by the early twentieth century. The extreme impact of human activity upon animals has been, of course, their destruction but a more general impact has been fluctuation in the size of particular animal populations. Over-hunting of the North American bison almost led to its extinction; the last surviving dodo was killed on Mauritius in 1681.

Let me flesh out these bones, this skeletal account of human impacts upon plants and animals, with some exemplary geographical work on domestication and dispersal. Environmental historians are acquainted with the works of Sauer, whose geographical writings ranged over the 'theme of plant and animal destruction in economic history', the 'early relations of man to plants', and agricultural origins and dispersals (Sauer 1938a, 1947, 1952). But they exhibit much less familiarity with the work of Sauer's 'disciples'. A few other examples here might therefore be illuminating. I will take one classic regional study in historical environmental geography, by Clark, and one set of modern systematic studies, by Donkin. Following in the intellectual footsteps of Sauer as one of his research students, Clark (1949) researched the invasion of New Zealand's South Island by people, plants and animals. He opened his study with an account of the island's 'primitive habitat', its physiography, its climate, its vegetation, its fauna and its soils before the arrival of European colonists. There then followed accounts of the island's Polynesian occupation since 'some unknown period in the remote past', of early exploration and contact by Europeans from the early seventeenth century (especially resulting from the whaling trade), and of the island's peopling after 1840 by settlers from Australia and Europe (and especially, of course, from Britain). Thus, in meticulous detail, Clark had set the natural and cultural stage for his detailed analysis of the 'invasion' of South Island by animals (sheep, cattle, 'minor domesticated animals' – horses, pigs and goats – and animal pests – rabbits, exotic game animals – deer, chamois and thar) and by plants (potatoes, wheat, brassicas, grasses and clovers, and numerous exotic trees and shrubs). As a historical geographer, Clark's purpose was to demonstrate the contribution of these plant and animal migrations to changing the 'regional character' of South Island, 'to report on a revolutionary change in the character of a region, which occurred in a period of less than two centuries', to study 'the invasion of the area by armies of plants and animals, which, with the help of man, mingled with or displaced the native flora and fauna'. Clark hoped that his study 'might be exemplary of the themes of historical geography' (Clark 1949: 381 and v). It certainly anticipated by a long time-span the more recent interest in 'ecological imperialism' (Crosby 1986). More esoteric are Robin Donkin's studies of the historical geographies of plants and animals. Donkin was strongly influenced by Sauer's work and his own came to be increasingly based upon it (Donkin 1997). His studies have embraced a wide range of individually distinctive plants and animals, such as cochineal and the opuntia cactus, the peccary (a species of pig), the Muscovy duck, the guinea fowl, and camphor (Donkin 1977, 1985, 1989, 1991, 1999).

But I must return to more familiar ground, in fact to *soils*. Goudie emphasised that 'humans live close to and depend on the soil. It is one of the thinnest and most vulnerable human resources and is one upon which, both deliberately and inadvertently, humans have had a very major impact.' Anthropogenically induced changes to soils have included 'chemical changes (such as salinisation and laterisation), structural changes (such as compaction), some hydrological changes (including the effects of drainage and the factors leading to peat-bog development), and, perhaps most important of all, soil erosion' (Goudie 1993: 138–9). Such themes have featured largely in work by historical geographers. I will cite just a few examples, both of soil degradation and of soil amelioration as a result of human activity. It was a French geographer, Pierre Gourou, who highlighted the ways in which human activities in the tropics – the removal of forest and the practices of agriculture – aggravate what he called 'the dangers of laterite' and 'increase the rate of the process of laterisation' – laterite being an iron and/or aluminium-rich duricrust, hardening on exposure to air and through desiccation and thus becoming unfavourable to plant growth (Gourou 1961: 21–2). Goudie (1973) has presented considerable evidence from many parts of the tropics of accelerated induration brought about by forest removal. He has also offered some general observations on 'dust storms in time and space', of wind-generated soil erosion created in part by dry climatic conditions but often exacerbated by poor land-management techniques, such as over-grazing (Goudie 1983). But as long ago as 1938, Sauer drew specific attention to soil erosion in his general criticism of the destructive exploitation associated with modern colonial expansion. He said: 'We may well consider whether the theme of soil erosion should not be moved up to the first category of problems before the geographers of the world. It is very important for the future of mankind. It has critical significance for certain chapters of historical geography' (Sauer 1938b: 497). Since Sauer made that plea, there have been numerous studies of soil erosion, including many by historical geographers. One such study of importance was Trimble's account of human-induced soil erosion on America's Southern Piedmont from 1700 to 1970 (Trimble 1974) and Trimble has been restating Sauer's plea, arguing for more rigorous historical studies of soil erosion (Trimble 1992; Trimble and Crosson 2000).

Not all human impacts upon the soil have been deleterious, and considerable human ingenuity and energy have long been expended in improving the fertility and workability of soils. Again, a few examples will suffice to underpin this point. Kenneth Cumberland (1961), in his review of the role of 'man in nature' in New Zealand's historical geography, showed how, long before European settlement there, the Maoris had used thousands of tons of gravel and sand, carried in baskets made of flax, to improve soil structure. The practice of marling in eastern England, probably also of considerable antiquity but intensified during the eighteenth and nineteenth centuries, not only improved its light soils but also pocked its landscape with thousands of pits and hollows (Prince 1962, 1964). One of the most impressive, recent historico-geographical studies of soil improvement endeavours is A. D. M. Phillips' (1989) account of the under-draining of heavy soils on England's farmlands during the nineteenth century. His study showed how the more productive use of soils was tied, in some circumstances, to the more effective management of water.

So now I will turn more generally to the human impact on *water* in the environment. There are myriad issues here. Water is so vital to human life that considerable efforts have been made to manage it as a resource. Riverine and coastal floods have often been a threat to human life, welfare and property so that actions have been taken to contain them. Many human activities have had unintended consequences on water. For example, deforestation and urbanisation have both had hydrological consequences, affecting such matters as the nature of run-off and the rates of erosion and the delivery of pollutants to rivers. Human activities have significantly and often adversely influenced lake levels, ground-water conditions and water quality.

Even studies which focus upon present-day aspects of the 'effects of human activity on the interface of the hydrological cycle with the physical environment' (Meade and Trimble 1974) usually adopt a historical approach in order to assess, preferably to monitor, the changing nature of those effects. Goudie's (2000) overview of these matters is very thorough and I will therefore focus here on just two human impacts upon water in the environment: first, the deliberate modification of rivers, and secondly, the reclamation of wetland environments. I will illustrate these themes by reference to some major studies by historical geographers.

The direct modification of river channels has been practised for centuries, indeed for thousands of years. It has taken varied forms (such as the construction of dams and reservoirs, and channel improvement through straightening, widening and deepening) and it has had varied purposes (including water storage, flood prevention, power generation and transportation). One (I would venture to suggest, *the*) classic study by a historical geographer of river management is that by Dion (1934a) of the embanking of the Loire in France. Dion provided a fascinating account of the enduring and epic efforts of individuals and authorities in the Loire Valley to bring the longest river in France under control. Frequent flooding of the valley imposed serious restrictions on early settlement and agriculture, while changes in the river's channel interfered with navigational use of the Loire for transporting goods and people. Dion demonstrated that from the mid-twelfth century onwards there were constructed along various parts of the valley, beginning downstream in Anjou, *levées* or embankments, built in the belief that they would be an effective flood-prevention measure. But given that the embankments were for a long time discontinuous, they served to protect some sections of the valley while worsening the flooding of its unprotected sections. Moreover, as the length of the embankments grew over the centuries, the river, while being increasingly constrained within a narrow artificial channel, increased its level within that channel and flooding remained a recurrent problem, with the river overflowing and/or breaking through its embankments. The local populations, believing in the theoretical possibility and practical utility of building insubmersible embankments, constructed ever-higher embankments with increasingly stronger materials. That belief persisted for centuries, despite continued and recurrent flooding of the valley floor and the frequent damaging and occasional destruction of many of the wooden and later stone bridges built over the river. Dion demonstrated that the solution adopted to manage the problem of flooding in the Loire Valley, far from solving it, had even exacerbated it. Not until after massive floods and the severe damage which they inflicted in 1846, and then again in 1856 and in 1866, was there begun a serious search for an alternative solution. From the late 1860s onwards, there were constructed a series of *déversoirs* (overspill areas) in the middle and lower reaches of the valley, to act as safety valves into which 'flood water' could be harmlessly diverted. Although these measures prevented further serious floods through to the early 1930s when Dion published his regional monograph, he was not totally convinced that a permanent solution to the problem had been found.

Later, with the construction of dams and reservoirs in the middle and higher sections of the valley, the river's regime has come to be more precisely controlled and the danger of serious flooding appears to have been removed. Dion's classic study of anthropogenic river modification over almost 800 years remains unsurpassed. It has no modern equivalent in terms of the breadth of its historical and geographical coverage of river channel management.

I will, therefore, now turn to the second main watery theme pursued by historical geographers, that of the reclamation of wetland environments, for which I am able to call upon both classic and modern studies to provide testimony. The former were provided by Darby in his portrayals of the medieval Fens of eastern England and of their subsequent reclamation (Darby 1940a, 1940b). The Fens occupied some 1,300 square miles (almost 3,500 km^2) and their reclamation could be claimed as having constituted the most dramatic case of anthropogenic environmental transformation in England's history. Darby argued that although there had been some attempts to drain parts of the Fens since Roman times, they had been essentially piecemeal efforts and they were by no means continuously successful, so that even by the early seventeenth century the Fens were a wetland environment which had been only partially modified by human activity and which was valued mainly for its wetland products, such as fish and fowl, timber and turf, sedge and salt, and some pastures for grazing livestock. From the seventeenth century there were initiated major, more or less integrated, schemes of drainage drawing at first upon Dutch expertise of water engineering and increasingly upon general developments in pumping technology. The work involved the construction of vast new 'drains' (to evacuate water from the Fens more rapidly) and the creation of a vast overspill area between two major drains to act as a reservoir for what would otherwise have been the flood waters. But Darby, like Dion for the Loire, showed that such management systems in the Fens had unforeseen consequences. Pumping water into straighter, more efficient drains certainly made the area more agriculturally productive, but pumping also produced another unexpected effect: the surface of the peat lowered, owing in part to the shrinkage of the peat as it dried and also in part to the wasting away of the drying peat surface because of increased bacterial action. Lowering of the surface-level was most acute in the peat zone of the southern Fens, but it was encountered also, to a considerably lesser extent, in the silt zone to the north. As the surface of the Fens lowered, so the necessity arose for even more pumping into the network of now relatively higher drains. Pumps powered by wind gave way in the nineteenth century to pumps powered by steam, and those were in turn in due course replaced by pumps powered by diesel and by electricity. While the wetland environment of the Fens has been dramatically transformed by the investment of vast amounts of capital and engineering expertise, the control of its hydrology requires constant vigilance, for the 'nature' of the Fens has not been completely 'tamed' – reflecting which fact, Darby's epic narrative, first published in 1940, was updated as a second edition in 1956 and a third edition in 1968, to bring into account the new drainage measures implemented in the interim periods.

Darby's description of the reclamation of the Fens of eastern England has served directly as a model for similar studies of the environmental transformation of wetlands in other places, such as pre-revolutionary Russia (French 1964), parts of Australia (Williams 1974) and the Somerset Levels of western England (Williams 1970). But signs of Darby's influence are also detectable in studies of the drainage of the wetlands of the American Midwest (Hewes and Frandson 1952; Prince 1997). Water management more generally continues to be a well-researched theme in historical geography. It has, for example, been a special interest of Powell in his wide-ranging work on the historical geography of Australia. In his *Watering the Garden State: Water, Land and Community in Victoria, 1834–1988* (1989) and his *Plains of Promise, Rivers of Destiny: Water Management and the Development of Queensland 1824–1990* (1991), Powell provided detailed and illuminating accounts of the centrality of water management in the history of regional development, conservation and environmental appraisal in Australia. In particular, he examined the roles of private individuals, communities and public authorities in the formulation and implementation of policies and practices of water management. His works provided insight into the historical geographies of those two states through the optic of competing demands for water from agricultural, industrial and urban interests. Powell emphasised the organisational, socio-political aspects of water management: for example, he examined the relation of the holistic and ecological concept of the river basin to the emergence of regionalism and community identity in the Murray-Darling Basin since 1850 and he showed the provision of water supplies to have been important in consolidating mining and farming frontier districts in Western Australia during the nineteenth and twentieth centuries (Powell 1993, 1998).

The human impact upon water has often involved the environmental transformation of large areas. That on *landforms* has often been more localised and I want now to consider the role of human agency in creating landforms and in modifying the operation of geomorphological processes such as weathering, erosion and deposition. In relation to this set of questions, the approaches of physical geographers and of human geographers can be clearly differentiated, more so than in relation to their studies of other components of environmental systems. Those coming as physical geographers to such questions have viewed human activity as a geomorphological process, seeing people as geomorphological agents. The emphasis of their interest has been more on the processes than on the structures which resulted from those processes. By contrast, those coming to these issues as human geographers have tended to focus on the physical structures which human activities have produced, seeing those structures as cultural contributions to physical environments and landscapes. Their emphasis has been more on the 'landforms' as cultural constructions than upon human agency as a geomorphological process.

Support for this general argument is to be found in the fact that almost all of the overviews of the human impact upon landforms have been provided by physical geographers and not by historical and cultural geographers. One of the earliest such surveys was R. L. Sherlock's *Man as a Geological Agent* (1922), since when the field has been reviewed on a number of occasions (Jennings 1966; Brown 1970; Nir 1983; Goudie 1993). Goudie listed 'anthropogenic landforms' separately from the direct and indirect 'anthropogenic processes' producing or modifying landforms. In his first list are 'landforms' which have been the focus of interest for many historical geographers: they include pits, ponds and spoil heaps produced by mining and marling; terracing, lynchets and ridge-and-furrows crafted for agricultural purposes; cuttings and embankments created to improve transportation systems; embankments, reservoirs and dikes associated with river and coastal management; and mounds and moats built as defensive measures. While to a physical geographer such phenomena are 'landforms', for many historical geographers they have been 'relict cultural features' which have generated often-protracted debates about their origins and functions. For his second list, Goudie employed M. J. Haigh's (1978) classification of direct and indirect anthropogenic processes, with the former being constructional and excavational activities together with measures of hydrological interference, and the latter being the acceleration of erosion and sedimentation, subsidence, slope failure and earthquake generation. In his own treatment of human agency in geomorphology, Goudie considered a wide range of anthropogenic landforms and processes: for example, he deals with landforms produced by excavation and by construction and dumping, and by the deliberate and non-deliberate modification of river channels; with the impact of human activity in accelerating sedimentation, weathering, mass movements, and coastal and peat erosion; and with the impact of human activity on ground subsidence, on sand dune instability, and even on seismic activity and volcanoes.

Whether studies of such anthropogenic forms and processes have been executed by physical or by human geographers, they have usually encountered the same difficulty, that of determining the relative importance of natural and cultural processes in the formation of such structures. As Goudie has argued,

landforms produced by indirect anthropogenic processes are often less easy to recognise [than those produced by direct anthropogenic processes], not least because they tend to involve, not the operation of a new process or processes, but the acceleration of natural processes. They are the result of environmental changes brought about inadvertently by human technology. None the less, it is probably this indirect and inadvertent modification of process and form which is the most crucial aspect of anthropo-geomorphology. (Goudie 1993: 237)

The case for such studies being undertaken collaboratively, therefore, by both physical and human geographers has been made very convincingly: they bring to the same problem different knowledges and skills which can together enhance understanding (Hooke and Kain 1982). When work is not undertaken in that way, then the same forms (or at least very similar forms) might well be interpreted in very different ways. Thus depressions in the chalklands of Dorset in southern England have been debated as being either naturally formed dolines or culturally constructed marl pits (Sperling et al. 1979; Prince 1979). By contrast, the benefits which can be realised from close collaborative work have been dramatically demonstrated in studies of the Broads, a group of twenty-five freshwater lakes in Norfolk, in eastern England. Because of their area and size, the Broads were originally considered to be natural features, formed in natural peaty hollows or in tributary valleys whose mouths were blocked by clay (Jennings 1952). But detailed work undertaken co-operatively by historical and physical geographers revealed that the Broads were products of human activity, that they resulted mostly from peat-cutting in the Middle Ages, with the depressions thus created becoming subsequently filled with water (Lambert et al. 1970). This was a truly remarkable set of research findings, the result of magnificent historico-geographical detective work using evidence garnered in the field and in archives and libraries.

Work of comparable quality and significance by historical geographers cannot yet be cited in relation to the human impact on *climate* and *atmosphere*. While there are, as I have shown, historical geographers who have contributed usefully to studies of the climate change, none has – to my knowledge – conducted extensive and significant study of the human impact on climate. There are probably a number of reasons for this. First, few historical geographers feel as 'at home' with climatology as they do with biogeography and even with geomorphology: this limitation is, I suspect, a by-product of the uneven nature of their school and university education, for climatology seems to be a weak link – indeed, possibly the weakest link – in the training which schools and colleges provide for geographers. Secondly, historical data on the human impact upon climate over time are by no means abundant and tend to be relatively soft in character. Thirdly, and perhaps most importantly, it is probably only during the past two centuries that human agency has become a significant factor in climate change. Fourthly, the anthropogenic impact on observed trends in climate is not easily distinguishable from the role of natural processes.

The contribution of historical geographers (and, unsurprisingly, of the newer environmental historians) to this 'field' of enquiry has as yet been negligible. The main opportunities here lie, as Goudie (2000) indicates, in examining the unintentional effects of human activity on atmospheric quality and on the albedo of land masses (with the latter being much more contentious than the former). Thus there have been some, and could well be more, studies of the atmospheric impacts of the Agricultural and Industrial Revolutions. Goudie summarises those which have been undertaken, treating, for example, levels of methane gas (which, having been stable for most of the past 10,000 years, have risen more than two-fold since 1700), and of various forms of pollution in the atmosphere (including smoke haze and petrochemical smog), as well as the development of urban 'heat islands'.

My treatment of the human modification of natural environments has been organised systematically, because this approach dismantles the environment into its components and makes the subject manageable. The dual complexity of natural environments and of human activities impacting upon them have militated against the researching and writing of 'total' historical environmental geographies of individual areas. As few such holistic studies exist, it would be faint praise indeed to describe any particular study as being 'one of the best' of its kind. But I do want to mention the monumental study by David Watts (1987) of environmental and cultural change and development in the West Indies from the 1490s until the 1980s (Fig. 3.1) and the much briefer but none the less excellent study by Geoffrey Buckley (1998) of the environmental transformation of an Appalachian valley in America during the second half of the nineteenth century. Other beginnings have been made. Georges Bertrand (1975) sketched what he, as a geographer, termed 'an ecological history' of rural France; Wynn (1998) provides a glimpse of the historical environmental geography of Canada which he is writing and which is awaited with much anticipation; A. T. Grove and O. Rackham (2001) combine their respective geographical and ecological expertises in their 'ecological history' of Mediterranean Europe; and Eric Pawson (a geographer) and Tom Brooking (a historian) bring together not only geographers and historians but also an archaeologist, an anthropologist, an ecologist and an environmental lawyer to write a set of environmental histories of New Zealand (Pawson and Brooking 2002). Assessments of environmental appraisals and impacts also feature largely in John Wright's (1993) study of the Rocky Mountains, in essays edited by William Wyckoff and Lary Dilsaver (1995) on the mountainous West, and in Paul Starrs' (1998) examination of cattle ranching in the American West.

Environmental transformations, both deliberate and unintentional, have by no means been confined to rural areas. There is a sharpening focus on historical urban environmental geography. Especially during the past two hundred years or so, urbanisation coupled with industrial systems of production created environmental problems and degradation on a scale not previously encountered. Dense concentrations of people and industrial activities produced pollution and environmental problems (especially of health and hygiene) to which both public authorities and private individuals responded with management policies of very varying effectiveness. Christopher Boone's (1997) pioneering, edited essays on this theme demonstrate the promise and potential rewards of new research on urban environments from a historico-geographical perspective.

Before terminating this discussion of human modifications of natural environments, I must insert one significant caveat. I noted earlier that ecologists are rethinking their discipline. Revisionists are questioning some long-held 'principles', such as those of ecosystem and equilibrium, of community and climax, and promoting instead ideas about, for example, disturbance and dynamism. This in turn means that other scholars – be they historians or geographers – need to exercise caution when adopting and applying ecological concepts to their own investigations. This point has been debated by geographer Demeritt (1994a) and environmental historian Cronon (1994). The cautionary tale told by Demeritt about the extent to which ecologists themselves are currently debating some of the key concepts

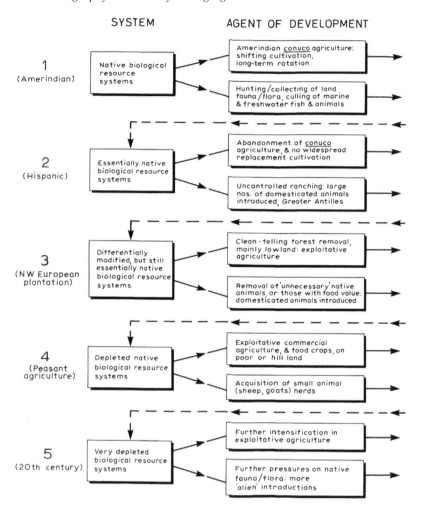

Figure 3.1 'A general model of the effects of development on environment within the West Indies since 1492.' The effects were 'overwhelmingly negative'
Source: Watts (1987: 534–5 and 533)

being taken for granted and borrowed almost unquestioningly by some environmental historians is not seriously challenged by Cronon. But Cronon does part company with Demeritt on broader issues. When Demeritt draws upon recent debates about the nature of knowledge and upon postmodern critical theory to challenge work in environmental history, Cronon poses fundamental problems about the writing of any kind of history, be it environmental or whatever. Those questions – about the legitimation of historical narratives, about the realist–idealist,

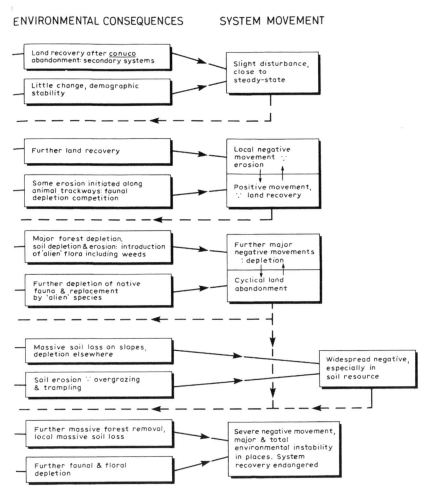

Figure 3.1 (*cont.*)

objectivist–relativist dualism – are so crucial that they cannot be ignored, and yet so basic that philosophers and historians have meditated upon them for centuries. Cronon prefers answers which permit the practice of a pragmatic, consensual history rather than the more philosophical and also more committed, engaged answers provided by Demeritt. While readily accepting pleas for caution in interdisciplinary enterprises, I find Cronon's approach to the practice of historical enquiry much more facilitating than Demeritt's, to which an indirect rejoinder has also been penned by Matthew Gandy (1996) in his review of the postmodernity debate and the analysis of environmental problems.

Throughout this discussion of the human modification of natural environments, I have repeatedly emphasised that human activities often had unintended environmental consequences. Such surprises often stemmed from the incomplete or inappropriate appraisal of environments by those exploring them and by those exacting their livelihoods from them. I will now, therefore, turn attention away from the 'real' environments to environments as they were 'perceived' by those encountering them.

The perception of natural environments: historical geosophy

Conceptions of nature, and ideas about natural environments and about a society's relationship to nature and with natural environments, have their own histories and geographies. Both have been studied by historians and by geographers, as well as by others. For example, Keith Thomas (1983), a historian, examined the differing and changing ways in which theologians, scientists, moralists and aesthetes in England between 1500 and 1800 conceived the natural world of plants and animals around them, while Clarence Glacken (1967), a geographer, traced the Western conception of the relations between nature and human societies as that view evolved from ancient times through to the eighteenth century. More recently, Simmons (1993: 157–88) summarised the literature on cultural constructions of 'wilderness', ranging from desert to paradise, showing how such ideas both change from time to time and differ from place to place – in effect, such ideas have their own historical geographies. Other good examples of this genre are the historian François Walter's (1990) book on the changing attitudes of the Swiss to nature from the early eighteenth century to the late twentieth century and the geographer Williams' (1998) paper on such attitudes in the Western world in general during the first half of the twentieth century. But my concern here is less with the history and geography of conceptions of nature in general and more with the perceptions of specific environments by individuals and groups in the past.

Studies of past environments from the perspectives of contemporaries who observed them have a long pedigree within the practice of historical geography. For example, S. W. Wooldridge's (1936) account of the Anglo-Saxon settlement of England was based on the premise that it was necessary 'to see the country in its former state through the eyes of a practically-minded immigrant farmer'. The rationale for such an approach was set out independently in two key papers, by J. K. Wright (1947) and W. Kirk (1951). Despite modestly but naïvely claiming not to be doing so, Wright introduced the term 'geosophy' into the literature of geography, defining it as 'the study of geographical knowledge from any or all points of view'.

For Wright, geosophy covered 'the geographical ideas, both true and false, of all manner of people – not only geographers, but farmers and fishermen, business executives and poets, novelists and painters, Bedouins and Hottentots – and for this reason it necessarily has to do in large degree with subjective conceptions'.

Logically, therefore, Wright saw 'historical geosophy' as the history of geographical knowledge but as possessed by all sorts and conditions of men and women – and even children – in the past and not just by geographers. Given that such knowledge, whether accurate or otherwise, was (and is) the basis for action, for exploration and for exploitation, it has much more than intrinsic interest: its recovery through research is fundamental to the wider project of historical geography (and its role in education remains fundamental to development of informed individuals and of an informed society). A collection of essays in historical geosophy published to honour Wright testified to the wide applicability of the concept (Lowenthal and Bowden 1976).

For Kirk, there was a distinction to be drawn between the phenomenal environment and the behavioural environment. Concern with people as agents of environmental change, with the sequence of occupance of environments, and with the physical relics of human actions, Kirk saw as belonging to a phenomenal environment. Concern with the changing knowledge of an individual or a society's natural environment and of changing environmental values, he envisaged as part of a behavioural environment. Kirk saw facts of the phenomenal environment entering people's behavioural environment, but only in so far as they are perceived by human beings with motives, preferences, modes of thinking, and traditions drawn from their social and cultural context. The same empirical data may be arranged into different patterns by, and have different meanings for, people of different cultures or at different periods in the history of a particular culture. Kirk's main purpose was to warn against the danger of attempting to explain the actions of a past community in terms of the values and knowledge of our own, present-day culture. While Kirk's 1951 paper did not inaugurate an entirely new line of work, it was published in a more accessible form in 1963 and was acclaimed by Harold Brookfield (1969) as being the earliest in geography to separate the perceived environment as a distinct surface and to frame it in terms of Gestalt psychology. Kirk's paper has been shown to have had its antecedents and even one which anticipated it to a remarkable extent (J. Campbell, 1989; Philo 2001). Be that as it may, Kirk's influential paper did make explicit a view of the world which was implicit in the writings of a number of others, including Wright.

Studies in historical geosophy (or, as they now tend to be termed, studies of past geographical knowledges) constitute a significant research cluster within historical geography (Chambers 1982): one issue of the field's leading international journal included eight articles on historical geosophical topics (*Journal of Historical Geography* 18 no. 1, 1992) and the sections on 'Popular images and evaluation' in an authoritative bibliographic guide to geographical writing on the American and Canadian past cite hundreds of works in this genre (Conzen et al. 1993). All of which lends support to what might otherwise be thought to be an extravagant claim by Ralph H. Brown (1948: iii) that 'no phase of historical geography is more important than that of weighing the effectiveness of beliefs as distinct from actual knowledge in the occupancy and settlement of regions'. Studies in historical geosophy fall into two broad categories: those which depict past environments using the 'language' and knowledge of an individual contemporary observer or of a group of observers, and those which identify the nature and extent of the gap between what Wright called the 'false' and 'true' ideas of people in the past about their environments. I will consider each in turn.

Observations made by learned men, by topographers and by travellers are often the basis for historical geosophies which fall into the first category. There is a long line of such studies, many of which have become classic studies. J. N. L. Baker (1931) wrote an account of Daniel Defoe's knowledge of England's geography, as evidenced in Defoe's publications; H. C. Darby (1935, 1954) extracted from the writings of the Venerable Bede some of the geographical ideas shared by learned men in England in the eighth century and from topographies and reports for the Board of Agriculture the ideas of their authors about the agricultural regions of England; E. G. R. Taylor (1936) compiled essays on the geography of England in the sixteenth century as observed and recorded by two topographers, John Leland and William Camden; F. V. Emery (1958, 1965) explored the regional geography of England as depicted in topographies of the seventeenth and early eighteenth centuries and the geography of the Gower peninsula in South Wales as depicted by a natural scientist, Edward Lluyd, and some of his Glamorgan correspondents; W. R. Mead (1962) drew upon a Swedish traveller's account of his journeys through the Chiltern Hills of England in the eighteenth century and T. H. Elkins (1956) upon an English traveller's perceptions of the Siegerland. Clark (1954) argued that 'in attempting to see the area of his interest as it was, the best view for the historical geographer is through the eyes of observers contemporary with the time of his interest'. Clark used the journals of Titus Smith, junior – 'a farmer by occupation; a surveyor by avocation; a scientist, philosopher, and a writer for recreation' – to reconstruct the geography of Nova Scotia in 1801 and 1802. Clark pushed his case too far, however, in claiming that through the eyes of such observers, 'as in no other way, may we hope to see the lands we study, as nearly as may be, *as they really were*' [my italics]. Smith's view, undoubtedly perceptive and authentic, would none the less now be accepted as just one geographical account of Nova Scotia.

More comprehensive have been studies which have drawn not upon a single source or narrow set of sources but upon a very wide range of contemporary observations in order to demonstrate the multiple geographical knowledges which were often constructed of a given environment. An excellent example was provided by H. R. Merrens' (1969) study of the physical environment of colonial South Carolina as 'imagined' and described by five sets of observers. First, there were the publications of those promoting settlement in the colony. Printed in different European languages and distributed widely in major European cities, this promotional literature portrayed the physical environment of South Carolina as a kind of terrestrial paradise ripe for settlement. Secondly, reports by officials such as missionaries, administrators and military officers also tended to describe the environment positively, perhaps in part because this is what they thought their superiors wanted them to do. Thirdly, accounts by more independently minded individual travellers were, Merrens argued, more informative and more reliable, although regrettably few in number. Fourthly, notebooks compiled by natural scientists were based on careful observations and tended to be systematically presented accounts, but only of one or a limited number of facets of the colony's physical environment. Fifthly, there were statements recorded by settlers in the colony which indicated the reactions of people for whom the suitability of the physical environment for settlement and development was their most immediate concern. Merrens showed clearly that what Wright had termed 'the subjective conceptions' of these different groups of observers varied markedly. An earlier study by Merrens (1964) of North Carolina in the eighteenth century had also shown how widely the evaluations of its physical environment by its native populations differed from those of immigrant settlers and those in turn from a modern geographer's 'real' assessment of the land.

The notion of multiple knowledges of a single environment has permeated many other excellent works by historical geographers. There is today a renewed interest by historical geographers in travel writings and their role in the construction of 'imaginative geographies' of 'foreign' places and peoples (for example, Blunt 1994; McEwan 1994; Gregory 1995; Kearns 1997). Robin Butlin (2001) compares and contrasts many representations of Palestine in the nineteenth century in the writings of English and French scholars and travellers, while Laura Cameron's (1997) intriguing narrative of the draining of Sumas Lake in British Columbia during the 1920s uses oral histories and written accounts to reconstruct the negotiated and contested knowledges of the lake and its draining. Remarkably, Cameron's concluding chapter is an imaginative account of the environment and its transformation from the perspective of a mosquito. Another example is Yehoshua Ben-Arieh's (1979) account of what he called 'the rediscovery of the Holy Land in the nineteenth century' by explorers and travellers, missionaries and clergymen, military officers and administrators, artists and poets, and surveyors and scientists. Many other examples in this genre could be cited, for example, Douglas McManis' (1964) analysis of initial evaluations of the Illinois Prairies 1815–40, and to them must be added studies which emphasise the ways in which ideas about environments not only differ among individuals and groups but also change through time, such as G. Malcolm Lewis' (1962) account of the changing emphases in descriptions of the natural environment of the American Great Plains region. A recent and excellent example of this latter category is Prince's (1997) recovery of changing attitudes towards the wetlands of the American Midwest since the early nineteenth century, moving from their evaluation and use by Native Americans through their assessment by speculators, landowners, farmers and railway companies to the views of modern environmentalists and conservationists.

There is, then, a long tradition of studies in historical geosophy within historical geography. But during the past decade or so they have been given a new lease of life in reconstructions of the geographical knowledges of particular individuals or groups of individuals in the past. For example, Alan Lester (2000) argues that historical geographies of imperialism within the English-speaking world have largely focused on how that ideology was understood in European metropolitan centres. He examines the sorts of knowledge about other races, climates and landscapes produced, for example, by European geographers as well as within popular circuits of knowledge. In similar vein, Ploszajska (2000) analyses the sorts of geographical knowledge produced and communicated within the textbooks and by the teaching practices used in England's schools between 1870 and 1944. Looking at the other side of the imperialist coin, Brenda Yeoh (2000) examines the knowledges not of the colonisers but of the colonised, using the Chinese community in nineteenth-century Singapore as her case study. Others have been concerned with the geographical knowledges of, for example, scientists and politicians.

But I want now to focus instead upon those studies which explicitly examine what they consider to be the gap between the 'image' and the 'reality' of an environment, because some of the most interesting work in historical geosophy has emphasised that 'false' geographical knowledge has been as significant historically as 'true' knowledge. One relatively simple illustration of this point is the way in which much of the exploration of North America during the sixteenth and seventeenth centuries was driven by the search for the North-West Passage to China, based upon the illusion that the St Lawrence River and the Great Lakes were somehow connected to rivers and seas which provided direct access to China (Watson 1969). This is but one example of the general point that geographical imagination has played a leading role in the history of exploration (Allen 1976). But the idea has a wider purchase within historical geosophy.

The conception of an opposition between a 'myth' and a 'reality' has underpinned major studies in historical geosophy and has done so very significantly, because it emphasises the importance of establishing the perceptions of past environments not only by those who visited them and by those who lived in them but also by ourselves, with historico-geographical hindsight. A classic in historical geosophy is R. L. Heathcote's (1965) study of land appraisal and settlement in the semi-arid plains of eastern Australia between the early nineteenth century and the mid-twentieth century. Heathcote's aim was 'to describe and if possible account for the sequence of attitudes to, knowledge and appraisal of, and finally the use of, the pastoral resources of semi-arid Australia'. He distinguished both between 'popular' and 'official' ideas about the plains, and between knowledge derived from the application of foreign and general standards to local conditions and knowledge derived from local and unique experience, a transformation from a 'colonial' to an 'autonomous' view of the Australian environment. From this reconstruction of differing assessments of the plains' environment, Heathcote revealed the conflict between official attempts to intensify the occupation of the land and the actual land use which tended to remain relatively extensive and exploitive. In particular, he showed how traditional geographical knowledges derived from more humid areas had to be modified in the semi-arid interior of Australia. A somewhat similar study by Powell (1970) of settlement and land appraisal in the Australian colony of Victoria during the nineteenth century highlighted the dichotomy between popular and official environmental assessments, between the practice of settlement and development as it happened and the theory of settlement and development as officials thought it should have happened. In a broader study, Powell (1977) demonstrated the role of images and of image-makers in the settlement geography of the New World.

Geographical knowledges could indeed be transformed, but they could also be remarkably fixed even when they were false. The idea of a Great American Desert east of the Rockies provides a good illustration of this. Martyn Bowden (1969, 1971, 1976) has shown how the desert image of the western interior of the United States was cultivated during the period 1820–70 in advanced school textbooks which drew upon the report of Stephen Long's expedition to the area in 1819–20. But he also showed that the desert belief was far from being universally held in America: it disseminated first to the educated elite of New England and then to that of the North-East, but he doubted whether the primary-school educated of the South or the Interior shared that image. Bowden argued that not even among the well-educated in New England, among whom the desert belief was strongest, did the view persist for longer than forty years that a vast desert existed east of the Rockies. More significantly, Bowden showed that the dominant images of the nineteenth-century Plains' environment as conveyed in the writings of historians and geographers were not constant. From 1880 to 1905 the Great American Desert concept was accepted by 'romantic historians' as an accurate appraisal of the arid plains as a true desert, settled by glorified pioneers; from 1905 to 1931 the Great American Desert was portrayed as an erroneous popular concept which had been applied to sub-humid prairie-plains, and the frontier was seen to be important more as a location and less as an environment; and then from 1931, as drought and depression made their impact, the Plains were interpreted as a semi-arid, difficult environment. Bowden argued that these changing images of the Plains reflected the region's variable climate, governmental and popular concern for a problem region, and the views and preconceptions of prominent historians, notably Turner and Webb. Bowden's study of the Great American Desert clearly demonstrated, in a variety of ways, the role of imagination and even of myth making in history and geography. Widening his horizon to the general American scene, he has shown how bodies of belief about space, environment, landscape and people could become so internalised by a nation or social group that it was practically impervious to scholarship that showed it to be largely erroneous (Bowden 1992). He termed this process 'the invention of traditions' (Fig. 3.2).

Historical geosophies of the kind so far considered rely upon mainly documentary sources, ranging from private correspondence, diaries and notebooks to

Invented American traditions of space, environment, landscape and people

West				East	
Time					
Warrior	Savage			Ignoble	Pre-American People
PRISTINE WILDERNESS Far tougher to conquer than it really was					Pre-American Environment
Sterile Wasatch Desert	Great American Desert	Infertile Virgin Prairies	Forest Primeval	Howling Desart Wildernesse	
FRONTIER					Place & Process of American Encounter
Scarred American Hostile to Nature					Results of Encounter
Saint	Superhuman Over-Achieving American Cowboy Pioneer			Saint	
GARDEN of American Yeoman					American Landscape Result
	Garden of Puritan Yeoman in Two-Storey Arks			Fabled Colonial Agricultural Village on the Green	New England Landscape Result
19th Century	18th Century			17th Century	

Figure 3.2 'Invented American traditions of space, environment, landscape and people'
Source: reprinted from *Journal of Historical Geography*, 18, M. Bowden, 'The invention of American traditions', 3–26. Copyright (1992), with permission from Elsevier

official surveys, reports and policy documents, using such materials to reconstruct past imaginings of environments. But there have also been a few endeavours in historical geosophy which have been exceptionally imaginative in themselves. Some studies have invented, imaginary authors and produced accounts of environments using only information that would have been available to such authors. The classic work in this genre is Ralph Brown's (1943) *Mirror for Americans: Likeness of the Eastern Seaboard, 1810*. Brown, creating a fictional writer of the early nineteenth century, one Thomas P. Keystone, wrote the book that he imagined Keystone might have written in 1810, using only the sources, knowledge, understanding and skills that would have been available to Keystone at that time.

The style of presentation, the language and the illustrations were also those of the period. This is an ingenious, if extreme, example of the reconstruction of a past environment, of an application of the principle underpinning historical geosophy. Brown's study was recognised by Darby as 'a *tour de force* and an intellectual exercise that throws light upon some of the problems involved in the creation of the "historic present"', but Darby expressed two reservations about it. First:

the idiosyncrasy of the treatment has a limiting effect in the sense that the reconstruction does not avail itself of modern knowledge of the relief and soils and climate of the eastern seaboard. The imaginary Keystone was obviously a man who not only had something to say but who could say it well, yet a study by Ralph Brown, writing as Ralph Brown, would have given us an even clearer view of the geography of the area in 1810.

It would have indeed, but that quite explicitly was not Brown's intention: his was an exercise in historical geosophy specifically rather than in historical geography more generally. Secondly, Darby argued that 'the method of *Mirror for Americans* is not one that can be followed generally with the likelihood of any great success. As one looks back in time, the language, the outlook, and the method of exposition, become more and more different from our own, until one reaches a point when a "reconstruction" in Brown's manner could have little but antiquarian value' (Darby 1962a: 129–30). On that point Darby would seem to have been correct, for there have been very few similar endeavours. One was Eric Ross' (1970) *Beyond the River and the Bay. Some Observations on the State of the Canadian Northwest in 1811 with a View to Providing the Intending Settler with an Intimate Knowledge of That Country*. Ross invented an imaginary writer of the book, one Ian Alexander Bell Robertson, for whom he provided detailed biographical information.

Such accounts are certainly rare, perhaps because they highlight what is potentially the fundamental problem in historical geosophy – its closeness to idealist history and thus to the limitations of that approach to historical understanding. Studies which address exclusively the geographical ideas and knowledges of individuals and of groups in the past, however fascinating and challenging they might be, prohibit those who undertake them from evaluating those ideas and knowledges with the benefit of historical hindsight. To focus exclusively on the thinking of the historical actors is to require the historical practitioner (whether historian or geographer) to deny his or her own thinking, to suspend his or her own ideas and knowledge. Such an approach fails to recognise a fundamental distinction between the actors in and the observers of a historical drama: historical practitioners are in the audience, not on the stage.

Fortunately, as I have shown, many studies in historical geosophy rise successfully above this problem by seeking to demonstrate the extent to which past geographical knowledges may be seen as 'myths', the extent to which they failed to correspond with what a modern scholar puts forward as the 'reality'. But of course that 'reality' might well in due course be shown to have been just another 'myth'. For historical environmental geographies of all kinds – as also historical ecologies and environmental histories – are socially constructed and competing narratives (Harris 1978a; Cronon 1992). Geographical discourses are likewise socially constructed and differing ways of seeing the world. The environmental and landscape discourses have so much in common that they are often confused and even conflated, but they are distinguishable perspectives. What, then, is the distinctive perspective of the landscape discourse?

4

Landscape geographies and histories

The landscape discourse in geography

'Describing the Earth' is the literal and the most basic definition of 'Geography' as an activity, but that apparently simple task has provoked many long-standing debates, not only about the art and science of geographical description but also about the nature of the object to be described. One such debate for more than a century has focused on the concept of 'landscape' and there persists to this day some ambiguity and confusion about it. I will, therefore, set out my own understanding and use of the term 'landscape', not least because I consider it to be significantly different from 'environment' and 'region' with which it has been – and still is – often confused. I will explore first the use of the concept of landscape in modern Western geography and then consider the idea of landscape more generally, both in earlier times and in other cultures. This will serve as a context for examining the connections of the landscape discourse in geography with the study of landscapes in history and other disciplines before considering in greater depth the specific concerns and contributions of historical geography to landscape studies.

The history of the word which gave rise to the concept of 'landscape' in different European languages has yet to be written (Besse 2000: 40), but it is clear that the term *Landschaft* became part of modern geographical currency in Germany towards the end of the nineteenth century. It did not do so unambiguously, however, and this has had unfortunate consequences for the translation of the term into 'landscape' in the English-speaking (and especially in the American) literature. *Landschaft* was employed to describe either the appearance of part of the earth's visible surface or a restricted area or region of the earth's surface. Hartshorne, in his monumental study of *The Nature of Geography* (1939: 149–58), carefully dissected the confused use of *Landschaft* in the German literature, including the different uses of the term by Siegfried Passarge and Otto Schlüter (with the former initially referring exclusively to physical landforms and the latter including cultural features in his conception of *Landschaft*). This multiple and confused meaning of *Landschaft* was unfortunately introduced into the American geographical literature by

Carl Sauer in his none the less very significant essay on the morphology of landscape, for he defined 'landscape' as 'the English equivalent of the term German geographers are using largely, and strictly has the same meaning: a land shape, in which the shaping is by no means thought of as simply physical. It may be defined, therefore, as an area made up of distinct associations of forms, both physical and cultural'. Sauer initially considered 'landscape', 'area' and 'region' as 'equivalent terms' (Sauer 1925; citation from Leighly 1963: 321) and this conflation had led to some confusion.

The fundamental importance of Sauer's own work ultimately surmounted that obfuscation. He argued influentially that the kind of morphological methods used to analyse physical landforms could also be employed in the study of cultural features. Moreover, he introduced into the English-speaking geographical world the distinction between a 'natural landscape' (*Naturlandschaft*) and a 'cultural landscape' (*Kulturlandschaft*), the former being the landscape of an area largely or wholly untouched by human hands and the latter being that landscape as transformed by human activities and attitudes. This was to become a central focus of the landscape tradition in geography.

Because of his own background, Sauer drew mainly upon the work of German geographers but French geographers were debating similar issues in the late nineteenth and early twentieth centuries. For example, Paul Vidal de la Blache and Jean Brunhes, one of Vidal's disciples and colleagues, saw landscape (*paysage*) as an expression of human activity, as a human imprint upon the land. Although the French distinguished conceptually between locality (*pays*) and landscape (*paysage*), the distinction between landscape and area or region was often blurred in practice. Thus Vidal de la Blache famously and evocatively referred to the way in which, through time, a country (*contrée*) became 'a medal struck in the image of a people' (*une médaille frappée à l'effigie d'un peuple*). Jean-Marc Besse claims that Vidal was using the term *contrée* to mean either a landscape or a place, and perhaps even both. Vidal was fond of this marvellous metaphor and it had its antecedents, for example in Elisée Reclus' claim in 1870 that 'man shapes in his own image the country in which he lives' (*L'homme pétrit à son image la contrée qu'il habite*) (Besse 2000: 106).

The continuing ambiguity of the term 'landscape' was emphasised a century later by a distinguished American historical geographer, D. W. Meinig, in his preface to an edited collection of essays on the 'interpretation of ordinary landscapes'. Recognising that the term 'landscape' was attractive, important and ambiguous, Meinig decided to clarify it by differentiating 'landscape' from some closely related concepts. For Meinig, landscape is related to, but not identical with, 'nature'; every landscape is a scene, but landscape is not identical with 'scenery'; landscape is related to, but not identical with, 'environment'; landscapes are related to, yet not identical with, 'places'; landscape is a portion of the earth's surface, related to, but not identical with, 'region', 'area' or 'geography'. More positively, for Meinig landscape is 'the unity we see, the impressions of our senses rather than the logic of the sciences'; it is ubiquitous, something to be observed but not necessarily admired; it is defined by our vision and interpreted by our minds; it is a continuous surface rather than a point, focus, locality or defined area (Meinig 1979a: 1–7).

Sauer's concern with landscape stemmed in part from his acceptance of Hettner's argument that to identify the core of geography in terms of some abstract *relationship* (such as the relationship between people and their environment) was fundamentally misconceived, because a field of knowledge needs substantive *content*. Without a category of objects to call its own, geography had only, in Hettner's phrase, a 'parasitic existence'. Hence Sauer's attention to landscapes as objects and to his promotion of the transformation of natural landscapes into cultural landscapes as 'a satisfactory working programme' for geography. But Sauer went further. Because such landscape transformations were what materially differentiated cultural areas from each other, he saw landscapes as the basis of regional geography, of a geography which conformed to Richthofen's view of geography as 'chorology', the science of regions (Livingstone 1992: 297). Landscape had been elided into region.

Such an elision could be provided with some historical justification not only from the German geographical literature with which Sauer was very familiar. This is seen clearly in Besse's (2000) essays exploring the relationship between landscape and geography. In sixteenth-century Europe, the term used to describe geographical representations was the same as that used for landscape painting. Cosmographers of the period drew upon Ptolemy's assertion that geography was a graphical, pictorial representation of the known world. German, Dutch and Italian painters and cartographers of the sixteenth century came to employ the terms *Landschaft, landschap* and *paese* in an aesthetic sense but these words initially had a territorial, thus geographical, significance. A 'landscape' was first defined by its site, by it own position, whose characteristics were distinct from those of its neighbours: it had natural and cultural boundaries and could thus be mapped as well as painted. Moreover, in these maps and paintings the land itself became an object for a spectator, for a cartographer and for a painter as subject. This was in clear contrast to medieval maps and paintings, which recounted historical narratives, inserting both the earth and people as part of the physical and theological story of the creation of the world. Furthermore, this view of landscape encouraged its contemplation – often from an elevated viewing point and from a distance – as a theatre, as a spectacle, as a representation. This is seen *par excellence* in the *Grands Paysages* of Bruegel, a series of prints produced in 1555–6. Such maps, prints and paintings brought not only a new way of looking at places but also a new way of experiencing them and a new way of judging them. 'Landscape' thus became the visible world, to be described not only graphically in maps, prints and paintings but also verbally in books published as topographies and geographies. 'Landscape' became in the sixteenth century a new way of looking at the world (Besse 2000: 35–68; Cosgrove 1985), with paintings and maps produced as representations of landscapes (Casey 2002).

That was at least the case in Western Europe but it was not necessarily so else-where. Augustin Berque (1995) provides a comparative and evolutionary analysis of the idea of landscape from classical China through to the 'virtual realities' of today's Western world. Recognising that concepts of landscape are not universal but both historically and geographically specific, Berque's central concern is to explore why some cultures have been more conscious than others of landscapes. While all societies have existed within, and interacted with, environments, only some have explicitly conceived and recognised landscapes. The latter, Berque ar-gues, can be identified through their representations of landscapes, which can be four-fold: linguistic, literary, pictorial or physical (notably in the form of gardens, which constitute an aesthetic appreciation of nature). While one or more of the last three can be found in many societies, Berque claims that all four are to be found together only in those which can properly be said to have embraced the idea of landscape.

Some societies, it follows, were not landscape-aware. Berque, citing the famous assertion by Cézanne that the peasants of Provence had never 'seen' the Montagne Sainte-Victoire, argues that peasant societies in general have worked with envi-ronments but never wondered about landscapes, and that rural landscapes were first conceived or 'invented' by city-dwellers. The civilisations of ancient Greece and of India did not have in their languages a word for 'landscape' and the Abo-riginal civilisation of Australia (which lasted for some 50,000 years or more) produced pictorial representations of mythical, dream worlds rather than of the actual, real places they inhabited. An aesthetic conception of landscape in the full sense emerged for the first time in the world in China about two thousand years ago and then diffused to other parts of eastern Asia. That region's languages have a rich terminology relating to landscape as well as powerful representations of landscapes in literature, in pictures and in gardens. Berque shows that the idea of landscape in China and eastern Asia at that time was sophisticated: it was not just a visual concept but embraced an appreciation of landscapes by all of the senses, and it included landscapes of imagination and of memory, incorporating them into a sense of place.

These brief excursions into the idea of landscape have revealed that the ambi-guity of the concept results both from the extent to which it overlaps with related concepts and from the changes in meaning which it has itself undergone. But they have also suggested that it is indeed a powerful and important concept. It has, as will shortly become clear, contributed very productively to work in modern and postmodern geography. The landscape discourse within geography both needs and deserves to be considered apart from others. It is concerned with the visible appearance of surfaces of the earth; it recognises landscapes as being cultural constructions and also cultural representations realised in imagination, in literary forms, in art or on the ground itself.

Perhaps the complex nature of landscape geography is best illuminated by the metaphor of *physionomie* which has long been employed by many French geographers. For them, describing and understanding landscape has been a fundamental geographical objective and they have examined landscapes as cultural constructions. Landscapes reflected the actions and ideas of the societies that produced them. Landscapes were seen as the earth's facial expressions, as its countenance, its physiognomy. And of course surface expressions have to be accurately described and interpreted but never taken at 'face' value – just like faces, landscapes have to be read carefully.

An American geographer, Peirce F. Lewis (1979), has set out seven axioms for 'reading' the American landscape that are so widely applicable that I will list them here in full:

1 The man-made (*sic*) landscape provides strong evidence of the kind of people we are, and were, and are in the process of becoming.

2 Nearly all items in human landscapes reflect culture in some way. There are almost no exceptions. Furthermore, most items in the human landscape are no more and no less important than other items – in terms of their role as clues to culture.

3 Common landscapes – however important they may be – are by their nature hard to study by conventional academic means.

4 In trying to unravel the meaning of contemporary landscapes and what they have to 'say' about us as Americans, history matters.

5 Elements of a cultural landscape make little sense if studied outside their geographical (i.e. locational) context.

6 Most cultural landscapes are intimately related to physical environment. Thus, the reading of cultural landscapes presupposes some basic knowledge of physical landscape.

7 Most objects in the landscape – although they convey all kinds of 'messages' – do not convey those messages in any obvious way.

Landscape geography may be seen initially as an art and science of visual perception, of studying the role of people in changing the face of the earth, but it extends beyond that to encompass decoding the significance of cultural expressions in landscapes. To the question 'How and why was this landscape made?' is added the question 'What does this landscape mean?' I will use these two questions, which have been so fundamental to the landscape discourse in geography, to structure my argument in this chapter. But before addressing those questions I want to acknowledge – and learn from – the approaches to landscape that have been adopted by scholars in history and other disciplines, because geography can clearly claim no monopoly of this holistic concept.

Interdisciplinary connections and landscape representations

Historians have been incorporating landscapes into their studies for a very long time, but landscape history as an identifiable sub-discipline is a relatively recent and not always appreciated addition to history's extended family. From an early acceptance of landscape as a repository of historical evidence and as a backcloth to historical dramas, many historians have now come to adopt landscape as an object of historical enquiry in its own right.

For historians in the late nineteenth century accustomed to working with literary sources in record offices and libraries, it must have been something of a shock to hear 'the ground itself' being asserted by J. R. Green as 'the fullest and most certain of documents' for his study of *The Making of England*. Green urged historians to 'read' the information 'afforded' by landscapes (Green 1881: vii). Not long afterwards the legal historian and Domesday scholar F. W. Maitland described the Ordnance Survey map – an outstanding representation of the British landscape – as 'that marvellous palimpsest, which . . . we are beginning to decipher' (Maitland 1897: 15). It became a tradition within history to see features in the 'present-day' landscape as survivals, as relics from past periods, which could be interrogated as witnesses to history. For example, A. L. Rowse in his *Tudor Cornwall* claimed that 'there is no research more fascinating than to attempt to decipher an earlier, vanished age beneath the forms of the present and successive layers that time has imposed. So it is that beneath the towns and villages, the roads and fields of today, we may construct under our eyes out of the evidences that remain, a picture of a former age' (Rowse 1941: 13). It was another, more scholarly, Tudor historian, R. H. Tawney, who proclaimed that what economic historians needed was stouter boots (cited in Darby 1962a: 147). But probably the most powerful advocate of fieldwork by historians has been Maurice Beresford. Both in his book *History on the Ground* (1957) and in his lecture *Time and Place* (1961), delivered on his being inaugurated as Professor of Economic History at the University of Leeds, Beresford set out his own approach to history as 'an emphasis on visual things', on those 'visible remains in [today's world] by which past economic activity can be detected' (Beresford 1961: 3). He put that credo into practice in many ways: in his studies of medieval England from the air, of deserted medieval villages, of the new towns of medieval England, Wales and Gascony, and of the streets of early-modern and modern Leeds. In many of these ventures, Beresford worked closely not only with geographers but also with archaeologists and aerial photographers (Beresford 1951, 1967, 1988; Beresford and St Joseph 1958; Beresford and Jones 1967; Beresford and Hurst 1971). In his 'detection' of past activities in present-day landscapes, Beresford viewed landscapes primarily as evidence. But his work on what he termed 'the face' of Leeds indicated additionally a wider concern, with the appearance of places in the past as a legitimate object of historical enquiry.

Historians have also long argued the need to know about the landscapes of their own preferred periods of study. In the mid-nineteenth century, Thomas Macaulay, in his history of England from the accession of James II, argued that in studying our ancestors we must never forget that 'the country of which we read was a very different country from that in which we live'. Thus his famous third chapter described the landscape of England in 1685 as a backcloth to its subsequent political history (Macaulay 1848; Firth 1932). In the twentieth century, other historians prefaced their works with geographical sketches. Thus G. D. H. Cole (1927) and G. M. Trevelyan (1930) both provided descriptions of England in the early eighteenth century, based principally on Daniel Defoe's portrayal of it in his *Tour thro' the Whole Island of Great Britain*. Then the economic historian who was to be a powerful influence on the development of British historical geography, J. H. Clapham, included in his study of modern Britain two descriptions of what he called 'the face of the country', one in 1820 and the other in 1887 (Clapham 1926: 3–52; 1932: 489–529). Other historians followed suit, prefacing their studies with descriptions of 'the face' of the country or area being studied (for example, Rowse 1950 and Mackie 1952). Such studies viewed landscape principally as the backcloth to history, as the scenery in front of which historical dramas were enacted. But others have seen landscapes as having their own histories, as having been produced by, rather than for, those dramas.

Landscape history has not been welcomed into the family of history as warmly as some other new perspectives and perhaps not even as cordially as its close relation, environmental history, which itself has had to struggle to be recognised by its elders. In 1962, a collection of essays on the major approaches to history did not include landscape history (Finberg 1962a). Almost thirty years later, a similar collection treating new perspectives on historical writing again did not embrace landscape history (Burke 1991a). Landscape history remains, it would seem, the Cinderella of history. By contrast, historical geographers are full of admiration for the achievements of two of its most distinguished proponents, an Englishman, W. G. Hoskins, and an American, J. B. Jackson – and by 'achievements' I mean both their own scholarly studies and the very considerable influence they have had upon the emergence and development of landscape history as a distinctive field of enquiry.

'The English landscape itself, to those who know how to read it aright, is the richest historical record we possess. There are discoveries to be made in it for which no written documents exist, or have ever existed' (Hoskins 1955: 14). With this challenge, Hoskins both introduced what was to become a classic – even *the* classic – study of the making of the English landscape and intentionally initiated what he called 'a new kind of history' which he hoped would 'appeal to all those who like to travel intelligently . . . and to unearth the reason behind what they are looking at'. Hoskins emerged from the chrysalis of local history as a magnificent landscape historian. For him, landscape was both a record, a rich body of evidence about the past, and a problem to be investigated, a complex set of questions to be addressed in the present. 'What I have done', claimed Hoskins in the introduction to his book on *The Making of the English Landscape*, 'is to take the landscape of England as it appears today, and to explain as far as I am able how it came to assume its present form, how the details came to be inserted.' His concern was with what he termed 'the visible landscape' and he considered historical processes only in so far as they had impacted upon landscape forms. He approached his subject 'chronologically as far as possible, to show how the pattern developed as a whole, even if in patches'. He rejected the alternative notion of systematically considering in turn major landscape features, such as field patterns and country houses, or roads and towns, because for Hoskins it was 'important to show the logic behind the changing face of the English landscape, and only a chronological treatment can bring this out'. Thus he opened his book with a chapter on 'The landscape before the English settlement' and concluded it with one on 'The landscape today' (Hoskins 1955: 13–15).

That Hoskins contributed very significantly to the construction of a new landscape history is beyond doubt. He did so both directly through his own writings and indirectly through those who followed his example. Hoskins' own output was prodigious and wide-ranging: his many books and articles married local history and landscape history (for examples, see Hoskins 1957, 1959, 1963, 1966, 1967). They also fostered links between landscape historians and historical geographers, a point which I will pursue further shortly. Hoskins also had an enormous indirect impact, stimulating others to venture – both literally and metaphorically – into the field of landscape history. He established and edited a series of landscape histories of individual English counties, with twenty-one volumes being published by Hodder and Stoughton between 1954 and 1985 (the later volumes in this series being co-edited with a geographer, Roy Millward). Historical geographers wrote some of the volumes, like those on Cornwall, Lancashire, Shropshire and Oxfordshire, while that on Cambridgeshire was written by Christopher Taylor, a historical geographer-turned-archaeologist (Balchin 1954; Millward 1955; Rowley 1972; Emery 1974; Taylor 1973). These books went some way to fulfilling Hoskins' mission to make landscape history accessible to as wide an audience as possible, an aim which he furthered in a series of radio and television broadcasts. Others have taken up the challenge, as evidenced in Edward Hyams' account of 'the changing face of Britain', in S. R. J. Woodell's edited collection of essays on the past, present and future of the English landscape, and in P. Coones and J. Patten's Penguin guide to the landscape of England and Wales (Hyams 1977; Woodell 1985; Coones and Patten 1986). In addition, there are two other series, one being a 'history of the British landscape' (Cantor 1987; Reed 1990; Howard 1991; Whyte and Whyte 1991; Palmer 1994) and another focusing on the histories of specific landscape forms, such as fields, villages and towns (Taylor 1975; Rowley 1978; Aston and Bond 1976). The seed sown by Hoskins has resulted in a rich harvest, the portents for which were clearly set out in a brief but informative survey of landscape history, published by the Historical Association (Knowles 1983). Hoskins' hyperbolic description of landscape as 'the richest historical record' is used as the title for a collection of essays celebrating the twenty-first anniversary of the founding in 1979 of the Society for Landscape Studies (Hooke 2001a). Among the essays in this volume are two (rather disappointing, largely uncritical and dominantly Anglo-centric) appraisals of the development and achievements of landscape history (Hooke 2001b; Taylor 2001).

While acknowledging fully Hoskins' achievements, some assessments of his contribution have come to be tempered with cautious criticism (Meinig 1979d;

Phythian-Adams 1992; Matless 1993; Muir 1999: 27–32). Hoskins' love of the past was accompanied by disquiet, even disgust, at the changes being wrought upon the English landscape in the twentieth century. More than that, Hoskins loved the countryside, or more precisely he loved the towns and countryside of pre-industrial England, but he was uncomfortable with landscapes of the Industrial Revolution of the eighteenth and nineteenth centuries. He was blatantly more at home in the Midlands and in his beloved Devon than in the North of England. While Hoskins' influence is clearly identifiable in a recently published survey of the history of the English rural landscape (Thirsk 2000), it is not so readily detectable in its companion volume on the English urban landscape (Waller 2000). None the less, publication of this latter volume confirms the enhanced standing of landscape history among English historians, even if it does not openly declare the debt which it owes to Hoskins. A new journal, *Landscape History*, launched in 1979 by the Society for Landscape Studies, could perhaps be seen as marking the coming of age of landscape history in Britain, but by then its American forerunner, *Landscape*, had been in existence for almost thirty years, having been established by J. B. Jackson in 1951. The launching in 2000 of another journal of landscape history, *Landscapes*, serves to confirm the considerable interest in Britain in this field.

Landscape history in America owes much to the enterprise and ideas of Jackson (Meinig 1979d). Born in France of American parents, Jackson went to school in America, Switzerland and France before graduating in history and literature from Harvard in 1932. He then spent some time working for a newspaper, some working on his uncle's ranch in New Mexico, some studying architecture at the Massachusetts Institute of Technology, and some visiting Europe. After serving as an intelligence officer during World War II, Jackson returned to New Mexico and leased a ranch south of Santa Fe. His wartime and other experiences acquainted Jackson with the immense diversity of Europe's geography and he acquired considerable geographical knowledge from maps, aerial photographs, guidebooks, talking with people and travelling widely. Furthermore, his curiosity led him to read about human geography in the writings of French geographers like Maurice Le Lannou, Pierre Deffontaines and Max Sorre. Jackson was, as Meinig puts it, 'no ordinary rancher'. In 1951 he decided to combine his interests in history, geography, architecture and literature by launching his own journal, *Landscape*. Initially established to focus on the South-West of the USA, within a year it broadened its scope and came to include articles on any part of the world. Jackson edited and published *Landscape* for seventeen years, by which time the journal was well established and internationally recognised. For the next ten years he turned to teaching and researching landscape history and then from 1978 concentrated exclusively on research.

Meinig has distilled the essential characteristics of Jackson's approach to landscape. For Jackson, landscapes are best viewed from the air, for air travel has provided a new perspective, a new way of looking at the geographical diversity of the world, but he was equally emphatic about the historical complexity of landscapes, of their ever-changing character. Jackson's idea of landscape is anchored in *human life*, not just something to look at but also to live in, and not alone but with other people. Landscape is a *unity* of people and environment, not a false dichotomy of people and nature. Landscape is to be understood as *a place for living and working*, to be judged in terms of those living and working there. The elementary unit of landscape is the *individual dwelling*, for Jackson the oldest and by far the most significant 'man-made' component of a landscape. Understanding a landscape in living terms requires giving primary attention to the *vernacular*, to the features of the workaday world. For Jackson, all landscapes are *symbolic*: landscapes reflect the societies responsible for creating and maintaining them and ultimately they are 'expressions of a persistent desire to make earth over in the image of some heaven'. Finally, landscapes are always undergoing change (Meinig 1979d: 228–9).

Jackson, through his editing and his writing, has very effectively promoted landscape studies in America. His own major works include *American Space: the Centennial Years, 1856–1876* (1972), *The Necessity for Ruins and Other Topics* (1980) and *Discovering the Vernacular Landscape* (1984). Studies in American landscape history owe much, but not of course everything, to Jackson's idea of landscape. Some excellent work has been produced by historians, as witnessed by, for example, John Stilgoe's *Common Landscapes of America, 1580 to 1845* (1982) and Allen Noble's *Wood, Brick and Stone: the North American Settlement Landscape* (1984). But Conzen was able to assert without contradiction that his edited collection of essays on the making of the North American landscape, written largely by historical geographers, was the first attempt to cover the history of the American cultural landscape in a single volume (Conzen 1990: 4–5). Conzen's book includes an essay by Jackson on the house in the vernacular landscape as well as essays by David R. Meyer, a sociologist, on 'the new industrial order' of the nineteenth and twentieth centuries and by Edward K. Muller, who trained as a historical geographer and now works as a historian, on 'the Americanisation of the city' during the twentieth century. The overlapping interest in landscape by scholars from different backgrounds is manifest.

Given that my concern in this book is the relation between geography and history, I have in this chapter concentrated so far on the approaches of historians to landscapes. I will now consider, more briefly, historical perspectives upon landscapes identifiable in some other disciplines. Understanding the visible appearance of places and their representation in words (both in prose and poetry), in pictures (for example, in maps, paintings and photographs), in numbers and even in sounds has been among the objectives of a wide variety of scholars and artists. As a holistic concept, 'landscape' invites and even demands interdisciplinary approaches. For most of us, this involves learning from, and sometimes co-operating with, colleagues in cognate disciplines while retaining our own disciplinary identity, as a matter not of principle but of pragmatics. But for a few it means becoming an interdisciplinarian, a polymath. For example, George Seddon (1997), in his book *Landprints*, offers stimulating reflections on place and landscape from the rich perspective of an Australian scholar whose academic career has encompassed English literature, geology, environmental studies, and the history and philosophy of science.

To understanding and explaining landscapes has been added the task of exploring the meanings of places and of the experiences that they provide for those who live in them or visit them. There are dozens of journals published in the English-speaking world that include the word 'landscape' in their title. Some concern themselves with the landscapes of defined places, such as Ireland (*The Irish Landscape Journal*) or China (*The Journal of Chinese Landscape Architecture*), but most address a particular aspect of landscape systematically. This latter category is itself overwhelmingly dominated by journals devoted to landscape architecture. It is, therefore, to this field that I will turn first, before considering more briefly the concern for landscape in archaeology, anthropology, literature and art.

Landscape architecture focuses on the planning and design of landscapes both today and in the past – and, of course, it has its own history. Modern concern in the Western world with planned and designed landscapes is essentially a product of the development of interest during the European Renaissance in the great architectural achievements of antiquity and of the emergence of 'the landscape idea' and of landscape as 'a way of seeing', as a perspective upon the world (Cosgrove 1984, 1985). Then during the eighteenth and nineteenth centuries archaeologists and historians increasingly revealed the wide range of design concepts that had been applied to built environments in the past. The growth of both nationalism and romanticism stimulated the serious study of landscape architectural history and landscape design. The American journal *Landscape Architecture* was founded in 1910, since when it has contributed, along with similar but later-established journals, to the construction of landscape architectural history as a distinctive and distinguished discipline (Newton 1971; Tobey 1973; Jellicoe and Jellicoe 1975; Mann 1993).

Philip Pregill and Nancy Volkman (1999) demonstrate the broad and interdisciplinary approach of landscape architectural history in their monumental survey of landscapes in history, an extraordinarily wide-ranging review of landscape design and planning in both the Eastern and Western traditions. They argue that it is necessary not only to consider traditional as well as modern ideas about land planning and design but also to situate those ideas within their social and environmental contexts. Their book, treating European, Asian and North American landscapes from the prehistoric period to the present day, addresses six issues: 'the relationship of people to the natural environment; the effect of technology; human values concerning urban, rural, and natural landscapes; symbolism of the landscape; the social role of design; and the role of aesthetics in land planning and design'. Pregill and Volkman argue that people have established a relationship to the landscape as master, servant, steward or interpreter of the natural world, with those roles in considerable measure being dependent upon the level of technology possessed by a particular society at a given time and upon the attitudes and values of that society. They emphasise that the relationship of people to landscape is usually much deeper than merely a desire to satisfy material needs, for every culture has had some symbolic attachment to landscape. Furthermore, they emphasise that not only societies collectively but also powerful individuals have left their impressions upon landscapes, both to demonstrate their status and to express their aesthetics. Part One of their book examines the European and Asian regions and traces the development of human activity in the landscape from early settlement to modern times. Much of this section deals with landscape design and planning before the emergence of a self-conscious landscape architectural practice during the European Renaissance. Part Two considers the North American landscape from pre-Columbian to modern times, examining especially the birth and growth, the ideas and impact, of landscape architecture as a profession and practice. Pregill and Volkman probably have most to say about urban design through time and across cultures: 'new towns' have been planned in many places and periods. But the breadth of their study is staggering, embracing such disparate 'built environments' as Roman military colonies and classical Chinese gardens, early Egyptian ceremonial sites and modern American cemeteries.

Similar landscape forms have, of course, attracted the attention of landscape archaeologists. Although a journal of *Landscape Archaeology and Ecology* was not established until 1993, the close link between landscape and archaeology was firmly established almost a century ago by O. G. S. Crawford, the British Ordnance Survey's first archaeological officer, whose experiences during the Great War as a navigator in the Royal Flying Corps had convinced him of the significance of aerial photography as a source of archaeological intelligence. Crawford's pioneering work led to the systematic application of aerial photography to archaeological enquiry, notably promoted by J. K. St Joseph (Crawford 1953; St Joseph 1977, 1979; Maxwell 1983). A summary of the fruits of this work is to be seen in an admirable set of studies of historic landscapes of Britain from the air (Glasscock 1992). Landscape archaeology focuses not only on individual forms within landscapes (such as deserted villages, moated farmsteads and field boundaries) but also – and perhaps most especially – on assemblages of features, on the combination of natural, semi-natural and cultural forms which collectively constitute the landscape of a locality, region or area (Fowler 1972, 1977; Hall 1982; Roberts 1987). Confirmation of the overlapping interests of landscape archaeologists and historical geographers is provided in the exemplary work of Christopher Taylor. Trained initially as a geographer but not enthused by the intellectual hegemony at that time being exercised by the locational analysts in geography, Taylor moved into archaeology, taking with him ideas about landscape and fieldwork which made him welcome and allowed him to feel 'at home' among the archaeological fraternity. Taylor's work on, for example, villages, farmsteads and gardens shows that the terms 'landscape history' and 'landscape archaeology' have become virtually interchangeable and that they have a close affinity with work on landscape by historical geographers (Taylor 1974, 1983a, 1983b, 2001). Landscape features are viewed both as problems to be investigated and as witnesses to be interrogated for their knowledge of the past.

Interest in landscape encompasses far more disciplines than those of history, architecture and archaeology. All of the social sciences and humanities express their own concerns with landscape. As an anthropologist, Barbara Bender (1992a) brought together a set of edited essays on landscape politics and perspectives in order to demonstrate the complexity and power of landscapes. 'In contemporary Western societies', Bender emphasised,

they involve only the surface of the land; in other parts of the world, or in pre-modern Europe, what lies above the surface, or below, may be more important. In the contemporary Western world we 'perceive' landscapes, we are the point from which the 'seeing' occurs. It is thus an ego-centred landscape, a landscape of views and vistas. In other times and other places the visual may not be the most significant aspect, and the conception of the land may not be ego-centred. (Bender 1992b: 1)

For Bender, landscape is not so much artefact as in process of construction and reconstruction:

The landscape is never inert; people engage with it, re-work it, appropriate it and contest it. It is part of the way in which identities are created and disputed, whether as individual, group, or nation-state. Operating therefore at the juncture of history and politics, social relations and cultural perceptions, landscape has to be . . . 'a concept of high tension' (Inglis 1977). It also has to be an area of study that blows apart the conventional boundaries between the disciplines. (Bender 1992b: 3)

Bender's edited collection includes essays by anthropologists, geographers, historians and archaeologists. In brief, the essays embrace such themes as the politics of vision and of place, landscapes as memory and landscapes of memory, gendered perspectives upon landscape, and the roots of Western, modern sensibilities and conceptualisations of landscape. Bender conceded that her book offered a seemingly eclectic coverage: prehistoric, historic, contemporary; overdeveloped and underdeveloped world; town and country. Her three-fold intention was to force a recognition of the multiplicity of the experience of landscape through time and place; to relativise 'our' own experiences and to recognise both their particularity and their being part of a process and therefore continually open to change; and, finally, to permit an exploration of the ways in which people, differentially engaged and differentially empowered, appropriate and contest their landscapes (Bender 1992b: 17). In short, her emphasis is not on landscapes *per se* but on their significance for people. Erich Hirsch (1995) provides another valuable overview of the anthropology of landscape and of anthropological approaches to place and space. He sees landscape unproblematically as a cultural process and indicates that anthropologists seek to uncover the perspectives on a landscape held by its 'insiders', by those who relate directly to the land. Hirsch takes issue with those – like geographer Denis Cosgrove (1984: 32 and 269–70) – whom he sees as arguing that landscape implies the denial of process and whose focus is on the perspectives on landscape of 'outsiders', of those who relate to landscape as a form of exchange value. Hirsch's representation of Cosgrove's concept of landscape is not wholly judicious and he seems to be unaware of work by geographers in historical geosophy (addressed in chapter 3) and on the meanings of landscapes to those who made and experienced them (which I will consider later in this chapter). None the less, Hirsch demonstrates the necessity for, and the difficulty in achieving, genuinely interdisciplinary understandings of landscapes.

Intriguingly, Bender, in her essay on 'landscape – meaning and action', considered at length the landscapes portrayed in V. S. Naipaul's autobiographical novel *The Enigma of Arrival* (1987), in which he wrote about his adult encounters with an English landscape and his childhood memories of a Trinidadian one in order to tease out his own life story. Naipaul, as a novelist, wrote about what Bender, as an anthropologist, terms 'the politics of landscape' (Bender 1992b: 3–9). The politics and the aesthetics of landscape have certainly been a concern not only of professional academics but also of novelists and poets, of painters and musicians. How have the interests of geographers in landscape led them to these artistic creations?

As far as literature is concerned, Marc Brosseau points out that geographers are exploring its relevance to different points of view: he recognises 'regionalists in search of more vivid description of place; humanists seeking evocative transcriptions of spatial experience; radicals concerned with social justice; others trying to establish parallels between the history of geographical and literary ideas; or more discursively-oriented researchers addressing the problems of representation' (Brosseau 1994: 333). There has been a long tradition in historical geography of using novels as a source for regional geography, as mines of information about the landscape and character of a place (Gilbert 1960, 1972). An early model for this approach was provided by Darby (1948) in his account of the regional geography of Thomas Hardy's Wessex and has been continued in reconstructions of the 'real' locales and landscapes of, for example, the Black Country of Brett Young and the Paris of Simenon as the stages upon which the novelists' stories have been enacted (Jay 1975; White 1984). Undoubtedly the most extensive examination of this kind has been that conducted by M. Chevalier (1993) into the geographical 'reliability' of some 250 nineteenth- and twentieth-century French novels. Brosseau is critical of approaches which endeavour to assess the documentary qualities of the novel, to compare the 'fiction' with the 'actuality'. 'It is legitimate', he argues, 'to wonder why one would resort to novels when more "reliable" sources are available, or when geographers can do their own fieldwork. The interest of such an exercise lies within the scope of literary history: what were the degrees of realism and to what extent were novelists accurate with regards to description of geographical realities?' (Brosseau 1994: 337).

Of course, many novels have an apparently 'real' locale, which can be identified and recovered, and many non-geographers have looked for the geography, for landscape and place, within literature. For example, D. Daiches and J. Flower (1979) produced a 'narrative atlas' of the literary landscapes of the British Isles, Margaret Drabble (1979) explored landscapes in writings on Britain, examining the links between landscape and literature in order to understand better the human condition, while Stephanie Foote (2001) explores regional culture and identities in nineteenth-century American literature. But novelists also endow landscapes with meaning and significance, allocating to them active, not merely passive, roles. For them, landscapes and locales play metaphorical roles in their stories. Gillian Tindall (1991) showed how familiar landscapes – such as the moors of Yorkshire and the streets of Paris – acquire the force of powerful metaphors when ascribed meaning by authors ranging from Charles Dickens and Emile Zola to Alain Fournier and Evelyn Waugh, who refashioned familiar landscapes as 'countries of the mind'. Rural scenes, for example, can be used to embody regret for the loss of a golden past; cities can be made to stand, paradoxically, not only for decay and alienation but also for hope and revival.

In this vein, historical geographers too turn to novels to provide insights into landscape, place and region that are *not* available in other sources. Their concern here is with the experience of landscape, with the meaning of place, with the subjective qualities of a region as revealed in novels (Pocock 1981a, 1988; Noble and Dhussa 1990). Of course, novels are by no means straightforward accounts of a sense of place and they have to be interpreted within their own historical and geographical contexts. But, as Raymond Williams made clear in his classic study *The Country and the City* (1973), novels and other literary forms can be made to reveal historically embedded structures of feeling about a place in a specific period. Moreover, the representation of landscapes in novels and travel writings plays a central role in the moulding of geographical imaginations about them. For example, many of our ideas about cities and city life are derived from novels, from what has been termed 'writing the city': Peter Preston and Paul Simpson-Housley's (1994) edited essays on the city as seen through the eyes of novelists, poets and their fictional characters capture the human experience, both individual and collective, contained in portrayals of cities as different as, for example, Jerusalem and Johannesburg, Manchester and Montreal, and Odessa and Osaka. Equally good examples are provided by studies of the representation of the modern city in the Nottingham novels of Alan Sillitoe (Daniels and Rycroft 1993) and of the depiction of safe and dangerous urban spaces in detective fiction (Schmid 1995). That the frontier between geography and literature is a very fruitful meeting ground for the two disciplines has been amply demonstrated in two collections of essays, one edited by Douglas Pocock (1981b) and the other by William Mallory and Paul Simpson-Housley (1987). The former included, for example, discussions of the 'real' and 'symbolic' landscapes and geographies in the novels of D. H. Lawrence, Doris Lessing, George Eliot, John Steinbeck, William Dean Howells and Mary Webb, and in the poetry of George Crabbe and in the criticism of John Ruskin. The latter collection embraced landscapes in the novels of Arnold

Bennett, José Maria Arguedas, Willa Cather, Harriette Arnow, Ivan Turgenev, Mikhail Lermontov and Thomas Hardy, and in twelfth-century Arthurian romance and the poetry of John Donne.

'Poets make the best topographers,' according to Hoskins (1955: 17). The depiction of southern African landscapes in the 1820s in the poetry of Thomas Pringle, a Scottish journalist, provides support for this claim (Bunn 1994), as do also John Clare's better-known poetic portrayals of, and responses to, the remaking of parts of the English open landscape undergoing enclosure in the early nineteenth century (Barrell 1972). Landscape poetry is a distinctive, difficult and delightful genre that encompasses *inter alia* Shakespeare and Wordsworth, John Betjeman and Ted Hughes (K. Baker 2000). But landscapes are most explicitly represented visually, in paintings and photographs. Geographers have themselves for centuries been representing landscapes graphically in maps and field sketches, but they have more recently turned seriously to the representations of landscapes by others in paintings and photographs. Landscape paintings have been used as documentary evidence for the geographical study of historical landscapes, although – like all documentary sources – they have to be conceptualised and interpreted with circumspection. As Denis Cosgrove and John Thornes emphasised: 'The "landscape of fact" is always mediated through a set of rules, limitations and individual intentions on the part of the painter, of which the geographer employing his work as a documentary source is not always fully aware' (Cosgrove and Thornes 1981: 21). But paintings have also come to be used to illuminate historical attitudes towards landscapes, towards the relations of culture and nature, and towards the meanings of place. Here geographers and art historians find common ground, even though they view landscape aesthetics from different perspectives and for different purposes (Howard 1991). Denis Cosgrove and Stephen Daniels have probably done more than any other historical geographers to draw our attention to 'the idea of landscape', to landscape aesthetics and to the visual representation of landscape, to the link between landscape geography and art history, and to landscape as a painterly and elitist way of seeing the world (Cosgrove 1979, 1984, 1985; Daniels 1993).

Until a generation ago, the canons of art history in relation to landscape painting were those established by Kenneth Clark in his *Landscape into Art* (1949) and more especially by Ernst Gombrich in his essay on 'the Renaissance theory of art and the rise of landscape' (1953). They argued that the idea of landscape was a western European phenomenon, which emerged during the sixteenth and seventeenth centuries and reached a peak in the nineteenth century, and that it was initially and fundamentally constituted as a genre of painting associated with a new way of seeing. This long-established orthodoxy has come to be challenged and not only by Marxist art historians who insist upon placing landscape paintings within their specific historical (often class- or gender-based) contexts (Barrell 1980; Bermingham 1986). Thus W. J. T. Mitchell (1994a) points out that it is mistaken to believe that the appreciation of natural beauty in landscape began only with the invention of landscape painting. The testimony of poets from Hesiod and Homer to Milton and Dante shows that Europeans did not, as Ruskin thought, acquire an entirely 'new sense of seeing' sometime after the Middle Ages. Furthermore, the historical claim that landscape is a post-medieval invention overlooks the earlier Hellenistic and Roman schools of landscape painting and the overwhelming richness, complexity and antiquity of Chinese landscape painting. Mitchell prefers to interpret the European discourse of landscape as a crucial means for enlisting 'Nature' in the legitimating of modernity and even of imperialism. For him, 'landscape is already artifice in the moment of its beholding, long before it becomes the subject of pictorial representation' (Mitchell 1994a: 14).

Landscape paintings, like cultural landscapes, are social codes. For example, Ann Bermingham (1986) analysed the underlying ideology of English rustic landscape painting between 1740 and 1860; Ann Jensen Adams (1994) argues that Dutch landscape painting in the seventeenth century provided a site for the working out, not of rural issues, but of urban ones, a set of images of different communities with which (or from which) individuals might imaginatively affiliate (or distance) themselves; and Elizabeth Helsinger (1994) claims that J. M. W. Turner's drawings in his *Picturesque Views in England and Wales* depict a contested land, for they are full of transgressive, working-class figures whose assertive presence puts the title of Turner's work into question. The approaches exhibited to landscape painting by these art historians are virtually replicated in work by historical geographers. For example, Prince (1988) wrote about art and agrarian change in England during the nineteenth century; Trevor Pringle (1988) examined the contribution of Edwin Landseer's paintings to the construction of a mythical image of the Scottish Highlands; and Brian Osborne (1988) analysed the iconography of nationhood in Canadian art. The painterly tradition in landscape geography, James Duncan (1995) argues, 'is good at showing us that the landscape is a way of representing the world and that representations have very real political consequences'.

Probably the best demonstration of this point is found in Daniels' work on the paintings of Turner (1775–1851). 'Turner's pictures of places', Daniels (1993) argued, 'are not merely local in their meaning. They situate places in regional, national and international contexts. Nor are such pictures merely factual . . . Above all Turner was intent to endow landscape painting with extensive power, to concentrate issues of history and historical destiny in an apparently momentary view of a particular place, to intersect the epic with the everyday.' Thus Turner's watercolour *Leeds* (1816) 'is not itself a simple transcription of what he saw' but 'part of a long tradition of prospects celebrating the city of Leeds and its commercial power' (Fig. 4.1). What Turner depicts is a 'wholly industrialized landscape. He shows various processes, some mechanized, some not, from the spinning of yarn in the valley to the tentering of cloth on the hill. It is a scene of energy – signified by steam, sun, wind and human labour – co-ordinated to industrial expansion.' Turner's oil painting *Rain, Steam and Speed – the Great Western Railway* (1844) was stylistically very different from *Leeds*: it is much less detailed and more abstract. Daniels identified none the less correspondences of subject and symbolism in the two

Figure 4.1 *Leeds* by J. M. W. Turner, 1816
Source: Reproduced from the Paul Mellon Collection, with permission from the Yale Center
for British Art, New Haven, Connecticut

pictures: they both feature the main icons of industrial advance in their time, textile mills in 1816 and railways in 1844, and both pictures 'break the traditional frame of visibility to co-ordinate features as part of a larger network of space and time'. Most of the features in *Rain, Steam and Speed* are 'reduced to pictograms and dissolve into flux'. Turner here provides a hint of the difficulty which early rail travellers encountered when trying to adhere to old painterly ways of seeing when looking out from trains: railway journeying promoted and demanded new ways of looking at landscapes as they sped evanescently past the train's window (Schivelbusch 1986). Moreover, Daniels argued that in showing the Great Western Railway crossing the River Thames, Turner portrays these major routeways as integral parts of a system with regional, national and international dimensions. Here the Thames is itself an icon of state power and the Great Western offered a new prospect of state power (Daniels 1993: 116–38). Daniels is here emphasising the reciprocal relevance of landscape painting to geography and of geography to landscape painting. This latter point he makes even more forcefully in his demonstration, using John Constable as well as Turner as examples, of how the remapping of England affected landscape painting (Daniels 1994), while the interconnected relations of landscape painting, landscape gardening and landscape literature are laid bare in a study of a Georgian estate in Hertfordshire (Daniels and Watkins 1994).

Much of what I have said here about landscape paintings as representations of landscapes also applies to other visual images, such as advertisements, film, maps, portraits, prints and photographs: they are cultural messages which diverse scholars endeavour to decode; they are products of what Peter Burke (2001) calls the 'eyewitnessing 'of history. The example of photography will suffice here to illustrate the point. Raphael Samuel anatomises beautifully the cultural value of 'old photographs' to historians willing to use them as 'the eye of history' (1994: 313–77) By the late 1850s, improvements in photographic practice meant that the photographic prints could no longer be mistaken for pictures made in other media. Moreover, because of their technical, scientific characteristics and their portrayal of detail, they were often thought by contemporaries to be precise and accurate representations of the landscapes, people and objects which they depicted. But photographs, be they, for example, of the American West's landscape between 1860 and 1880, of British colonial landscapes, of landscapes of the Great War, or of the slums of east London in the 1930s, must be understood in terms of their production and the uses to which they were put in the past both by their producers and by their consumers (Snyder 1994; Rose 1997; Ryan 1997; Griffin 1999). Photographs have to be interpreted as documents offering historically, culturally and socially specific ways of seeing the world (Brennen and Hardt 1999; Schwartz 1996, 2000). Moreover, as Gillian Rose (2000) argues, geographical researchers have their own ways of seeing and interpreting past worlds: research is itself a practice with its own effects on the photographs.

I suspect that similar points could be made about the representation of landscape in 'sound images' or 'soundscapes'. This remains a relatively uncultivated field as far as historical geographers are concerned, although a start has been made to explore the geography of music. Studies are emerging of the geographies of different musical genres, in terms of their distribution and diffusion, in terms of identifying and understanding music regions and regional music and the spread of musical cultures (Carney 1987, 1990; Nash and Carney 1996; Leyshon and Matless 1998). Connections between geography and music are legion. Some music is an expression and celebration of a local or regional folk culture or of a wider nationalism; some has been composed for particular places or particular environments; and some – the most pertinent for my purpose here – represents landscapes (and seascapes). For example, onwards from the completion in 1725 of Vivaldi's four violin concertos *The Four Seasons*, pastoral landscapes have been portrayed in music: most notable are Beethoven's *Pastoral Symphony* and Vaughan Williams' *The Lark Ascending* (1920) and *A Pastoral Symphony* (1922) (Revill 1991, 2000a). So, too, have urban landscapes, as in Vaughan Williams' *A London Symphony* (1913) (Cox and Naslas 1984). While it is being increasingly recognised that some music can be read as historically and geographically specific representations of landscapes and of the cultures which produced them, serious analysis of music for this purpose has been taken up only gradually by historical geographers (Pocock 1989; Monkman 1997; Revill 2000b). There is considerable scope for more work both on the cultural significance of music in place histories and on the portrayal of past landscapes in music.

Although I have emphasised the visual paramountcy of landscapes, places can be experienced by all of the senses. Just as there are landscapes to be viewed, so too there are, for example, 'soundscapes' to be heard and 'smellscapes' to be scented. Few excursions have been made into either of these territories by geographers. Examples that can be cited are in fact exceptions, such as D. Pocock's (1987) sound portrait of Durham as an English cathedral city and R. Johnston et al.'s (1990) exploration of the historical geography of English church bells. These are territories which French geographers and historians are more ready to enter, it seems, than are their English-speaking counterparts. Thus R. Dulau and J-R. Pitte (1998) edit diverse essays on the geography of smells, both historically and in the present day in various parts of the world, while Corbin (1982, 1994) writes intriguingly on the history of odours and of sounds in nineteenth-century France.

Scholars from different disciplines – and indeed non-scholars from different backgrounds – look at landscapes in different ways: a single landscape can be viewed in multiple ways. *Reading Landscapes: Country–City–Capital* (Pugh 1990), a collection of essays based on the premise that landscapes and their representations are 'texts' which are 'readable' like any other cultural form, included contributions by specialists in literary criticism, cultural studies, art history, geography and photographic history. For some geographers, this is perplexing and provokes an unstructured response (Coones 1985). For others, it is challenging and stimulating. Meinig (1979b) argues that there are at least 'ten versions of the same scene'. Different observers of the 'same' prospect might see the landscape before them, depending upon their 'perspectives', as representing *nature* (emphasising the insignificance of people), *habitat* (as people's adjustment to nature), *artefact* (reflecting people's impact on nature), *system* (a scientific view of interacting processes), *problem* (for solving through social action), *wealth* (in terms of property), *ideology* (revealing cultural values and social philosophy), *history* (as a record of the concrete and the chronological), *place* (through the identity that locations have) and *aesthetic* (according to some artistic quality possessed). More succinctly, another American historical geographer, Michael Conzen, has codified landscape studies into four principal approaches, reflecting respectively concerns with *environmental awareness*, with *symbolic representation*, with *landscape design* and with *landscape history*. In practice, as Conzen recognised, these four approaches collapse into one because:

to view the landscape historically is to acknowledge its cumulative character; to acknowledge that nature, symbolism and design are not static elements of the human record but change with historical experience; and to acknowledge too that the geographically distinct quality of places is a product of the selective addition and survival over time of each new set of forms peculiar to that region or locality. (Conzen 1990: 3–4)

Studies of landscape necessitate a historical approach. Landscapes are, as Marwyn Samuels (1979) put it, 'expressions of authorship' and to comprehend what he termed 'the biography of landscape' requires a historical knowledge of the role of individuals, of their ideas and actions, in the making of landscapes.

Work on the historical geographies of landscape has recently been reviewed by a number of its practitioners and it is worth pausing here briefly to note their approaches. First, Williams (1989c) considered the role of landscape in the writings of Darby, defending his work in the mistaken belief that specific criticisms of Darby's limited approach to landscape had been generalised into a rejection of the study of landscape. Williams' survey focused narrowly on 'change in the landscape' and on three particular 'processes of landscape change' (the draining of marshes, clearing the forests and reclaiming the heathlands). Secondly, Robin Butlin, after comparing landscape studies by historical geographers in turn in Britain, Ireland, Europe, the USA and Canada, reviewed work more systematically but selectively on the ideologies and symbolisms of landscape, on the nature of landscape myths and on landscape as heritage (Butlin 1993: 131–46). Thirdly, Richard Muir's (1999) survey explores different approaches to landscape. His book embraces 'the structure and scenery approach', 'landscapes of the mind', 'landscape, politics and power', 'the evaluation of landscape', 'symbolic landscape', 'the aesthetic approach to landscape' and 'landscape and place'. Although a professional geographer, Muir describes himself in his book as a 'landscape historian'. Fourthly, Suzanne Seymour's (2000) selective survey of 'historical geographies of landscape' is heavily biased towards studies of landscape symbolism and representation: it pays scant and dismissive attention to other approaches.

These diverse approaches to landscape may be reduced to attempts to answer two basic questions: 'How and why was this landscape made?' and 'What did and does this landscape mean?' How successfully can those questions be addressed, given that answers must necessarily be sought in historical contexts? I will now consider those questions at greater length than I was able to do in an earlier and brief essay on the relations between ideology and landscape (Baker 1992a).

The making of landscapes

Sauer and Darby established frameworks for the landscape tradition in historical geography, at least in the English-speaking world. Their ideas and examples have inspired considerable research in this genre and continue to do so, even though their views have encountered criticisms. They merit special attention, because of the fundamental and enduring contributions which they made to this tradition.

Drawing heavily upon his knowledge of European (and especially German and French) geographical ideas, Sauer undertook a broad survey of the field of geography in his extended essay on the morphology of landscape (Sauer 1925). As an examination of the nature of geography, Sauer's essay can be challenged, for example for its conflation of 'landscape' with 'area' and even with 'region', and for its insistence upon the organic quality of landscapes (Duncan 1980). But many of its tenets remain valid and have strongly influenced landscape studies in historical geography (Schein 1997). Thus Sauer argued that 'we cannot form an idea of landscape except in terms of its time relations as well as of its space relations. It is in a continuous process of development or of dissolution and replacement.' Sauer elaborated the distinction between natural and cultural landscapes, the former being untouched by human activity and the latter being modifications of the former by human agency. Cultures were seen as making use of the natural forms, in many cases altering them, in some cases destroying them. For Sauer

the cultural landscape is fashioned from a natural landscape by a culture group. Culture is the agent, the natural area is the medium, and the cultural landscape is the result. Under the influence of a given culture, itself changing through time, the landscape undergoes development, passing through phases, and probably reaching ultimately the end of its cycle of development. With the introduction of a different – that is, an alien – culture, a rejuvenation of the cultural landscape sets in, or a new landscape is superimposed on the remnants of an older one. The natural landscape is of course of fundamental importance, for it supplies the materials out of which the cultural landscape is formed. The shaping force, however, lies in the culture itself. (Sauer 1925; citation from Leighly 1963: 343)

From his perspective upon the nature of geography, Sauer was concerned with the morphology of the cultural landscape, with its forms and structures: he was explicitly *not* concerned with 'the energy, customs or beliefs of man but with man's record upon the landscape' (Sauer 1925; citation from Leighly 1963: 342). Thus for Sauer historical geography could be considered 'as the series of changes which the cultural landscapes have undergone and therefore involves the reconstruction of past cultural landscapes . . . From this difficult and little-touched field alone may be gained a full realization of the development of the present cultural landscape out of earlier cultures and the natural landscape' (Sauer 1925; citation from Leighly 1963: 344). Reconstruction of the landscape of an area at successive periods was thus for Sauer a component of its cultural history, leading up to its present-day geography. He wished 'to reckon historical geography as a part of culture history' (Sauer 1941a: 9).

Such thinking has underpinned those numerous studies which begin with the reconstruction of a natural landscape and then trace the impact of human activities upon it and the consequential construction (as well as destruction and renewed construction) of a series of cultural landscapes. Such thinking has especially permeated studies that focus upon the creation of primitive landscapes as a result of early encounters of peoples with natural landscapes, in effect upon cultural landscapes within which natural features continue to play an important role. But such thinking is also influential within studies that emphasise the dominant role of culture and the almost total destruction of nature in the development of almost totally 'unnatural' urban-industrial landscapes. Many of the world's landscapes treated in the series edited by J. M. Houston are considered first in terms of 'the land', 'the natural landscape' or 'the landscape without man' – treating the physiography, climate, vegetation and soils that constituted the physical landscape prior to human settlement and development. Their subsequent treatments of the making of land-scapes are more varied: most adopt a sequential approach and identify landscapes of particular periods with specific cultures, such as 'indigenous', 'colonial' and 'neo-colonial'; others take a more systematic approach, recognising landscapes as being associated distinctively with specific systems of production, such as land-scapes of 'non-commercial agriculture', of 'mining' and 'small towns'; some con-sider 'media landscapes', such as those created by tourism and by literature. This formulaic approach has been applied effectively to very different countries of the world, such as Brazil, Ireland, Nigeria and South Africa (Dickenson 1982; Orme 1970; Morgan 1983; Christopher 1982). This is the formula adopted in Conzen's edited collection of essays on the making of the American landscape: its first chapter, 'Nature's continent' by Trimble, provides a 'portrait' of America's natu-ral regions 'through the broad brush strokes of climate, landform, vegetation and soil', thus (changing the metaphor) setting 'the stage upon which the human drama has unfolded' (Conzen 1990: 9).

This was also the approach adopted in many of the classic French regional monographs, upon which Sauer drew to some extent for his own ideas, as he did also upon German ideas about primitive landscapes and their transformation into cultural landscapes. Thus Otto Schlüter (1872–1952) had distinguished between a natural landscape (*Naturlandschaft*) and a cultural landscape (*Kulturlandschaft*) but he, with others, soon realised that the distinction between the two is not as easy to recognise in practice as it is in theory: natural landscapes are not static and human impacts can be both accidental and deliberate. He therefore also developed the idea of the *Urlandschaft*, to refer to a wild or primitive landscape, one in which nature is dominant because of the low density of human settlement and the low level of technology being used by the settlers (Dickinson 1969: 126–36). Many of the classic French monographs began with an account of the region's physical geography and continued with a narrative of the historical development of the area and its landscape, from prehistoric times onwards. Their collective emphasis was upon 'the taming of the land' and the formation of rural, agricultural, and of urban, industrial, landscapes. Then, usually, a third concluding section considered the region and its landscape in the 'present day'. These geographical descriptions of the major regions of France were simultaneously historical narratives about them. Their authors acknowledged, as Maurice Le Lannou stated in his study of Brittany, that 'historical knowledge is always necessary in order to appreciate a region geographically' (Le Lannou 1952: 13).

The methodology and the phraseology employed by these French authors, as well as the content of their works, powerfully influenced Darby who was in turn, together with Sauer, to have a major impact upon the character of historical ge-ographies of landscapes in the English-speaking world. Initially immersed in a historical geography practised in Britain as the reconstruction of past geographies,

Darby turned increasingly to studies of the processes by which people have altered landscapes. This was Darby's 'methodological turn' from 'horizontal cross-sections' to 'vertical themes' as part of his self-conscious drive to establish a new kind of historical geography in Britain and beyond. In this reorientation from 'past geographies' to 'changing landscapes', Darby drew explicitly upon the ideas of French geographers (Clout 2002). He concluded that the processes of landscape change 'are almost entirely concerned with man's work – with the house he builds, the road he travels, the field he tills, the mine he exploits' (Darby 1962a: 141). He acknowledged that Jean Brunhes, who made that point, went on to say: 'It is in fact work and the direct consequences of work which form the true connection between geography and history' (Brunhes 1920: 544). This underpins the view of landscape as primarily a product of economic activity, as a visible, material expression of economic history.

In 1951 Darby published a seminal paper on the changing English landscape. Although by no means 'a radical departure', as that paper has been described by Williams (1989c: 95), for it was building on foundations laid much earlier, in 1925, by E. H. Carrier (Baker 1999b), Darby's paper was certainly seminal. It provided a model for the historical study of landscape change that could readily be applied to other countries and areas. Population migrations and growth, the colonisation and settlement of territory, were seen as the basic agents of landscape change. Darby then identified some key themes in the changing English landscape: clearing the woods, draining the marshes, reclaiming the heaths, changing 'arable' (agriculture), landscape gardens, and towns and seats of industry. Each of these vertical themes was traced through from early times to the then 'present day' (Darby 1951a; see also 1953a). Two of the themes – clearing the woods and draining the marshes – Darby himself pursued further (Darby 1940a, 1940b, 1951b, 1956), but all of them have also served as models for others, both explicitly and implicitly. Moreover, Darby recognised that his list of vertical themes was not definitive and could be extended, for example by including the setting-up of national parks and the draining of the claylands (Darby 1961, 1964). Williams has best exemplified the value of Darby's programme. Williams' work on the draining of the Somerset Levels and on the clearing of the American forests (Fig. 4.2) – and latterly more generally on the world's wetlands and forests – has realised in large measure some of the potential so clearly identified by Darby (Williams 1970, 1989a, 1989b). In addition, Williams (1974) employed this Darbian approach in his monograph on the making of the South Australian landscape: an introductory chapter on the sequence of (European) settlement from the early nineteenth century to the early twentieth century was followed by chapters on 'clearing the woodland', 'draining the swamps', 'irrigating the desert', 'changing the soil', 'building the townships' and 'the making of Adelaide'. Darby's approach to changing landscapes was thus fundamentally thematic, in contrast, for example, to that of Hoskins, which was principally chronological.

Accounts of changing landscapes can, of course, be organised very differently. Conzen (1990), in the preface to his edited essays on the making of the American landscape, acknowledged openly his book's debt to Hoskins and to Jackson, but the influences of Sauer and Darby are also very evident. The book begins with an account of the continent's physical geography. It then has essays on, respectively, the Indian, Spanish and French legacies in the American landscape. It includes essays on the clearing of the forests, settlement of the American grassland, challenging the desert and the new industrial order. It presents chapters on the house in the vernacular landscape, on the emergence of a national landscape, on the imprint of central authority, and on landscapes of power and wealth. This is probably the best example of what can be achieved by combining different approaches to the historical geography of a landscape. It provides a more coherent account than does that of Stephen Mills, whose essays on the American landscape are individually stimulating and perceptive but collectively not greater than the sum of their parts (Mills 1997).

How best to organise historical studies of landscapes has been a question addressed by geographers for decades and there is clearly not a single, optimal solution: there is no methodological Holy Grail in historical geography, however diligently and ingeniously it is sought. In considering explicitly the puzzle posed by Derwent Whittlesey (1945) of how to incorporate the factor of time into incontestably geographical studies, Darby's exploration of the problem of geographical description set out six possible solutions and recognised that there were variants and combinations of those six methods that also provided challenges to literary skill and ingenuity (Darby 1962b). Most of Darby's solutions were in effect literary devices (the use of introductory narrative, of parentheses, of footnotes and of the present tense), but others were more methodological (retrospective cross-sections and sequent occupance). Whittlesey had himself introduced the concept of 'sequent occupance' in 1929 and it influenced significantly a generation of American and British historical geographers. 'Human occupance of an area', stated Whittlesey, 'like other biotic phenomena, carries within itself the seed of its own transformation' and he drew an analogy between a succession of stages of human occupance and those of plant succession in botany. For Whittlesey, 'the view of geography as a succession of stages of human occupance establishes the genetics of each stage in terms of its predecessor'. While Whittlesey recognised that external interruptions meant that 'normal sequences are rare, perhaps only ideal', others fastened upon his notion of an ideal sequence because it seemed to provide a widely applicable model and even the promise of prediction. Whittlesey illustrated his concept with reference to northern New England, where he identified three stages of occupance: first, the Indian stage of hunting and gathering in the 'virgin mixed forest'; secondly, farming and forest clearance; and thirdly, the decline of farming and growth of secondary forest.

While Whittlesey's 1929 paper – like Darby's 1951 paper on the changing English landscape – was not itself a radical departure in geographical thinking, it

Figure 4.2 'Change in the American forest, 1600–1859'
Source: Williams (1989b: 126–7)

did bring a concept into much sharper focus than hitherto and it stimulated similar studies of other areas, such as that by Stanley Dodge (1931) of an Illinois prairie and that by Edward Ackerman (1941) of a Boston suburban community. Many American studies employed the concept of sequent occupance, doing so either explicitly or implicitly, through to the 1950s when it more or less fell out of use. The rise and decline of the concept as a chapter in the history of American geography has been charted by Marvin Mikesell (1976), who concluded that sequent

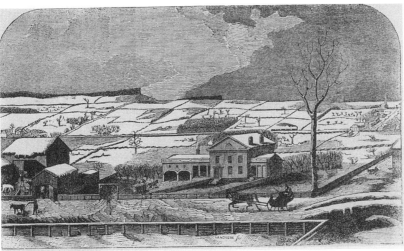

Figure 4.2 (*cont.*)

occupance became popular because it was an 'analogue model', built in emulation of the erosion cycle in geomorphology and the concepts of succession and climax in plant ecology. The concept, Mikesell argued, seemed also to promise a historical determinism as a replacement for a questionable environmental determinism. But it was Whittlesey's case study rather than his generalisations about landscape change that encouraged the proliferation of sequent occupance studies. Moreover, Mikesell argued, the large literature thus inspired 'proved to be additive rather than cumulative'. Given that the concept was not subjected to serious criticism while it was in widespread use, Mikesell could only speculate on the reasons for its decline. His suggestions included the influence of an ahistorical methodology in American geography in the decade after the publication of Hartshorne's *The Nature of Geography* in 1939 and the formidable practical difficulties in reconstructing a succession of geographies. 'In addition', Mikesell argued, 'few geographers interested in the past viewed with favour a conceptual framework that emphasised local development rather than diffusion and that required acceptance of the Davisian assumption that process is implicit in stage.' The case of the rise and fall of the concept of sequent occupance serves as a clear cautionary signal to those seeking a definitive solution to Whittlesey's puzzle.

Of the diverse solutions considered by Darby, a variant of sequent occupance came to be the one he himself preferred. He concluded that an ingenious solution to the problem of combining description with explanation had been found by Broek (1932) in his study of the Santa Clara Valley in California, in which four cross-sections were separated by three studies of the processes which led to successive landscapes. Cross-sections of 'the primitive landscape', of 'the landscape in Spanish-American times' and of 'the present [1932] landscape' were connected by intervening essays on 'the social-economic determinants' of, respectively, the Spanish-American period, the early American period and the (then) recent American period. Darby adopted this solution for his new historical geography of England, interleaving 'vertical' chapters addressing questions of change and process within a series of 'horizontal' chapters presented as cross-sections of the geography of England in 1086, 1334, 1600, 1800, 1850 and 1914 (Darby 1960, 1973). Broek's study had itself been inspired by an earlier work, that of a German geographer, A. Rühl (1929), who had employed cross-sections of data at significant dates linked by explanatory narratives in a study of the historical economic geography of eastern Australia (Heathcote and McCaskill 1972).

That multiple approaches to changing landscapes can be productive is exemplified by Pitte's (1983) history of the French landscape. For Pitte, the uncomplicated definitions of 'landscape' and the comprehensive approaches to changing landscapes adopted by English-speaking geographers and historians like Darby, Hoskins and Jackson have resulted in work of considerable originality. As a geographer, Pitte drew upon the classic studies of the history of the French landscape by Marc Bloch (1931), Gaston Roupnel (1932) and Roger Dion (1934b), as well as upon both the many regional geographical monographs which had the evolution of landscapes as one of their principal concerns and recent work by archaeologists, architectural historians, landscape architects and ethnologists. The first organising principle of Pitte's approach was chronological, from the Quaternary to the present day. The second was based on the fundamental distinction between rural and urban landscapes, which are accorded more or less equal treatments at different historical periods. His focus was less upon the destruction of natural landscapes and more upon the construction of cultural landscapes. Pitte emphasised the structures that constitute landscapes, the built-forms that comprise them. His study therefore considered rural and urban house and settlement forms in some detail but it also embraced, for example, prehistoric megaliths, Roman roads, hedgerows, medieval moated sites, vineyards, gardens and railways.

This emphasis on the morphology of landscape, upon the material components of landscape, is an integral part of the practice of historical geography both in Europe and in America. There is ample testimony to the former, for example, in the papers presented to a series of meetings of what was to become the Permanent European Conference for the Study of the Rural Landscape. The first meeting was held in Nancy (France) in 1957. Since then these conferences have contributed enormously to our understanding of the origins and transformations of field boundaries, field forms and field patterns (including notable studies of cultivation terraces, of hedgerows and of parcellation), of settlement plans, settlement structures and house structures (including important studies of planned villages, of deserted settlements and of distinctive rural house types), and of specific rural land uses (including valuable studies of village greens, of vineyards and of woodlands). In addition, the conferences have thrown considerable light upon some of the principal processes at work in changing the landscapes of Europe: in general, clearing the woodlands, draining the marshlands, reclaiming the heathlands, proto-industrialisation and urbanisation; and more specifically, colonisation and land allocation, the origins and transformation of field and settlement systems, enclosures and agrarian reforms (Baker 1988).

In America, Sauer's ideas promoted a rich vein of studies of the material content of the cultural landscape. One of his leading doctoral students, Fred Kniffen, published in 1936 a study of Louisiana house types, which marked the beginning of a career devoted to Louisiana's cultural landscape structures and to American cultural landscapes in general (for examples, see Kniffen 1951, 1965). As Conzen has stated:

Kniffen made a career of studying rural house types . . . Indian tribes and Indian mounds, agricultural fairs, covered bridges, outdoor ovens, Spanish moss, and iron rock captured his attention from time to time, but no topic proved so absorbing as the multitudinous forms that folk housing could take. Whatever the object of study, his method was straightforward: choose a cultural form, identify the key elements, plot the distribution of different types, locate the probable hearth area from which it expanded, and trace the paths of diffusion. His work on folk housing and the processes that distinguished its many forms emphasised the contribution of ordinary people as opposed to elites in the making and remaking of regional cultures and cultural landscapes. (Conzen 1993: 47–8)

Kniffen's (1965) seminal paper on folk housing as a key to diffusion set out a research project which involved tracing the construction of European house types by early settlers on the eastern seaboard of North America and monitoring their westward diffusion and structural modification.

Focusing upon the history of specific cultural landscape forms came to be the distinguishing – and distinguished – feature of this school of historical/cultural geography in America, splendidly exemplified in Terry Jordan's (1978, 1982) books on Texas log buildings and Texas graveyards, and in Ennals and Holdsworth's (1998) study of the making of the Canadian domestic dwelling during the past three centuries. Collectively such studies have contributed significantly to our knowledge of contrasting cultural landscapes, but less so, it could be argued, to our understanding of them because, as Holdsworth (1993) points out, many of them – including Allen Noble's (1984) immensely detailed study of the houses, barns and other farm structures in the North American settlement landscape – do not connect closely enough the cultural landscape forms being investigated to the transforming economic and social fabrics in which they were constructed.

Jordan's (1982) study of Texas graveyards was subtitled 'a cultural legacy'. Within the broad canvas of studies of the making of landscapes of specific regions or areas were embedded narrower studies of features in the present-day landscape that have survived as legacies, as relict features, as visible remains of the past. Within a European context, there have been studies of relict features such as deserted villages, strip lynchets, ridge-and-furrow and moated farmsteads. These individual landscape structures need to be investigated, to be described and explained, in terms both of their origins and historical significance and of the reasons for their survival into the present-day landscape. They are themselves proper objects of historical and geographical enquiry. Prince's (1962, 1964) studies of the numerous pits and ponds of England's East Anglia are excellent examples of work in this genre. But, as I have emphasised earlier, a landscape may also be read as a document, as a witness to the past geography of a place. A landscape has to be both read and allowed to speak. There are basic logical difficulties encountered here, involving the principles of equifinality and of indeterminacy: different cultural processes can give rise to similar landscape structures and any one process can give rise to different structures. For these reasons, landscape structures cannot be interpreted exclusively in terms of themselves: evidence gained in the field has to be supplemented by that in the archives. This might be an obvious point, but perhaps because it is so obvious it can be overlooked too easily. Landscape studies – whether of landscapes at certain periods in the past, of landscapes changing through time or of landscape features that have survived into the present as relicts from the past – self-evidently depend upon work in the field, but they also necessitate research in record offices and libraries (Holdsworth 1997). Della Hooke's (1998) excellent study of the landscape of Anglo-Saxon England combines both field and documentary evidence in an exemplary manner, as did – for a very different place and period – Richard Francaviglia's (1978) study of the creation of the Mormon landscape of the American West.

Citing these two very different landscape studies reminds me how difficult it is to make sustainable generalisations about such projects. They could serve to emphasise the differences among such studies, at least in terms of their aims if not in terms of their methods. But I am citing them here in order to emphasise how somewhat different aims can be achieved by remarkably similar means. That point is made very forcefully in the more than thirty volumes which have been published since 1990 in the series *Creating the American Landscape*, edited by George Thompson and published by The Johns Hopkins University Press. They include Richard Harris' (1996) examination of the sprawling of Toronto's unplanned suburbs during the first half of the twentieth century, John Jakle and Keith Sculle's (1994) study of the gas station in America, and James Vance, Jr's (1995) assessment of the origins, evolution and geographical impact of the North American railroad.

The making of cultural landscapes has often been seen in materialist terms, interpreting structures straightforwardly as the products of work, of the results of people labouring to meet their basic needs for food, water, clothing and shelter, and transforming landscapes in doing so. This approach to landscape, fundamentally utilitarian and economistic, was grounded in a weak conceptualisation of culture that separated off economy from consciousness, action from ideology. Neither Hoskins nor Darby, for example, allowed much room for the ideas and attitudes that underpinned the making of landscapes. Non-economic, aesthetic considerations and intentional ideas about landscape design entered into their studies mainly in relation to gardens and country houses in England. For long, the making of landscapes was seen for the most part as by-products of economic activity. Many landscapes are indeed the unintentional products of, *inter alia*, the struggle for survival and the need to 'make a living', but even that activity is engaged in by conscious human beings. As Denis Cosgrove – drawing in part upon Vidalian reserves – has aptly put it: 'Any mode of production is a "mode of life", a *genre de vie*, constituted by men [*sic*] and symbolic *ab initio*' (Cosgrove 1982: 221). Landscapes of material cannot avoid also being landscapes of meaning. Moreover, it has become increasingly recognised that many landscapes were deliberately designed at the outset, or have been redesigned subsequently, often in accord with some explicitly stated principles. Schein (1997) pinpoints this issue in emphasising that a particular landscape should be viewed as a tangible, visible articulation of numerous discourses, that a landscape is in effect 'materialised discourse'. What, then, do landscapes signify?

The meaning of landscapes

The discovery and recovery of meaning in landscape is a challenging and difficult task, both in theory and in practice. Perhaps for that reason it has been described using a great variety of metaphors, most of which emphasise the duality of the 'apparent' and the 'hidden' in landscapes.

Pitte's likening of a landscape to *the visible tip of an iceberg* is echoed by the use of Lawren Stewart Harris' oil painting *Icebergs, Davis Strait* by Cosgrove and Daniels on the dust-jacket of their influential, edited collection of essays on the iconography of landscape (Pitte 1983: 23; Cosgrove and Daniels 1988). For Pitte, a landscape was also 'an act of liberty: it is a poem written on a blank sheet of climax vegetation' (Pitte 1983: 24). For Audrey Kobayashi, landscape was like a *dance* because it, too, is 'organised, choreographed' and 'like the dance, it can produce profound emotional effects on the beholder'. She argued that 'both land-scape and the dancer require a practised eye to appreciate their finer qualities. Both are irreducible to their constituent elements, both transcend their moments of ex-pression, yet neither exceeds its physical features: buildings or props, movements, expressions in flux' (Kobayashi 1989: 164). Some take this argument further by insisting upon the importance not only of physical features but of people them-selves as components of, even as actors within, landscapes. Thus landscape has been viewed as *theatre*, or as *carnival*, or as *spectacle* (Jackson 1979; Ley and Olds 1988; Cosgrove and Daniels 1989; Cosgrove 1990; Daniels and Cosgrove 1993). Other interpreters of landscapes have employed *geological metaphors*, referring to the 'sedimentation' of meaning in landscapes, to 'layers' and 'strata' and to 'underlying structures' of meaning.

More frequently, however, landscape is being likened to a *written document* to be read, as James Duncan and Nancy Duncan argued, like a 'deeply-layered text' (Duncan and Duncan 1988). Lewis (1979), as I have already noted, provided some 'axioms for reading the [American] landscape', but his guidance notes have a much wider purchase and the textual analysis of landscape has moved much further than he ventured, penetrating into the realm of landscape study as literary criticism (Smith 1993). Like texts, landscapes are being opened to Derrida's strat-egy of deconstruction and, to borrow Brian Harley's (1989b) phrase, 'searched for alternative meanings'. To deconstruct a landscape or a text is, in Terry Eagleton's revealing metaphor, 'to reverse the imposing tapestry in order to expose in all its unglamorously dishevelled tangle the threads constituting the well-heeled image it presents to the world' (Eagleton 1986: 80). Deconstructing landscapes is easily stated as an aim but much less easily accomplished because, as Roland Barthes (1970) emphasised, the landscape is the richest of our system of signs. A common metaphor currently in use in landscape studies is that of a landscape as a *message, which has to be decoded* (Besse 2000: 95–114). But while a landscape is composed of a multiplicity of signs it may also contain a plurality of meanings: it is not a simple matter of 'one landscape/one message'. This characteristic led Daniels to refer to the 'duplicity' of landscape, a cultural term carrying meanings of both surface and depth which gives it analytical potential 'not despite its difficulty as a comprehensive or reliable concept, but because of it' (Daniels 1989: 197).

A landscape is a resultant of attitudes and actions; but to the extent that actions are themselves outcomes of attitudes, the latter deserve – but have by no means always been granted – a privileged status over the former in historico-geographical studies. To my mind, the process of landscape creation and reformation was captured tangentially in Marx's view of history as being specific to particular places. At every period in history there is 'a material outcome, a historically created relationship to nature and of individuals towards each other', a sum total of production forces 'that is transmitted to each generation by its predecessor' and 'on the one hand is modified by the new generation but on the other itself prescribes its own living conditions and imposes upon it a definite development, a special character of its own – so that, in other words, circumstances make men just as men make circumstances' (Fleischer 1973: 21–2). Historical specificity can thus be envisaged as underpinning the individuality of a landscape, which is a resultant of both environmental and social struggles in particular periods at particular places. Such an approach to landscape change allows for, indeed requires, consideration of both intended and unintended consequences of actions, of material and non-material motivations. It recognises the possibility of a false consciousness on the part of people who have enacted historical roles assigned to them by forces that they did not understand and which can only be comprehended by an observer, while it also allocates a role to ideology as a system of ideas that aspires both to explain the world and to change it. Historical studies of landscapes must be grounded in an analysis of material structures: they are properly concerned with tangible, visible expressions of different modes of production, with hedgerows and field systems, with canals and factory systems. But such material structures are created and creatively destroyed within an ideological context: such studies must therefore also acknowledge that landscapes are shaped by mental attitudes and that a proper understanding of landscapes must rest upon the historical recovery of ideologies (Baker 1992a).

Of the many characteristics of ideology, three are of especial relevance to the making and meaning of landscapes: the connections of an ideology to a quest for *order*, to an assertion of *authority* and to a project of *totalisation*. An ideology is seen by Edwards Shils as 'the product of man's need for imposing intellectual *order* on the world'. Ideologies offer ordered, simplified visions of the world; they substitute a single certainty for a multiplicity of ambiguities; they tender to individuals an ordered view both of the world and of their own place within its natural and social systems. The function of an ideology in this regard is to furnish assurance; it does so, paradoxically, either by highlighting perfect patterns in the present or by promising utopian forms in the future (Shils 1968). In both cases, the concept of order comes to be represented in landscapes, both unintentionally and intentionally. Ideologies also involve the assertion of *authority*, transcendental or earthly. Consequently, they are concerned with struggles for power between conflicting interest groups. Moreover, ideologies compete with each other, so that a given landscape might have several different systems of symbolic representation existing within it simultaneously and antagonistically. Ideologies create, both unthinkingly and deliberately, a landscape as a system of signification, expressive of authority. Historical landscapes were, for example, rich in signs of identity, linking an individual with a social group: coats of arms, flags, totems, uniforms, decorations, tattooings, hairstyles, trademarks. It was also replete with expressions of social codes – protocols, rituals, fashions and games – which were elements of communication: gestures and dances, customs and ceremonies, parades and processions, eating and drinking, all provided opportunity for a social message to be communicated, for authority to be asserted, for prestige and power to be proclaimed. This argument is without closure because 'everything is a sign: presents, our houses, our furniture, our domestic animals' (Guiraud 1975: 90). Moreover, an ideology often employs individual, sacred symbols to signify its own *holistic* character, its 'claim to offer an overall representation of a society, its past, present and future, integrated into a complete *Weltanschauung*' (Duby 1985: 152). It follows that the reorganisation of landscape signifies to some degree a realignment of social authority.

Considerable movement towards a redefinition of landscape and towards a theory of cultural landscape change has been made by Cosgrove, in a series of studies on symbolic landscapes initiated some years ago in his paper on 'place, landscape and the dialectics of cultural geography' (Cosgrove 1978). But before considering his extended argument, I think it appropriate to take cognisance of two other earlier and significant contributions to our rethinking about approaches to landscapes. In 1971 Paul Wheatley published his weighty enquiry into the origins and character of the ancient Chinese city under the title *The Pivot of the Four Quarters*. Wheatley's purpose was a specific and deceptively esoteric one: to elucidate the manner in which there emerged on one part of the North China Plain during the second millennium BC hierarchically structured, functionally specialised institutions organised on a political and territorial basis, and to describe the way in which, during subsequent centuries, they were diffused through much of the rest of north and central China. To this end, he marshalled a vast amount of evidence: archaeological, epigraphic and literary, together with inferences from the morphology, symbolism and function of later cities and with information derived from folklore and mythology. Wheatley's exploration took him far beyond the narrow confines of his specific problem and specific sources, for the second half of his book viewed the early Chinese city in comparative perspective – other areas of the world and the varied fields of social science were explored for any light which they might, by reflection, throw upon the ancient Chinese city. Examination of the earliest urban forms in six regions of primary urban generation (Mesopotamia, Egypt, the Indus Valley, Mesoamerica, the central Andes, south-western Nigeria) and in four regions of secondary urban generation (Crete, Etruria, Japan, south-east Asia) prefaced a systematic analysis of the nature and genesis of early cities. A comparative search for similarities resulted in Wheatley's proposing a model of the ancient city as a symbolic, ceremonial centre:

Whenever . . . we trace back the characteristic urban form to its beginnings we arrive not at a settlement that is dominated by commercial relations, a primordial market, or at one that is focussed on a citadel, an archetypal fortress, but rather at a ceremonial complex . . . Naturally this does not imply that the ceremonial centres did not exercise secular functions as well, but rather these were subsumed into an all-pervading religious context . . . Operationally they were instruments for the creation of political, social, economic and sacred space, at the same time as they were symbols of cosmic, social and moral order. Under the religious authority of organised priesthoods and divine monarchs, they elaborated the redistributive aspects of the economy to a position of institutionalised regional dominance, functioned as nodes in a web of administered (gift or treaty) trade, served as foci of craft specialisation, and promoted the development of the exact and predictive sciences. Above all, they embodied the aspirations of brittle, pyramidal societies in which, typically, a sacerdotal elite, controlling a corps of officials and perhaps a praetorian guard, ruled over a broad understratum of peasantry. (Wheatley 1971: 225–6)

Wheatley's argument was that, of the components of the ecological complex customarily adduced as being involved in the generation of urban forms, environment, population and technology should be regarded as independent variables, but social organisation as a dependent variable. Of the generalised activities that have either singly or together been held to induce social differentiation, the only one that seemed to fit the case of the ceremonial centre, with its emergent class and concomitant occupational and spatial differentiation, was religion. Once the ceremonial centre had been established as a symbol of that ideology, other factors then operated to produce culturally, economically and temporally distinct configurations, so that each nuclear realm came to exhibit its own particular urban (or proto-urban) style. But the ancient city – represented hieroglyphically as a cross within a circle – was a landscape symbolising its social formation.

Not only ancient but also modern civilisations have their symbolic landscapes. In a short but significant essay on some idealisations of American communities, Meinig argued that 'every mature nation has its symbolic landscapes. They are part of the iconography of nationhood, part of the shared set of ideas and memories and feelings which bind a people together' (Meinig 1979c: 164). He claimed that certain landscape images – especially of the New England village, of Middle America's Main Street, and of Californian suburbia – became distinctive and powerful national symbols as idealised communities for American family life. Meinig's was a pioneering essay, 'the product of reflection rather than focused research', which sought to ask not the traditional question 'What were the landscapes which have served as the bases for these symbols "really like"?' but also a set of 'newer' questions, for example, about how 'actual' landscapes become 'symbolic' landscapes and about how the power of landscape symbolism can be assessed. Meinig made the point forcefully that landscapes are 'at once a mould and a mirror of the society that creates them'.

Following these pioneering forays into landscape symbolism by Wheatley and Meinig, Cosgrove produced an important series of essays, which explored in depth the notion that landscape is an ideologically charged and very complex cultural product (Cosgrove 1982, 1984, 1985, 1989, 1993a). In his early essay on the problems of interpreting the symbolism of past landscapes, Cosgrove identified the basic problem as follows: 'Understanding the meaning of past human landscapes demands a theory of collective behaviour or culture appropriate to their context.'

He set out to provide such a theory, given that historical and cultural geography were, in his view, weak on this front. For him, 'such theory must be dialectically constituted: between individual subjectivity and culture, and between social and spatial structure'. He was critical of Wheatley's reading of the Chinese urban landscape because it was not fully reciprocal, for the cultural, symbolic landscape remained a secondary expression and the social order theoretically pre-existed its constitution as a symbolic order. 'Too easily', argued Cosgrove,

the claimed dialectic of social order and symbolic order becomes subsumed in practice under a more powerful linear logic wherein the symbolic is the outcome of an existing social structure . . . Once the symbolic becomes superstructural to an economic or productive base the symbolic character of the system itself is lost, and the dialectical unity of cultural and practical reason, nature and consciousness, the 'real' and the symbolic is eliminated.

For Cosgrove,

social order and symbolic order are dialectically unified, and they cannot be read off from a notion of practical reason which underlies theories of economic base or universal structures. Dialectically related to material forces and constraints and to each other, they produce a 'mode of life' structuring and structured by symbolic production whose prime location is not necessarily in material production. All human landscapes may thus be regarded as symbolic. In [a] class society, culturally constituted and reproduced, symbolic production is appropriated by the dominant class, either through its control of the means of material production in capitalist society, or of sacred production in [a] redistributive society.

Thus Cosgrove identified as 'a crucial question for historical geographers' the change from one mode of life to another as it is expressed in and underpinned by landscape change (Cosgrove 1982: 220–3).

Cosgrove has both elaborated these ideas in general terms and exemplified them in specific circumstances, especially those of the ideal city of Renaissance Europe. The form and structure of the Renaissance ideal city Cosgrove generalised as follows. A circular or polygonal, closed urban space of fixed dimensions was centralised upon an open *piazza* – a civic and sacred precinct – itself of ordered proportions. From this square radiated roads lined with monumental buildings whose own proportions both in plan and elevation conformed to the mathematical regularity of the city as a whole. Minor open spaces, monuments, gates and so on were symmetrically arranged around the city to give an overall plan of perfect regularity, symmetry and proportion.

Cosgrove considered three ways in which such structures might be interpreted. First, he recognised that the form of the Renaissance city had obvious similarities to that of other urban plans in other periods and places and that it might be related to common psychological structures that derive ultimately from human physiology and biology. But, for Cosgrove, while that might account in part for the cross-cultural regularity of the form it did not explain its specific historical occurrence, nor why it should achieve such explicit realisation at an important juncture of northern Italian history when centric redistribution was far weaker than it had been at the high point of European feudalism. Secondly, Cosgrove considered the suggestion that studies of Renaissance cosmology and humanist philosophy might have a strong bearing on the ideal city as an architectural and geographical manifestation of a new conception of man and cosmos particularly promoted in early fourteenth-century Florence and rapidly diffused throughout northern and central Italy. Cosgrove thought that such an interpretation was superficially attractive because it located the ideal city in a historically specific cultural movement, but rejected it because it depended upon an assumption that ideas and beliefs develop autonomously from their social and material context, and failed to account for the emergence of such ideas in the particular historical and geographical moment. Thirdly, Cosgrove examined the materialist interpretation of the ideal city, which located it as a superstructural expression of the particular material circumstances obtaining in Italy during the transition from feudalism to capitalism, so that the ideal city communicated in landscape terms the self-image of a feudal aristocracy rather than a merchant patriciate. The central *piazza*, for example, was dominated by church, signorial palace and military building and was for discourse and display. Markets were relegated to the periphery, and symmetry and monumentality stated wealth, power and lineage rather than serving the needs of production and exchange.

While this interpretation grounded the symbolic landscape in prevailing material conditions, for Cosgrove it failed to locate the production of symbolic order outside the economic realm of practical reason, it failed to account for its structuring role, and it failed to derive the form of the ideal city from the nature of the material forces and constraints seen as giving rise to it. For Cosgrove, 'symbolic production must be regarded as more than the almost unmediated reflection of economic and class forces'. Cosgrove's own interpretation of the ideal city was that its symbolism was culturally determined. He emphasised that, as a symbolic system, Renaissance humanism and its articulation in the form of ideal city plans contains a major contradiction. Humanism was secular and individualistic, yet the ideal city as a landscape is manifestly aristocratic and rank-ordered. 'It is an iconographic programme evoking a classical past and in its formal, monumental order requiring a ritualised form of behaviour which recalled an imagined heroic past rather than an egalitarian and individual future.' Renaissance humanism was originally developed, and its expressions produced, by the middle class as part of their struggle against the landowning aristocracy: material conditions were implicated but did not structure the terms of the debate, although they affected its outcome. The struggle was won in northern Italy by the landowning class who appropriated the humanist symbolic system: in its hands the ideal city became one aspect of their system of symbolic power, evoking a classical past whose virtues were imperial and aristocratic rather than republican and secular. As a symbolic landscape, argued Cosgrove, the ideal city sustained the cultural hegemony of the landowning nobility under the guise of a universal ideal (Cosgrove 1982: 223–30).

Although focused on Renaissance Italy, Cosgrove's studies expanded into other periods and places, applying his general idea of landscape as an ideologically charged cultural product to specific circumstances in England and America from the seventeenth century to the present day (Cosgrove 1984, 1990, 1993a, 1993b). In addition, his general idea has been elaborated in a very influential essay, written jointly with Daniels, on iconography and landscape (Cosgrove and Daniels 1988) and in a wide-ranging review of culture and symbolism in landscapes where he provided, just as an organising device, a typology of cultural landscapes which differentiates landscapes of dominant cultures from alternative landscapes of residual, emergent and excluded cultures (Cosgrove 1989).

The recovery of meaning in landscapes and the theorisation of culture have become important components of 'the new cultural geography' (Cosgrove and Jackson 1987; Duncan and Duncan 1988; Barnes and Duncan 1992; Duncan and Ley 1993; Duncan 1995; Crang 1998; Mitchell 2000) and of historical geographies of landscape (Seymour 2000). Indeed, Suzanne Seymour's contribution to a collection of review essays on modern historical geographies, allocating only one paragraph to 'traditional' studies of the making of landscapes, focuses largely on the symbolic qualities of landscape. After an excursion into landscape as 'a way of seeing', Seymour chooses to consider the representation of 'landscapes of property', 'landscapes of labour' and 'landscapes of improvement' in England during the eighteenth and early nineteenth centuries, as well as British colonial landscapes. In so doing, Seymour emphasises that a landscape should not be considered as an end product, for a landscape does not simply mirror or distort underlying social relations; it 'needs to be understood as enmeshed within the processes which shape how the world is organised, experienced and understood'.

Discourses of landscape design and improvement in England during the eighteenth and nineteenth centuries combined aesthetic, social, economic and patriotic imperatives: improvement required restructuring the landscape and, by extension, restructuring the lives of those who lived in it, worked in it and looked upon it (Daniels and Seymour 1990). Similar processes can be seen at work in the British and other European empires of that period. A good example is Duncan's (1990) study *The City as Text: the Politics of Landscape Interpretation in the Kandyan Kingdom.* Broad views of the role of imperialism in shaping the landscapes of modern European cities (Driver and Gilbert 1998, 1999) can now be set alongside reconstructions of imperial legacies in the North American landscape (Conzen 1990; Mills 1997). Of course, much of the American landscape is post-colonial but it none the less reflects other struggles for authority, for hegemony, within a developing capitalist economy. Many of its urban landscape forms, for example, signal competing claims for status, power and domination by individuals, groups and institutions. Studies of the skyline of American cities in general (Ford 1973, 1992) and in particular of New York's skyscrapers (Domosh 1987, 1988, 1989, 1992, 1996) reveal their dependence on the changing technology of building and, just as importantly, on the economic and social imperatives of corporate capitalism.

The symbolism of capital and power in the offices, and especially in the headquarters, of British banks both at home and overseas is being revealed in studies by Iain Black (1996, 1999a, 1999b, 2000).

In effect, all forms of social tension – including political, economic, class, ethnic, religious and gender conflicts – are inscribed in landscapes. To take just one example, that of gender. Janice Monk (1992) showed that many monuments in public landscapes express with varying degrees of blatancy the masculinist, patriarchal power that structures the appearance and use of those places. In essence, women are either largely absent from such monuments or depicted in unrealistic and (as seen by men) idealised (often nude or semi-nude) forms. Landscapes are increasingly being interpreted in terms of the ideologies and discourses which underpin them. Landscapes are recognised as having a moral dimension, being material expressions of ideas about the nature of society. Both individual structures within a landscape and entire landscapes are symbolic of moral values and moral orders. For example, both 'liberal' and 'neo-conservative' landscapes have been identified in Vancouver (Ley 1987). Explicit studies of 'moral landscapes' are multiplying (Smith 2000). For example, the middle-class perception of unacceptable behaviour in the Victorian city provided justification for mapping the moral geography of the city as a basis for social intervention (Driver 1988a). Similarly, moral discourses underpinned decisions about the 'right' place in landscapes for certain social institutions in Victorian England, such as hospitals and reformatories (Ogborn and Philo 1994; Ploszajska 1994). Different but equally striking examples of work in this genre are David Matless' (1994, 1997) studies of the competing moral codes expressed in the landscape of the Norfolk Broadlands of eastern England from the late nineteenth to the mid-twentieth century and of how the concept of good citizenship found expression in the English landscape during that period.

There has been a palpable shift in landscape studies by geographers in recent decades. None the less, continuities can also be detected running from Vidal de la Blache's concern with the concepts of *pays* and *paysage* through the ideas of structuralism to those of deconstruction (Claval 1968). For example, Kobayashi's argument that 'the geographical theory of landscape can provide the third component in a triad of action, discourse and object, for a comprehensive, dialectical understanding of social history' provides clearly audible echoes of concepts enunciated deep within the salons of the French geographic tradition (Kobayashi 1989: 182; Buttimer 1971). This is hardly surprising because, as Cosgrove has remarked, 'the issues raised by landscape and its meanings point to the heart of social and historical theory: issues of individual and collective action, of objective and subjective knowing, of idealist and materialist interpretation' (Cosgrove 1984: 38). Such issues are fundamental to a humanistic geography, indeed to any humanistic study, and together with the holistic character of landscape they explain why the geographical study of landscape must involve many disciplines in addition to geography.

The making and meaning of landscapes in the past both reflected and structured the societies who worked and lived in them, who created, experienced and represented them. But to the extent that those landscapes have survived, or are thought to have survived, into the present day they have a continuing significance as one of the components of cultural memory and identity.

Memory and identity in landscapes

Memory and heritage

Traditional studies in historical geography of 'the past in the present' focused somewhat narrowly on the survival of relict features, on the need to describe and explain such features as historical phenomena in the 'present-day' landscape. Modern studies, by contrast, focus much more on the continuing cultural significance of historical survivals and on related questions about heritage conservation and presentation. Here, of course, historical geographers are warm admirers of works by those in other disciplines. They have been inspired recently, for example, by Simon Schama's panoramic perspective on *Landscape and Memory* (1995) and by Raphael Samuel's magnificent meditations on *Theatres of Memory* (1994, 1998). Schama evokes in enormous detail and sweeping generalisation the richness and antiquity of the landscape tradition: metaphorically, he 'excavates' landscapes 'below our conventional sight-level to recover the veins of myths and memories that lie beneath the surface'. Similarly, Samuel examines landscapes of memory, ranging over both the diverse ways in which history is being represented and 'the wholly different versions of the [British] national past on offer at any given point in time'. Both authors focus especially on the visual and on the role of landscapes – past and present – as stores of cultural myths and memories.

A pioneering work in this field by a historical geographer was Robert Newcomb's (1979) *Planning the Past: Historical Landscape Resources and Recreation*. Drawing extensively on European and North American experience, Newcomb examined the recreational and planning issues affecting what he termed 'the visible past'. His broad canvas embraced historic landscape attractions and the planned preservation of the past, the past as recreation and as preservation. Newcomb emphasised that both indoor and outdoor museums can be used to promote particular interpretations of history. For example, they can be used as symbolic expressions of a national ideology: while providing information and instruction, they can serve also as patriotic shrines. He showed that complex and contrasting legal frameworks had been established in many countries to ensure the preservation of the past into the present, and he examined many problems associated with the intensified and diversified recreational uses of the past. Newcomb systematically considered both rural and urban historical landscape features, as well as landscapes specifically bearing the imprints of industrial activities and those carrying imprints of the state. His wide-ranging book broke much new ground in historical geography, for the existing literature in this field was limited when he was writing (for examples, see Fieguth 1967; Baker 1969; Ford 1975; Rowley and Breakell 1975). Newcomb's book can now be seen as having anticipated what has become a major preoccupation of many historical geographers: heritage studies.

A review of historical geography and heritage studies by Dennis Hardy (1988) distinguished between heritage as a 'conservative' concept and heritage as a 'radical' concept. In the former case, Hardy argued, a key feature is nostalgia, with the past being represented in sentimental terms and often in defence of the present, in support of the *status quo*. He drew substantially on the analysis of heritage as a cultural production in Patrick Wright's (1985) book *On Living in an Old Country*, which aimed to clarify some of the ways in which the past has been secured as a cultural presence in modern Britain. This view holds that to some extent 'heritage' has been ideologically appropriated by the 'right wing', to promote concepts like nationalism and patriotism, even if people find heritage themes attractive in part because they can identify some 'truth' in them. Heritage as a radical concept, Hardy argued, is a more honest and open approach, one which recognises particularities within past societies and which engages in a critical dialogue between past and present. Hardy suggested two ways in which historical geographers might become more involved with heritage studies: first, by applying their traditionally strong empirical skills to the identification and interpretation of relics of past landscapes and communities, and, secondly, by grounding such work in theory, so that the past meanings and present significance of such relics can be understood. Historical geographers contribute significantly to debates about heritage preservation and representation (for examples, see Datel and Dingemans 1988; Lamme 1989; Jakle and Wilson 1992; Johnson 1996).

In a recent review of aspects of 'historical geographies of the present', Nuala Johnson (2000) considers some of the theoretical, moral and practical questions raised by heritage studies. She focuses on two themes. She examines first the cultivation of a collective, public memory and the creation of landscapes of remembrance in the aftermath of the Great War, drawing especially upon studies by Heffernan (1995) and Morris (1997) of the ways in which an official and quintessentially English landscape of remembrance, of memorials and cemeteries, was constructed along the Western Front of the Great War in Belgium and France: by 1930 there were almost 900 such cemeteries containing more than 540,000 headstones. Secondly, Johnson addresses the debates surrounding the representation of the past through heritage tourism, examining through an Irish case study some of the challenges and opportunities encountered at heritage sites. She considers the links between heritage and the construction of national identity and the questionable distinction between 'true history' and 'false heritage', the problems of translating and interpreting the past for the present. A more extended consideration of the relationships among heritage, history, memory and landscape is the collective analysis of the geography of heritage by Brian Graham, G. J. Ashworth and J. E. Tunbridge (2000). They define heritage straightforwardly as 'the contemporary use of the past': their focus is upon heritage as part of the 'present'. They are not, therefore, concerned with whether one representation of the past is historically more correct, intrinsically authentic and innately valuable or qualitatively more worthy than another. They see the 'present' as creating the heritage it requires and managing it for a variety of purposes, well or badly, and for the benefit or at the cost of few or many. Their book addresses three main themes. First, the plurality of use and consumption of heritage as a cultural and economic resource; secondly, the conflicts and tensions that arise from this multiple construction of heritage, dealing especially with struggles for the ownership of heritage; thirdly, the relationship between heritage and identity at a variety of geographical scales, from the local through the national and continental to the global. Throughout, theirs is a postmodern approach that stresses the polyvocality and hybridity of meaning and purpose in heritage: dissonance, they argue, is intrinsic to all heritage. They claim that their book 'represents the first significant attempt to place heritage in geography'. This may be so, and they certainly impose – in a paradoxically modernist fashion – a new structure upon this field of enquiry. But although the rich harvest from heritage studies in geography is only now being brought home, there have been labourers in the field for some time.

The geographer who has laboured most productively and imaginatively in this field for decades is David Lowenthal. A stream – nay, a torrent – of papers and books on landscape, heritage and memory has flowed from his pen for almost fifty years. He has done more than any other geographer to shape the discipline's perspective on this field, even though his approach is principally anecdotal rather than analytical. I will here refer only to some of his major contributions. In 1965, Lowenthal co-authored with Hugh Prince a study of English landscape tastes, a paper which constructed from a wide range of mainly literary sources, historical and contemporary, what they identified as the essence of English attitudes towards landscape. In 1975, Lowenthal published a key paper on landscape and memory, on what he called 'past time, present place'. In that discursive essay, he explored the concept of nostalgia, argued that the past is inevitably in the present landscape and that past landscapes provide cultural continuity. He examined why it is that many people have expressed a preference for the past over the present, while others deny the presence of the past. He emphasised that it is 'through awareness of the past that we learn to remake ourselves. Through awareness of our own experience, we also refashion the past and replace what is all the time being altered or lost' (1975: 24).

The ideas discussed in a preliminary and provocative way in that paper were pursued in much greater depth and with even more provocation ten years later in Lowenthal's (1985) hugely impressive *The Past is a Foreign Country*. He explored there our need for the past, the ways in which we come to know the past, and the ways in which we change the past. With enormous erudition, drawing upon a vast array of sources from different periods, places and social contexts, Lowenthal showed how memory, history and relics of earlier times shed light on the past, but also and more significantly how the past they reveal is not simply 'what happened': 'it is', he argued, 'in large measure a past of our own creation, moulded by selective erosion, oblivion and invention'. This book showed how these forces have reshaped the known past for every individual and epoch, and how since the Renaissance that past has become more and more a foreign country distinct from the present, yet at the same time increasingly manipulated by present-day aims. In his recent sequel, *The Heritage Crusade and the Spoils of History*, Lowenthal (1998) tries to explain 'the growth, exponential in pace and global in sweep, of current obsessions with the past, above all with what we enjoy or endure as patrimonial legacies' (p. ix). He explores the tensions generated by heightened patrimonial concerns, the disputes about who should own and interpret heritage. And he insists upon a distinction between heritage and history, for he sees heritage as not being history at all: Lowenthal argues that, 'while it borrows from and enlivens historical study, heritage is not an enquiry into the past but a celebration of it, not an effort to know what actually happened but a profession of faith in a past tailored to present-day purposes' (p. x). His book is thus an explication of phenomena as apparently different as the Acropolis in Greece and Colonial Williamsburg in Virginia, the Plimoth Plantation in Massachusetts and the Holocaust Museum in Jerusalem.

Such historical geographies of memory have become a new research cluster, focusing on questions about the politics of landscape and on questions of how the past is viewed and valued. Considerable attention is being given to memorial landscapes, to the social construction of a past in the present. This 'topology of memory' (Farmer 1995) includes, for example, studies of how Mughal tomb-gardens combine personal memorials and imperial status (Westcoat 1994), of the political and aesthetic battles over the memorialisation of the dead of the Great War (Heffernan 1995), and of the memorialisation of the Great War in Ireland and in Canada and its role in the construction of Irish and Canadian histories and identities (Johnson 1999; Osborne 2001). Heritage and memory are here being engaged in the creation of social identity.

Heritage and identity

In Europe the concepts of heritage and of landscape emerged during the early-modern and modern periods in parallel with that of nationalism. The intertwining of heritage and nationalism has become a major focus of studies in historical geography, analysing the association between cultural landscapes and cultural identities (Graham 1998, 2000). In addressing here the connection between landscape and nationalism, I am certainly not arguing that it is the only or even necessarily the most important expression of landscape identity. But it is an especially appropriate case to consider because as an ideology nationalism incorporates notions about the appropriation not only of space, of clearly defined but not inelastic territory, but also of time, of a heroic and progressive past. I have already touched upon the ways in which *heritage* landscapes are used as tools in the construction and maintenance of a national identity. In fashioning *new* landscapes, a nation-state asserts its dominant culture; it creates distinctive and recognisably national landscapes, intending to impose a national cultural homogeneity upon pre-existing local and regional diversity. As John Agnew (1998a) points out, 'the agents of every modern state aspire to have their state represented materially in the everyday lives of their subjects and citizens. The persisting power of the state depends upon it. Everywhere anyone might look would then reinforce the identity between state and citizen by associating the iconic inheritance of a national past with the present state and its objectives.' The idea of a national landscape and also that of a national identity is, however, complex. As Agnew argues,

a national identity involves a widely shared memory of a common past for people who have never seen or talked to one another in the flesh. This sense of belonging depends as much on forgetting as on remembering, the past being construed as a trajectory to the national present in order to guarantee a common future. National histories, monuments (war memorials, heroic statues), commemorations (anniversaries and parades), sites of institutionalised memories (museums, libraries and other archives) and representative landscapes are among the most important instruments for ordering the national past. They give national identity a materiality it would otherwise lack. (Agnew 1998a: 214–16)

Moreover, heritage as a national political instrument and economic resource both reflects and perpetuates the divisions within European society and culture (Tunbridge 1998: 236).

One of the aims of a nation-state is to establish both its internal homogeneity and its difference from other states. For example, Italy, historically a land of city-states and of regional-states, only became a nation-state during the second half of the nineteenth century. Agnew demonstrates that the new state was built on what foreigners had found exceptional in Italy, on foundations that would lead to respect from others. Thus it was to ancient Rome, both Republican and Imperial, and to certain Renaissance landscape ideals (notably those of Florence and Tuscany) that the visionaries of the new nation-state turned. Both of these represented powerful landscape images that would, they hoped, not only mobilise the disparate populations of the new state behind it but also impress outsiders with the revival of a glorious past, only now in an Italian rather than a Roman or a Renaissance form (Agnew 1998a: 217–32).

Post-Revolutionary France provides an outstanding example of the use of landscape in the creation and maintenance of a sense of national identity. Three volumes of essays on the construction of the French past set out to study national sentiment by analysing the places in which the collective heritage of France was crystallised, the principal *lieux*, in all senses of the word, in which collective memory was rooted (Nora 1996, 1997, 1998). The third volume explores some national symbols, including the tricolour flag and the republican slogan 'Liberty, Equality, Fraternity' which came to adorn public buildings; the playing and parading of the national anthem, the *Marseillaise*; and the annual Bastille Day (14 July) celebrations. It also examines the symbolism of some major cultural sites where Pierre Nora considers it is possible to hear the heartbeat of France itself: the prehistoric cave drawings at Lascaux; Reims, the city in which the kings of France were for centuries anointed and crowned; the Louvre, a royal residence transformed into a 'temple of the arts'; the palace and gardens of Versailles, monuments to regal power and imagination but also explicit and intentional statements of the richness of France's geography and history; the Pantheon, a petrification of the cult of great men and of the notion of national unity; the Eiffel tower, taken by foreigners to be the very image of France so that, according to Nora, the country has itself strongly internalised the world's regard; and Verdun, which it is argued occupies a unique place in France's national memory because the battle in 1916 was not simply one episode among others but rather the apogee of nineteenth-century patriotism. And there are essays on the Gallic cock and Joan of Arc, both of which pepper the French landscape in varied forms, as well as on the wonderfully symbolic landscape of Paris (Nora 1998). From the early nineteenth century the centralised French state was administered from the council offices (*mairies*) established in each of its more than 30,000 communes and from the 1830s, and most especially from the 1870s, a sense of French identity was taught in the country's primary schools. In these and other public buildings – such as hospitals, military barracks and prisons – the modern state signalled iconographically its take-over from the medieval Church (Baker 1992b).

Nation-states were to become significant landscape architects not only in Europe but also in the New World. Lowenthal (1976, 1991) has reflected not only upon British national identity in the English landscape but also upon the place of the past in the American landscape. Holdsworth (1986) examined varied architectural expressions of the Canadian national state, ranging from the singular Parliament Building in Ottawa to the many federal buildings (such as post offices) constructed by the Department of Public Works in smaller towns and cities. Although borrowing heavily from European architectural traditions, the hybrid Canadian federal architecture provided a focus for a country that stretched across a continent. Wilbur Zelinsky (1986, 1988, 1990) traced the changing face of nationalism in the American landscape and examined the imprint of central authority on the landscape, ranging from administrative boundaries and buildings to public parks and patriotic parades.

Nation-states have clearly been instrumental in the creation of landscapes, but landscapes have themselves been agents in the construction of national images. Victor Konrad (1986) considered recurrent symbols in the image of Canada, emphasising that many of them are drawn from romanticised landscapes and physical environments distinct to Canada, notably the pervasive Shield which both nurtured Canada's early development through the provision of furs, timber and minerals and also inspired poets, novelists and painters. Images of Canada employ many environmental icons, such as red maples and white pines, Rocky Mountain peaks, and caribou and polar bear. In similar vein, Osborne (1988, 1992, 2001) explores the iconography of Canadian nationhood in art. Daniels (1993) examined how landscapes, in various media from painting to photography, have articulated national identities in England and the United States from the late eighteenth century. He concentrated on the representation of their landscapes by painters – Joseph Wright, J. M. W. Turner, Thomas Cole, Frances Palmer and John Constable – and the designing of landscapes by Humphrey Repton in late Georgian England. Daniels showed that

landscape imagery is not merely a reflection of, or distraction from, more pressing social, economic or political issues; it is often a powerful mode of knowledge and social engagement. Running through many of the images is a variety of discourses and practices, from engineering to political economy. Not all of them were put there by the artists. They are often activated, or introduced, by the various contexts in which the images are displayed, reproduced and discussed. (Daniels 1993: 8)

Daniels demonstrated the power of landscape as an idiom for representing national identity. He argued that landscapes such as the American West and the English landed estate provide images of the nation itself; as exemplars of moral order and aesthetic harmony, they achieve the status of national icons.

Such images contribute, some intentionally and others unintentionally, to the creation of a national consciousness. David Matless (1998) examines the intertwining of landscape and senses of Englishness during the period roughly from 1918 to the 1950s. Initially, he traces 'the emergence in the 1920s ands 1930s of a movement for the planning and preservation of landscape which sought to ally preservation and progress, tradition and modernity, city and country in order to define Englishness as orderly and modern'. Then he considers 'a counter-current of Englishness, which far from seeking a modern form of progress in city and country set an organic sense of rural life against modern city living and upheld traditional authority against progressive expertise'. He finally returns to his initial themes but in the context of war and reconstruction, arguing that the Second World War allowed the planner-preservationist mode of Englishness to achieve a position of considerable cultural and political power (Matless 1998: 14–15). Just as there are different visions of landscapes, so there are different versions of Englishness historically and geographically. While Matless demonstrates that there are connections between landscape and national identity, his book emphasises the multiplicity of both concepts and the complexity of their relationships. In doing so, incidentally, Matless considers W. G. Hoskins' post-war contribution to English landscape attitudes, emphasising his attachments to the local and to the past and his distaste for planning, science, industry, the military and modernity. Hoskins' turning away from the present, his escape into history, has had, Matless argues, 'enormous contemporary effect, its particular formulation of despair acting as a powerful force for conservation'. Matless points out the irony of Hoskins' being opposed to landscape change in the present after having studied so many changing landscapes in the past: modern change was for Hoskins the regrettable erasure of a historic document of Englishness (Matless 1998: 274–7).

Nationalism is not, of course, the only cultural identity to be expressed in landscapes. So, too, are resistances to nationalism as well as other ideologies. While all cultural landscapes may be constructed and interpreted as landscapes of power, as resultants of struggles both with the physical environment and among social groups and individuals, the power sources are many and often contested. Communities may be identified not only by their nationality but also, for example, by their religion, their race, their class and their gender, and each of these can express their identity in landscape and all have their own histories and geographies. W. J. Darby (2000) examines expressions both of nation and of class in the English landscape. Within national landscapes there have persisted regional and local landscapes reflective of sub-national cultures (McQuillan 1993; Lowenthal 1994). The hegemony of the nation-state over landscapes has always been far from complete and I have been using it here only as an exemplar. Moreover, in drawing attention to the role of landscapes as national symbols I have not been arguing that other aspects of a nation's history and geography have necessarily contributed less to its sense of identity. On the contrary, the face of a nation is but one of its features. In considering the identity of a nation, its whole personality must be taken into account. Such issues have been the central concern of the fourth tradition of historical geography, that which addresses the character of areas and places, of localities, regions, countries and continents.

Intellectual histories of geography emphasise the contested nature of its development. The discipline has been conceived and nurtured differently by its leading philosophers and practitioners at different periods in its history (Hartshorne 1939; Dickinson 1969; Livingstone 1992). I have so far considered three discourses within geography: the locational, the environmental and the landscape discourses. Each of these has contributed significantly to the making of geography as a discipline, but none of them individually could claim justifiably to be more than a contributor, to be more than a part of the whole. They are what Haggett (1965: 10–13), following Hartshorne (1939: 102–9), termed 'deviations' from the main geographical discourse. If the quality and quantity of work that has been produced, and is still being produced, within those discourses suggests that use of the term 'deviation' to describe them was probably rather harsh, nevertheless that description made the key point that none of these fundamentally analytical approaches could make a comprehensive claim upon the nature of geography. For that, one has to turn to the core discourse in geography, to areal differentiation and regional geography. How does historical geography fit into that discourse and how do studies in historical regional geography relate to regional and other area histories?

5

Regional geographies and histories

The regional discourse in geography

The region as a core concept in geography

Just as there is a basic human desire to know about the past, to understand our individual and collective histories, so too there is a comparable need to know about places and to understand how and why they differ. Geography as an academic subject has developed over more than two thousand years to meet in a disciplined way people's curiosity about places. The origins of modern Western geography are traceable to classical Greece. The writings of Herodotus (*c.* 484–425 BC), Eratosthenes (*c.* 275–193 BC), Strabo (63 BC–*c.* AD 25) and Ptolemy (*c.* AD 100–178) provided descriptions of the lands and peoples of the known, inhabited world, the *ecumene*. Herodotus wrote a descriptive work called *Geographica*: it included the first recorded use of the word 'geography', derived from the Greek *ge*, meaning 'the earth', and *grapho*, meaning 'I write' or 'I describe'. Compiling maps and drawing upon travellers' accounts, Greek scholars described the different physical and human geographies of the world, both 'real' and 'mythologised'. They considered places both as discrete units, in what they termed topographies, and as interconnected systems, in chorographies. Thus the Greeks have been credited with 'inventing' regional geography. Thereafter, geography as an organised body of knowledge in the Western world made little progress until the Renaissance and the Age of Discoveries. During the sixteenth, seventeenth and eighteenth centuries there was a vast expansion of geographical knowledge associated with developments in cartography and navigation, in exploration and empire building, and in theology, science and technology. An early and significant codification of that burgeoning knowledge was provided by a German, Bernhard Varenius (1622–1650), in his *Geographia Generalis*, published in 1650. Varenius argued that geographical knowledge was partitioned into two divisions, general (or universal) and special (or particular). The former considered properties and processes in relation to the whole earth without regard to particular countries; the latter treated the properties of and processes operating in individual countries. Varenius thus identified the basic distinction between what came to be termed systematic geography and regional geography, with the former focusing analytically on sets of forms and functions (such as in geomorphology or in urban geography) and the latter looking synthetically at particular places, especially at a regional scale. Immanuel Kant (1724–1804), a Prussian philosopher, drew upon the ideas of Varenius in his highly influential discussion of the nature of geography. Kant argued that both history and geography are synthesising bodies of knowledge: both are descriptive, the former in relation to events in time and the latter in relation to circumstances in space. Kant's idea of *Raum* (area or space) was a holistic concept in which the findings of the divisive systematic sciences could be cohered and understood as parts of a whole. He thus provided a philosophical justification for the prosecution of geography as a study of areas in terms of their particularities and in terms of their differences (Hartshorne 1939; Dickinson 1969; May 1970; Livingstone 1992).

These ideas were pursued further during the nineteenth century. The growth of national geographical societies encouraged exploration and helped to meet the growing commercial, military, political and popular demands for knowledge about the different areas of the world. German geographers like Alexander von Humboldt (1768–1859), Carl Ritter (1779–1859) and Alfred Hettner (1859–1941) built on foundations laid earlier, promoting the regional concept in geography. But it was a French geographer, Paul Vidal de la Blache (1845–1918), who did most to advocate regional knowledge and understanding as the core of geography. Vidal de la Blache viewed the distinctive landscape and life-style of each local 'region' or *pays* as the resultant of the interactions of peoples with their physical environments over (usually long) periods of time. His conception of regional geography underpinned much of geography as practised in the Western world during the first half of the twentieth century. In 1939, Hartshorne, in *The Nature of Geography*, concluded that geography 'studies the world, seeking to describe, and to interpret, the differences among its different parts, as seen at any one time, commonly the present time' (Hartshorne 1939: 460). Hartshorne viewed geography as 'the science of areal differentiation', a term which he borrowed explicitly from Carl Sauer's paraphrasing in 1925 of Alfred Hettner's statement two years earlier of his concept of geography (Hartshorne 1959: 12). Hartshorne argued that 'to comprehend the full character of each area in comparison with others, we must examine the totality of related features . . . found in different units of area – i.e., regional geography' (Hartshorne 1939: 468). Hartshorne's critical survey of Western geographical writings led him to conclude that 'geography is concerned to provide accurate, orderly, and rational description and interpretation of the variable character of the earth surface' (Hartshorne 1959: 21). Sauer, in his 'foreword to historical geography', had advised young geographers to immerse themselves in a region (Sauer 1941: 10). I agree with Haggett (1965: 10) that 'there is little doubt that Hartshorne's definition represents one of the common denominators that runs through the greater part of geographical works from the Greeks onwards'.

This is not to be blind to the many problems associated with the regional concept in geography, some of which I will consider in due course. For now I want only to emphasise the epistemologically central and historically enduring role of the regional concept in geography, notwithstanding its problematic nature. For a variety of reasons, the regional concept came under heavy attack from the 1960s onwards. Its emphasis upon uniqueness and its inductive approach were criticised during a period in geography's history in the 1960s and 1970s that attached greater value to universality and a deductive approach. The undoubted weaknesses of the regional concept were exaggerated, as were also the alleged strengths of the positivist and nomothetic geography which came into favour during that period. For at least a couple of decades regional geography was unfashionable, being seen as overly descriptive and non-scientific. Given the intellectual climate of the time, few were prepared to 'come out' as its practitioners. Traditional regional geography withered. But gradually during the 1980s and 1990s, as the limitations of nomothetic geography came increasingly to be revealed, there developed a revived interest in regional studies. A 'new' regional geography has emerged as an integral part of postmodern human geography (Gregory 1989a; Thrift, 1990, 1991, 1993). Unsurprisingly, the concept of a 'new' regional geography is much debated: Hans Holmen (1995) even argues that what has been created is neither 'new' nor 're-gional'. None the less, a renewed emphasis on the cultural significance of area, of place and of region has given geography a rejuvenated relevance to the social sciences and humanities (Entrikin 1991, 1994). For some the 'new' regional geography might be more theoretically informed, less empirical, and might pay more attention to narrative, less to analysis, but for Nicholas Entrikin what distinguished new work from more traditional studies was 'the greater willingness to move beyond the traditional "facts" of place to examine the more subjective experience of place. Such a shift adds richness to studies of place and region, at the cost of adding the logical complication that results from a concern with both subjective and objective reality' (Entrikin 1991: 133).

I have already noted that regional geography rests upon synthesis but I do not hesitate to emphasise the point again. I subscribe to the Kantian notion that history and geography epistemologically focus not upon a special category of phenomenon but rather upon totalities – with history doing so from a temporal perspective and geography from a spatial perspective (which is not to assert that history has a prior claim on time and geography a prior claim on space by comparison with other disciplines). The synthesising concepts of 'total history' (as propounded by the *Annales* school) and of regional geography have much in common. They approach the same problem but from different perspectives. Period history and regional geography are closely related synthesising concepts. Synthesis logically requires the integration of the two dimensions of history and geography. That the regional concept has been central to the development of geography is beyond dispute. While the systematic (disintegrative) branches of geography overlap considerably with cognate analytical disciplines (such as ecology and economics) that are also focused on specific phenomena or systems in the natural and social worlds, regional (integrative) geography can more justifiably claim its own distinctive ground. But the concept itself has been much debated.

The region as a problematic concept in geography

Both theoretical and practical problems face those engaged in researching and writing regional geography. I need treat those difficulties only briefly here, because they have created a substantial literature (for reviews, widely separated in time, see Whittlesey 1954; Dickinson 1976; Mead 1980; Claval 1993). My main purpose here is to note some of the similarities that exist between the problematics of regional geography and of period history.

The problems of regional geography stem fundamentally from its dual endeavour to identify the specific character of each 'region' and to delimit its spatial boundary. The former theoretically requires an ability to know and understand the whole range of the forms and functions within a given area, from its Atmospheric conditions to its Zoogeography, while the latter theoretically assumes either a homogeneity of, or at least a distinctive and interdependent set of, characteristics within the bounded area. Hartshorne dissected the theoretical complexities of regional geography, revealing for example the difficulties involved in a choice of geographical scale for the areas being studied and the complications introduced by recognising that regions are not static but dynamic and that they are not discrete but interconnected. He recognised, therefore, that there was likely to be a disjuncture between the theory and the practice of regional geography. But the intrinsic difficulties of regional geography do not, Hartshorne argued, allow geographers 'to shirk the task of organising regional knowledge into areal divisions determined by the best possible judgement'. For Hartshorne, regional geography might aim to be objective but it cannot avoid being to some degree subjective (Hartshorne 1939: 436–44). Harvey, in his analytical discussion of explanation in geography, argued that 'characteristically geographers tend to work with human and physical differentiation at the "regional" level although it is difficult to pin this down with any precision . . . the geographer tends to filter out small-scale variation and large-scale variation and to concentrate his attention upon systems . . . which have meaning at a regional scale of resolution' (Harvey 1969: 484).

The concept of the region in geography is logically related to that of the period in history. It has been a common practice in history both to identify the specific character of each 'period' and to delimit the temporal boundary of each 'period'. Such a process has encountered precisely the kind of problem I have just outlined (Green 1995). It requires a sound knowledge and understanding of an almost infinite number of historical variables and of their interconnections, and it assumes a continuity of characteristics within the bounded 'period'. Furthermore, historians encounter difficulties in choosing a temporal scale for the periods being studied and with the complexities introduced by recognising that the societal characteristics identified for particular periods are not necessarily uniform through either the space or the time being studied. Some periodisations in history have rested on reigning monarchs (such as 'Tudor' or 'Victorian' England) or on political regimes (such as France's 'Second Empire' or 'Third Republic'). Others have reflected broader but distinctive cultural, economic, social or political characteristics (such as 'The Renaissance', 'The Age of Empire' or 'The Great Depression'). More commonly, periodisation has rested on broad slices of time (such as 'Ancient', 'Medieval' and 'Modern') or on precise but often arbitrary time periods (such as specified decades or centuries). Different kinds of history necessitate different kinds of periodisation. Like geographical regions, historical periods may be sought objectively but they have to be constructed subjectively. Both are best seen as ways of organising knowledge and understanding, as the means of achieving a kind of synthesis.

Regional geography became discredited from the 1960s in part because of the apparent intractability of the problems I have been discussing and in part because of the ways in which it had come to be practised. Guelke (1977) argued that regional geography had been undermined by its widespread adoption of an unsuitable framework (that of spatial analysis), by its failure to take – as he saw it – proper account of the ideas and thinking behind human activity, and by its lack of historical understanding because of the methodological problems encountered in incorporating a temporal dimension into geography. Many French regional monographs by the 1960s had become encyclopaedic descriptions rather than imaginative interpretations of areas. Moreover, the concept of the *pays* was criticised as being suited more to pre-industrial and basically rural societies than to industrial and significantly urban societies (Wrigley 1965). Such criticism ignored the fact that Vidal de la Blache himself had emphasised the importance not only of the *milieu* and the *genre de vie* of each *pays* but also its *connectivité*, its links with other places through flows of people, commodities, capital and ideas. The concept of the *pays* was sufficiently flexible to embrace studies which focused upon the urban organisation of space and the interconnectedness of places (Juillard 1962), but this was overlooked by some of its critics. Quite simply, the ideographic regional monograph became unfashionable among a new generation of nomothetic geographers more enthused by spatial theory and model building. It is tempting to argue that regional geography became neglected because prosecuting it is so difficult. A leading regional geographer, John Paterson (1974), certainly set out very clearly six key problems in writing regional geography: the logical impossibility of providing a complete regional description in verbal form; the problem of identifying the regions themselves; the problem of handling scale variations in presentation; the growing shortage of subordinate regional information; the submergence of regional distinctiveness; and the limited amount of stylistic innovation possible. Paterson made it abundantly clear that the task of writing regional geography is intellectually very challenging. But 'adopting other lands', as Mead (1963) poetically described regional geography, dedicating oneself to the study of areas (Farmer 1973), has its rewards: it can provide what Clark (1962a) termed 'the tremendous satisfaction in feeling that one has gotten under the skin of any such region'.

The problem of geographical description, often but not always coupled with that of historical narration, has been and is likely to remain an enduring concern in the practice of geography (Darby 1962b; Meinig 1983; Watson 1983; Sayer 1989; Daniels 1992). Haggett (1990) also made the point that the problem of writing regional geography has been exacerbated because the pace of regional change has itself accelerated, so that information about a region is soon outdated. But Haggett further emphasised another barrier to the practice of regional geography: 'understanding a region involves something much deeper than statistics: it means adopting its culture, learning its language, travelling its byways, scouring its archives, acquiring a specialist understanding of its landscapes and economy. It is costly in time, a business of many years, and not one that fits easily with short project grants or the imperatives of quick results for publication' (Haggett 1990: 85). Not surprisingly, many geographers seek refuge in the easier option of systematic geography.

There are, then, many reasons for the turbulent history of regional geography. They include the restless histories of regions themselves. In this connection, Andrew Sayer (1989) has pointed out that the 'new' regional geography originated in radical geography and involved what he termed an empirical turn towards works of geohistorical synthesis. Each region has its own history and its 'present' condition is seen most clearly when illuminated by the light of that history. As Darby proclaimed in his inaugural lecture delivered in the University of Liverpool on 7 February 1946: 'If it is the purpose of the geographer to portray the character of a region, he [*sic*] cannot hope to do so without some understanding of how it has come to be.' Darby was a powerful advocate not only of the necessity for historical understanding in geography but also of regional geography itself. 'Our systematic enquiries', he stated, 'are after all means to an end, and it is regional geography that is the culmination of our work' (Darby 1947: 19–20). A very similar conclusion was reached by Harvey in his exploration of explanation in geography: 'It may be that the domain of the geographer can best be approached by an analysis of the particular resolution level at which he works rather than by an examination of the kind of subject-matter he discusses . . . I am prepared to suggest that another basic tenet of geographic thought is that its domain is defined in terms of a regional resolution level' (Harvey 1969: 484–5). Defining a 'regional' scale has been one of the main problems in regional geography. For some, it lies between 'local' and 'global'; others prefer to recognise a nested hierarchy of 'regional' systems; still others acknowledge both individual localities and the globe as a whole as 'regions'. Sometimes it seems that what is accepted as a 'region' depends as much upon the aims and interests of the geographer as it does upon any attempt to define objectively an appropriate resolution level for geographical study.

While the region is again being acknowledged as geography's central object of study, the concept of the region is itself being rethought once more. One current think-tank (Allen et al. 1998) accepts the validity of regional geographical studies 'as exemplars of wider phenomena, symptomatic of broader changes; as laboratories for the exploration of particular issues, both theoretical and empirical; and for themselves, to aid attempts by people living and working within an area to understand what is going on around them and maybe to change it for the better'. But they also advocate a different way of approaching regional geography: they see regions as constituted of spatialised social relations, and narratives about them, which not only lay down ever-new regional geographies but also work to reshape social and cultural identities and how they are represented. Moreover, Allen et al. conceive a region, viewed in this way, as being a series of open, discontinuous spaces constituted by social relationships which stretch across spaces in a variety of ways – they thus present an alternative way of thinking about the region. More conventionally, they also see regional studies as always being produced for a purpose, with a specific aim in view, there being multiple ways of seeing 'one' region (Allen et al. 1998: 1–5). Regions and regional knowledges, like histories and historical knowledges, are socially constructed, both by 'insiders', those living in them, and by 'outsiders', those observing them from beyond (Buttimer et al. 1999).

No matter the many problems inherent in the regional conception of geography, it has been and remains the central discourse in geography. My immediate concern is to examine historical geography's participation in that discourse before considering the regional contexts of historical studies.

Historical regional geographies

During the 1960s, the role and status of regional geography came increasingly to be questioned, even threatened, by those advocating the development of a theoretical and universal geography of spatial relations, and this impacted upon work in historical geography. In his 1972 review of progress in historical geography in North America, Clark sounded an alarm, suggesting that 'perhaps the most critical question for historical geographers today is the place of the regional historical study'. Clark believed that the kind of theoretical and statistical work then being aggressively pursued in geography might be charged with 'its failure to relate in an interpretative way to the general and specific characteristics of particular regions'. For Clark, geography's 'full and only purpose' was 'making sense of the world', providing what he termed the 'world knowledge' which he saw as being 'absolutely vital to the intellectual health of mankind' and 'of great importance to his social, economic and political well-being' (Clark 1972: 131–3).

Clark's brief but forcefully expressed concern about the development of spatial analysis and spatial theory in geography was considered at much greater length and with even greater strength in two significant and influential essays by Harris. In his thoughtful examination of theory and synthesis in geography, Harris (1971) developed a powerful three-fold argument. First, he contested the limited view of geography as the study of spatial relations (because spatial considerations are the legitimate interest of any subject matter specialist). Secondly, he challenged all attempts to develop geographical theory (because such theories are necessarily exercises in abstraction and simplification in which the complexities of particular situations are eliminated, whereas geography's concern is precisely with those complexities). For Harris, the geographical point of view is characterised by 'the habit of seeing the complex of factors that make up the character of places, regions, or landscapes: in a word, by a breadth of synthesis' (Harris 1971: 162). Thirdly, Harris summarised the long debate about the nature of history and argued that the points of agreement in that debate applied also to geography. Geography, like history, is primarily concerned with the particular; explanation in geography, like that in history, may take into account the thoughts of individuals lying behind action; explanation in geography, like that in history, may make use of general statements, theories or laws; and explanation in geography, like that in history, relies heavily on the reflective judgement of individuals. 'In short, to understand a particular region, place or landscape, or to treat a theme which itself embraces a complex set of relationships bearing on the character of a particular place, is to achieve a synthesising understanding analogous to that in history' (Harris 1971: 167–8). In his essay on the historical mind and the practice of geography, Harris (1978a) expanded these ideas with great subtlety, power, conviction and – ultimately – influence.

Both Clark's anxiety about the place of regional historical geography and Harris' advocacy of historical geographical synthesis cited past exemplars in the field while looking to the future. In effect, they reasserted the central, regional discourse in geography. I will now consider two of its specific components, those of geographical personality and of culture area.

Geographical personality

Each person is unique and so is each place; each has its own distinctive personality, a product in part of its own history. The concept of geographical personality became one of the central themes of human geography during the first half of the twentieth century (Dunbar 1974; Claval 1984; Guiomar 1997).

Paul Vidal de la Blache lodged the concept of personality in the geographical literature in 1903, in his contribution to Ernest Lavisse's multi-volume *Histoire de France*. Vidal's *Tableau de la géographie de la France* opened with an essay bearing the title 'Personnalité géographique de la France'. Gary Dunbar (1974), who has traced the origins and use of the concept, emphasised that although French geographers had used the term 'personality' previously, it was its frequent and emphatic use in Vidal's *Tableau* that established its place in the geographer's lexicon. It seems that Vidal borrowed both *tableau* and *personnalité* from the great French Romantic historian, Jules Michelet (1798–1874), whose *Histoire de France* included a lengthy (130 pages) geographical scene-setting 'Tableau de la

France'. Michelet famously claimed that 'history is at first entirely geography' but that gradually 'society overcomes nature' and 'history effaces geography' (Michelet 1833: 2 and 128). For Michelet, geography provided a passive stage upon which the drama of history was enacted. While that limiting view has probably blinkered the geographical perspective of many historians, another of Michelet's aphorisms certainly expanded the horizons of geographers. 'La France est une personne,' stated Michelet (1833: 126). For him, the personality of France as a nation, as a people, had been forged in the centuries-long struggle with England. Vidal appears to have taken this concept and applied it to France as a place, as a country, as a landscape. For him, the personality of France was forged in the centuries-long struggle of its people with their physical environment. For Vidal de la Blache, geographical personality is something that grows with time, until a country becomes 'a medal struck in the image of its people' (Vidal de la Blache 1903: 8). Dunbar argued that Vidal consistently regarded the depiction of the physiognomy or personality of places as perhaps the central task of geography (Dunbar 1974: 28).

The principal users of the concept of geographical personality in the English-speaking world have been H. J. Fleure and his students in the 'Aberystwyth school' of geography and Carl Sauer and his followers in the 'Berkeley school'. Fleure (1921) wrote a brief paper on 'countries as personalities', while Estyn Evans' (1970) Presidential Address to the Institute of British Geographers was on 'the personality of Ulster', a prelude to his broader book *The Personality of Ireland: Habitat, History, Heritage* (1973). Fleure and his students were interested in places in remote rather than recent periods, and with broadly cultural rather than narrowly economic and social questions. They had strong links with archaeologists and anthropologists (Langton 1986, 1988a). In 1932 the archaeologist Cyril Fox published his book on *The Personality of Britain* in prehistoric and early historic times, and other archaeologists have used the term in titles of books on other countries, such as India (Subbarao 1958) and Rhodesia (Summers 1960). Sauer certainly knew Vidal's work, but he stated that the inspiration for the title of his own essay on 'the personality of Mexico' came directly from Fox. For Sauer, 'the designation of "personality" applied to a particular part of the earth involves the whole dynamic relation of life and land' (Sauer 1941b: 353). Thereafter the term 'personality' was employed by some of Sauer's students, such as Clark (1962b) in his article on geographical diversity and the personality of Canada and Dan Stanislawski (1963) in his book on the Algarve.

Although 'geographical personality' has often been employed loosely, both as a concept and as a term, it has underpinned considerable work in geography and been central to its practice. For some, it defines the role of geography. For example, E. W. Gilbert (1960: 158) declared that geography is 'the art of recognising, describing and interpreting the personalities of regions'. Sometimes the term 'individuality' has been used as a synonym for 'personality', as in Dan Stanislawski's (1959) study of *The Individuality of Portugal*. Moreover, the concept has been adopted and modified by a historian, Braudel (1986), in his portrayal of the 'identity' of France. Interest among geographers in the personalities of regions declined as part of the general retreat of regional geography during the 1960s. David Turnock, reviewing the role of the region in modern geography, suggested that the concept of geographical personality should be abandoned, despite his own professed interest in historical regional geography, later exemplified by his study of the historical geography of Scotland since 1707 (Turnock 1967, 1982). But Haggett, one of the new frontiersmen in geography during the 1960s, accepted that although regions had come under some heavy crossfire, they continued to be 'one of the most logical and satisfactory ways of organising geographical information' (Haggett 1965: 241). And even Harvey, in his relentless search for rigorous explanation in geography, conceded that the classic works of French regional geographers struck a balance between the presentation of factual information and skilfully constructed literary accounts which succeeded in evoking an image of the personality of a region (Harvey 1969: 296). Samuels' (1979) exposition of what might constitute 'a biography of landscape' developed implicitly – although not explicitly – the Vidalian concept of personality. Allan Pred's (1984) presentation of a theoretical foundation for what he claimed was 'a different type of place-centred or regional geography' opened by citing Vidal de la Blache's claim that 'modern geography is the scientific study of places'. The conception of places as having personalities has undoubtedly permeated through much modern geography. A related influential idea has been that of 'culture areas'.

Culture areas

The concept of 'culture areas' in geography is most closely associated with the American geographer Carl Sauer. For Sauer, geography's distinctive concern was with 'synthetic areal knowledge': 'no other subject has pre-empted the study of area' (Sauer 1925; citation from Leighly 1963: 317). To him, regional geography had 'meaning only as a study of culture areas': he deplored lightweight regional descriptions and enthused about the need for a geographer to 'really get into the problems of one region' (Sauer in correspondence, cited in Leighly 1978: 103).

Sauer's development of the concept of culture areas was derived in part from studies by American anthropologists and in part from German geographers' notion of a *Kulturprovinz*. For him, 'the whole task of human geography . . . is nothing less than the comparative study of areally localised cultures' (Sauer 1941a; citation from Leighly 1963: 359). Sauer explicitly 'equated' regional geography and historical geography, and his elaboration of that relation is worth citing fully:

The historical geographer . . . must be a regional specialist, for he must not only know the region as it appears today; he must know its lineaments so well that he can find in it traces of the past, and he must know its qualities so well that he can see it as it was under past situations. One might say that he needs the ability to see the land with the eyes of its former occupants, from the standpoint of their needs and capacities. This is about the most difficult task in all human geography: to evaluate site and situation, not from the standpoint of an educated American of today, but to place one-self in the position of a member of the cultural group at the time being studied. It is, however, a rewarding experience to know that one has succeeded in penetrating a culture that is removed in time or alien in content from ours. (Sauer 1941a; citation from Leighly 1963: 362)

Sauer phrased his remarks in the light of his own interests in the discovery and settlement of areas, but his point may readily be generalised to all research in historical geography.

When referring to culture, Sauer embraced both the material objects and the ideas characteristically associated with a group of people. He argued that a

culture trait or complex originates at a certain time in a particular locality. It gains acceptance – that is, is learned by the group – and is communicated outwards, or diffuses, until it encounters sufficient resistance, as from unsuitable physical conditions, from alternative traits, or from disparity of cultural level. These are processes involving time; and not simply chronologic time, but especially those moments of culture history when the group possesses the energy of invention or the receptivity to acquire new ways. (Sauer 1941a; citation from Leighly 1963: 359–60)

For Sauer, a geographer

is interested in discovering related and different patterns of living as they are found over the world – culture areas. These patterns have interest and meaning as we learn how they came into being. The geographer, therefore, properly is engaged in charting the distribution over the earth of the arts and artefacts of man, to learn whence they came and how they spread, what their contexts are in cultural and physical environments. (Sauer 1952: 1)

Those employing the culture area concept often recognise three contiguous subdivisions of an area: first, a core, over which the culture being studied has exclusive or almost exclusive influence; secondly, a domain, over which its identifying traits are dominant but not exclusive; and thirdly, a realm, in which its traits are located but sub-dominant to those of another culture. An excellent individual example in this genre is Meinig's (1965) identification of a Mormon culture area in North America centred on the Great Basin of Utah. Perhaps the most ambitious and provocative use of the concept was Wilbur Zelinsky's (1973) attempt to map the culture areas of the United States. His three-level hierarchical classification of the country into cultural-genetic regions and sub-regions has been hailed as representing 'a major benchmark of synoptic mapping in American historical geography' (Conzen 1993: 65).

A culture area or culture region is one over which a functionally coherent way of life dominates: culture areas or regions are identified using key traits or combinations of traits. The process of identification encounters the boundary problem familiar to all regional geographers: a boundary defined by one criterion might not, often does not, correspond with the boundary defined by other criteria, and in any event the boundary of any culture area is more likely to be changing than fixed.

Moreover, the concept of culture area shares with that of regional personality the fundamental question of the geographical scale at which an area or region should, or can, be studied. There have been many and varied answers to that question.

Regional and area studies in historical geography

Syntheses in historical geography are produced at very different geographical scales, many of which have been loosely termed 'regional' when the less specific term 'area' might have been more accurate. Of course, the problem here is that the 'regional' scale can have no clear boundaries to it. The geographical scale of a study will reflect both the cultural and physical character of the area and the personal preferences of its researcher. While it could be argued that regional studies should logically be conducted at meso- rather than micro- or macro-scales, such a qualitative claim simply avoids the problem of precise definition and ignores the fact that researchers have produced 'regional' studies of quite small areas (or 'localities') as well as of very large areas (or 'world regions'). There is no point in trying to be prescriptive about what properly constitutes a historical 'regional' geography in terms of its scale. 'Regions' exist in the eyes of their beholders – with the beholders being in this case both historical geographers as passive observers of the past and contemporaries as active participants in their own 'historic presents'. It might, none the less, be instructive to look at the production of historical geographies at different scales. I will start with what came to be termed the French school of geography, both because it laid foundations for Western 'regional' geography and because it has been practised at a variety of spatial scales.

Historical geographies of France

Vidal de la Blache's *Tableau de la géographie de la France* (1903) continues, a century later, to be reassessed and to provoke new thinking about a wide range of concepts in human and regional geography (Robic 2000). Vidal's concern was with the personality of France as a country. He was operating at the national scale, seeking to understand the identity of France as a nation constructed both historically and geographically. His achievement was to demonstrate that the national, historical unity of France was complemented by a regional, geographical diversity. Moreover, there was a local diversity within the regions, among their localities or *pays*. Each locality, each region, was seen as a vital component of the whole nation. Although deriving some of his ideas about regional and local diversity from the work of geologists, and although acknowledging the significant role of physical geography in the formation of distinctive areas in France, Vidal saw *pays,* regions and nations as cultural constructions, as products of the interactions of people with their environments and with each other over long periods of time.

Many French regional monographs, beginning with the first, Albert Demangeon's (1905b) study of Picardy, were emphatically historical in their approach. Typically, such monographs treated their regions and their constituent *pays* sequentially in terms of their physical geography, their historical geography and their 'present-day' geography, although in detail these monographs were very varied both in their style and in their substance. Many treated past geographies and changing geographies for their own sakes, being in effect historical geographies *sensu stricto*. For example, Jules Sion's (1908) study of eastern Normandy included cross-sections of its geography in the thirteenth and eighteenth centuries, as well as one of its 'present-day' geography in the early twentieth century. Others, like Théodore Lefebvre's (1933) study of the eastern Pyrenees, focused clearly upon the 'present', delving into the past not for its own sake but in order to enhance understanding of the region in the 'present'. Such studies are historical geographies *sensu lato*, and might perhaps more aptly be read as retrospective regional geographies. As French geography after the Second World War became increasingly applied in character and orientated towards planned reconstruction and development, so the historical component of regional monographs was diluted. Almost one-third of Maurice Le Lannou's (1952) study of Brittany was devoted to its history, but Le Lannou considered it necessary to express the hope that he would not be reproached for having presented so much history in a geographical monograph, insisting that 'historical knowledge is always necessary to appreciate a region geographically' and asking rhetorically how the 'personality of an area', especially one like Brittany, can be understood 'if we do not appreciate the efforts that have been made to adapt to external changes that are imposed continuously, sometimes slowly, sometimes rapidly' (Le Lannou 1952: 9 and 13).

The regions presented in French monographs were themselves often identified partly in terms of their geological and topographical characteristics and partly in terms of their cultural and historical significance as provinces under the *Ancien Régime*. Thus they focused on 'regions' like Brittany and Burgundy, or the Pyrenees and Provence. Within them, *pays* were often similarly identified on a combination of local physical and historical criteria. The 'regions' studied in these monographs varied considerably in size as well as in almost every other way. The nature of these accounts reflected not only the diverse histories and geographies of the regions themselves but also the differing histories and concerns of their authors. There is no single formula for researching and writing a 'regional' geography. Each has to be judged on its merits and in the light of its author's objectives and of her/his knowledge and understanding, insight and imagination. I am able here only to give a hint of the abundant harvest produced by historical geographers who have laboured in this particularly difficult field, synthesis being much more challenging than analysis.

Area studies in historical geography possess intrinsic interest and are justifiable on their own terms: they endeavour to satisfy the author's and the readers' historical and geographical curiosity about a particular place, however large or small. But local and regional studies may also be considered theoretically as contributing cumulatively to the production of historical geographies of countries, of continents and even of the world. If a regional synthesis is difficult, then how much more challenging it must be to produce a historical geography of a country. Despite the host of regional studies produced for France since the beginning of the twentieth century, it was not until almost the end of the century that the first comprehensive historical geography of France was published (Planhol 1988). True, two works bearing the title or sub-title 'géographie historique de la France' had been published earlier but they were both limited in their topical scope, focusing on the history of France's territorial divisions (Mirot and Mirot 1929; Fierro-Domenech 1986). There had also been published an edited collection of essays on the historical geography of France, but this treated selected themes and was explicitly not intended to be an overall view (moreover, most of the essays were written, and the book edited, by British historical geographers) (Clout 1977). Xavier de Planhol's book was a masterly synthesis of the huge mass of works produced by the French geographical school (as well as by cognate disciplines) over the past century. Published a few years later and written for a much wider audience, Trochet's *La géographie historique de la France* (1997) is much narrower in scope, focusing on the spatial organisation of France's economy, society and culture from the end of the Greco-Roman period to the middle of the nineteenth century. Most recently, and for a narrower student audience, Philippe Boulanger's *La France: espace et temps* (2002) is a practical guide to the historical geography of France, providing critical commentaries on sources and suggesting structured approaches to key questions.

Historical geographies of North America

A similar course can be detected in writings on the historical geography of North America, where one can point to an early and continuing flow of regional monographs with strong historical emphases but only a relatively recent cascade of syntheses of the historical geography of the United States, of Canada and of the North American continent as a whole. I need illustrate this point only briefly here because Robert Mitchell (1987), Conzen (1993), Wynn (1993) and Knowles (2001) collectively provide full and thoughtful surveys of geographical writing on the American and Canadian pasts. Regional studies have been a rich seam running right through the practice of the historical geography of North America. A cursory exploration soon reveals that it links Sauer's studies of the Ozark Highland of Missouri (1920) and of Spanish America, particularly Mexico (1941b, 1966), with Clark's studies of the South Island of New Zealand (1949), of Prince Edward Island, Canada (1959) and of Nova Scotia (1968), and with works by Meinig on the Great Columbia Plain (1968) and on the Southwest of the United States (1971). The number of excellent historical regional geographies by North Americans runs into hundreds. In addition, there have been some attempts to identify the historical significance of regional ways of life and of regionalism within North America. For example, J. Wreford Watson (1965) examined regionalism, the feeling of regional individuality, expressed in Canadian 'life and letters' alongside a growing sense of Canadian nationhood during the nineteenth and twentieth centuries, while Harris (1978b) discussed from a historico-geographical perspective the processes of regional differentiation and the problems of regional consciousness in North America as a whole. But syntheses at national or continental scales have been slow to appear.

Two early overviews of the historical geography of America were published simultaneously in 1903, but they both had a focused, analytical approach and can scarcely be considered to be syntheses. Brigham's *Geographic Influences in American History* and Semple's *American History and its Geographic Conditions* addressed a common question but differed in their searches for answers to it. Brigham's book, reflecting his own interests in geology and physiography, treated regions which he considered were more or less distinct physically and which also often showed what he termed 'a good measure of historical unity' (Brigham 1903: ix). For example, his book included chapters on the 'eastern gateway of the United States', on 'shoreline and hilltop in New England' and on 'prairie country'. But he also wrote of regions defined more by their staples, such as 'cotton, rice and cane' and 'mountain, mine and forest', and some of Brigham's chapters were more historical and systematic than regional, such as those on the geography of the Civil War and of American destiny. For her part, Semple sought to 'define the relationship between historical movements in the United States and the natural environment as the stage upon which history unfolds' (Semple 1903: v). She discussed such key themes as exploration, immigration, transportation and cities and included chapters on the War of 1812 and the Civil War and on the United States as a Pacific Ocean power. Both of these books were important pioneering ventures that stimulated much further research, but neither was a balanced synthesis.

Much closer to that objective was Brown's (1948) *Historical Geography of the United States*. Conforming to the orthodoxy of his time, Brown considered the aim of historical geography to be the reconstruction of the regional geographies of past periods. Its principal method was to be the detailed examination of documentary evidence, which he prioritised over field evidence. Brown argued that such reconstructions were at their best when they treated relatively limited areas and periods; consequently, 'the flow of history must frequently be stopped in order to inspect the relatively static conditions of geography' (cited in Coppens 1985: 17). Brown's own research focused on the Atlantic Seaboard of America and included his imaginative cross-section of the Eastern Seaboard in 1810 that relied not only for its information but also for its ideas and style exclusively on original sources from that period (Brown 1943). Brown's belief in regional geography underpinned his 1948 synthesis of the historical geography of the United States. An opening chapter on the period of colonisation was followed by five regionally based essays on 'the Atlantic Seaboard at the opening of the nineteenth century', 'the Ohio River and Lower Great Lakes region, to 1830', 'the new Northwest, 1820–1870', 'the Great Plains and bordering regions, to 1870', and 'from the Rocky Mountains to the Pacific Coast, to 1870'. Although uneven in both its areal and temporal coverage, Brown's was arguably the first modern synthesis of America's historical geography and remains the only single-authored, single-volume such study (Conzen 1993: 38 and 42). It has been supplemented but not entirely replaced by subsequent publications.

Regions of the United States, a set of essays authorised by the Association of American Geographers and edited by John Fraser Hart (1972) to be presented to an International Geographical Congress, was, in effect if not necessarily in intention, a multi-authored synthesis of America's historical regional geography. The essays provided historical perspectives on the development of the mosaic of American regions. A collection of readings on the historical geography of the United States, edited by David Ward (1979), brought together essays previously published separately. The essays, grouped into three sets under the headings 'The land and its people', 'The regional mosaic' and 'Urbanisation', were selected to demonstrate 'how a geographic perspective contributes to our appreciation of the American past'. Meinig has taken a great leap forward in that process in his multi-volume study of *The Shaping of America*, sub-titled 'a geographical perspective on 500 years of American history' since 1492. Three volumes have been published to date, covering the periods 1492–1800, 1800–1867 and 1850–1915, and a volume on the twentieth century is in preparation (Meinig 1986, 1993, 1998). This is a vast enterprise, covering the historical geography of a continent (although focused on the United States, the project also embraces Canada) over five centuries. While displaying close attention to detail, Meinig's approach is distinguished by his willingness to offer broad, provocative generalisations about the changing geographic character of a continent over five centuries. He is throughout concerned with the formation of regional societies and with the geopolitics of the emergence and consolidation of the United States as a nation. Only a mature and disciplined scholar at the height of his powers could produce such a massive, hugely ambitious work of synthesis. It is an astonishing undertaking which has been widely acclaimed by both historians and geographers. Of course, it also has its critics who point, for example, to Meinig's focus on place and pattern at the expense of people and process, and to his sweeping generalisations and broad-brush graphics (Fig. 5.1). But there can be no doubt that Meinig's study will stand as one the major achievements of American historical geography.

There is as yet no comparable study of Canada. Meinig's study embraces Canada from time to time, but its focused and sustained relationship is with the United States. For the continent as a whole, Robert Mitchell and Paul Groves (1987) edited *North America: the Historical Geography of a Changing Continent*. Arranged in four broad chronological periods extending from the 1490s to the twentieth century, the eighteen original essays provided a mix of topical and regional treatments. Inevitably lacking the coherence that a single author (such as Meinig) would have brought to such a work, this book none the less provided very effectively an accessible summation of the vast and burgeoning literature on the historical geography of North America. It remains the only single-volume treatment of the historical

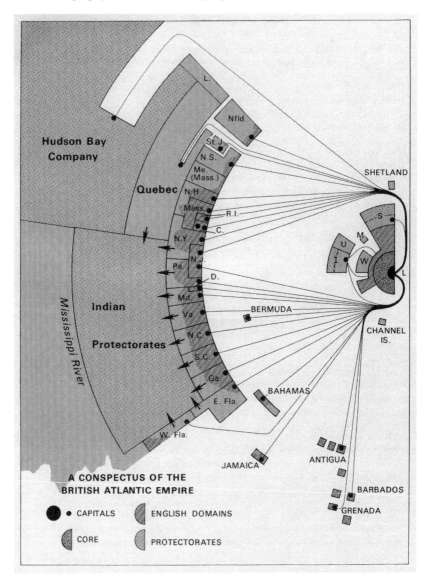

Figure 5.1 'A conspectus of the British Atlantic Empire'. The initials in the British Isles denote London, Scotland, Wales, Isle of Man, Ulster and Ireland
Source: reprinted from D. W. Meinig, *The Shaping of America: a Geographical Perspective on 500 Years of History, Vol. I: Atlantic America, 1492–1800.* Copyright (1986), with permission from Yale University Press

geography of the North American continent. A second, considerably revised edition has recently been published: many of the chapters from the first edition have been thoroughly updated and some new ones added, most significantly three which treat rural and urban change during the twentieth century. Within its fundamentally chronological and regional framework, this book self-confessedly displays a variety of approaches into past geographies (McIlwraith and Muller 2001). As for Canada alone, historical geography as a discipline there is not much more than one generation old; there were few trained historical geographers in Canada and little research in historical geography before the 1970s (Harris 1967). None the less, by 1974 Cole Harris and John Warkentin had jointly written a regionally structured historical geography of Canada before Confederation in 1867. This has served as a foundation for much later work. It remains the only such study, although it has been usefully supplemented by an edited collection of seventeen previously published articles providing outstanding examples of some geographical perspectives on the Canadian past (Wynn 1990).

If there persists a dearth of textual syntheses of the historical geography of Canada and even, notwithstanding Meinig, of the United States, the same cannot be said of England and Wales.

Historical geographies of England and Wales

The first book-length treatment of the historical geography of England and Wales was published in 1925. Elsé Carrier's *Historical Geography of England and Wales (South Britain)* opened by claiming: 'Historical Geography may be regarded as the Study of the Regional Environment of Human Societies, which latter, in actual fact, had already reached a noteworthy degree of development thousands of years before the beginnings of written History.' Notwithstanding this regional emphasis, Carrier's book had a first-order structure which was chronological and a second-order which was systematic. This was a semi-popular narrative of the making of the land of southern Britain, of the geographical changes which it had experienced from the prehistoric period to the 'present' day. It addressed some of the themes which were to become the staple fare of historical geographies of England and Wales. For example, its early chapters provided an account of the colonisation and settlement of territories by 'waves of invaders' and they emphasised the contributions of each invading group to the peopling of southern Britain, to its place-names, settlement forms and politico-administrative organisation. Later chapters included some tracing the progressive 'mastery' of the physical environment during the Middle Ages, in, for example, 'The battle of land and sea: disappearance of forest and fen'. Others dealt with the later 'revolutions' in transport and industry, in village life and in town growth. Although not a work of great scholarship, Carrier's book has not been accorded the recognition it deserves as a pioneering work of synthesis which identified some key strands in the historical geography of England and Wales (Baker 1999b). Her work soon came to be overshadowed by a more

scholarly enterprise, a collection of fourteen essays on the historical geography
of England edited by H. C. Darby (1936), published more than half a century before a comparable volume appeared on the historical geography of North America
(Mitchell and Groves 1987).

Darby's (1936) *An Historical Geography of England before AD 1800* was
'concerned with the reconstruction of past geographies' and aimed 'to provide
a sequence of cross-sections taken at successive periods in the development' of
England (although Wales did not come within the scope of the book, the editor and
authors explicitly referred to it where it seemed 'desirable' to do so). Darby claimed
in his editorial preface that no 'substantial' historical geography of England had
yet appeared and that his book was, therefore, 'in a sense, experimental'. Notwithstanding its uneven coverage and the fact that many of the essays were narratives
of changing geographies rather than reconstructions of past geographies, Darby's
volume soon became acknowledged as a benchmark publication. Darby himself
led, and also encouraged others to undertake, both major geographical explorations
of historical sources and serious quests for solutions to what he termed the 'problem of geographical description'. These concerted endeavours ultimately led to the
publication in 1973 of *A New Historical Geography of England*, an edited volume
of twelve essays, each individually tied to a cluster of sources and collectively
organised to combine sequentially 'horizontal' and 'vertical' approaches, with reconstructions of past geographies separated by studies of geographical changes
through time, covering the period from the Anglo-Saxon settlement to *c.* 1900
(Darby 1973). That volume was more coherent and based upon more original research than was its predecessor, and it stands as a remarkable achievement. But in
contemplating the result, Darby could 'only be very conscious of what remain[ed]
to be done', both on relatively neglected historical sources and in the application
of statistical techniques and concepts of locational analysis. In his editorial preface, Darby acknowledged that 'in another generation or so the materials for an
historical geography of England will not be as we know them now. A wider range
of sources will have been explored and evaluated. Fresh ideas will have prepared
the way for a more sophisticated presentation' (Darby 1973: viii).

In fact, the accelerating pace and growing volume of research in historical geography during the 1960s and 1970s meant that it was not another generation but only
five years before the next synthesis of the historical geography of England (and
Wales) was published. Robert Dodgshon and Robin Butlin's *An Historical Geography of England and Wales* (1978) both reflected a dissatisfaction with an approach
which emphasised past geographical patterns to the relative neglect of the historical
processes which underpinned them and capitalised upon the ideas and researches
of a new generation of practitioners, many of whom contributed to that volume of
fourteen essays. Their book placed an emphasis on interpretation, on the periods
after 1500, and on a systematic, topical (rather than a primarily chronological)
organisational framework. Its objective was to provide an up-to-date, stimulating,
interpretative portrayal of the historical geography of England and Wales from the
prehistoric period to 1900 as a counterpoint to the more descriptive, more tightly

organised and (despite the editorial disclaimer) seemingly authoritative account to be found in Darby's volume. Dodgshon and Butlin's more ambitious objective inevitably carried within itself the seeds of its own transformation; in recognising explicitly the relative rather than absolute, interpretative rather than authoritative, nature of research and writing in historical geography, they were not only permitting but also promoting the need for a new edition of their book. In fact, they published a second edition in 1990, separated from the first by only twelve years, whereas the two edited by Darby were separated by thirty-seven years (or by thirty-one years if one discounts the interruption of the Second World War). Dodgshon and Butlin's second edition incorporated not only the substantial amount of work published since 1978 but also, and more significantly, the changing character of historical geography itself: it thus deliberately reflected a dramatic broadening of themes, a widening of methodologies, an expanding variety of sources and a greater ideological awareness. This was a fully revised and substantially enlarged edition, an impressive fruit of the vigorous growth of British historical geography since the mid-1970s.

Alongside the five volumes on the historical geography of England (and Wales) so far considered, there stands one other which has made a distinctive, if less influential, contribution. Michael Dunford and Diane Perrons' *The Arena of Capital* (1983) provided, from a Marxist perspective, an account of the geographically uneven transition from feudalism to capitalism in Britain from the early medieval period to 1945. Drawing upon a materialist conception of geography, Dunford and Perrons offered an analysis of the connections between modes of production and spatial development, which, they argued, produced over the long term a regionally differentiated space-economy. In their insistence upon the sustained use of an explicit, theoretically informed framework and their adoption of a Marxist perspective, Dunford and Perrons were distanced from most work in historical geography and their contribution has not received much attention – there is, for example, only one reference to it in the second edition of Dodgshon and Butlin (1990: 126). It constituted, none the less, a carefully argued but clearly different interpretation of Britain's historical geography from that to be found in the 'standard' textbooks, for its authors sought to connect the literature on historical geography with wider conceptions of social change. Another distinctive approach to the historical geography of England is being taken in a set of essays focused on both the material and the imagined geographies of the North–South divide in England from the present day retrogressively to the eleventh century (Baker and Billinge, forthcoming).

Historical geographies of Europe

The first books claiming to portray the historical geography of Europe were written by historians, before historical geography had become established in the universities as a sub-field within geography. E. A. Freeman, Professor of Modern History at Oxford, published his book *The Historical Geography of Europe* in 1881. In his first chapter, under the heading of 'Definition of historical geography', Freeman stated the aim of his book as being 'to trace out the extent of the territory which the different states and nations of Europe and the neighbouring lands have held at different times in the world's history, to mark the different boundaries which the same country has had, and the different meanings in which the same has been used' (Freeman 1881: 1). Similar concerns were addressed in 1929 by another historian, J. M. Thompson, in his *An Historical Geography of Europe, 800–1789*. It was not until the 1930s that such studies incorporated broader geographical perspectives, being written by geographers and reflecting new thinking about the nature of historical geography. Thus W. G. East's *An Historical Geography of Europe* (1935) was a sweeping geographical synthesis not only of political and territorial history but also of economic and social change. So too was N. J. G. Pounds' *An Historical and Political Geography of Europe* (1947). These two works still relied heavily on work by historians even though they adopted a broader geographical perspective than had been evident in their predecessors. With more original work on the historical geography of Europe being undertaken by geographers themselves and with new ideas in contemporary human geography (such as those relating to locational analysis and spatial diffusion) impacting upon historical geographers, it became possible for a different, more spatially analytical emphasis to be provided by Smith in his *An Historical Geography of Western Europe before 1800* (1967). Less conceptual but displaying an astonishing grasp of a wide range of historical and geographical literatures in many European languages were the two volumes on the historical geography of Europe between 1500 and 1914 by Pounds (1979, 1985). Few individuals can be expected today to have the knowledge and understanding required to write single-handedly a book-length account of the historical geography of so vast and complex an area as 'Europe'. The challenge of writing such a synthesis is enormous and I hope that someone in each future generation will continue to rise to it. Failing that, however, a good compromise is provided by edited collections of essays, such as Butlin and Dodgshon's (1998) *An Historical Geography of Europe*. These essays, by sixteen scholars whose combined expertise embraces not only geography but also archaeology and history, collectively span the period from the prehistoric to the present. For the most part, each individual essay has a topical, systematic focus (for example, on towns and trade, or on rural issues). Like all such edited collections, the treatment is uneven, but Butlin and Dodgshon's enterprise does provide an informed review of thinking on the major themes of Europe's historical geography. Understandably and probably pragmatically, it leaves to one side the problem of defining 'Europe' – the boundary problem faced by all regional geographers.

Boundary problems in historical regional geography

Delimiting a study in historical geography both in time and in space is often difficult and sometimes arbitrary. Attempts are made to solve the first part of the problem either by bounding a study with specific dates that are considered to be significant or by general temporal periods, such as decades or centuries or periods which are claimed to have distinguishing characteristics. Such solutions are more or less satisfactory, accepted as being pragmatic compromises which are necessary if any study is to be conducted. There are, of course, disputes about the dates and periods selected but not about the need to put some kind of temporal boundary around a historical study. Pragmatically, there have to be limits. The spatial boundary problem is at least as difficult and sometimes more so. The historical 'region' or 'area' being studied often did not have boundaries which were clearly defined at the time being studied; and such boundaries as were defined were often not static but themselves changed through time. Attempts to identify regions in the past with precision are thus fraught with difficulties, with both historical actors and modern observers holding different views and defining the 'same' area or region differently according to the varied criteria being employed. This was well portrayed in K. A. Sinnhuber's (1954) study of the concept of 'central Europe' and in Lewis' (1966) study of regional ideas and what he terms 'reality' in the Cis-Rocky Mountain West in North America. Heffernan (1998) also demonstrated the problem more broadly in his study of 'the meaning of Europe'. As a consequence of all these difficulties, pragmatic solutions are often provided to the spatial boundary problem as well as to the temporal boundary problem in historical geography.

A common solution has been to study the historical geography of a modern 'nation' or country, such as France, the United States of America, Canada or England, as already noted. There have been many other excellent historical geographies in this genre, such as those of Russia (Parker 1968), Australia (Powell 1988) and South Africa (Lester 1996). National geographies are integral to national histories. Claval (1994) has emphasised how descriptions of the distinctive *regional* geography of France by Vidal de la Blache and others contributed to the construction of a specific *national* French identity, and historical geographies of other nations have often followed a similar course. Meinig presents the fundamental rationale for this approach:

National geography, like national history, must be a staple product of professional work. Nation-states have become the most powerful agents in the division and administration of earth-space. They serve as the primary territorial frameworks in such profound and pervasive ways that it seems logical and appropriate that geography – 'earth description' – order much of its works within such frameworks (a logic powerfully reinforced by data collection, funding, public policies, and much else). Furthermore, geography, like history, provides a knowledge and shared understanding important in the basic civic education of a citizenry. It is fundamental to a sense of who and where a people are with reference to a larger world. For these obvious (and other) reasons, the nation-state will long continue to be the most important unit for many kinds of human geography. (Meinig 1999a: 80)

Meinig rightly emphasises the many opportunities which national historical geographies provide. They enable historical and contemporary human geography to become more effectively bound together; they contribute to the formation of an informed citizenry, developing and conveying a clear view of the changing human geography of a country and of its relevance to a general understanding of that country's history. But at the same time, and perhaps more importantly, Meinig wisely cautions us about what national historical geographies should not be. First, 'national' must not mean exclusion of all that lies beyond the national boundaries – each 'nation' must be set within its larger context, as part of a world system of interdependent nations. Secondly, 'national' must not mean nationalistic – it must treat all areas of the nation and all inhabitants of the country: 'As we trace the changing human geography of area after area, we must account for the people who get eliminated or subordinated as well as those who advance and dominate.' Thirdly, 'national' must not exclude other scales and types of loyalties and asso- ciations – we need to be alert to various kinds of group identities that may not be congruent with the national territory, such as identities based upon ethnicity or re- ligion or indeed upon sub-national territories (Meinig 1999a: 84–8). On this point, I would also add identities based upon class or gender and also upon supranational territories. Intriguingly, Meinig's cautionary tale is published in a *Festschrift* for a distinguished Israeli historical geographer, Yehoshua Ben-Arieh, who has been the driving force behind the development of historical geography in Israel. Like many other national 'schools' of historical geographers, the Israelis have focused their research and publications mainly on their own country, where the question of national identity is much debated and contested (Kark 1989; Ben-Artzi et al. 1999). There can be little doubt that the work of Israeli historical geographers is intended as, and is comprehended as, a contribution to the making of Israel's na- tional identity. Meinig's cautionary note was not a narrow one, however, because the other example of a national historical geography which he cites is that of the *Historical Atlas of Canada,* an explicitly national project, described by Harris in his preface to the first of three volumes as a 'public project, an opportunity . . . for Canadian scholarship to report to the Canadian people about the nature of Canada' (Harris 1987; Kerr and Holdsworth 1990; Gentilcore 1993).

A logical progression from national historical geographies would be to historical geographies of colonies and empires, although the change in scale and complexity involved in such a step is no doubt one reason why relatively few such studies have been essayed. Additionally, the spatial boundary problem confronted by such stud- ies is more complex because the 'area' being treated comprises non-contiguous units as well, of course, as continually changing itself as an entity as new colonies are gained and old ones lost. Interest in the historical geography of colonialism was, unsurprisingly, at a peak during the late nineteenth and early twentieth century when colonialism itself was a powerful economic force and political issue. There has also been a renewed interest during the late twentieth and early twenty-first century in the historical geography of colonies and empires, but for very different reasons. Between 1887 and 1924, Sir Charles Lucas edited a multi-volume series under two general titles, *A Historical Geography of the British Colonies* and *A*

Historical Geography of the British Dominions, the title varying from volume to volume according to the areas being treated. Historical events necessitated frequent revisions of some of the volumes. Together they provided a panorama of the historical geography of the Mediterranean and Eastern Colonies, the West Indian Colonies, West Africa, South and East Africa, Canada, Australasia and India. Written by different authors, these volumes did not present standardised treatments. But taken together they were colonial histories which took cognisance of the specific geographical sites and situations of the colonies. They were histories in their geographical settings. This view of historical geography as being 'the geography behind history' also underpinned *A Historical Geography of the British Empire* by H. B. George, first published in 1904 and subsequently as revised editions, the seventh of which appeared in 1924. Much more adventurous was the work of Harold Innis who, as a geographically informed economic historian, explored the connections between empire and communications in Canada specifically but also in the Western world generally. Innis was concerned with the development and extension of the institutional control of space and time and with its role in asymmetric, centre–margin patterns of knowledge, power and wealth (Innis 1923, 1950, 1951; Parker 1993).

In the closing decades of the twentieth century and opening years of the twenty-first century, a very different emphasis is discernible in historical geographies of imperialism written under the influence of postcolonial perspectives in literary and cultural studies. Now the concern is more with the cultural transactions between Europeans and the peoples they colonised and with the ways in which Europeans (mis)represented and (mis)understood those peoples. There is currently a very productive focus by historical geographers upon this colonial or imperial discourse (Lester 2000). Some interrogate directly the connections between geography and imperialism (for example, Hudson 1977; Godlewska and Smith 1994; Driver 1992b; Bell et al. 1995). Others examine the colonial experiences of European travellers, explorers, missionaries, settlers and officials, and their representations of colonial peoples, environments, landscapes and regions (for example, Blunt 1994; Blunt and Rose 1994; Gregory 1995). An especially distinctive contribution is Ploszajska's (2000) analysis of both verbal and visual representations of colonial peoples and landscapes in geography textbooks used in London schools between 1870 and 1944. Recent historical geographies of colonialism are certainly enriching, but Yeoh (2000) argues that such studies overshadow historical geographies of the colonised world. She argues persuasively for fewer Eurocentric studies of colonialism and for more studies of what she calls 'the politics of space' in the colonised world where people resisted, responded to and were affected by colonisation – in effect, for more historical geographies of colonialism from the perspectives of those who were colonised.

An institution such as an empire clearly constitutes one very specific optic through which to examine the interconnected historical geographies of non-contiguous areas. Thus A. J. Christopher (1988) has provided an overview of the geography of the British Empire at its zenith. Many studies in historical geography could be envisaged of what Wayne Moodie (1976) termed 'the geographical impress' of an institution or organisation. Moodie was concerned with the macro-historical geographies of the great chartered companies, in his case specifically the Hudson's Bay Company (Moodie and Lehr 1981). Cecil Houston and William Smyth (1980, 1984, 1985) have produced an excellent series of studies in this mould on the historical geography of the Orange Order in Canada and the United States. There remains a rich vein here awaiting further exploitation: historical geographies of institutions and organisations, especially of trans-national companies and associations. This is an unusual solution to the boundary problem in historical geography but one which merits more application. It echoes the new view, previously noted, of regions as a series of discontinuous spaces connected by social relations (Allen et al. 1998).

More traditional solutions have been provided by studies of groups of countries bound together by their geographical proximity and/or by the cultural and historical affinity. I am thinking here of studies like those of W. M. Ramsay (1890) on the historical geography of Asia Minor, but especially of more recent examples, such as Mead's (1981) on Scandinavia and Catherine Delano-Smith's (1979) on the 'western Mediterranean world' of Italy, Spain and southern France.

Many historical geographies use cultural or political units as the areal context for their study. But there have been radically different solutions, using 'natural' or physical units, notably river drainage basins and sea and ocean basins. Smith (1969) noted that the idea of the drainage basin as a suitable framework for geographical study has roots going back into at least the eighteenth century. Unlike cultural regions and areas, the drainage basin was considered to have a well-defined boundary, its watershed. Moreover, water provided a link between the earth and people's activities. Rivers provided water supplies for people and their crops and livestock; fish and game; a means of transportation; and a source of power. In addition drainage basins provide systematically arranged patterns of resources (such as soils and vegetation).

For all of these reasons, the river basin was viewed as a significant organising principle in the French school of regional geography. Brunhes (1920), for example, in his study of the human geography of France, based his major divisions of the country on the drainage basins of the Garonne, Loire, Seine and Rhône-Saône and their major towns. Some French regional monographs were based on parts of basins: for example, those on the middle Garonne (Deffontaines 1925), on the middle Rhône (Faucher 1927), on the lower Rhône (George 1935) and on the middle Durance (Veyret 1944). And one of the very best of the French monographs, that by Dion (1934a), took the Loire Valley as its study area. But the concept of the drainage basin as the historical basis for human activity has also been applied outside France. Broek's (1932) study of the Santa Clara Valley in California was to become significant methodologically because of its interweaving of 'horizontal' cross-sections with 'vertical' narratives of change, but it is also noteworthy for having used the drainage basin as the unit of study. Somewhat differently and more speculatively, Clark (1975b) offered some observations on the role of what he called the 'Empires' of the St Lawrence and the Mississippi drainage basins in the historical geography of North America. For England, historian Charles Phythian-Adams (1991) has argued for the fundamental importance of drainage basins in the social organisation of territory and community, at least until the 'age of urbanisation' and the Industrial Revolution of the modern period. He was here building on work by fellow-historian Alan Everitt (1985) and historical geographer Harold Fox (1989) on the roles of rivers, wolds and *pays* in pre-industrial English local history.

Going beyond individual drainage basins, it would be logical to expect there also to be studies in historical geography which employ sea and ocean basins as their organising frameworks. Only a few such studies exist. Among them are Darby's brief – but typically pioneering – essays on the medieval sea state and on the two European worlds at the end of the Middle Ages, one focused on the Mediterranean and the other on the Baltic and North Seas (Darby 1932, 1957). Much more substantial were O. H. K. Spate's (1979, 1983) two volumes on the Pacific since Magellan. Meinig's (1989b) 'geographical transect of the Atlantic world, *c.* 1750' produced a broad perspective on the commercial, political and social systems which embraced and connected America and Europe in the mid-eighteenth century. He offered his trans-oceanic systems framework as a geographical perspective upon history which emphasised connectivity, arguing that the standard conceptual frameworks (such as those of homeland and colonies, metropolis and frontier, centre and periphery) were inadequate and 'loaded with meaning, carrying as they do implications of old and new, dominance and subordinance, innovation and diffusion'. But historians have made more use than have geographers of sea and ocean basins as frameworks for historical analysis. There is, for example, not only the classic study by Braudel (1949) of the Mediterranean and the Mediterranean world in the sixteenth century, but also the emergent field of 'Atlantic history' which focuses on the complex flows of people, commodities, ideas and capital across that ocean (Bailyn 1996). Jerry Bentley (1999), reviewing the use of sea and ocean basins as frameworks for historical analysis, argues that they are especially useful for bringing focus to the trans-national processes of commercial, biological and cultural exchange which have profoundly influenced the development of both individual societies and the world as a whole. Such studies are not simply a different way of constructing regions: they are becoming central to the writing of post-colonial history.

A similar general point could be made about studies on a world scale. There are few studies by historical geographers offering perspectives on world history (Bigelow 1989). I can point to some studies in systematic historical geography conducted at a global scale, such as David Grigg's (1974) of the agricultural systems of the world, Hugill's (1993) of world trade since 1431 and Langton's (1996) much briefer account of the origins of the capitalist world economy. Perhaps the most ambitious shot at a world historical geography was Jim Blaut's (1992) *1492: the Debate on Colonialism, Eurocentrism and History*. Blaut argued that the 'West' did not rise before its ability to harness bullion and the resources and labour of the 'New World'. He challenged the ideas of Eurocentred historians, ascribing no intrinsic value or advantage to Western culture. Blaut (1993) mounted a strong challenge to the widely held belief that 'European civilisation – "The West"– has had some unique historical advantage, some special quality of race or culture or environment or mind or spirit, which gives this human community a permanent superiority over all other communities, at all times in history and down to the present'. Blaut aimed to refute the theory of a Eurocentric diffusion, of Europe as the source of most cultural diffusions to the non-European world. He questions the idea of 'the European Miracle', the notion that Europe was more advanced and more progressive than all other regions prior to 1492, prior, that is, to the beginning of the period of colonialism, the period in which Europe and non-Europe came into intense interaction. While offering a powerful critique of diffusionism, Blaut had no over-arching alternative interpretation of the historical geography of the world since 1492: he offered not a conclusion but merely 'an introduction' to the problem. Agnew's (1998b) *Geopolitics: Re-visioning World Politics* also paints a 'broad-brush, big picture' of the geopolitical ideas and impacts of European states, and states of European origin, since the mid-seventeenth century. He argues that major geopolitical changes reflected redefinitions of the authority of the state as being vested successively in monarchs, in territory and in the people.

Constructing a historical geography of the world remains a major challenge. To date, it has been met only partially in *historical atlases*, to which I will turn in due course. Also, having considered a range of regional and areal historical geographies, I will need shortly to turn the coin over and to consider the closely related topic of *regional and areal histories*. I want for the moment to remain with historical geographers and to consider the ways in which they have addressed the question of *regional transformation*.

Regional transformation

I have already considered (in chapter 2) the ways in which spatial diffusion theory can illuminate our understanding of regional change: both contagious and hierarchical diffusion processes transform areas, bringing about areal differentiation in some circumstances and a greater uniformity among areas in other circumstances. Although those processes cannot always be plotted on maps and graphs with great precision, the concept of diffusion can often provide a useful framework within which to interpret geographical change at a variety of scales from the local to the global. I have also already noted (in chapter 4) the geographical concept of sequent occupance. What other specifically geographical concepts, or at least concepts put forward by historical geographers, might aid historical understanding of regions? I focus here not on the problem of geographical description, of how to write historical geography, but on aspects of the more fundamental question of how to prosecute it and specifically how to conceptualise and investigate regional change.

Does a region have potential as a laboratory within which to study change? This would be to study regions not for their own sake but as a means of testing, and also developing, general ideas and theories about cultural and environmental change. The past has sometimes been viewed as such a laboratory, so why not also the region? If both a (historical) period and a (geographical) region can be used as laboratories, then does not historical geography, concerned with both period and place, offer even greater possibilities for improving our knowledge and understanding of cultural and environmental change? It is tempting to think so. Clark, a very distinguished North American historical geographer, initially fell to that temptation. As a graduate student of Sauer, Clark was clearly very impressed by his mentor's willingness to proffer broad generalisations on, for example, the morphology of landscape, cultural geography, the origins of agriculture and the relation of people to nature. Clark's doctoral research examined what he called 'the invasion of New Zealand by people, plants and animals' (Meinig 1978b). Although in practice the book which Clark (1949) wrote on this theme was restricted to the South Island of New Zealand, it was conceived explicitly as part of a grand project. It was, claimed Clark, intended to be the first in a series of studies 'dealing with similar problems of the development of patterns and practices of land use in mid-latitude areas overseas which were settled by folk from the shores of the North Sea'. He planned to include in his project studies of Southern Africa and of North America. These regions were to be used, in effect, as laboratories in which to test and develop some generalisations about such European colonisation (Clark 1949: iv). In practice, Clark was to lose that general perspective and to focus instead on much more specific studies of Prince Edward Island (1959) and Nova Scotia (1968). He became increasingly immersed in the historical geographies of particular places and played down the significance of the search for broad generalisations, models and theories. He developed instead into a forceful advocate of historical regional geographies, of empirical studies of regional change, having modified his earlier view for both epistemological and practical reasons: he gave primacy to making sense of a region's geography and to recognising that an individual geographer can hope to obtain mastery of information and interpretation for only limited parts of the world and for limited periods of time (Clark 1972). Intriguingly, Harris, a pupil of Clark, for a while took up the challenge which his mentor had abandoned. Harris (1977) essayed what he explicitly called a 'model' of 'the simplification of Europe overseas', doing so by examining colonisation by Europeans in early Canada, South Africa and New England. He argued that regional differences in the settlers' collective background were lost in a process of simplification and generalisation. It might be fairer to Harris to call his study an exercise in comparative historical regional geography than a rigorous use of regions as laboratories: his generalisations were specific to the periods and places studied and his 'model' has not seen wide application elsewhere. Geography, like history, does not provide isolated, closed laboratories. No matter how precisely a study in historical geography is bounded in time and in space, the region being studied was caught up in processes which originated in other periods and places. No region can be explained exclusively in its own terms: change is generated both exogenously and endogenously. Every region must be situated within its appropriate historical and geographical context in the fullest of senses. It has to be recognised, as it came to be by Clark, that regional closure is a pragmatic and to some extent arbitrary necessity, while acknowledging also that for full understanding regional studies must be contextualised to the greatest possible degree.

Regions, then, cannot be viewed as spatially isolated laboratories: each region has connections to other places, periods and peoples. Additionally, no region is static, all regions are dynamic. This latter characteristic was the central point of the concept of 'geographical change' which Clark (1960) set out as a theme for economic historians and as an axiom for historical geographers. Clark was convinced that there had been too few studies of geographies 'as continually changing entities' and that there should be 'more emphasis on the geographical structure of change; on the changing patterns of phenomena and relationships in and through area'. Of particular interest to Clark was 'the focus on the locational aspects of change itself, and of rate of change, in the distribution of individual significant phenomena, of multiple functions of phenomena, or of important interactive processes' (Clark 1960: 611–12). Clark's concept was applied with increasing conviction in his own three meticulously detailed regional studies. As Meinig has pointed out, Clark's 'main concern was "area" and his main geographic method was to map populations, productions, and various elements in order to make a "fine-grained analysis" of areal patterns and changes in those patterns' (Meinig 1978b: 13). Many of Clark's graduate students undertook and published historical regional geographies, although often adopting a systematic perspective within a limited regional context (Conzen 1993: 60), in a manner somewhat reminiscent of the later generation of French regional monographs. While Clark's concept of regional geographical change provided a general framework, the approaches adopted by authors for particular regions reflected both their own individual interests and the specificities of their chosen regions. James T. Lemon (1972) wrote one of the best such monographs: his study of south-eastern colonial Pennsylvania was a magnificently researched and written historical regional geography which simultaneously challenged the orthodox views of historians about the origins of liberal republicanism in America.

The Clarkian concept of geographical change has certainly been influential. Meinig has significantly extended the notion. He has written some powerful historical regional geographies of the great Columbia Plain (1968), of Texas (1969) and of the south-west of the United States (1971). Drawing from the deep well of that very considerable experience, Meinig (1978a) offered a refreshing and ambitious prospectus for both geographers and historians on 'the continuous shaping of America'. In a lecture to the American Historical Association in 1976, Meinig noted the want of 'a coherent conceptual framework for the overall historical geography of the United States' and set out to meet that need. He did so mainly within the locational and regional discourses of geography, rather than those of environment or landscape. His prospectus was based on two fundamental questions: (1) why do major cultural patterns and movements begin where they do (the problem of the 'cultural hearth')? and (2) how do they spread to other peoples and areas (a problem of 'spatial diffusion')? What Meinig sketched in his paper was:

a view of America as a gigantic 'geographic growth' – not as a quasi-natural phenomenon but simply as a cultural historical fact, as a continuously expansive pattern that can be traced on the surface of the globe from its tiny, variegated beginnings as tenuous transoceanic outposts of various European agencies to its solid transcontinental and oceanic national presence and multifarious penetrations of many other parts of the earth. It is a view that is at once fundamentally historical and geographical. It is a view of America as an ever-changing place, an ever-changing congeries of places, an ever-changing structure of places, and an ever-changing system of places. Those several points of view are held together by regarding places as the creations of particular peoples working over a period of time in particular locations and physical environments that are thereby stamped with a distinctive landscape and social character and organised as segments of spatial systems, all of which can be examined consistently at scales ranging from the local to the global. (Meinig 1978a: 1202)

Meinig's was an approach which viewed regions as abstractions, as complex, ambiguous and changing phenomena, and for that reason he argued that it was more properly labelled geographical than regional (he reserved the latter term to a spatial scale of generalisation). Meinig's objective was to see America as a historical phenomenon in geographical terms. His prospectus is being implemented in his study of *The Shaping of America: a Geographical Perspective on 500 Years of History* (Meinig 1986, 1993, 1998). Although self-admittedly pursuing a limited form of historical geography, Meinig has amply demonstrated an approach which others with his courage and energy could apply to other countries and continents. This is 'big-picture' historical 'regional' geography (Conzen 1993: 77–82). But remarkably few individual historical geographers have had the nerve – or the ambition – to offer long-term analyses of change over large areas of the earth's surface. Among the exceptions are Earle (1992), who offered some brief reflections on periods of American growth over almost four centuries using Kondratieff longwave cycles, and Hugill (1993), who examined the global spread of Western technology and its links to capitalism during the past five hundred years, again drawing upon the concept of longwaves and their relationship to technical innovation.

A very different, much more theoretical, 'big-picture' historical systematic geography is provided by Dodgshon (1998) in his wide-ranging exploration of 'a geographical perspective on change'. Paradoxically, however, Dodgshon focuses on the importance of geographical *inertia* as an integral component of societal *change*. After reviewing critically theories of social change and considering how effectively they address change as not only a temporal but also a spatial process, Dodgshon examines the experience of change at a variety of geographical scales, from world systems and empires to nation-states and regions. He emphasises not how easy change is but how problematic it may be. Although Dodgshon is impressed by how some empires, states and regions maintained their positions as centres of power, wealth and innovation for lengthy periods, his general conclusion is that advantage is never sustained. Moreover, he argues that radical change can be shown frequently to have erupted around the edges of established systems at all scales, from world systems down to recent industrial complexes. Thus he argues that change has an intrinsically geographical dimension, one that redraws advantage and disadvantage between core and periphery in a periodic fashion. He suggests that the way in which a society organises itself in space forms a powerful source of inertia for societal systems, one that ultimately retards or deflects change. Dodgshon examines carefully three different types of inertia: the cultural and symbolic construction of landscape; institutional or organisational sources of inertia; and the built environment as a source of inertia. He views inertia 'not as a dysfunction of society, as if it were something left as an abandoned and anachronistic relic of the past, but as a functioning and necessary part of societal systems and how they are constituted' (Dodgshon 1998: 163). Dodgshon's complex argument cannot be treated both justly and briefly, but its essence may be detected in one selection from his work, where he states:

Logically, change has a greater likelihood in those areas where there are greater resources of 'unused freedom', that is, greater resources of flexibility or plasticity about how available choice over the use of resources might be expended. Whereas areas held firm by the stasis of inertia have an experience or history of change that is necessarily convergent, reinforcing consecutiveness, areas which have greater reserves of 'unused freedom' are, by contrast, those which combine a greater capacity for divergence, novelty and macroscopic diversity, with the flexibility that could feed runaway growth. Seen in this way, the geography of flexibility and inflexibility provides us with the foundation for a geographically informed concept of change, a structural reason for supposing that change may be more likely in some areas than on others through the way inertia maps constraint and, as a consequence, creates a geography of relative opportunity. (Dodgshon 1998: 180)

Dodgshon's theoretical argument is grounded in substantial empirical studies and he would readily admit, I am sure, that what matters for most historians and geographers is how general ideas about geographical change and inertia can be used to enhance our understanding of specific historical geographies.

Similar in its objective, and sometimes in its argument, has been Harvey's grand project to reconstruct the historical geography of capitalism and its regional transformations, and to promote historical-geographical materialism as an open-ended and dialectical mode of enquiry rather than a closed and fixed body of understandings (Harvey 1989). There have been a number of examinations of the processes of uneven regional development within the historical geography of capitalism (for example, Smith 1984, 1986; Soja 1985; Dunford 1998) but Harvey's has been the most sustained. Harvey argued that the recurrent crises of capitalism happen because investments in the built environment are irrecoverable. Harvey argues that capital, while it needs to be mobile, cannot recover that part of itself that is sunk into fixed capital. A compromise is the reworking of built environments as a process of creative destruction. Harvey's (1985) reworking of the literature on the reconstruction and construction of Paris during the 1850s and 1860s provided an excellent example of his general ideas. An often related consequence is for capital to be diverted into new areas (at any geographical scale), to seek greater returns elsewhere, a process referred to by Harvey (1981) as a 'spatial fix'.

The rise of modern capitalism had significant regional expression and was itself a regional process. Soja (1989: 157–89) has generalised the historical geography of urban and regional restructuring, while significant, specific studies of urban economic and social restructuring as part of the march of capitalism are those on North American cities by Richard Harris (1993, 1994), Robert Lewis (1994, 2000), both separately and jointly (Harris and Lewis 1998), and also by Lemon (1996). There have been some excellent studies by historical geographers which demonstrate the interplay of the micro-, meso- and macro-poitical economies of regional restructuring. Such would be Gregory's (1982b) study of regional transformation during the Industrial Revolution in woollen-manufacturing west Yorkshire and Langton's (1979) of coal mining in Lancashire. There has also been a lively debate among historical geographers about the extent to which regional identities were strengthened or weakened in England during the Industrial Revolution (Freeman 1984; Langton 1984, 1988b; Gregory 1988, 1990a; Butlin 1990). In addition, there have also been some perceptive studies of the ways in which geographical change has been structured inter-regionally by urban systems. I am thinking here of Pred's (1966, 1973) examination of the spatial dynamics of urban-industrial growth and of the circulation of information in the system of cities in America during the nineteenth century, and also of Robson's (1973) book on the connections between urban growth and broader geographical changes in England during the same period. Pred (1984, 1990) has also presented the theoretical foundation for a different type of place-centred or regional geography. He proposed an integration of time geography and of structuration theory in order to conceptualise place (or region) as 'a constantly becoming human product as well as a set of features visible upon the landscape'. He envisaged place as 'a process whereby the reproduction of social and cultural forms, the formation of biographies, and the transformation of nature ceaselessly become one another at the same time that time-specific activities and power relations continuously become one another'. He further contended that the ways in which these phenomena are interwoven in the becoming of place or region are not subject to universal laws but vary with historical circumstances. Pred (1986) applied his ideas in a study of social and spatial transformation in southern Sweden between 1750 and 1850. The rich documentary sources of Sweden permitted the amazingly detailed application of Pred's approach, as they did also in Hoppe and Langton's (1994) study of the transformation from peasantry to capitalism in western Östergötland in the nineteenth century.

Changing regional geographies and the problems of regional transformation have, then, engaged the attentions of many historical geographers. So, too, have they of historians and I want now to consider some of their approaches to this major bridge between their two perspectives.

Regional and area histories

Geographies take time, histories take place. Although perhaps principally concerned with period and process, a historian has also to confront the problem of place. Historians do, of course, identify themselves and their subject in varied ways. One method focuses on the time period being studied: thus we encounter, for example, ancient, medieval and modern historians. Another is based on the topic being examined: thus we have, for example, political, economic and social historians. Yet another approach endeavours to fuse these two, emphasising the cultural character of a period: thus there are, for example, European Renaissance historians and French Revolution historians. In these two last examples, specific places have also crept into view. But the explosion of historical studies during the second half of the twentieth century was notable mainly for its fragmentation into more and more systematic specialisms.

In 1962, a survey of the main approaches to history embraced political history, economic history, social history, the history of art, the history of science, universal history and local history (Finberg 1962a). A generation later, in 1991, perspectives on historical writing had widened to include women's history, 'history from below', oral history, histories of reading, of images, of political thought, of the body and of events, as well as microhistory and overseas history (Burke 1991a). That list could be extended further, to encompass for example historical demography, labour history, urban history, environmental history and landscape history. But no matter the kind of history being practised, and no matter the time period involved, the question of place has also to be addressed. While many historians have viewed place as a passive stage, others have come increasingly to recognise knowledge of place as being crucial to a full understanding of history. Where history takes place is not incidental but central to the way in which its dramas unfold. Moreover, the geographical scale of historical enquiry has become a significant issue for many historians.

During the nineteenth century, with the rise of nation-states, national history was dominant and continued to be so for much of the twentieth century. Much history was focused on the institutions, constitutions, foreign policies, politics and economic developments of national communities. On the premise that history was made by nation-states, it was logical (and practical, using national archives) for historians to work within the national framework. The place or area, the 'geography', that mattered was that within a nation's boundary. Increasingly, that premise came to be questioned during the second half of the twentieth century, with the growing recognition that a nation has both backward linkages, to its regions and localities, and forward linkages, to other nations with which it is interconnected in a world system. Historians no longer take the geographical scale of their study for granted but consider it to be an integral part of their enquiries. Furthermore, it has come to be claimed that areas other than the nation also deserve to be studied for their own sakes and not necessarily as components of a national or wider system. National history continues to flourish, albeit in different guises from those it donned in the nineteenth century, but it now sits alongside histories at other geographical scales, from the local to the global. What might we learn from histories at different geographical scales?

Local history

Local history itself has a long history, rooted in the many topographies which came to be written from the sixteenth century onwards and in the numerous publications of local and regional literary and scientific societies of the eighteenth and nineteenth centuries. Often practised by amateurs and antiquarians, it was for a long while excluded from the circle of professional historians. Even towards the end of the twentieth century it was still not included in a major encyclopaedia of the 'new history' (Le Goff et al. 1978), nor in a voluminous dictionary of the 'historical sciences' (Burguière 1986). The case for local history has been forcefully argued in Britain by H. P. R. Finberg (1952, 1962b) and W. G. Hoskins (1959), who may be seen as having established a distinctive school of local history at the University of Leicester. The central concern of local history is the local community, a social grouping intermediate between the family and the nation (Rogers 1977; Phythian-Adams 1987; Sheeran and Sheeran 1998). Some local historians focus on *people*, on the community – and so have promoted what they see as a new community history (Pryce 1994). Others focus upon *place* – recognising that the territory occupied by a local community can range in size from a parish to a county, from a *pays* to a region (Everitt 1977; Phythian-Adams 1991). Some study such communities or localities for their own intrinsic interest; some see them as components of a national mosaic (Everitt 1979; Phythian-Adams 1991; Hudson 1995). Others view them as case studies exemplifying non-local (regional, national or international, or even universal) themes – in this approach, which has come to be termed 'microhistory', detailed analysis of the most minute events is undertaken as a means of arriving at far-reaching conclusions (Skipp 1981; Levi 1991). Jean Jacquart (1990) saw local history as being both limited (it is microhistory, concerned with little facts and minor events in a small area) and unlimited (as a form of total history). The localities studied by local historians vary considerably in size, and their boundaries are often ill-defined and dynamic. But they tend to be 'small' and the term 'local' certainly no longer implies 'isolated', as it might once have done. Localities, whatever their size as communities and/or as places, are connected to wider worlds.

Regional history

Just as there are different forms of local history, so there are diverse justifications for regional history. Some have promoted it as an alternative to a national, metropolitan-dominated history. One historian, J-F. Soulet (1988), has argued that although French rural history flourished from the 1950s onwards, many of the numerous doctoral theses which were published had a common but limited aim: to determine the ways in which, and the extent to which, national (meaning Parisian) socio-economic and political ideas and practices diffused into, and were adopted and adapted by, the regions of provincial France. Given that a single problematic guided those studies, their results were strikingly similar: they all demonstrated that after a period of reticence people in the regions accepted the national model of change. The singularity of each region resided only in its local mode and degree of acceptance, in the particularity of the timing and spacing of the diffusion process. But such specificities were portrayed as regional nuances, not as fundamental differences from the national picture. Soulet argued that regions should be seen not only as responding to external, national stimuli but also as actively making their own histories: general, national influences should be seen as having been integrated with specific, local and regional circumstances. Particular social relations – such as the cohesion of certain groups, the importance of a sense of territoriality and conflicts between town and country dwellers – were often decisive processes in a region's history. Thus Soulet argued for regional studies founded on an internal, not an external, problematic, for studies which would analyse the *structures* and *conjonctures* specific to each region, as well as their own *événements*. Of course, national influences might well be a part, but only a part, of that specificity. An especially spirited advocacy of regional history has been provided also by Guy Thuillier and Jean Tulard (1992). They argued that regions should be studied for their intrinsic interest and not as appendages to a national history; that regional historians are able to capitalise on their own attachment to, on their own identification with, a particular place; and that regional histories can convey a real sense of continuity as well as of change, for regions often have a longer history than does the nation of which they became a part.

    Such a humanistic approach is far from the positivist position taken much earlier by Henry Broude (1960) in his discussion of the significance of regional studies for the elaboration of national economic history. He argued that the objective, preferably quantified, study of regional interaction could enhance understanding of national economic development. To describe accurately the dynamics of development, Broude claimed, we must be able to identify leading geographical sections (regions) as well as leading economic sectors. National economic histories, he argued, cloak the processes and patterns of regional differentiation, creating 'a more homogenous image than reality warrants'. Regional economic history stands here as the handmaiden to national economic history. But Broude also emphasised that regions are dynamic, not only because the boundaries related to a particular set of identifying criteria change, but also because the criteria employed to recognise relevant homogeneities over area also change.

That boundaries to regions are a matter of perception, usage and convenience was also recognised by J. D. Marshall in his extended analysis of why historians should study regions (Marshall 1985, 1986). Marshall noted that, whereas in France historians have long drawn upon geographical concepts and have produced a remarkable range and richness of regional history (Gibson 1983), in Britain the greater distancing of historians from geographers retarded the development of regional history there until the 1980s. Of course, Marshall was able to point to some distinguished classics of history set firmly within regional contexts, such as G. H. Tupling's (1926) economic history of Rossendale in Lancashire, A. H. Dodd's (1933) study of the Industrial Revolution in North Wales and J. D. Chambers' (1932) portrayal of Nottinghamshire in the eighteenth century. He was also able to note some more recent histories with clear regional themes, such as A. M. Everitt's (1966) *The Community of Kent and the Great Rebellion, 1640–1660* and A. Fletcher's (1975) *A County Community in Peace and War: Sussex, 1600–1660*. He could also have cited the numerous volumes of the Victoria County History, a project begun in 1899 and continuing today, aiming to narrate the history of England county by county (Sheeran and Sheeran 1998: 73–4).

But the regional awareness of British historians, and indeed their awareness of work by geographers on regions, has been sharpened only during the closing decades of the twentieth century. Everitt (1979) gave that process impetus with his paper on the role of localities, counties and towns in the making of English history. Marshall's advocacy of regional studies by historians was inspired initially by his reading of East's (1935) discussion of the geography behind history, but buttressed subsequently by a wide range of geographical literature on regions and the regional concept. This enabled him to advocate recognition of the 'region' as a spatial framework for human activities and thus for histories of such activities; it enabled him to argue for an awareness of a wide range of regions, including city regions; and it enabled him to promote the idea of the region as a 'laboratory' for the testing of theories of location and economic development or as a 'milieu' in which to study changing perceptions and cultures; and it enabled him to signal the importance of regional dynamism, citing approvingly works by historical geographers on regional transformation during the Industrial Revolution in Lancashire (Langton 1979) and in Yorkshire (Gregory 1982b). Marshall (1986) examined some major questions to be addressed and topics to be researched by regional historians. He argued not only for more studies of the linkages which constitute a region but also for inter-regional and intra-regional comparisons, as well as for studies of the perception of regions by, and the significance of regional loyalism to, people in the past. Regional history, as synthesis, is fundamentally interdisciplinary, calling upon the knowledge and understanding of many analytical disciplines. Marshall admitted that regional history is a vast and amorphous – and therefore very challenging – study. The concept of regional history as synthesis appears to me to be unavoidably a holistic one at a philosophical level, but Marshall's approach was exclusively pragmatic. He explicitly directed his argument away from what he saw as 'two possible quagmires': the notions of total history and of a region as an objective reality. Regional histories should be essayed, Marshall argued, even though he considered total histories to be unachievable and even though regions do not exist as objective realities.

Perhaps for these reasons, regional histories in Marshallian mode remain relatively rare but some of those existing are excellent. Marshall himself, working with John Walton, produced a history of the Lake District of England between 1830 and the mid-twentieth century (Marshall and Walton 1981); J. K. Walton (1987) wrote a social history of Lancashire between 1558 and 1939, and Norman McCord (1979) provided an economic and social history of north-east England. During the 1980s, Barry Cunliffe and David Hey edited a series of regional histories of Britain. They included, for example, two books on south-east England, one addressing the region up to AD 1000 and the other the region from that date – the former was written by archaeologists/historians, the latter by historical geographers (Drewett et al. 1988; Brandon and Short 1990). Many briefer glimpses of regional histories have been published in the *Journal of Regional and Local Studies* since it first appeared in 1981. Similar trends – the growth of regional history, a productive combination of urban and regional history, and a fruitful borrowing of geographical concepts – have been identified among American historians (Kulikoff 1973; Goldfield 1984), while the concept of metropolitan dominance has been expanded as an explanatory framework for a regional history of Canada before 1914 (Careless 1954, 1989). In Australia, regional history has received less attention than has urban history and the latter has been more concerned with the internal structures and processes of urban development than with cities in their regional contexts, but these imbalances are being corrected (Laverty 1995).

Even situating a city within its regional context cannot provide closure around an urban history, because the region itself (and thus its cities) also needs to be situated in a national and ultimately an international context. A city exists as part of a system of cities; a region exists as part of a system of regions. A city and regional historian's net has logically to be cast wider than the specific city and the region under examination. This is clear in such contrasting works as Peter Hall's (1998) massive and comparative assessment of the role of some key world cities as crucibles of culture, innovation and order and Peter Clark's (2000) magnificent edited survey of the urban history of Britain from *c.* 600 to 1950. Both of these works stand, in different ways, as testimony to the benefits of a very close relation between history and geography: the former, written by a geographer, employs a deeply historical perspective, while the latter not only draws upon geographical perspectives but also engages historical geographers in the enterprise.

National history

Much history – perhaps most history – continues to be written within a national framework. For over a century and a half, the study of European history has been dominated by the idea of the nation. As Benjamin Sax comments, 'this was understandable when the nation-state with its foreign policy and domestic politics clearly formed the main object of historical knowledge. But even with the more recent interest in social history, the main lines of research and the frameworks of interpretation . . . have most often followed national lines in practice' (Sax 1992: 845). National history derives its inspiration from nineteenth-century state-building and state-reforming movements in Europe, an inspiration which was replenished in the twentieth century following the creation of new states within and beyond Europe as a result of two world wars and decolonisation (Hopkins 1999: 202–3). The development of a new kind of history by the French *Annales* school of history from the 1920s onwards involved both a challenge to the traditional national histories with their emphases on political, constitutional, military and diplomatic concerns and a new focus on social, economic and cultural issues at scales ranging from the local to the global (Clark 1999). None the less, national histories stood their ground. The more recent development of even newer forms of history – such as labour history, women's history and urban history – has still not escaped totally from national frameworks. Indeed, some of the newest strains of history are resolutely national histories, focused on questions about the construction and reconstruction of national identities and national memories – exemplified *par excellence* in a collection of essays on the construction of the French past (Nora 1996, 1997, 1998).

National histories rightly continue to be produced: nation-states have been powerful history-makers. But they too had their backward and forward spatial linkages and so cannot be considered in isolation. One very specific forward linkage merits special attention, for colonies and empires may be seen as extensions of nation-states beyond their borders. Studies of individual colonies may thus be seen as a special form of regional history, as histories of overseas regions of a nation-state. But a strong case has recently been made for reviving imperial history, for looking at empires as overall structures and for recognising that the big issues of the post-colonial era cannot be understood without acknowledging the extent to which they are a legacy of the empires that dominated the greater part of the world during the past three centuries. Empires were trans-national organisations created to mobilise the resources of the world (Hopkins 1999). But they were selective in spatial terms. Colonial history and imperial history are thus also special kinds of international history.

World history

In 1962, Geoffrey Barraclough made a powerful case for the prosecution of world history:

Of all the approaches to history none has been less explored than that which we usually call world-history or universal or 'oecumenical' history. And yet there is probably no type of history which is closer to our present preoccupations or more nearly attuned to the world in which we live. The reasons why the history most needed today is universal history lie all around us. They are a reflection of the unification of the world by science and technology and by the revolutionary advance of mass communications, a consequence of the familiar fact that we can no longer isolate ourselves from events in any quarter of the globe . . . Furthermore, the processes of industrial society, which originated in Western Europe and North America, are now world-wide, their impact universal . . . The emergence of the greater part of mankind from political subjection to political independence and political influence necessitates a shift in historical perspective. In short, the very forces which have transformed our view of the present compel us to widen our view of the past. It is this new situation which makes the need for universal history – by which we mean a history that looks beyond Europe and the west to humanity in all lands and ages – a matter of immediate practical urgency. (Barraclough 1962: 83–4)

Barraclough recognised that the concept of world history had deep historical roots: it fitted in with the Enlightenment notion of progress, of mankind advancing steadily from primitive barbarism to reason, virtue and civilisation. He argued that the first great historical achievement of the eighteenth century was to bring the extra-European world into the field of enquiry and thus to make universal history possible. Its second achievement was to debate the problems involved in the writing of world history. But world history waned from the end of the eighteenth century until the middle of the twentieth century, for a variety of reasons. As a more scientific attitude to history developed, so the superficiality of eighteenth-century historical writing was more deeply felt. Also, the feasibility of world history was called into question: the foundation of critical knowledge for such an ambitious project was considered by some to be insufficient, while others argued that writing world history made demands upon knowledge which were too great for any one individual, while co-operative histories tended to be encyclopaedic, not treating mankind as a unity, providing aggregates of national histories with little cohesion or connection. As Barraclough pointed out, to these technical reasons for the declining practice of world history has significantly to be added the rise of the nation-state during the nineteenth century and with it the notion that national history was the only type of history that mattered. It took two world wars to shake the foundations of that historical attitude, for it to be more generally recognised that by the mid-twentieth century the political groups which counted in the world were supranational.

Barraclough was explicitly not arguing for abandoning national histories: he admitted that it would remain appropriate to ask how far particular national characteristics affected the character of a civilisation, how far the expression of particular values was the work of a particular nation or state or people, and how far the actions of governments imposed a particular pattern on the life of a particular geographical area. Instead, for Barraclough, world history was a separate branch of historical enquiry. It was not the sum of national histories; nor was it history with national history left out; nor was it to be confused with what was sometimes described as 'meta-history', an attempt to survey the whole vista of the historic past in order to discover general trends, patterns and laws; and nor was it the purpose of world history to provide a single continuous narrative of the whole history of the world. For Barraclough, world history had aims and objectives which other types of history could not fulfil: it cut across national boundaries and addressed questions of international history which only a universal point of view could elucidate. It was, above all, a perspective upon history, and in particular it was an avoidance of Eurocentric history. Since it was essentially an attitude of mind, it could in principle cut into the past at any given period or moment: a world history of the Stone Age was as possible and as inherently necessary as a world history of the Space Age. Nor did every world history have to encompass the whole of the globe; it could interpret, say, European or Asian history in relation to its place in the world. World history was history conceived and written from a universal point of view. For Barraclough, world history was both possible ('there are no insuperable obstacles on a practical level to the study of world history') and necessary ('every age needs its own view of the past, and the present age of global politics and global civilisation needs a global view of history') (Barraclough 1962: 107–8).

The growth of a renewed world history has been more hesitant than perhaps its proponents had anticipated. More than thirty years after Barraclough's incisive advocacy, world history could still be described as 'struggling to achieve its own identity' (Mazlish 1998: 385), with many historians remaining 'relatively ignorant about it as a developing field' (Pomper 1995: 1). But Michael Geyer and Charles Bright (1995), in their wide-ranging survey of 'world history in a global age', maintain that since the late 1980s world history has become one of the fastest growing areas of history teaching in America and that a significant body of new scholarly writing has been emerging in world history, while Philip Pomper's commentary on world history and its critics is a useful stock-taking of what he calls 'a lively and creative, but still small subdiscipline of history' (Pomper 1995: 1).

World history as studied during the past thirty years or so has taken a variety of forms. One significant strand has been comparative historical studies of civilisations, often focusing on the history (and geography) of power and on the nature of 'civilisation'. Another strand has been the history of globalisation, focused on the history of flows of people, capital, commodities and ideas throughout the world. A third strand now argues that the main concern should be to try to understand the practices and processes both of global integration and of regional and local differentiation that have come into play (mainly, it is usually argued, during the twentieth century) (Geyer and Bright 1995; McNeill 1995). Some historians consequently now argue for a distinction between world history and global history (Mazlish and Buultjen 1993; Mazlish 1998).

Probably the most forceful advocate of a new world history has been William McNeill (1967, 1973, 1992, 1995), following explicitly in the footsteps of Oswald Spengler and Arnold Toynbee but going further than they did along the trail leading to the comparative study of civilisations. McNeill argues that historical change was largely provoked by cultural contact, with one civilisation borrowing (or sometimes rejecting or holding at bay) novelties encountered in another. He traces the developments in communications networks which accelerated and extended human encounters across the centuries. He identifies two sets of especially significant encounters; first, biological and ecological (which diffused, for example, diseases and crops from what McNeill terms 'the Eurasian ecumenical world' across larger and larger areas, until after 1500 the process became global); and secondly, cultural encounters (which have frequently and even chronically involved conflict and power struggles among human groups). McNeill argues that these processes have not resulted in global uniformity, but in increased ecological and cultural variability in time and space. Global communications made world history a palpable reality.

Better known to geographers than the works of McNeill are those of Immanuel Wallerstein on the modern world-system – better known, perhaps, because of his use of geographical metaphors and certainly because of the interdisciplinary debate his approach has promoted. Wallerstein (1974, 1979, 1980, 1983, 1984) argued that there have been historically many local or regional societies ('mini-systems') in which exchange was based on reciprocity, as well as many 'world-empires' founded on the redistribution and the payment of tributes. But, Wallerstein contended, there has been only one successful 'world-economy' based on continuous capital accumulation through the operation of free markets. That world-economy, in his view, originated in Europe from the mid-fifteenth century and spread to embrace the whole world by the end of the nineteenth century. Wallerstein's world-system analysis thus required historical studies not to examine individual regions or single countries; instead, they had to embrace the whole world-system. Wallerstein claimed that the world-system had three spatial components ('core', 'semi-periphery' and 'periphery') that were not geographically static but continually changing, with particular countries moving from one category into another. Additionally, Wallerstein argued that the process of capital accumulation did not proceed at a constant rate but was marked by 'long waves', consecutive periods of growth and stagnation, with the latter providing the conditions needed for restructuring the world-economy. Wallerstein's world-system analysis drew upon systems theory (which emphasises the functional interdependence of the components of a system), upon neo-Marxist dependency theory (arguing that the expropriation of surplus value occurs not only from an exploited class to a dominant class, but also across space from underdeveloped and dependent areas to more developed areas), and upon a structural view of history as embracing recurrent economic and geopolitical reorganisation. Wallerstein's world-system analysis is not, of course, the only structural theory of uneven development and others also deserve consideration (Smith 1987), but Wallerstein's ideas have attracted a very considerable interest among world historians.

To some extent, Wallerstein's notions extended and formalised ideas expressed by Braudel (1949, 1967, 1979a, 1979b) in his classic study of the decline of the Mediterranean 'world' as the economic and political centre of Europe in the sixteenth century and the associated rise of the North Sea and Baltic Sea 'world' and in his sweeping, three-volume study of material culture and capitalism from the sixteenth century. Planned originally as a book on Europe, this latter work approached a world history, embracing Asia and America and (to a lesser extent) Africa. One of Braudel's main arguments was the necessity to understand changes in individual regions, countries and continents in global terms. Wallerstein's own ideas have been extended back in time by Janet Abu-Lughod (1989, 1995), who argues that the period between 1250 and 1350 was a crucial turning point in world history. Although the world-system she identifies at that time lacked an international division of labour, her world-system comprised interconnected trading cities in Europe, India and China. Such an approach also enables Abu-Lughod to refer to the Roman Empire as the first nascent world-system. The world-system approach as set out by Wallerstein has spawned an immense literature, much of it challenging the approach itself (Geyer and Bright 1995). I am not concerned here, however, with the merits or otherwise of the world-system perspective, nor with contributions by geographers to the debate about world-systems (for examples, see Nitz 1987; Kearns 1988; Berry 1991; Hugill 1993; Taylor 1999a, 1999b). My concern here is simply to emphasise the fundamentally geographical nature of world-system theory and indeed of all world histories and all historical studies of globalisation.

Most studies of regional transformation, whether by geographers or by historians, represent it primarily in words and only secondarily in numbers or pictures, as verbal text rather than as tables, diagrams and maps. But how has historical and geographical change been represented in studies which foreground maps, that is to say, in historical atlases?

Histories in place, geographies in time: historical atlases

Understanding places requires a historical perspective, and understanding periods requires a geographical perspective. Each needs the other; each is impoverished without the other. More importantly, each is enriched by the other. Historical atlases bring the two perspectives together. Historical atlases portray cartographically cultural change (in its broadest sense) in defined areas (which range from the local to the global). They provide both a geographical perspective upon the history of an area and a historical perspective upon the geography of an area. They do so using maps as the primary (but not the only) means of communication. Historical atlases offer a distinctive way of understanding and representing the changing character of places and peoples in the past. At the same time, and with the passage of time, historical atlases themselves become sources: the materials selected for inclusion in atlases are reflections of the ideologies of the people who produced them and of the periods in which they were produced. The compilers of historical atlases in France during the seventeenth and eighteenth centuries considered such works to be 'the eyes of history', but they can be considered today as mouthpieces voicing through their substance and style the idea of history held by those who compiled them (Hofmann 2000; Winearls 1995).

Cartography – including the production of historical atlases – has its own history and geography. This is being made abundantly clear in a major and multi-volumed interdisciplinary project on the history of cartography throughout the world (for the project's programmatic statement, see Harley and Woodward 1987: xv–xxi). The history of cartography is a systematic field in its own right, like the history of painting or of photography: it ought not to be confused with historical geography, even though maps can be made to tell us much about past geographies (Harley 2001). These points are made clearly in Jeremy Black's (1997) short but excellent study of constructing images of the past in historical atlases. The oldest printed historical atlas was produced in China in the twelfth century and Black shows that from the outset the selection of maps and presentation of material in such atlases involved politics and propaganda. In Europe, some individual maps depicting the Holy Land at the time of Christ and some maps of the Classical world were produced during the medieval period, but the first generally acknowledged historical atlas was produced by Abraham Ortelius and published in Antwerp in 1570 as the *Theatrum Orbis Terrarum* (*Theatre of the World*). His section on maps of the Classical world – the *Parergon* – represented a significant shift from the single-sheet historical map to the atlas. Black shows that interest in mapping the Classical world and the Holy Land persisted during the seventeenth century and that during the eighteenth century there developed an increasing interest in atlases of the post-Classical world, in atlases which embraced Asia and Europe. But Black shows that it was in the nineteenth century that historical atlases were produced in profusion, as part of the political projects of nationalism and imperialism. In the twentieth century, historical atlases continued to reflect those ideologies, but Black emphasises that they were also significantly influenced by other perspectives, including environmentalism, fascism, communism, conservatism, liberalism and of course commercialism. The last of these has also led to the increasing use in historical atlases of forms of graphical illustration other than maps, as well as to the inclusion of lengthy verbal texts and compact statistical tables. In addition, the presentation of historical atlases has been changed by the use of new mapping and printing technologies. Black's full and critical account of historical atlases, which he situates in their appropriate historical and geographical contexts, is an excellent review of the genre.

I have no need to repeat Black's findings in any detail here, nor to follow any further the historiographical approach which he adopts. I will, instead, consider briefly the relations of geography and history in a few, mainly recent, examples of the mapping of history. Mapping history means, at the most basic level, locating geographically events and phenomena considered (by the map-maker) to be historically significant. Depicting historico-geographical change is achieved, again at the most basic level, by a series of chronologically sequential maps, permitting change to be inferred through the method of comparative statics. More complex attempts to portray change involve the mapping of some indication or index of change between two specified dates or periods. This often employs arrows to depict movement qualitatively or isopleth or choropleth maps to depict change quantitatively, and sometimes other, non-cartographic, graphical portrayals of change, such as graphs, pie-charts and histograms. But the basic question facing producers of a historical atlas is whether its fundamental organising principle should be chronological, geographical or topical. These three solutions to the problem are found in differing combinations, reflecting the preferences and prejudices of their compilers. Further, as Joan Winearls (1995: xi–xvii) emphasises, an edited historical atlas reflects the ideas of its editor(s) about the relative importance of maps and text, the knowledge and interests of the author(s) of particular maps, and the skills and preferred techniques of its cartographer(s).

Brian Harley's (1982, 1988, 1989a, 1989b, 2001) pioneering and highly influential work on deconstructing maps, his analyses of the selection of information shown in maps and of the methods used to compile them, showed how individual maps and collections of them in atlases need to be read not only as sources of knowledge but also as icons of power. It is, therefore, relevant to note at this point that historians have compiled more historical atlases than geographers have done. Historical atlases produced during the nineteenth and early twentieth century were, in general, concerned more with locating and spatialising history than with dating and temporalising geography. They mapped mainly locations and distributions of political areas and activities, often doing so against the background of physical geography but not from a wider geographical perspective. From the 1930s, however, historical geographers were demanding more from maps and gradually this came to influence the contents and format of historical atlases – but only gradually, because such atlases continued until fairly recently to be produced more by historians than by geographers. But historical atlases have now become a seat of highly productive co-operation between the two sets of scholars.

Many of the general historical atlases produced in the nineteenth and twentieth centuries were, in effect, political (and to some extent military) histories with maps. Perhaps the classic of this genre was R. L. Poole's (1902) *Historical Atlas of Modern Europe from the Decline of the Roman Empire*. Such atlases focused on the changing boundaries and characters of political units at a variety of geographical scales. Many were published as school or college teaching aids, with geography being viewed as the handmaiden to history. They became gradually but discernibly broader in scope, so that today historical atlases address a wide range of issues, not only political and military but also social, economic and cultural. They also came to confront more directly the question of the distribution and changing distribution of phenomena at scales ranging from the global to the local.

Black argues that *The Times Atlas of World History* has been the most important of the global historical atlases, 'because with its innovative use of interesting perspectives and coverage of much non-political material, it has altered the general perception of what an historical atlas of the world should contain' (Black 1997: 144). English editions first appeared in 1978 and concise English editions in 1982, while the main atlas was available in seventeen languages by 1995. Before the appearance of *The Times Atlas of World History*, H. C. Darby and Harold Fullard (1970) had edited an atlas designed both to serve the needs of readers of *The New Cambridge Modern History* and to illustrate school or university courses on modern history. Their intentions were clear:

In planning the atlas we have tried to balance the amount of space given to maps of Europe by nearly as many maps dealing with non-European lands – with North America, Latin America, Africa, the Far East, Australasia and the world as a whole. A substantial number of maps showing economic and social conditions has been included [in addition to political and military maps]. We wish we could have included even more, but, only too often, we have drawn a blank in our search for reliable economic information for some areas at a number of periods . . . Some historical atlases have adopted a basic chronological plan; others have grouped maps of similar areas together. Each method can be defended, but we have followed the latter in the belief that it facilitates reference to individual areas at different periods. The maps within each group, so far as is possible, have been arranged in chronological sequence and have been produced on the same scale to enable easy comparison between them. (Darby and Fullard 1970: xvii)

Thus the section of their atlas treating North America included, for example, maps of its political territories in 1763, of military campaigns during the American Revolution 1775–83, of areas of virgin forest in 1650, 1850 and 1926, and of the 'coloured' population in 1900 (Fig. 5.2).

Other historical atlases cover not the entire globe but large portions of it. Good but very different examples are J. E. Schwartzberg's *Historical Atlas of South Asia* (1978), J. F. Ade Ajayi and Michael Crowder's *Historical Atlas of Africa* (1985) and G. S. P. Freeman-Grenville's *Historical Atlas of the Middle East* (1993). More common, certainly because more manageable and perhaps because more fundable, are historical atlases of individual countries. I will here take as examples atlases of the United States and Canada.

A number of historical atlases of the United States of America were published during the nineteenth and early twentieth century, couched in terms of its political, territorial and military history seen in the context of its physical geography. But a significantly new direction was taken by Charles Paullin (1932) in his *Atlas of the Historical Geography of the United States*. This substantial atlas was a major product of co-operation over almost thirty years between the Department of Historical

---

NORTH AMERICA

Atlantic coast colonies, *c.* 1650, and the Iroquois
Spanish, British, French in Eastern North America, 1603–1763 (before Treaty of Paris)
North-east America to 1763: British and French rivalry (before Treaty of Paris)
North America, 1756
North America, 1763 (after Treaty of Paris)
The American Revolution, 1775–83
United States, 1783–1803
United States: Density of population, *c.* 1790
California: The gold and silver rush, 1849–59
North America: Colonial economy in the 18th century
United States: Territorial expansion from 1803
United States: Exploration of the West, 1803–53
United States: Railroads and overland mail, *c.* 1860
United States: Rates of travel, *c.* 1860
United States: Slavery to *c.* 1860
The American Civil War, 1861–5
United Sates: Areas of virgin forest, 1650, 1850 and 1926
United States: Gold, silver, oil and gas, *c.* 1930
United States: Cotton growing, 1859 and 1919
United States: Cotton spinning, 1840 and 1926
United States: Iron and steel, 1858 and 1908
United States: Economic, *c.* 1900
United States: Coloured population, 1900
United States: Population 1900
European emigration to US: 1851–1910
United States: Foreign-born population, 1900
United States: Presidential elections, 1904–20
Alaskan boundary dispute, 1898–1903
Maine boundary dispute, 1783–1842
Canada: Exploration, 1768–1905
Eastern Canada: Settlement in the 18th and 19th century
Canada: Westward expansion of settlement
Canada: Development of provinces 1862, 1867 and 1882, 1898, 1912 and 1949
Canada: Origin of the population, 1911
Canada: Population, 1951

Figure 5.2 Maps in the section on North America in *The New Cambridge Modern History Atlas*
Source: Darby and Fullard (1970)

Research of the Carnegie Institution of Washington and the American Geographical Society. Paullin's aim was to illustrate the 'essential facts of geography and history that condition and explain the development of the United States'. But the geographical facts went beyond simple cartographic statements about location, distribution and physical background, because for Paullin 'historical judgement must rest on the recognition of fundamental relationships in space as well as in time' (Paullin 1932: xi). Although there was one map of 'Indian tribes and linguistic stocks' in 1650, this atlas ignored the earlier history of Native Americans and addressed instead the history of the settlement of America by Europeans. But this limitation apart, the atlas was an important break from tradition. It was organised thematically rather than chronologically, with maps grouped into major sections, for example, on population and on industries and transportation, and with many maps making effective use of statistical data. Its first group of maps dealt not with military history, which was both relegated to a later section and downgraded in the amount of attention given to it. Instead, the first set of maps drew inspiration from Turner's frontier thesis and included maps of exploration, colonisation and settlement in the distinctive American environment, of the use made of resources, and of the allocation of land and the creation of administrative units. Later groups of maps treated varied aspects of America's economic and cultural history, mapping a mass of statistical data. For example, the section on 'Industries and transportation, 1680–1932' included not only maps of the spatial spread of individual forms of transportation (with the spread of the motor car being shown in two maps indicating the ratio of people per car in 1913 and 1930), but also maps showing the length of time taken in 1800, 1830, 1857 and 1930 for people to reach different areas of the United States from New York by the normal means of travel in use at those dates. The atlas also significantly included maps showing the distribution of wealth, for example, by using valuations of houses and land in 1799, 1912 and 1922. Another group of maps portrayed the geography of reforms largely brought about by state legislation, such as the abolition of slavery and of the property qualifications for voting, and the introduction of female suffrage and of schooling. Black points out that Paullin's atlas did, of course, have faults. In addition to its neglect of Native Americans, it had little to say, for example, about environmental history or about poverty, and greater detail would have been revealed had the maps been compiled using smaller units than states (Black 1997: 117–21). Moreover, the atlas emphasised geographical distributions at specific dates or periods, largely leaving it to the reader to infer geographical change by the method of comparative statics. None the less, Paullin's atlas was a highly significant advance in the production of historical atlases: it has served as a model for later such works.

Paullin's atlas remains informative today, not having been entirely replaced by its successors. During the 1980s the National Geographic Society published under the banner 'The Making of America' a series of seventeen regional maps covering the historical geography of the United States and its borderlands (Meinig et al. 1982–8). Then in 1988 the Society published a new, imaginatively designed *Historical Atlas of the United States*, aimed at a popular audience (and the Society presented a copy to every junior and senior high school in the country). This was an important publishing event which extended the reach of historical geography well beyond its professional practitioners.

Very different but at least equally and probably more significant has been the *Historical Atlas of Canada* (Harris 1987; Kerr and Holdsworth 1990; Gentilcore

1993). Published in three volumes, this atlas has been very highly and appropriately praised. Graeme Wynn claims justifiably that this atlas:

stands as a major achievement of, and substantial tribute to, the work of Canadian historical geographers. Bold, comprehensive, integrative, informative, and indubitably geographical, the *Historical Atlas* offers a full and fascinating picture of Canadian development over several centuries. It is also remarkable in combining rich local detail with wider, albeit cautious, interpretations of regional and subcontinental development in a manner relatively uncharacteristic of, although not unknown in, geographical writing on the Canadian past during the last two decades. (Wynn 1993: 119)

The first volume of the *Historical Atlas of Canada* covered the period from pre-history to 1800. Its sixty-nine plates were presented in three groups: 'prehistory' (addressing the physical environment and its early occupants), 'the Atlantic realm' (dealing with exploration and the development of fisheries) and 'inland expansion' (treating exploration, colonisation, settlement and the development of trade in the St Lawrence Valley and the interior). The second volume, on the nineteenth century, comprises fifty-eight plates on a very wide range of cultural, demographic, economic, political and social topics. The third volume, on the twentieth century, has sixty-six plates: they present collectively an overview of Canada's changing geography in its many guises. Although appropriately dominated by the plates, the *Historical Atlas of Canada* includes interpretative essays. Moreover, each 'plate' is itself not just one map but a set of maps accompanied often by diagrams, sketches, photographs and statistics. The sources for each plate are fully documented and critically noted. The *Historical Atlas of Canada* stands as one of the major achievements of Western historical geography during the twentieth century.

Three scholars who participated in the making of this atlas present their personal reflections on the practical aspects of atlas editing. William G. Dean (1995) examines the elements of an atlas which give it 'structure' (direction, purpose and appearance) and the evolution of the modern thematic atlas. Harris (1995) discusses the first volume of the *Historical Atlas of Canada* as a 'text', a narrative of the early history of Canada as seen through the eyes of modern historiography, arguing that as maps are 'about power', this atlas is best seen not as a dogmatic and nationalistic conception of Canada but as a 'morality play' portraying Canada as an evolving, culturally complex, political construction. Holdsworth (1995) sets out what he terms 'the politics' underpinning the third volume, identifying some of the key conflicts which had to be resolved editorially in producing the atlas: he cites, for example, 'the politics of interpretation' (although the atlas portrays a nation, it is also about a nation versus the regions and a nation versus the conti-nent), 'the politics of power' (here attempting to recognise the role of social power and so presenting different 'takes' of the same phenomenon), and 'the politics of representation' (explicitly adopting an *Annaliste* view, the editors wanted to represent the great diversity of Canadian life, including its popular culture). The *Historical Atlas of Canada* has set a new standard for the genre. Following quickly in its footsteps is the *New Zealand Historical Atlas/Ko Papatuanuku e Takoto Nei* (McKinnon 1997). This remarkable production shows a keener sensitivity than does even the atlas of Canada to key topics such as aboriginal (first nation) worlds, to environmental issues and to colonial questions.

Historical atlases are also being produced of sub-national units, such as states, provinces, regions and counties. For example, the *Atlas historique du Québec* is a remarkable set of thematic atlases produced by interdisciplinary teams of scholars, designed to give a spatial dimension to their historical studies. The series as a whole is edited jointly by a historical geographer, Serge Courville, and a social historian, Normand Séguin, with some volumes being produced also by them and others by different scholars. Individual atlases cover topics ranging from the *pays* of the St Lawrence Valley to the city of Quebec, from the role of the *Nord* in the province of Quebec to the historical geography of health and medical facilities (Courville and Séguin 1995, 1997, 1998, 2001a, 2001b, 2001c). In France, the Société de l'Atlas Historique Français was established in 1969 to promote the production of a series of regional historical atlases which would ultimately cover the whole of France. The first volume dealt with Provence, Comtat, Orange, Nice and Monaco (Baratier et al. 1969). In England, admirable regional historical atlases are being published, such as one on the south-west (Kain and Ravenhill 1999), and also county historical atlases, such as those on Lincolnshire (Bennett and Bennett 1993) and on Norfolk (Wade-Martins 1993).

Descending the geographical scale, there are some outstanding historical atlases of towns. Mary Lobel (1969, 1975) has edited atlases of historic towns of the British Isles which aimed, in a series of maps and an essay on each of a number of towns, to recreate and record the condition of the major British towns which existed before 1800. Thus the section on Cambridge has maps of its situation, its site, its street names *c.* 1300 and *c.* 1500, its medieval hostels, its parishes *c.* 1800 and its layout *c.* 1800. Jean-Luc Pinol's (1996) *Atlas historique des villes de France* aims to be a synthesis of the histories of the ten principal French urban agglomerations, portrayed in maps, photographs, diagrams and essays. This atlas was in fact the second volume in a series on European towns, initiated by Manuel Guàrdia, Francisco Javier Monclús and José Oyón of the Centre de Cultura Contemporània of Barcelona. Some atlases are devoted to individual towns. *The Times London History Atlas*, edited by a historical geographer, Hugh Clout (1991), and contributed to by a team of historians, museum curators, archaeologists and geologists as well as by geographers, is a lavishly illustrated portrayal of London's history chronologically, from Roman time to the 1980s, and then thematically, with sections on, for example, Royal London, the London of Charles Dickens, underground London and unrealised schemes of the London that never was. China's leading historical geographer, Ren-Zhi Hou, edited a *Historical Atlas of Beijing City* (Ren-Zhi 1985).

Theoretically, a historical atlas could be prepared for an area of any size, down to the smallest unit of human habitation and organisation, even including domestic interiors (although the graphics in this extreme case would be plans rather than maps, so it might not be appropriate to title such a collection an 'atlas'). But historical atlases can also be 'scaled-down' by limiting the topics and/or periods which they address. For example, the aim of J. Langton and R. J. Morris' (1986) *Atlas of Industrialising Britain 1780–1914* was to depict the geography of industrialisation in modern Britain rather than its total geography. None the less, it covered some thirty topics, including inevitably such themes as agriculture, coal and steam power, textiles, and shipbuilding but also, somewhat more surprisingly, embracing such subjects as popular institutions, sport, education and religion. D. Hill's (1981) *An Atlas of Anglo-Saxon England* presented 260 maps in five sections called 'The background', 'The events', 'Administration', 'The economy' and 'The church'.

If the range of topics is narrowed more strictly, then the theme(s) addressed can be considered throughout a long time period and over a wide area. Religion provides good specific examples here, as in a *Historical Atlas of Christianity* (Franklin 2001), in a *Historical Atlas of Mormonism* (Brown et al. 1994) and in *An Historical Atlas of Islam* (Brice 1981). A more general example is the series of thematic historical atlases of America being published by Routledge, such as those of religion (Gaustad and Barlow 2001), of the railroads (Stover 1999) and of presidential elections (Mieczkowski 2001).

The ways in which historical atlases have been developed vindicate a point made by P. Foncin towards the end of the nineteenth century in his treatise on *Géographie historique*. In a book intended for use in schools, Foncin considered the influence of geography on history. He argued that historical atlases being produced in the nineteenth century were of limited use because without a text which explained the maps, and which was reciprocally explained by the maps, the maps themselves were incomprehensible (Foncin 1888: 2). Jeremy Black, towards the end of the twentieth century, notes the increasing use of text in historical atlases but none the less asserts that 'the sense of change is not one that is catered for by most historical atlases, other than by turning the pages and hopefully noting alterations' (Black 1997: 211). While that may be the case for many historical atlases, it is by no means true for all of them. The problem of describing geographical change as well as distribution is one that some historical atlases, the best of them, address very directly, not only cartographically but also graphically, verbally and statistically.

Historical atlases have a dual significance: they permit an effective combination of history and geography as fields of enquiry and they enable productive co-operation between historians and geographers as researchers. This chapter has shown that historical atlases, regional histories and historical regional geographies not only permit but require the 'Great Divide' between history and geography to be bridged – and, moreover, that many have crossed it successfully. It is, therefore, now time to reflect upon the general question of the relations between geography and history in the light of this and the previous chapters.

6

Reflections

Retrospect

The academic battlefields of geography and history are littered with aphorisms about each other, as well as about their 'mysterious' offspring, historical geography. One of the earliest and best known comes from Peter Heylyn's *Microcosmus, or a Little Description of the Great World*: 'Geographie without Historie has life and motion but at randome, and unstable; Historie without Geographie like a dead carcasse has neither life nor motion at all' (Heylyn 1621: 11). Such aphorisms provide flashes of insight rather than a sustained illumination of the relations of geography and history. I have not sought to add to that inventory of aphorisms. My objective has been to examine critically the relations of geography and history generally and the practices of historical geography and geographical history specifically. At a time when the social sciences and humanities are moving increasingly towards both historical and geographical modes of explanation and understanding, when there is discernible both a 'historical turn' and a 'geographical turn' in those realms, there is both a need and an opportunity to contribute to the long-standing discourse between history and geography. I have done so here through a critique of the intellectual status of historical geography, their principal 'hybrid' – a descriptive term which portrays the product of the union of history and geography more positively (and certainly more politely) than does 'bastard Science', which is how historical geography was once described (Auerbach 1903: 897). 'Hybridity' in this context implies intellectual diversity and strength. The heterogeneity of historical geography, if not self-evidently its vigour, is discernibly exemplified in a series of *Studies in Historical Geography* published during the past thirty or so years (Fig. 6.1).

My central concern has been to examine the relations of geography and history, to explore both the similarities and the differences of these two perspectives upon the world. While acknowledging the distinctive natures of geography and history, I have sought to bridge the divide which too often separates them, doing so by emphasising the characteristics which unite them. While a distinguished historical

STUDIES IN HISTORICAL GEOGRAPHY
Edited by Alan R. H. Baker and J. Brian Harley

Published by David Charles, Newton Abbot

1970 Baker, A. R. H., Hamshere, J. D., and Langton, J. (eds.) *Geographical Interpretations of Historical Sources*
1972 Russell, J. C. *Medieval Regions and their Cities*
1972 Baker, A. R. H. (ed.) *Progress in Historical Geography*
1974 Perry, P. J. *British Farming in the Great Depression 1870–1914*

Published by Dawson, Folkestone and Archon, Connecticut

1976 Christopher, A. J. *Southern Africa*
1977 Roberts, B. K. *Rural Settlement in Britain*
1977 Powell, J. M. *Mirrors of the New World: Images and Image Makers in the Settlement Process*
1977 Jones, M. *Finland: Daughter of the Sea*
1978 Parry, M. L. *Climatic Change, Agriculture and Settlement*
1978 Patten, J. *English Towns 1500–1700*
1979 Newcomb, R. M. *Planning the Past: Historical Landscape Resources and Recreation*
1980 Turner, M. *English Parliamentary Enclosure: Its Historical Geography and Economic History*

CAMBRIDGE STUDIES IN HISTORICAL GEOGRAPHY
Edited by Alan R. H. Baker with J. Brian Harley and David Ward
(and then with Richard Dennis and Deryck Holdsworth)

Published by Cambridge University Press.

1982 Baker, A. R. H. and Billinge, M. (eds.) *Period and Place: Research Methods in Historical Geography*
1982 Turnock, D. *The Historical Geography of Scotland since 1707*
1982 Guelke, L. *Historical Understanding in Geography: an Idealist Approach*
1984 Dennis, R. *English Industrial Cities of the Nineteenth Century*
1984 Baker, A. R. H. and Gregory, D. (eds.) *Explorations in Historical Geography: Interpretative Essays*
1985 Kain, R. J. P. and Prince, H. C. *The Tithe Surveys of England and Wales*
1986 Sack, R. *Human Territoriality: Its Theory and History*
1987 Watts, D. *The West Indies: Patterns of Development, Culture and Environmental Change since 1492*

(continued)

Figure 6.1 The intellectual diversity of historical geography: an edited series of *Studies in Historical Geography*, 1970–2003

1988	Powell, J. M. *An Historical Geography of Australia: the Restive Fringe*
1988	Denecke, D. and Shaw, G. (eds.) *Urban Historical Geography: Recent Progress in Britain and Germany*
1988	Cosgrove, D. and Daniels, S. (eds.) *The Iconography of Landscape*
1989	Galloway, J. H. *The Sugar Cane Industry: an Historical Geography from its Origins to 1914*
1989	Ward, D. *Poverty, Ethnicity and the American City, 1840–1925*
1989	Cleary, M. C. *Peasants, Politicians and Producers: the Organisation of Agriculture in France since 1918*
1989	Phillips, A. D. M. *The Underdraining of Farmland in England during the Nineteenth Century*
1990	Robinson, D. J. (ed.) *Migration in Colonial Spanish America*
1991	Kearns, G. and Withers, C. W. J. (eds.) *Urbanising Britain: Essays on Class and Community in the Nineteenth Century*
1992	Baker, A. R. H. and Biger, G. (eds.) *Ideology and Landscape in Historical Perspective: Essays on the Meanings of Some Places in the Past*
1992	Driver, F. *Power and Pauperism: the Workhouse System, 1834–1884*
1994	De Planhol, X. *An Historical Geography of France*
1994	Carter, F. W. *Trade and Development in Poland: an Economic Geography of Cracow, from its Origins to 1795*
1995	Hoppe, G. and Langton, J. *Peasantry to Capitalism: Western Östergötland in the Nineteenth Century*
1996	Overton, M. *Agricultural Revolution in England: the Transformation of the Agrarian Economy 1500–1850*
1996	Friedman, S. W. *Marc Bloch, Sociology and Geography: Encountering Changing Disciplines*
1997	Short, B. *Land and Society in Edwardian Britain*
1998	Cliff, A., Haggett. P. and Smallman-Raynor, M., *Deciphering Global Epidemics: Analytical Approaches to the Disease Records of World Cities, 1888–1912*
1998	Dodgshon, R. *Society in Space and Time: a Geographical Perspective on Change*
1999	Baker, A. R. H. *Fraternity among the French Peasantry: Sociability and Voluntary Associations in the Loire Valley, 1815–1914*
1999	Bassin, M. *Imperial Visions: Nationalist Imagination and Geographical Expansion in the Russian Far East, 1840–1865*
2000	Meyer, D. R. *Hong Kong as Global Metropolis*
2000	Campbell, B. M. S. *English Seigniorial Agriculture 1250–1450*
2000	Hannah, M. G. *Governmentality and the Mastery of Territory in Nineteenth-Century America*
2002	Barton, G. A. *Empire Forestry and the Origins of Environmentalism*
2003	Johnson, N. C. *Ireland, the Great War and the Geography of Remembrance*

Figure 6.1 (*cont.*)

geographer can legitimately claim that 'it is not at all uncommon for historians to be slow in getting acquainted with pertinent work in geography' (Meinig 1997: 2), I am sure that equally distinguished historians could claim with similar legitimacy that geographers are often slow to familiarise themselves with relevant work in history. Believing that division and conflict are often at best based on misunderstanding and at worst on ignorance, my aim has been to widen simultaneously the historical perspectives of geographers and the geographical perspectives of historians. I write as a historical geographer and this book reflects my greater knowledge and understanding of my own field than of history.

I have considered four discourses of geography as master-narratives while recognising the simultaneous existence within them of local-narratives and of counter-narratives. Employing these discourses and narratives facilitates coherent dialogue; it creates a common language in which to conduct debate, although it carries with it also the danger of being accused of imposing order on diverse (some would argue, chaotic) knowledges. In which case, my plea is: 'Guilty'. I will now connect those discourses and narratives back to the question of the relations of geography and history. I will do so by considering the relation of historical geography first to history and then to geography. This will lead to a discussion of both geography and history as 'place histories' and to a brief consideration of the prospect for historical geography. In what follows, I am modifying my presentation elsewhere of some basic characteristics of historical geography. The seven principles which I set out may not be the only ones underpinning the practice of historical geography, but they do permit me to bring the relations of geography and history into sharper focus (Baker 1995, 1996b).

Historical geography and history

The first of my seven principles is that *historical geography, like history, asks questions about the past*. Unlike history, it addresses essentially geographical questions, but unlike contemporary geography it does so about places in the past rather than in the present. Historical geography's concern is with geographical problems, but its focus is upon those problems at some time in the past or during some period in the past. Historical geography is thus the geographical study of the past. Given the wide range of questions posed by geographers in general, there is an equally wide range of studies produced by historical geographers in particular. Some examine the changing location and distribution of human activities, particularly in studies of cultural diffusion; others examine the relationships of peoples with their physical environments in the past; some trace the making of landscapes or decode the meaning of landscapes in the past; others concern themselves with reconstructing the geography of regions or places in the past. But instead of examining these problems in particular places today, in the 2000s, historical geography does so in relation to past times or periods, such as 1086 or 1801, or the 1790s or the 1490s. Historical geography remains primarily a geographical enquiry even though it uses historical

Figure 6.2 The loneliness of research in the records' office: the author in the Archives Départementales, Nancy, France, in July 2000
Source: Author

data, research methods and techniques, and even though it focuses on the past rather than the present. Historical geography does not cease to be geography when it gazes upon the past; nor does it thereby become history. Historical geography is geography because it poses geographical questions, because it brings a variety of geographical perspectives to studies of the past. The problems investigated by geographers and historians – and, indeed, by those in cognate disciplines – often have a great deal in common, but the ways in which those problems are addressed reflect their differing perspectives, their differing geographical or historical – or other – imaginations.

The second of my principles is that *both the sources and the theories of historical geography, like those of history, are problematic.* The practice of historical geography involves an attempt to resolve the dialectical tension between 'fact' and 'interpretation'. Facts do not speak for themselves, interpretations must speak to others: both need to be contextualised. The geography we reconstruct from the 'facts' discovered in historical sources is not factual at all; it is instead a series of judgements which one scholar puts forward for acceptance (or rejection) by others (Fig. 6.2). Here a historical geographer has to be as attentive as any historian to the two classic discussions, by E. H. Carr (1961) and G. R. Elton (1967), on how to research, write and read history. In brief, and in caricature, the former presented the case for the subjectivity of history and the latter that for the objectivity of history. The former sought relative truth in history, the latter sought absolute truth. That these two books are still very well worth reading more than a generation after they were first published reflects their having addressed fundamental questions about the pursuit of history which even today each and every practising historian – and thus every historical geographer – must answer, at least to his or her own satisfaction, in order to conduct and to communicate research. The contrasting views of Carr and Elton have both been challenged to varying degrees since the 1980s by postmodernists who view history as just one discourse among many. Evans (1997) provides a judicious and poised critique of the Carr–Elton divide and a subtle (and, to my mind, very successful) defence against the postmodernist attack upon history and historians. He creates a balance among these competing views of history, making a convincing case for both the necessity and the possibility of history as an academic enterprise.

Our knowledge and understanding of the past is undoubtedly constrained (as well, paradoxically, as being enhanced) by our own ideas and ideologies, and by our own theories and techniques. Furthermore, our geographical knowledge of the past must always be incomplete because of the partial (in all of its senses) nature of historical sources. A complete record of the past was never compiled and only a small portion of the historical record which was compiled has survived and has been read critically by historical geographers. Moreover, a historical document or other source comes to us, not as a pure source about the past, but as one which has been refracted through the mind of the historical recorder and which in turn has now to be viewed though the eyes of present-day scholars. Strictly speaking, we are not reconstructing an 'actual' geography of the past; instead we are constructing an 'imagined' past geography. But this is most certainly not to argue that historical geography is simply in the minds of individuals, and that consequently there is not one but an infinity of interpretations with none any more 'correct' than any other: to reject the wholly 'objective' view of historico-geographical enquiry does not lead inevitably to an embrace of the wholly 'subjective' view.

Adopting, as I have done, a historiographical approach to the relations of geography and history reveals the tension which existed and to some extent persists between empirical and theoretical approaches in historical geography. There has been and to some extent remains a divide between empirically driven and theoretically driven work, between work which prioritises the historical sources and their geographical interpretation and work which focuses on today's social theories and their application to past geographies. The empirical emphasis which characterised much historical geography during the 1950s and 1960s came to be challenged by a social theoretical thrust during the 1980s and 1990s. In the process, a gulf also developed between a 'traditional', empirical, historical geography and a 'new', critical, cultural geography. While some of the former was characterised by mind-numbingly 'factual' accounts, some of the latter engaged in blindingly pretentious 'theorising'. I maintain that both the divide within historical geography and the gulf between it and cultural geography can be bridged by a wider recognition of the interdependence of 'fact' and 'interpretation', of the necessity to consummate the marriage of empirical and theoretical approaches: in this context, the whole is indeed greater than the sum of its parts. I also maintain that the best work in historical geography has always situated specific studies within their general contexts and it has always engaged general ideas to illuminate particular past geographies.

Circumspect use of a broadening spectrum of sources has long been a trademark of historical geography and it should remain so. A similarly cautious but extended use of theory has significantly modified the practice of historical geography in recent decades. Whereas, hitherto, theory was engaged only implicitly, now it is employed explicitly and rightly so. The best work in historical geography has been theoretically informed and, as a by-product, theoretically informative: it is the nature of historical geography to be more consumptive than productive of theory. The 'theoretical turn' in historical geography led initially to the application of geographical theory (notably central place theory and spatial diffusion theory) to past geographies and subsequently to an appeal to social theory, as the limits as well as the merits of spatial theories came increasingly to be revealed. But just as a historical geographer must select among the available sources, so s/he has to choose among the range of available social theories. Moreover, both preferences should be exercised explicitly and argued assiduously. As historical geographers, we co-opt both the sources and the theories which we consider to be best suited to our purposes – which places on us the obligation to define our purposes very carefully and very fully. Most historical geographers are aware of the wide spectrum of literary, graphical and statistical sources available to them and delight in expanding the range of sources which they are able to interrogate as witnesses to past geographies. Many are also becoming aware of the wide register of social theories which can be called upon to illuminate past geographies, recognising that they shed their lights from different vantage points.

Much work in historical geography has been grounded, not always consciously or critically, in modernisation theory (derived from sociologists like Herbert Spencer, Emile Durkheim and Max Weber) which posits an evolutionary change from a 'traditional' to a 'modern' society. But in recent decades historical geographers have enlisted other theories of social change. Most notably, the practice of historical geography has come under the influence of social theorists like Karl Marx, Michel Foucault and Anthony Giddens. Some work in historical geography has engaged directly with social theory in an attempt to 'geographicise' it, while other studies have sought to harness social theory to their own empirical studies. (For examples of the former, see Harvey 1973, 1982a, 1989; Gregory 1989b, 1990b, 1991; Harris 1991; Driver 1992a; Philo 1992a. For examples of the latter, see Philo 1992b; Driver 1993; Harris 1997; Hannah 2000). Mitchell has noted that 'there is actually something afoot in historical geography, something that is good not just for this small corner of the discipline, but for geography as a whole and even more for critical scholarship in general'. That 'something', Mitchell emphasises, is a body of work, encompassing such diverse works as Anne Knowles' (1997) *Calvinists Incorporated*, George Henderson's (1999) *California and the Fictions of Capital*, Matthew Hannah's *Governmentality and the Mastery of Territory in Nineteenth-Century America* (2000), Dan Clayton's (2000) *Islands of Truth* and Robert Lewis' (2000) *Manufacturing Montreal*, which is 'deeply theoretical without sacrificing – indeed that relies on – empirical richness. This empirical richness is exactly what licenses and grounds the theory, that gives it force (a force well beyond the vast majority of what is being produced in cultural studies or social theory in general)' (Mitchell 2002: 95–6). The marriage of theory and empiricism in (historical) geographical studies advocated many years ago by Harvey (1967) is proving to be very fertile.

A historical geographer faces the dual challenge of acknowledging the problematic character both of his or her sources and of his or her theories, and of persuading other scholars to accept his or her own preferred interpretation of some past geography. I subscribe to consensual historical geography. Of course, any consensus in history can be sought, and sometimes achieved, only by debate. This brings me to my third principle of historical geography: *debate is central to the practice of historical geography*. Rethinking and revising current, orthodox interpretations should be the norm in historical geography: it should be conventional to be radical. Current ideas and assertions must be, and must expect to be, revised as new evidence comes to light, as new techniques of analysis become available, as new problems deserving attention are identified, and as new ideas and theories are brought into play. Debate, both about substantive issues and about research methodologies, lies at the heart of historical geography as it does also of history (Fig. 6.3). Within historical geography, as within history, there should be an unrelenting criticism of all orthodoxies and conventional wisdoms, as well as an unremitting awareness of discourses in cognate disciplines.

Discussion and controversy are at the heart of the body of historico-geographical knowledge, pumping new life-giving blood around; they should not be thought of, or used as, an appendix. This is not to deny that it is the task of the historical geographer and of the historian to provide new knowledge about the past, but it is to assert the importance of also offering new understandings or interpretations of the past. Of course, these should be seen as interdependent rather than independent objectives. For example, mapping the changing distribution of wealth in England from the mid-eleventh century to the mid-sixteenth century has added considerably to our knowledge of the regional geography of England during that period, but it has not *per se* expanded very much, if at all, our understanding of the processes of regional transformation which underpinned that changing pattern. While bridge-building brick by brick requires diligence and tenacity as well as specific technical skills, designing the bridge as a whole calls for imagination; and once the bridge has been built, the task remains of persuading others to cross it with you. It is, of course, easier to destroy bridges than it is to construct them. Herein lies the challenge and the excitement of historical research: discovering new 'facts' and trying to convince others of the appropriateness of your 'interpretation' of them.

Figure 6.3 The conviviality of debate among historical geographers: participants at a symposium on research methods in historical geography at Cambridge in July 1979: (from left to right) Paul Koroscil (Simon Fraser University, Canada), Derek Gregory (University of Cambridge), Brian Harley (University of Exeter) and Ulla Göranson (University of Stockholm)
Source: Author

Given the nature of history and thus of historical geography, there is no possibility of writing a definitive historical account of any period, place or topic. Any such account will, sooner or later, need to be revised in the light of new theories, new evidence, new techniques and new concerns. We must all expect – and indeed wish – our work to be challenged. We must all expect – reluctantly or enthusiastically – to modify our own 'facts' and 'interpretations' partially or even to change them radically. All 'new' historical geographies are destined to become 'old' ones, and not just because, in the words of the first voice in Dylan Thomas' play, *Under Milk Wood*, 'time passes' (Thomas 1954: 3).

Historical geography and geography

The relations between historical geography and contemporary geography have been in turn brumal and thermal. Much of the blame for antagonism between their practitioners must rest with Hartshorne's (1939) insistence on a clear dividing line between history and geography (and thus in effect between historical geography and geography). His later (1959) concession of a limited historical licence to geographers blurred that line but certainly did not erase it. But some blame must also rest with those human geographers who have insisted on the need for all geographical work to have relevance to the 'contemporary' world. There are, however, logical grounds for reasserting the relevance of historical geography to geography in general. This I will argue in relation to two further principles of historical geography.

My fourth principle is that *historical geography is essentially concerned with geographical change through time*. While retaining a link here with history's concern with cultural and environmental change, historical geography's specific attention to the geographical aspects of change reflects its umbilical link to geography. The geographies of inhabited regions, areas and places are always changing, never static, so that all geography must be concerned with changing patterns and forms, and with the processes producing those changes. Concepts of geographical change constitute common ground for historical and contemporary geographers. This has been most apparent in studies of spatial diffusion but the point has much wider purchase, as was shown, for example, in Harvey's (1967, 1969) essays on models of the evolution of spatial patterns in human geography and on temporal modes of explanation in geography. Those essays are now very dated, but at the time they provided a significant bridge between historical and contemporary human geography. A shared interest in the processes of geographical change both enables and requires dialogue between historical and contemporary human geographers, while the broader concern with cultural and environmental change enables and requires both sets to engage with scholars in a wide range of cognate disciplines. Somewhat paradoxically, an excellent example of such intra- and interdisciplinary discussion of the concept of geographical change is that of Dodgshon (1998), who argues that society's use of space is a powerful source of inertia and that radical change has to be steered around such spaces.

Historical geography is fundamentally diachronic rather than synchronic in character. During the 1920s and 1930s historical geography was seen in the English-speaking world as being the description of the geography of an area at some past time, following the dictum that a historical geography of any region is in principle possible for any period of its history and that it must be written separately for each period. The reconstruction of past, static geographies was the orthodox view of historical geography and it often found expression in the mapping of historical sources. That notion was questioned, but extended rather than rejected, by those who added historical narratives, or 'vertical themes' of landscape and geographical change to the orthodox historical geographer's geographical descriptions, or 'horizontal cross-sections' of places in the past. The concept of the 'horizontal cross-section' does, however, have some profound weaknesses which render it questionable as a research method: for example, it is based on the false premise that history is concerned with time and geography with space, history with change and narration and geography with distribution and description – it creates a false dichotomy between history and geography instead of recognising the interdependence of, and connections between, the two disciplines. Furthermore, the cross-sectional method is based on the dubious assumption that the geography of a place can be stable, unchanging for a given period or time in the past; it assumes a balance, an order, among the components of an area's geography at a particular moment or period in time. Such an assumption is questionable both theoretically and empirically: any place is constantly changing, although not necessarily at a uniform rate.

In practice horizontal cross-sections have often been reconstructed not as being of interest *per se* but as one way of approaching the problem of studying geographical change, doing so through the (theoretically limited) method of comparative statics. A sequence of cross-sections may provide a description of change, but any explanation or understanding must address directly the question of geographical change by examining the processes at work as well as their products, the mappable patterns. Even a (laboriously, meticulously) reconstructed distribution pattern raises questions about how it came into being. Quintessentially, historical geography is the study of geographical changes through time rather than of geographical distributions at one time. The understanding of geographical change lies at the core of historical geography, as it does of geography generally.

This leads to my fifth principle: *historical geography is central to geography as a whole, not peripheral to it.* Geography has always been a historically grounded enterprise. In the broadest sense, Western historical geography has been basically concerned with the geographical impact of the growth and spread of capitalism and of liberal democracy throughout the world, with the impact of the Industrial Revolution and of the French Revolution upon different countries and continents. Historical geographers have been concerned with describing, explaining and understanding the changes that have taken place historically in the localities and regions, the countries and continents, of the world. In parallel, the concern of contemporary human geographers with changing geographical structures has required them to adopt a historical perspective in their studies of the present-day modern world.

That position differs not at all from the view long held by many French historical geographers, including for a time France's leading historical geographer, Roger Dion, that historical geography could be equated with retrospective human geography (*géographie humaine rétrospective*). Dion, inaugurating his Chair of Historical Geography at the Collège de France in 1948, argued that present-day cultural landscapes must be viewed as reflections of their histories and that the human geography of France must of necessity be a historical geography; almost ten years later, in a general essay on historical geography, he argued that it was in essence a retrospective human geography, looking to the past in so far as it was necessary to explain the geography of the 'present day' and that it was geography rather than history precisely because its concern was primarily to explain the 'present' (Dion 1949, 1957). These two methodological statements gave historical geography in France a logical but limited realm; they also tied it perhaps too closely to contemporary human geography, placing it a disadvantage when the latter (during the post-Second World War decades of social and economic re-construction) turned towards planning and applied geography, towards *géographie humaine prospective*. Historical geography as retrospective human geography gave it the limited role of handmaiden not to history, as some historians have seen it, but to geography. While it had the merit of not separating off historical geography from contemporary human geography, its relation was restricted to one of temporal and explanatory proximity rather than being based on a shared set of geographical concepts applied in some instances to the 'present' and in others to the past. Histor-ical geography is much more than retrospective human geography: it studies past geographies in general and views the 'present-day' geography as just one of many geographies. But too often the arbitrary division between 'present' and 'past' has been employed in an attempt to divide the sheep (in the guise of contemporary human geographers) from the goats (the historical geographers). Dennis (1989) has made a strong case for dismantling the inhibiting barriers between the past and the present in studies of urban geography and it could and should be logically extended to encompass other systematic studies.

The case against distancing historical geography from geography in general has frequently been stated but often ignored. But it has not always been necessary to make the case at all. Langton (1986) has pointed out that leading members of the Aberystwyth 'school' of historical geography – H. J. Fleure, Daryll Forde and Emrys Bowen – made no attempt to define historical geography separately from the rest of geography, except in terms of the time to which it related. A leading American historical geographer, A. H. Clark (1960), emphasised that all of the systematic branches of geography, such as political geography or climatology, could and should be studied historically: historical geography is not itself a 'topical specialty'. In my own 1972 essay on 'rethinking historical geography', I argued for a closer relation between historical geography and the rest of geography:

The dichotomy between historical geography and geography could be broken down, to be replaced by historical studies in the branches of systematic geography. Studies in, for example, 'historical agricultural geography', 'historical urban geography' and 'historical economic geography' seem to offer possibilities of fundamental development, particularly in terms of a better understanding of the processes by which geographical change through time may take place. (Baker 1972: 28)

Gregory (1976), reacting specifically against Guelke's (1975) attempt to distin-guish historical geography from the rest of the discipline and to advance an ide-alist approach within it, suggested the need for a more critical approach which would integrate historical materialist scholarship into geography by relating the experiences of individuals to the deeper structures which frame their actions. On a different tack towards the same objective, Langton (1988a: 17) claimed that there was no basis at all in the intellectual tradition or practice of many of those who had worked on the human geography of the past to justify the separation of historical geography from human geography as a whole. Haggett (1990: 118) noted with regret that historical geography is sometimes viewed as a separate part of geography because for him the role of time had always been such an integral element – in physical, human and regional geography – that he preferred to see it 'as a dynamic in all our studies'. Haggett made this comment notwithstanding the highest regard he has for work in historical geography. More outspokenly, Langton (1988a: 22) concluded that 'we must jettison the idea of a distinct subdiscipline of historical geography', because he subscribed to the notion that 'in so far as the relationships described in the present or the past can only be accounted for and made intelligible with reference to the way that they have developed through time, *all* human geography *must* be historical and therefore, in the same way that all history *must* be about some place and therefore geographical, the adjective is an entirely superfluous tautology'. Driver argued for the historicity of human geography and claimed that 'as human geography is profoundly historical (in more senses than have been acknowledged), thinking historically is no luxury; on the contrary it is an essential part of doing human geography' (Driver 1988b: 504).

Langton's and Driver's arguments are certainly logical but they do gloss over the simple, more pragmatically based fact that some geographers are enthused by studying geographies of the 'present' and others by studying past geographies. I have no difficulty in referring, for the sake of convenience, to the former as contemporary human geographers and to the latter as historical geographers: they are differentiated by the temporal focus of their geographical enquiries. Such tags serve merely to signal the broad objectives of those choosing to wear them. While not all historical geography must be retrospective human geography, no historical geography should be isolated from geography in general. With hindsight, it can be seen that the endeavour to establish historical geography as a self-conscious, separate discipline was not intellectually sustainable in the long term. Paradoxically, endeavours to create for historical geography a separate existence could be considered to have been too successful; isolating historical geography from contemporary human geography and distancing it from cognate disciplines (except economic history) deprived it of long-term nourishment. During the past decade or so, historical geographers and contemporary human geographers have especially been brought together in studies of modernity (Ogborn 2000) and of identity (Graham 2000), as well as of heritage and memory, which Johnson (2000) calls 'historical geographies of the present'. The last of these clearly also provides opportunities for those who seek to make manifest the relevance of historical studies by considering the diverse ways in which pasts are represented to the present, the various ways in which pasts are translated for, and made meaningful to, today's world.

Today, as contemporary human geography comes increasingly to reject the presentist and functionalist mode of interpretation and once again to recognise the necessity for a historical mode of explanation, there are renewed calls for a *rapprochement* between historical and contemporary human geography. In order to understand the geography of a place in the present it is necessary to take its past into account, to situate geographies historically. Even the so-called 'new cultural geography' (with its social theoretical emphasis), developed during the past ten years or so in Britain and America in part as a reaction against 'old cultural geography' (with its empirical emphasis), has come full-circle to stress that culture is constructed, that it is a process, so that it must be viewed in its historical context (Mitchell 2001). Earle and others (1989), in their contribution to a review of the condition of geography in America, argued that historical geography had long been viewed there as being peripheral to the broader field of human geography, but they detected and welcomed a growing convergence between the two. They stressed the growing recognition among geographers that historical context matters, specifically citing in support of their claim studies of geographical changes in the structure of capitalism and studies of the uneven development of the world economy. Harris (1991), acknowledging that there had been a change in the intellectual climate 'since historical geography emerged as a substantial geographical subfield', suggested that a growing conversation between historical geography and parts of social theory (especially those parts concerned with the concepts of power and modernity) could enrich both, while drawing historical geography into much closer relation with the rest of human geography. Within the post-positivist intellectual revolution, Harris saw historical geography and much of the rest of human geography 'converging – by backing into each other' (Harris 1991: 671). Agnew (1996), a leading political geographer, claims that all geographers are historical geographers now. For example, feminist geographers are adopting strongly historical perspectives in their endeavours 'to make sense of the world' (Domosh and Seager 2001). Entrikin (1998) sees the blending of historical geography into human geography as paralleling a broader tendency towards diminishing the distance between the social sciences and the humanities. The process may be viewed accordingly as part of the broader 'historic turn' in the human sciences (McDonald 1996). Meinig (1999a: 82) asserts that now 'is a strategic time for historical geography and human geography to become far more effectively bound together'. He rests his case on what he calls 'the growing chorus of voices' urging geographers to turn their main attention to the study of places and regions and their interconnections. Schein (2001) writes about 're-placing the past' in geography, noting the increasing attraction and importance both of the place of the past in geographical understanding and of past places themselves. There is considerable common ground for contemporary human geographers and historical geographers in what might best be termed 'place histories'.

Place histories

My final two principles of historical geography relate to its concern with the histories of places. My sixth principle is that *historical geography is fundamentally concerned with place synthesis, not with spatial analysis*. Historical geography is more sharply focused upon period and place than it is upon time and space.

Geography is no more the science of space than history is that of time: both space and time are as much the concerns of natural and social scientists as they are of geographers and historians. Concepts of spatial organisation and of temporal orga- nisation are essentially interdisciplinary rather than quintessentially geographical and historical. Ideologies shape time and space, so that temporal and spatial struc- tures must be seen as reflecting the decisions and actions of individuals and of social groups. Historical geographers examine the social organisation of space and time, not the temporal and spatial organisation of society. Time and space are viewed as being culturally appraised, like other resources and phenomena. This means that it is possible to research and write historical geographies of time and space with the same justification as researching and writing historical geographies of, say, timber, taxation and taboos or of sugar, sexual behaviour and socialism. Both history and geography clearly possess many systematic or 'vertical' divisions, but analytical studies of such individual forms, processes or ideas have value added to them if they are seen not as ends in themselves but as contributing towards a synthesis, towards a holistic understanding of particular 'horizontal' periods and places, towards the construction of period histories and regional geographies. As a historian, Phythian-Adams (1991) has argued for the superiority of 'integrative history' (which seeks 'to reconstitute and to explain the multi-dimensional nature of past experience') over 'the disintegrative historical approach' (or 'specialised thematic history'). While the latter examines past societies in terms of their specific components (such as demography, economics, class, gender or crime), the former explores 'society' over time and in a particular place (such as locality, region, na- tion or nations, or even the world). As a geographer, I agree with Phythian-Adams that such a broad interdisciplinary approach should be our 'ultimate aspiration' be- cause it is the most culturally relevant to the historical and geographical education of our fellow citizens.

This conducts me to my seventh and final principle of historical geography, that *historical geography highlights the historical specificity of particular places.* His- torical geography emphasises the distinctive and varying geographical patterns and geographical processes identifiable in particular places; it seeks to situate places within their own historical contexts. Each place is seen as being histori- cally and geographically distinctive, with its own personality, its own history and geography. Differences between places are of intrinsic interest and concern to historical geography, be they differences in the 'same' place at separate times or periods, or differences between separate places at the same time or period. The comparative method is employed to highlight both differences and similarities in order to enhance understanding of particular places rather than to contribute to some grand historico-geographical theory. The historical geography of individual places (and of the world as a whole, seen as the largest place available for geo- graphical study) is not essayed necessarily as part of some grand, developmental narrative, nor of some unified, modernisation or other historical theory. Instead, historico-geographical studies acknowledge the immensely varied routes of geo- graphical change taken by different places in the past. The practice of historical geography, aiming primarily to situate and to understand geographical patterns and processes in particular places, involves generalisation at a variety of historical and geographical scales and recognises the interdependence of places at a variety of geographical and historical scales, but it does not necessarily include on its agenda theoretical abstraction for its own sake and is even sceptical about any 'theories of history' or philosophies of universal evolution.

During the past decade or so there has been a remarkable revival of interest in the geographical concept of place, both by geographers and by historians and other scholars in cognate disciplines. Considerable attention is being given to interpreting the meaning of places from a cultural perspective and to examining the construction of places by social forces. In this, they are reflecting the view that places recall events, that geographies summon histories. 'Present' places are palimpsests of past events: they have been repeatedly written on, partially wiped out, and written on again. Some place histories focus on the sense of place, others on the perceptions and representations of places, still others on the symbolism of place and the role of place in the construction of social identities, and yet others on the consumption rather than the production of places (Lawton 1983; Entrikin 1991, 1994). An excellent example in this genre is Ogborn's (1998) study of some places/spaces of modernity – the Magdalen Hospital, the street, the Vauxhall pleasure garden, and the Universal Register Office – in London between 1680 and 1780. Superb examples by historians are the essays on some of France's major historical places – such as the caves of Lascaux, Verdun, Versailles and the Eiffel tower – in Pierre Nora's (1998) edited volume on symbols of the French past.

Daniels (1992), reviewing place studies in geography, saw this renewed emphasis on place awareness as a reclaiming of geography's imaginative ground. Massey (1995), in a perceptive set of reflections on places and their pasts, demonstrates most clearly the convergence of historical and contemporary studies, doing so in this instance as a geographer expressing her ideas about places to an audience of historians. She argues that 'the past of a place is open to a multiplicity of readings in the present. Moreover, the claims and counter-claims about the present character of a place depend in almost all cases on particular, rival, interpretations of its past.' The past, Massey stresses, can be present in places in a variety of ways, both materially and by resonance. The past, therefore, helps make the present but it is a two-way process. Thus Massey concludes that in trying to understand the identity of places we should not separate geography from history. But she goes beyond that to argue also that because places are culturally invented and reinvented historically, it might be useful to think of places not as areas on maps but as constantly shifting articulations of social relations through time. 'The description and identification of a place is', Massey concludes, 'always inevitably an intervention not only into geography but also, at least implicitly, into the (re)telling of the historical constitution of the present' (Massey 1995: 190).

With others, Massey is rethinking the concept of place/region and stressing its historical dimension: places/regions are being seen as 'constructed both materially and discursively, and each modality of this construction affects the other. Moreover, every place or region "arrives" at the present moment trailing long histories of economics and politics, of gender, class and ethnicity; and histories, too, of the many different stories which have been told about all of these' (Allen et al. 1998: 9). Without a memory, without a past, a place – just like a person – has no identity. Historical geographers thus have a significant role to play in the (re)construction of place identities. Moreover, most of us live our lives forwards, planning our futures, but we make sense of our lives backwards, by reflecting on our pasts. A painstaking acquaintance with the past makes possible a better understanding of our present condition. Our increasingly deracinated societies need constantly to be reminded of their historical and geographical roots. Hence the social importance of historical geography's role in (re)constructing the histories of places. The relevance of historical geography lies in its contribution to the construction of historically and geographically literate societies (and especially historically and geographically literate decision-makers). Historical geography empowers individuals and societies, enabling them to know and understand not only their own historical and geographical identities but also those of others. Twenty years ago Harvey (1982b) published a 'manifesto' for a materialist geography, arguing that it was imperative that all geography should become historical and that it should also become 'a people's geography'. He asserted:

The geography we make must be a people's geography, not based on pious universalisms, ideals, and good intents, but a more mundane enterprise that reflects earthly interests, and claims, that confronts ideologies and prejudices as they really are, that faithfully mirrors the complex weave of competition, struggle, and cooperation within . . . shifting social and physical landscapes . . . The world must be depicted, analysed, and understood not as we would like it to be but as it really is, the material manifestation of human hopes and fears mediated by powerful and conflicting processes of social reproduction. Such a people's geography must have a popular base, be threaded into the fabric of daily life with deep taproots into the well-springs of popular consciousness. But it must also open channels of communication, undermine parochialist world views, and confront or subvert the power of dominant classes or the state. (Harvey 1982b: 7)

That 'manifesto' remains pertinent today. Telling place histories for people is what historical geography is really about. There are so many stories to tell, so many ways of telling them and so many audiences to whom to tell them. The revived interest in the concept of place has been associated also with what Daniels calls some 'methodological renovations' in story telling. A renewed interest in the problem of geographical description has promoted an exploration of new forms of 'thick description' and narration (Daniels 1992: 311 and 319), of new ways of telling stories about 'making histories and constructing human geographies' (Pred 1990). Historians, too, are evaluating different narrative forms and assessing the implications of recognising their own stories as cultural constructions (Burke 1991b; Cronon 1992). But I have been concerned here only with the problems of geographical description and historical narration to the extent that they impinge upon the relations of geography and history. Detailed discussion of how to research and how to write history or geography, historical geography or geographical history, is beyond the scope of this book.

Prospect

Paradoxically, for the practice of historical geography it is the future that matters most. I will, therefore, conclude by considering briefly some of the implications of the arguments I have presented. Historical geography possesses both the coherence and the relevance necessary to ensure its survival. But in what form will it – or should it – survive? I will not endeavour either to predict or to prescribe the future for historical geography. In any event, it would be impossible to do so. Historiographical studies are poor predictors of the future shape of a discipline or sub-discipline: all that one may say with any degree of confidence is that the concerns of the next generation of historical geographers will almost certainly be different from those of the current and previous generations. None the less, my foundational premise is that there will also very probably be some basic continuities and that identifying them might enable us to reconcile some of the different positions taken by historical scholars about both methodological and substantive issues. Greater appreciation of the *structures* as well as of the *conjonctures* and *événements* of historical geography might lead to more intellectual tolerance. It should, at the very least, caution us against inflated claims that any one approach or theme is necessarily superior to that of others. Such claims have been made too often in the past – and too often turned out to be mistaken.

Let me refer to just one methodological example of such want of forbearance. When Donald Meinig (1978a) proposed in the *American Historical Review* his thesis on 'the continuing shaping of America' as 'a prospectus for geographers and historians', he was attacked by fellow-geographer Carville Earle (1978), not because Earle disagreed with Meinig's findings and suggestions but because he objected to Meinig's approach. Meinig was working mainly within the regional and locational discourses of geography, whereas Earle reproached him mainly from within ecological (environmental) discourse and to some extent from within the spatial (locational) discourse. Even more fundamentally, Meinig's essay was situated within the framework of the historical sciences (or humanities) and Earle's within that of the social sciences. Their views were, as Earle stated, 'worlds apart' – a fact which made him despondent, even though, as a geographer, he would in another context acknowledge the importance of recognising and understanding different 'worlds', both at present and in the past. Meinig had modestly drafted one agenda for historical geography; Earle had mistakenly read it as if it were the only such agenda. Earle (1999) has persisted in his criticism, objecting to Meinig's 'high Tory interpretation of the American geographical past' and making clear his own preference for a Marxist or at least a liberal approach to the historical geography of America.

Meinig's work has certainly aroused much discussion. He had published scholarly historical regional studies of Texas (1969), of the Great Columbia Plain (1968) and of the American Southwest (1971) before venturing a major synthesis of the historical geography of North America (1986, 1993, 1998). Both the style and the substance of Meinig's writings have given rise to considerable comment. Responding modestly to five (predominantly positive) critiques of his work published in *Historical Geography* (1995, vol. 24), Meinig affirms his commitment to 'free-wheeling interpretation', to 'large thematic suggestive treatments of an array of specific geographic topics', to geography as art rather than as social science, to not being a methodologist, and to not seeking 'any final determination of the character and meaning of our past'. He states his limited intentions as follows:

One is not proving anything, or solving problems, or refining theory, or providing detailed answers from the past to guide the present into the future. One *can* hope to provide a perspective, a way of looking at things, a help in making sense out of something far too vast to 'explain' – at best, perhaps, to provide the basis for a meditation. (Meinig 1997: 8)

Discussion of Meinig's work continues. He himself defends his major project as a historical geographer's critique of common presentations of American history and as a geographical complement to the ongoing task of reassessing and reconstructing American history (Meinig 1999b).

Harris (1999) is full of admiration for the 'huge stories' which Meinig tells, despite the fact that this 'vastly impressive work is added to the geographical canon at a time when the major trends in the discipline are in other directions' – there is little reflection in Meinig's work of current geographical interests in GIS, in environmental issues or in cultural studies. None the less, Harris argues, 'it is important that the tradition of scholarship exemplified so well in *The Shaping of America* be maintained. No one else will write a set of books remotely like this, but a great many people will be influenced by Meinig's extraordinary work. In myriad ways, large and small, it will enter the ongoing debate about America.' Earle (1999) continues his attack on Meinig's work, because of – in his view – Meinig's portrayal of the historical geography of America in terms of order and continuity rather than of disorder and discontinuity. Earle wants to bring into the foreground of the picture 'the unseemly struggles that have pitted workers against capital, egalitarians against elitists, anarchists against progressives, big producers against small, and nationalizers against regionalizers'. While Meinig argues for the continuous, Earle pleads for the discontinuous, shaping of America. A historian, Carl Abbott (2001), reviewing *Transcontinental America, 1850–1915*, admits that he and his colleagues can learn much from Meinig, especially about the mutability of regions. But he also registers his disappointment, because 'the trend within the historical profession has been away from structural analysis such as Meinig's and toward novelistic microstudies pivoted on the details of ordinary people and places'. Further, Abbott is also disappointed by the failure of Meinig's work to reflect the cultural turn in history. In short, Earle and Abbott would have preferred

Meinig to have written a different kind of historical geography: they identify the weaknesses of his work on their own terms rather than recognising the strengths of Meinig's work on his terms. Their views of historical geography are unnecessarily blinkered. They leave no room for multiple and differing perspectives upon the past. Earle wants a more Marxist approach, Abbott a more cultural approach: they judge Meinig's work from their own perspectives and not from that of Meinig himself.

One of my aims has been to demonstrate the diversity, the vigour, the coherence and the relevance of historical geography, to reconcile some of the oppositions perceived within it and also between historical geography and history. Richard Dennis wishes 'to reassert the importance of a diverse historical geography which gives equal value and attention to different approaches' (Dennis 2001: 20). Some disputes within historical geography may be interpreted as originating in one of the binary oppositions which are integral to its pursuit (and indeed to the pursuit of history and geography generally). Historical geographers encounter a number of such oppositions: for example, past/present; empirical/theoretical; material/imagined; and human/physical. Individual scholars adopting uncompromisingly different positions within any such pair can find themselves in unproductive conflict. I contend that our hope for greater knowledge and enhanced understanding of past geographies lies both in our reconciling such differences and in our recognising the creativity of such tensions. Reconciliation can be achieved by acknowledging the interdependence of the apparent oppositions: just as pursuit of the past cannot be disconnected from the present in which it is prosecuted, so the present is tied to varying degrees by links to its past; just as empirical work is, implicitly or explicitly, theoretically informed, so theoretical work needs to be empirically grounded if it is to have applicability; material geographies are products of imaginations, while imagined geographies are (often distorted) reflections of material geographies; human geographies cannot be removed entirely from their physical contexts, while physical environments are not immune from human activities. I am arguing here for the attraction of opposites and against opposition to such attractions. The nature of historical geography as I have described it – and indeed practised and experienced it – necessitates interdisciplinary and intradisciplinary perspectives and is nourished by intellectual tolerance.

I expect the apparently modernist approach which I have adopted in this book to be challenged by those who consider that the weaknesses of such a tack outweigh any strengths it might have. Some may consider that I have imposed order where none exists, projected an artificial coherence upon a real chaos. Some may consider that I have provided, as Earle might say, 'a tidily contrived narrative of historical geography's unified advance' (Earle 1995: 455), that the categories of knowledge and understanding which I have employed are subjective and used in what Livingstone has called (in another context) 'a bid to control conceptual territory by linguistic stricture' (Livingstone 1992: 265). My defence against such a charge would be that I have sought order and coherence in the relations of geography and history, and in the natures of historical geography and geographical history, not as ends in themselves but as a means of permitting more meaningful dialogue between and among geographers and historians. By apparently separating off categories of knowledge, as I do in this book, I lay myself open to being accused of seeking to police interdisciplinary and even intradisciplinary boundaries. But my purpose has been quite the opposite. While recognising for the convenience of argument the existence of 'boundaries' around fields of knowledge, I have both acknowledged their permeability and advocated more border crossings. It is the very hybridity of historical geography and geographical history which appeals to me. Indeed, I envisage and favour a realignment away from the traditional framework of geography, history and other disciplines (an institutional and epistemological framework inherited largely from the nineteenth century) and towards an interdisciplinary framework of spatial studies, environmental studies, landscape studies and area studies.

I also expect the essentialist approach which I have taken here to be contested. I defend my position in two ways. First, I accept the notion of geography and history as situated discourses. Every historian and historical geographer rewrites the past in the light of his or her own circumstances. That knowledge is situated is not a postmodernist discovery, more a reinvention. Over a century ago an American historian with a keen sense of geography, Frederick Jackson Turner, stated that 'each age writes the history of the past with reference to the conditions uppermost in its own time' (Turner 1891, cited in Meinig 1998: 312). I cannot avoid writing a historiography of the relations of geography and history which is embedded in present geographical and historical concerns, and in my own personal experiences. I readily accept the notion of knowledge as discourse. But for discourse to be effective there have to be rules of debate, there must be grounds not only for disagreement but also for agreement. I have engaged with four discourses of geography in order to provide salons within which to hold structured but occasional discussions, which I much prefer to Pinteresque 'conversations' in which people talk to each other without communicating or engaging with each other. Secondly, to the extent that the postmodernist critique of essentialism undermines it on the grounds that every intellectual position is caught in a subjective discourse, that 'weakness' applies equally and unavoidably to postmodernism itself.

While exploring the relations of geography and history, I have drawn attention to the richness and diversity of work produced by those who have ventured on to the bridge between them. Some have been professional historians, some professional geographers, and some professors of cognate disciplines. The bridge, marking the 'frontier' between geography and history, has been and is – and should be – an area of intellectual turmoil. We should expect to find there scholars of very different intellectual origins and with very different imaginations. Such cultural contact is potentially very exciting and productive. But it does not mean, *pace* Frederick Jackson Turner, that all those who venture to the 'frontier' will of necessity be reduced to having a common set of values. I do not envisage the 'frontier' of geography and history necessarily as an intellectual melting pot. On the contrary, I see such contact as promoting greater diversity and in the process strengthening both geography and history. Those who journey to the 'frontier' should not expect to find a monolithic historical geography; if that is their expectation, they will instead be surprised by the multiplicity of historical geographies to be found there. Adventuring to the 'frontier' ensures meetings with many 'others': with other scholars, of course, but also and just as fundamentally with other periods and other places. My own explorations of this 'frontier' lead me to conclude that the practice of history is becoming more geographical, with historians increasingly incorporating geographical concepts into their interpretations of the pasts they study. At the same time, contemporary geography is becoming more historical: geography's purchase upon the past is being reaffirmed. There is today much more meeting of minds – between historians and historical geographers and between contemporary and historical geographers – than has been the case for a considerable time.

I have tried to set out here what I consider to be the *benefits* of osculation between geography and history. There has been much more dialogue between historians and geographers than is assumed by an emphasis on the 'Great Divide' but there could be even more. I acknowledge that there could also be what some might judge to be *costs* associated with my argument, because I have also advocated the assimilation of historical geography within geography as a whole. Some historical geographers might consider my suggestion to be suicidal on the grounds that it could mean 'the end of historical geography'. On the contrary, it could represent a renewal of the marriage vows between geography and history; it could be 'a new beginning', a widening of the geographical horizons of historians and a deepening of the historical understandings of geographers. These two processes have made much headway since Hereford George's (1901) survey of the relations of history and geography. But the journey is 'without end'. Amen.

References

Abbott, C. 2001 review of D. H. Meinig (1998) *Journal of Historical Geography* 27, 598–9

Abu-Lughod, J. L. 1989 *Before European Hegemony: the World System AD 1250–1350* (New York)

1995 'The world-system perspective in the construction of economic history' *History and Theory* 34, 86–98

Ackerman, E. 1941 'Sequent occupance of a Boston community' *Economic Geography* 17, 61–74

Adams, A. J. 1994 'Competing communities in the "Great Bog of Europe"' in W. J. T. Mitchell (ed.) *Landscape and Power* (Chicago) 35–76

Ade Ajayi, J. F. and Crowder, M. 1985 *Historical Atlas of Africa* (Harlow)

Agnew, J. 1996 'Conference reports: Annual Meeting of the Eastern Historical Geography Association, Old Town, Virginia, 25–28 October 1995' *Journal of Historical Geography* 22, 327–32

1998a 'European landscape and identity' in B. Graham (ed.) *Modern Europe: Place, Culture, Identity* (London) 213–35

1998b *Geopolitics: Re-visioning World Politics* (London)

Allen, J., Massey, D. and Cochrane, A. 1998 *Rethinking the Region* (London)

Allen, J. L. 1976 'Lands of myth, waters of wonder: the place of the imagination in the history of geographical exploration' in D. Lowenthal and M. Bowden (eds.) *Geographies of the Mind: Essays in Historical Geosophy in Honor of John Kirkland Wright* (New York) 41–61

Antipode 1994, 26 [a set of reviews of Cronon 1991] 113–76

Arnold, B. and Guha, R. 1995 *Nature, Culture: Imperialist Essays on the Environmental History of South Asia* (Delhi)

Ashworth, G. J. 1998 'The conserved European city as cultural symbol: the meaning of the text' in B. Graham (ed.) *Modern Europe: Place, Culture, Identity* (London) 261–86

Aston, M. and Bond, J. 1976 *The Landscape of Towns* (Gloucester)

Auerbach, B. 1903 '*Le tableau de la géographie de la France* de M. Vidal de la Blache' *Revue générale des sciences* 14, 895–900

Bailes, K. E. (ed.) 1985 *Environmental History: Critical Issues in Comparative Perspective* (London)

Bailyn, B. 1951 'Braudel's geohistory – a reconsideration' *Journal of Economic History* 11, 277–82

1996 'The idea of Atlantic history' *Itinerario* 20, 19–44

Baker, A. R. H. 1969 'Keeping the past in the present: the preservation of French townscapes' *Town and Country Planning* 37, 308–11

1972 (ed.) *Progress in Historical Geography* (Newton Abbot)

1981 'An historico-geographical perspective on time and space and on period and place' *Progress in Human Geography* 5, 439–43

1982 'On ideology and historical geography' in A. R. H. Baker and M. Billinge (eds.) *Period and Place: Research Methods in Historical Geography* (Cambridge) 233–43

1984 'Reflections on the relations of historical geography and the Annales school of history' in A. R. H. Baker and D. Gregory (eds.) *Explorations in Historical Geography: Interpretative Essays* (Cambridge) 1–27

1986 'Historical geography in Czechoslovakia' *Area* 18, 223–8

1988 'Historical geography and the study of the European landscape' *Geografiska Annaler B* 70, 5–16

1992a 'Introduction: on ideology and landscape' in A. R. H. Baker and G. Biger (eds.) *Ideology and Landscape in Historical Perspective* (Cambridge) 1–14

1992b 'Collective consciousness and the local landscape: national ideology and the commune council of Mesland (Loir-et-Cher) as landscape architect during the nineteenth century' in A. R. H. Baker and G. Biger (eds.) *Ideology and Landscape in Historical Perspective* (Cambridge) 255–88

1995 'The practice of historical geography' in J-R. Pitte (ed.) *Géographie historique et culturelle de l'Europe: hommage au Professeur Xavier de Planhol* (Paris) 31–49

1996a 'On the history and geography of historical geography' *Rekishi Chirigaku (Historical Geography)* 38, 1–24

1996b 'On the principles and practices of historical geography' *Annals of Geography: The Chiri Shiso* 37 no. 2, 33–50

1997 ' "The dead don't answer questionnaires": researching and writing historical geography' *Journal of Geography in Higher Education* 21, 231–43

1999a *Fraternity among the French Peasantry: Sociability and Voluntary Associations in the Loire Valley, 1815–1914* (Cambridge)

1999b 'Historical geographies of England and Wales, 1925–1995' in Y. Ben-Artzi, I. Bartal and E. Reiner (eds.) *Studies in Geography and History in Honour of Yehoshua Ben-Arieh* (Jerusalem) 34–62

Baker, A. R. H. and Biger, G. (eds.) 1992 *Ideology and Landscape in Historical Perspective* (Cambridge)

Baker, A. R. H. and Billinge, M. (eds.) 1982 *Period and Place: Research Methods in Historical Geography* (Cambridge)

(forthcoming) *Geographies of England: the North–South Divide, Imagined and Real* (Cambridge)

Baker, A. R. H. and Gregory, D. (eds.) 1984 *Explorations in Historical Geography: Interpretative Essays* (Cambridge)

Baker, A. R. H., Hamshere, J. D. and Langton, J. (eds.) 1970 *Geographical Interpretations of Historical Sources* (Newton Abbot)

Baker, J. N. L. 1931 'The geography of Daniel Defoe' *Scottish Geographical Magazine* 43, 257–69

Baker, K. (ed.) 2000 *The Faber Book of Landscape Poetry* (London)

Balchin, W. G. V. 1954 *The Making of the English Landscape: Cornwall* (London)

Balée, W. (ed.) 1998a *Advances in Historical Ecology* (New York)

1998b 'Introduction' and 'Historical ecology: premises and postulates' in W. Balée (ed.) *Advances in Historical Ecology* (New York) 1–10 and 13–29

Baratier, E., Duby, G. and Hildesheimer, E. (eds.) 1969 *Atlas historique: Provence, Comtat, Orange, Nice, Monaco* (Paris)

Barnes, H. E. 1921 'The relation of geography to the writing and interpretation of history' *Journal of Geography* 20, 321–37

Barnes, J. 2002 *Something to Declare* (London)

Barnes, T. and Duncan, J. S. (eds.) 1992 *Writing Worlds: Discourse, Text and Metaphor in the Representation of Landscape* (New York)

Barraclough, G. 1962 'Universal history' in H. P. R. Finberg (ed.) *Approaches to History* (London) 83–109

Barrell, J. 1972 *The Idea of Landscape and the Sense of Place: an Approach to the Poetry of John Clare* (Cambridge)

1980 *The Dark Side of the Landscape* (Cambridge)

Barrows, H. H. 1923 'Geography as human ecology' *Annals of the Association of American Geographers* 13, 1–14

Barthes, R. 1970 *L'empire des signes* (Geneva 1970)

Barton, G. A. 2002 *Empire Forestry and the Origins of Environmentalism* (Cambridge)

Bastié, J. 1997 'Les rapports de l'histoire et de la géographie vus par un géographe' in J-R. Pitte (ed.) *Apologie pour la géographie* (Paris) 11–25

1999 'Du hazard en histoire et en géographie' in J-R. Pitte and A-L. Sanguin (eds.) *Géographie et liberté: mélanges en hommages à Paul Claval* (Paris) 127–34

Bayliss-Smith, T. P. 1982 *The Ecology of Agricultural Systems* (Cambridge)

Bell, M., Butlin, R. A. and Heffernan, M. (eds.) 1995 *Geography and Imperialism 1820–1940* (Manchester)

Ben-Arieh, Y. 1979 *The Rediscovery of the Holy Land in the Nineteenth Century* (Jerusalem)

Ben-Artzi, Y., Bartal, I. and Reiner, E. (eds.) 1999 *Studies in History and Geography in Honour of Yehoshua Ben-Arieh* (Jerusalem)

Bender, B. (ed.) 1992a *Landscape: Politics and Perspectives* (Oxford)

1992b 'Landscape – meaning and action' in B. Bender (ed.) *Landscape: Politics and Perspectives* (Oxford) 1–18

Benko, G. B. and Strohmayer, U. 1995 *Geography, History and Social Sciences* (Dordrecht)

Bennett, S. and Bennett, N. (eds.) 1993 *An Historical Atlas of Lincolnshire* (Hull)

Bentley, J. H. 1999 'Sea and ocean basins as frameworks of historical analysis' *Geographical Review* 89, 215–24

Beresford, M. W. 1951 'The lost villages of England' *Geographical Journal* 117, 129–49

1957 *History on the Ground* (London)

1961 *Time and Place: an Inaugural Lecture* (Leeds)

1967 *New Towns of the Middle Ages: Town Plantation in England, Wales and Gascony* (London)

1988 *East End, West End: the Face of Leeds during Urbanisation 1684–1842* (Leeds)

Beresford, M. W. and Hurst, J. G. (eds.) 1971 *Deserted Medieval Villages* (London)

Beresford, M. W. and Jones, G. R. J. (eds.) 1967 *Leeds and its Region* (Leeds)

Beresford, M. W. and St Joseph, J. K. S. 1958 *Medieval England: an Aerial Survey* (Cambridge)

Bermingham, A. 1986 *Landscape as Ideology: the English Rustic Tradition, 1740–1860* (Berkeley, Calif.)

Berque, A. 1995 *Les raisons du paysage de la Chine antique aux environnements de synthèse* (Paris)

Berr, H. 1925 'Foreword: The effect of environment on man and man's exploitation of the Earth' in L. Febvre *A Geographical Introduction to History* (London) v–xx

Berry, B. J. L. 1991 *Long-Wave Rhythms in Economic Development and Political Behaviour* (Baltimore)

Bertrand, G. 1975 'Pour une histoire écologique de la France rurale' in G. Duby and A. Wallon (eds.) *Histoire de la France rurale, I: La formation des campagnes françaises des origines au XIVe siècle* (Paris) 33–114

Besse, J-M. 2000 *Voir la terre: six essais sur le paysage et la géographie* (Arles)

Bigelow, B. 1989 'A geographical perspective of world history: contribution to an interdisciplinary course' *Journal of Geography* 88, 221–4

Billinge, M. 2001 'The "natural history" of the opera house: theatre, audience and socialisation in nineteenth-century Italy (with Parisian asides)' in I. S. Black and R. A. Butlin (eds.) *Place, Culture and Identity: Essays in Historical Geography in Honour of Alan R. H. Baker* (Laval, Quebec) 143–80

Bilsky, L. J. 1980 *Historical Ecology: Essays on Environment and Social Change* (London)

Black, I. S. 1996 'Symbolic capital: the London and Westminster Bank headquarters' *Landscape Research* 21, 55–72

1999a 'Imperial visions: rebuilding the Bank of England, 1919–1939' in F. Driver and D. Gilbert (eds.) *Imperial Cities: Landscape, Display and Identity* (Manchester) 96–113

1999b 'Rebuilding *The Heart of Empire*: bank headquarters in the City of London 1919–1939' *Art History* 22, 593–618

2000 'Spaces of capital: bank office building in the City of London, 1830–1870' *Journal of Historical Geography* 26, 351–75

Black, I. S. and Butlin, R. A. (eds.) 2001 *Place, Culture and Identity: Essays in Historical Geography in Honour of Alan R. H. Baker* (Laval, Quebec)

Black, J. 1997 *Maps and History: Constructing Images of the Past* (London)

Blanc, A. 1967 'Histoire sociale et géographie humaine' in *L'histoire sociale: sources et méthodes. Colloque de l'Ecole Normale Supérieure de St-Cloud (15–16 mai 1965)* (Paris) 207–22

Blaut, J. M. 1992 *1492: the Debate on Colonialism, Eurocentrism and History* (Trenton, N. J.)

1993 *The Colonizer's Model of the World: Geographical Diffusion and Eurocentric History* (New York)

Bloch, M. 1929 'Une monographie géographique: les pays du Rhône moyen' *Annales d'histoire économique et sociale* 1, 606–11

1931 *Les caractères originaux de l'histoire rurale française* (Oslo)

Block, R. H. 1980 'Frederick Jackson Turner and American geography' *Annals of the Association of American Geographers* 80, 31–42

Blunt, A. 1994 *Travel, Gender and Imperialism: Mary Kingsley and West Africa* (London)

Blunt, A. and Rose, G. (eds.) 1994 *Writing Women and Space: Colonial and Postcolonial Geographies* (London)

Boone, C. G. (ed.) 1997 'City and the environment' *Historical Geography* 25 (Special issue)

Botkin, D. B. 1990 *Discordant Harmonies* (New York)

Boughey, A. S. 1980 'Environmental crises past and present' in L. J. Bilsky (ed.) *Historical Ecology: Essays on Environmental and Social Change* (London) 9–32

Boulanger, P. 2002 *La France: espace et temps* (Nantes)

Bowden, M. J. 1969 'The perception of the western interior of the United States, 1800–1870: a problem in historical geosophy' *Proceedings of the Association of American Geographers* 1, 16–21

1971 'The Great American Desert and the American frontier, 1800–1882: popular images of the Plains and phases in the westward movement' in T. K. Hareven (ed.) *Anonymous Americans: Explorations in Nineteenth-Century Social History* (Englewood Cliffs, N.Y.) 48–79

1976 'The Great American Desert in the American mind: the historiography of a geographical notion' in D. Lowenthal and M. J. Bowden (eds.) *Geographies of the Mind: Essays in Honor of John Kirkland Wright* (New York) 119–47

1992 'The invention of American traditions' *Journal of Historical Geography* 18, 3–26

Brandon, P. and Short, B. 1990 *The South East from AD 1000* (London)

Braudel, F. 1949 [2nd edn 1966] *La Méditerranée et le monde méditerranéen à l'époque de Philippe II* (Paris)

1958 'L'histoire et les sciences sociales: la longue durée' *Annales économies sociétés civilisations* 4, 725–53

1967 [2nd edn 1979] *Civilisation matérielle et capitalisme. Les structures de quotidien: le possible et l'impossible* (Paris) [Translation published 1981 as *The Structures of Everyday Life: the Limits of the Possible* (London)]

1979a *Les jeux de l'échange* (Paris) [Translation published 1982 as *The Wheels of Commerce* (London)]

1979b *Le temps du monde* (Paris) [Translation published 1984 as *The Perspective of the World* (London)]

1986 *L'identité de la France* (2 vols., Paris)

Brennen, B. and Hardt, H. (eds.) 1999 *Picturing the Past* (Urbana)

Brice, W. C. 1981 *An Historical Atlas of Islam* (Leiden)

Brigham, A. P. 1903 *Geographic Influences on American History* (Boston)

1904 'Geography and history in the United States' *Journal of Geography* 3, 359–66

Broek, J. O. M. 1932 *The Santa Clara Valley, California* (Utrecht)

1941 'The relationships between history and geography' *Pacific Historical Review* 10, 321–5

1965 *Geography: Its Scope and Purpose* (Columbus, Ohio)

Brookfield, H. C. 1969 'On the environment as perceived' *Progress in Geography* 1, 51–80

Brooks, C. E. P. 1926 *Climate through the Ages* (London)

Brosseau, M. 1994 'Geography's literature' *Progress in Human Geography* 18, 333–53

Broude, H. W. 1960 'The significance of regional studies for the elaboration of national economic history' *Journal of Economic History* 20, 588–96

Brown, E. H. 1970 'Man shapes the earth' *Geographical Journal* 136, 74–85
Brown, R. H. 1943 *Mirror for Americans: Likeness of the Eastern Seaboard, c. 1810* (New York)
    1948 *Historical Geography of the United States* (Orlando)
Brown, S. K., Cannon, D. Q. and Jackson, R. H. 1994 *Historical Atlas of Mormonism* (New York)
Brunhes, J. 1910 *La géographie humaine: essai de classification positive* (Paris)
    1920 *Human Geography* (London)
Brunhes, J. and Vallaux, C. 1921 *La géographie de l'histoire: géographie de la paix et de la guerre sur terre et sur mer* (Paris)
Bryce, J. 1901 'Introductory essay' in H. F. Helmlot (ed.) *The World's History: a Survey of Man's Record, Vol. I* (London) xvii–lx
    1902 'The importance of geography in education' *Geographical Teacher* 1, 49–61
Buckatzsch, E. J. 1950 'The geographical distribution of wealth in England, 1086–1843: an experimental study of certain tax assessments' *Economic History Review* 3, 180–202
Buckley, G. L. 1998 'The environmental transformation of an Appalachian valley, 1850–1906' *Geographical Review* 88, 175–98
Bulmer, M. 1984 *The Chicago School of Sociology* (Chicago)
Bunn, D. 1994 ' "Our wattled cot": mercantile and domestic space in Thomas Pringle's African landscapes' in W. J. T. Mitchell (ed.) *Landscape and Power* (Chicago) 127–73
Burguière, A. 1986 *Dictionnaire des sciences historiques* (Paris)
Burke, P. (ed.) 1991a *New Perspectives on Historical Writing* (Cambridge)
    1991b 'History of events and the revival of narrative' in P. Burke (ed.) *New Perspectives on Historical Writing* (Cambridge) 233–48
    2001 *Eyewitnessing: the Uses of Images as Historical Evidence* (London)
    (n.d.) 'Reflections on the history of space' (unpublished manuscript)
Butlin, R. A. 1990 'Regions in England and Wales, c. 1600–1914' in R. A. Dodgshon and R. A. Butlin (eds.) *An Historical Geography of England and Wales* (London) 223–54
    1992 'Ideological contexts and the reconstruction of biblical landscapes in the seventeenth and early-eighteenth centuries: Dr Edward Wells and the historical geography of the Holy Land' in A. R. H. Baker and G. Biger (eds.) *Ideology and Landscape in Historical Perspective* (Cambridge) 31–62
    1993 *Historical Geography: Through the Gates of Space and Time* (London)
    2001 'A sacred and contested place: English and French representations of Palestine in the seventeenth century' in I. S. Black and R. A. Butlin (eds.) *Place, Culture and Identity: Essays in Historical Geography in Honour of Alan R. H. Baker* (Laval, Quebec) 91–131
Butlin, R. A. and Dodgshon, R. A. (eds.) 1998 *An Historical Geography of Europe* (Oxford)
Butlin, R. A. and Roberts, N. (eds.) 1995 *Ecological Relations in Historical Times: Human Impact and Adaptation* (Oxford)
Buttimer, A. 1971 *Society and Milieu in the French Geographic Tradition* (Chicago)
Buttimer, A., Brunn, S. D. and Wardenga, U. (eds.) 1999 'Text and image: social construction of regional knowledges' *Beiträge Zur Regionalen Geographie* 49
Butzer, K. W. 1990 'The Indian legacy in the American landscape' in M. P. Conzen (ed.) *The Making of the American Landscape* (London)
Cameron, L. 1997 *Openings: a Meditation on History, Method and Sumas Lake* (Montreal)
Campbell, B. M. S. 2000 *English Seigniorial Agriculture 1250–1450* (Cambridge)

Campbell, B. M. S. and Power, J. P. 1989 'Mapping the agricultural geography of medieval England' *Journal of Historical Geography* 15, 24–39

Campbell, J. 1989 'The concept of "the behavioural environment", and its origins, reconsidered' in F. W. Boal and D. N. Livingstone (eds.) *The Behavioural Environment: Essays in Reflection, Application and Re-evaluation* (London) 3–17

Cantor, L. 1987 *The Changing English Countryside, 1400–1700* (London)

Careless, J. M. S. 1954 'Frontierism, metropolitanism and Canadian history' *Canadian Historical Review* 35, 1–21

1989 *Frontier and Metropolis: Regions, Cities and Identities in Canada before 1914* (Toronto)

Carlstein, T., Parkes, D. and Thrift, N. (eds.) 1978 *Timing Space and Spacing Time, Vol. I: Making Sense of Time*; *Vol. II: Human Activity and Time Geography*; *Vol. III: Time and Regional Dynamics* (London)

Carney, G. O. (ed.) 1987 *The Sounds of People and Places: Readings in the Geography of Music* (Washington, D.C.)

1990 'Geography of music: inventory and prospect' *Journal of Cultural Geography* 10, 35–48

Carr, E. H. 1961 *What is History?* (London)

Carrier, E. H. 1925 *Historical Geography of England and Wales (South Britain)* (London)

Carter, P. 1987 *The Road to Botany Bay: an Essay in Spatial History* (London)

Casey, E. S. 2002 *Representing Place: Landscape Painting and Maps* (Minneapolis)

Chambers, J. D. 1932 [2nd edn 1966] *Nottinghamshire in the Eighteenth Century* (London)

Chambers, R. W. 1982 'Images, acts and consequences: a critical review of historical geosophy' in A. R. H. Baker and M. Billinge (eds.) *Period and Place: Research Methods in Historical Geography* (Cambridge) 197–204

Chaunu, P. 1969 'L'histoire géographique' *Revue de l'enseignement supérieur* 44–45, 67–77

1974 *Histoire science sociale: la durée, l'espace et l'homme à l'époque moderne* (Paris)

Chevalier, M. 1993 'Géographie et littérature' in M. Chevalier (ed.) *La littérature dans tous ses espaces* (Paris) 1–84

Christopher, A. J. 1982 *The World's Landscapes: South Africa* (London)

1988 *The British Empire at its Zenith* (Beckenham)

Clapham, J. H. 1926 *An Economic History of Modern Britain, Vol. I: The Early Railway Age* (Cambridge)

1932 *An Economic History of Modern Britain, Vol. II: Free Trade and Steel* (Cambridge)

Clapp, B. W. 1994 *An Environmental History of Britain since the Industrial Revolution* (London)

Clark, A. H. 1946 'Field research in historical geography' *Bulletin of the American Society for Professional Geographers* 4, 13–23

1949 *The Invasion of New Zealand by People, Plants and Animals: the South Island* (New Brunswick)

1954 'Titus Smith, junior, and the geography of Nova Scotia in 1801 and 1802' *Annals of the Association of American Geographers* 44, 291–314

1959 *Three Centuries and the Island: a Historical Geography of Settlement and Agriculture in Prince Edward Island, Canada* (Toronto)

1960 'Geographical change: a theme for economic history' *Journal of Economic History* 20, 607–13

1962a *'Praemia Geographia*: the incidental rewards of a geographical career' *Annals of the Association of American Geographers* 55, 229–47

1962b 'Geographical diversity and the personality of Canada' in M. McCaskill (ed.) *Land and Livelihood: Geographical Essays in Honour of George Jobberns* (Christchurch) 23–47

1968 *Acadia: the Geography of Early Nova Scotia to 1760* (Madison)

1972 'Historical geography in North America' in A. R. H. Baker (ed.) *Progress in Historical Geography* (New York) 129–43

1975a 'First things first' in R. E. Ehrenberg (ed.) *Pattern and Process: Research in Historical Geography* (Washington, D.C.) 29–21

1975b 'The conception of "Empires" of the St Lawrence and the Mississippi: a historico-geographical view with some quizzical comments on environmental determinism' *American Review of Canadian Studies* 5, 4–27

Clark, K. 1949 *Landscape into Art* (Harmondsworth)

Clark, P. (ed.) 2000 *The Cambridge Urban History of Britain c. 600–1950* (Cambridge)

Clark, S. (ed.) 1999 *The Annales School: Critical Assessment, Vol. I: Histories and Overviews; Vol. II: The Annales School and Historical Studies* (London)

Claval, P. 1968 'De Vidal de la Blache au structuralisme' in P. Claval and J. P. Narady *Pour le cinquantenaire de la mort de Paul Vidal de la Blache* (Besançon) 115–25

1984 'The historical dimension of French geography' *Journal of Historical Geography* 10, 229–45

1993 *Initiation à la géographie régionale* (Paris) [Translation published 1998 as *An Introduction to Regional Geography* (Oxford)]

1994 'From Michelet to Braudel: personality, identity and organization of France' in D. Hooson (ed.) *Geography and National Identity* (Oxford) 39–57

1995 'Les historiens, la géographie et le grand public en France' in J-R. Pitte (ed.) *Géographie historique et culturelle de l'Europe: hommage au Professeur Xavier de Planhol* (Paris) 171–87

Claval, P. and Sanguin, A-L. 1996 (eds.) *La géographie française à l'époque classique* (Paris)

Clayton, D. W. 2000 *Islands of Truth: the Imperial Fashioning of Vancouver Island* (Vancouver)

Cliff, A. D., Haggett, P., Ord, J. K. and Versey, G. R. 1981 *Spatial Diffusion: an Historical Geography of Epidemics in an Island Community* (Cambridge)

Clout, H. D. 1977 (ed.) *Themes in the Historical Geography of France* (London)

1980 *Agriculture in France on the Eve of the Railway Age* (London)

1983 *The Land of France 1815–1914* (London)

1991 (ed.) [2nd edn 1997] *The Times London History Atlas* (London)

2002 'H. C. Darby and the historical geography of France' in H. C. Darby *The Relations of History and Geography: Studies in England, France and the United States* (Exeter) 131–45

Clout, H. D. and Sutton, K. 1969 'The cadastre as a source for French rural studies' *Agricultural History* 43, 215–23

Cole, G. D. H. 1927 'Defoe's England' in D. Defoe *Tour thro' the Whole Island of Great Britain, 1724, 1725 and 1727* (London)

Collingwood, R. G. 1946 *The Idea of History* (Oxford)

Colten, C. E. 1998 'Historical geography and environmental history' *Geographical Review* 88, iii–iv

Colten, C. E. and Dilsaver, L. M. 1992 'Historical geography of the environment: a preliminary literature review' in L. M. Dilsaver and C. E. Colten (eds.) *The American Environment: Interpretations of Past Geographies* (Lanham, Md) 1–18

Colten, C. E., Hugill, P. J., Young, T. and Morin, K. M. (forthcoming) 'Historical geography' in G. Gaile and C. Willmott (eds.) *Geography in America at the Dawn of the Twenty-First Century* (New York)

Conzen, M. P. (ed.) 1990 *The Making of the American Landscape* (Boston)
1993 'The historical impulse in geographical writing about the United States 1850–1990' in M. Conzen, T. A. Rumney and G. Wynn (eds.) *A Scholar's Guide to Geographical Writing on the American and Canadian Past*, University of Chicago Geography Research Paper no. 235 (Chicago) 3–90

Conzen, M. P., Rumney, T. A. and Wynn, G. (eds.) 1993 *A Scholar's Guide to Geographical Writing on the American and Canadian Past*, University of Chicago Geography Research Paper no. 235 (Chicago)

Cook, E. M. Jr 1980 'Geography and history: spatial approaches to early American history' *Historical Methods* 13 no. 1, 19–28

Coones, P. 1985 'One landscape or many? A geographical perspective' *Landscape History* 7, 5–12

Coones, P. and Patten, J. 1986 *The Penguin Guide to the Landscape of England and Wales* (Harmondsworth)

Coppens, L. M. 1985: 'Ralph Hall Brown, 1898–1948' *Geographers: Biogeographical Studies* 9, 15–20

Corbin, A. 1982 *La miasme et le jonquille: l'odorat et l'imaginaire social XVIIIe–XIXe siècles* (Paris) [Translation published 1986 as *The Foul and the Fragrant: Odour and the French Social Imagination* (Leamington Spa)]
1994 *Les cloches de la terre: paysage sonoré et culture sensible dans les campagnes au XIXe siècle* (Paris) [Translation published 1999 as *Village Bells: Sound and Meaning in the Nineteenth-Century French Countryside* (London)]

Cosgrove, D. 1978 'Place, landscape and the dialectics of cultural geography' *Canadian Geographer* 22, 66–72
1979 'John Ruskin and the geographical imagination' *Geographical Review* 69, 43–62
1982 'Problems of interpreting the symbolism of past landscapes' in A. R. H. Baker and M. D. Billinge (eds.) *Period and Place: Research Methods in Historical Geography* (Cambridge) 220–30
1984 [2nd edn 1998] *Social Formation and Symbolic Landscape* (London)
1985 'Prospect, perspective and the evolution of the landscape idea' *Transactions of the Institute of British Geographers* 1, 45–62
1989 'Geography is everywhere: culture and symbolism in human landscapes' in D. Gregory and R. Walford (eds.) *Horizons in Human Geography* (Basingstoke) 118–35
1990 'Spectacle and society: landscape as theatre in pre- and post-modern cities' in P. Groth (ed.) *Vision: Culture and Landscape* (Berkeley, Calif.) 221–39
1993a *The Palladian Landscape: Geographical Change and its Cultural Representations in Sixteenth-Century Italy* (London)

1993b (ed.) *Nature, Environment, Landscape: European Attitudes and Discourses 1920–1970* (London)

1996 'Landscape' in A. Kuper and J. Kuper (eds.) *The Social Science Encyclopedia* 2nd edn (London) 449–50

Cosgrove, D. and Daniels, S. (eds.) 1988 *The Iconography of Landscape: Essays on the Symbolic Representation, Design and Use of Past Environments* (Cambridge)

1989 'Fieldwork as theatre: a week's performance in the Venice region' *Journal of Geography in Higher Education* 13, 169–82

Cosgrove, D. and Jackson, P. 1987 'New directions in cultural geography' *Area* 19, 95–101

Cosgrove, D. and Thornes, J. E. 1981 'Of truth of clouds: John Ruskin and the moral order in landscape' in D. C. D. Pocock (ed.) *Humanistic Geography and Literature* (London) 20–46

Courville, S. 1995 *Introduction à la géographie historique* (Sainte-Foy, Quebec)

Courville, S. and Séguin, N. (eds.) 1995 *Atlas historique du Québec: le pays laurentian au XIXe siècle* (Laval)

1997 *Atlas historique du Québec: le territoire* (Laval)

1998 *Atlas historique du Québec: l'institution médicale* (Laval)

2001a *Atlas historique du Québec: la paroisse* (Laval)

2001b *Atlas historique du Québec: le nord – habitants et mutations* (Laval)

2001c *Atlas historique du Québec: Québec – ville et capitale* (Laval)

Cowdrey, A. E. 1983 *This Land, This South: an Environmental History* (Lexington, Ky)

Cox, D. H. and Naslas, M. 1984 'The metropolis in music' in A. Sutcliffe (ed.) *Metropolis 1890–1914* (London) 173–90

Crang, M. 1998 *Cultural Geography* (London)

Crawford, O. G. S. 1953 *Archaeology in the Field* (London)

Cronon, W. 1991 *Nature's Metropolis: Chicago and the Great West* (New York)

1992 'A place for stories: nature, history and narrative' *Journal of American History* 48, 1347–76

1994 'Cutting loose or running aground?' *Journal of Historical Geography* 20, 38–43

Crosby, A. W. 1986 *Ecological Imperialism: the Biological Expansion of Europe 900–1900* (Cambridge)

1995 'The past and present of environmental history' *American Historical Review* 100, 1177–89

Crumley, C. L. (ed.) 1994 *Historical Ecology: Cultural Knowledge and Changing Landscapes* (Santa Fe)

Cumberland, K. B. 1961 'Man *in* nature in New Zealand' *New Zealand Geographer* 17, 137–54

Cunfer, G. 2002 'Causes of the Dust Bowl' in A. K. Knowles (ed.) *Past Time, Past Place: GIS for History* (Redlands, Calif.) 93–104

Daiches, D. and Flower, J. 1979 *Literary Landscapes of the British Isles* (London)

Daniels, S. 1989 'Marxism, culture and the duplicity of landscape' in R. Peet and N. Thrift (eds.) *New Models in Geography, Vol. II* (London) 196–220

1992 'Place and the geographical imagination' *Geography* 77, 310–22

1993 *Fields of Vision: Landscape Imagery and National Identity in England and the United States* (Cambridge)

1994 'Re-visioning Britain: mapping and landscape painting, 1750–1820' in K. Baetjer (ed.) *Glorious Nature: British Landscape Painting, 1750–1850* (New York) 61–72

Daniels, S. and Cosgrove, D. 1993 'Spectacle and text: landscape metaphors in cultural geography' in J. S. Duncan and D. Ley (eds.) *Place/Culture/Representation* (London) 57–77

Daniels, S. and Rycroft, S. 1993 'Mapping the modern city: Alan Sillitoe's Nottingham novels' *Transactions of the Institute of British Geographers* 18, 460–80

Daniels, S. and Seymour, S. 1990 'Landscape design and the idea of improvement 1730–1900' in R. A. Dodgshon and R. A. Butlin (eds.) *An Historical Geography of England and Wales* 2nd edn (London) 487–520

Daniels, S. and Watkins, C. 1994 'Picturesque landscaping and estate management: Uvedale Price and Nathaniel Kent at Foxley' in S. Copley and P. Garside (eds.) *The Politics of the Picturesque: Landscape and Aesthetics since 1770* (Cambridge) 13–41

Darby, H. C. 1928 'The architectural geography of south Britain' *Sociological Review* 29, 105–10

1932 'The medieval sea state' *Scottish Geographical Magazine* 48, 136–9

1934 'Note on the birds of the undrained fen' in D. L. Lack (ed.) *The Birds of Cambridgeshire* (Cambridge) 214–20

1935 'The geographical ideas of the Venerable Bede' *Scottish Geographical Magazine* 51, 84–9

1936 (ed.) *An Historical Geography of England before AD 1800* (Cambridge)

1940a *The Medieval Fenland* (Cambridge)

1940b [2nd edn 1956, 3rd edn 1968] *The Draining of the Fens* (Cambridge)

1947 *The Theory and Practice of Geography* (London)

1948 'The regional geography of Thomas Hardy's Wessex' *Geographical Review* 38, 426–43

1951a 'The changing English landscape' *Geographical Journal* 117, 377–98

1951b 'The clearing of the English woodlands' *Geography* 36, 71–83

1952 *The Domesday Geography of Eastern England* (Cambridge)

1953a 'Man and the landscape in England' *Journal of the Town Planning Institute* 39, 74–80

1953b 'On the relations of history and geography' *Transactions and Papers of the Institute of British Geographers* 19, 1–11

1954 'Some early ideas on the agricultural regions of England' *Transactions of the Institute of British Geographers* 11, 30–47

1956 'The clearing of the woodland in Europe' in W. L. Thomas (ed.) *Man's Role in Changing the Face of the Earth* (Chicago) 183–216

1957 'The face of Europe on the eve of the great discoveries' in G. R. Potter (ed.) *The New Cambridge Modern History* (Cambridge) 20–49

1960 'An historical geography of England: twenty years after' *Geographical Journal* 125, 147–59

1961 'National parks in England and Wales' in H. Jarrett (ed.) *Comparisons in Resource Management* (Baltimore) 8–34

1962a 'Historical geography' in H. P. R. Finberg (ed.) *Approaches to History* (London) 127–56

1962b 'The problem of geographical description' *Transactions and Papers of the Institute of British Geographers* 30, 1–14

1964 'The draining of the English claylands' *Geographische Zeitschrift* 52, 190–201

1973 (ed.) *A New Historical Geography of England* (Cambridge)

1977 *Domesday England* (Cambridge)

1979 'Some reflections on historical geography' *Historical Geography* 9 no. 1, 9–13

1987 'On the writing of historical geography, 1918–45' in R. W. Steel (ed.) *British Geography, 1918–45* (Cambridge) 117–37

2002 *The Relations of History and Geography: Studies in England, France and the United States* (Exeter)

Darby, H. C. and Campbell, E. M. J. (eds.) 1962 *The Domesday Geography of South-East England* (Cambridge)

Darby, H. C. and Finn, R. W. (eds.) 1967 *The Domesday Geography of South-West England* (Cambridge)

Darby, H. C. and Fullard, H. (eds.) 1970 *The New Cambridge Modern History, Vol. XIV: Atlas* (Cambridge)

Darby, H. C., Glasscock, R. E., Sheail, J. and Versey, G. R. 1979 'The changing distribution of wealth in England 1086–1334–1525' *Journal of Historical Geography* 5, 247–62

Darby, H. C. and Maxwell, I. S. (eds.) 1952 *The Domesday Geography of Northern England* (Cambridge)

Darby, H. C. and Terrett, I. B. (eds.) 1954 *The Domesday Geography of Midland England* (Cambridge)

Darby, H. C. and Versey, G. R. 1975 *Domesday Gazetteer* (Cambridge)

Darby, W. J. 2000 *Landscape and Identity: Geographies of Nation and Class in England* (Oxford)

Datel, R. E. and Dingemans, D. J. 1988 'Why places are preserved: historic districts in American and European cities' *Urban Geography* 9, 37–52

Davis, D. E. 2000 *Where there are Mountains: an Environmental History of the Southern Appalachians* (Athens, Ga)

Dean, W. 1987 *Brazil and the Struggle for Rubber: a Study in Environmental History* (Cambridge)

Dean, W. G. 1995 'Atlas structures and their influence on editorial decisions: two recent case histories' in J. Winearls (ed.) *Editing Early and Historical Atlases* (Toronto) 137–62

Deffontaines, P. 1925 *Les hommes et leurs travaux dans les pays de la moyenne Garonne* (Lille)

Delano-Smith, C. 1979 *Western Mediterranean World: a Historical Geography of Italy, Spain and Southern France since the Neolithic* (London)

Demangeon, A. 1905a *Les sources de la géographie de la France aux archives nationales* (Paris)

1905b *La Picardie et les régions voisines* (Paris)

1907 'Les recherches géographiques dans les archives' *Annales de géographie* 16, 193–203

Demeritt, D. 1994a 'Ecology, objectivity and critique in writings on nature and human societies' *Journal of Historical Geography* 20, 22–37

1994b 'The nature of metaphors in cultural geography and environmental history' *Progress in Human Geography* 18, 163–85

Dennis, R. 1989 'Dismantling the barriers: past and present in urban Britain' in D. Gregory and R. Walford (eds.) *Horizons in Human Geography* (Basingstoke) 194–216

1991 'History, geography and historical geography' *Social Science History* 15, 265–88

1994 'History and geography: at the intersection of time and space' in E. H. Monkkonen (ed.) *Engaging the Past: the Uses of History across the Social Sciences* (Durham)

2000 'Historical geographies of urbanism' in B. Graham and C. Nash (eds.) *Modern Historical Geographies* (Harlow) 218–48

2001 'Reconciling geographies, representing modernities' in I. S. Black and R. A. Butlin (eds.) *Place, Culture and Identity: Essays in Honour of Alan R. H. Baker* (Laval, Quebec) 17–43

Dickenson, J. 1982 *The World's Landscapes: Brazil* (London)

Dickinson, R. E. 1969 *The Makers of Modern Geography* (London)

1976 *Regional Concept: the Anglo-American Leaders* (London)

Dilsaver, L. and Colten, C. E. (eds.) 1992 *The American Environment: Interpretations of Past Geographies* (Lanham, Md)

Dion, R. 1934a *Le val de Loire: étude de géographie régionale* (Tours)

1934b *Essai sur la formation du paysage rural français* (Tours)

1949 'La géographie humaine rétrospective' *Cahiers internationaux de sociologie* 6, 3–27

1957 'La géographie historique' in G. Chabot, R. Clozier and J. Beaujeu-Garnier (eds.) *La géographie française au milieu du XXe siècle* (Paris)

Dodd, A. H. 1933 *The Industrial Revolution in North Wales* (Cardiff)

Dodge, S. D. 1931 'Sequent occupance on an Illinois prairie' *Bulletin of the Geographical Society of Philadelphia* 29, 205–9

Dodgshon, R. A. 1998 *Society in Time and Space: a Geographical Perspective on Change* (Cambridge)

Dodgshon, R. A. and Butlin, R. A. (eds.) 1978 [2nd edn 1990] *An Historical Geography of England and Wales* (London)

Domosh, M. 1987 'Imagining New York's first skyscrapers, 1875–1910' *Journal of Historical Geography* 13, 233–48

1988 'The symbolism of the skyscraper: case studies of New York's first tall buildings' *Journal of Urban History* 14, 320–45

1989 'A method for interpreting landscape: a case study of the New York World Building' *Area* 21, 347–55

1990 'Towards a feminist historiography of geography' *Transactions of the Institute of British Geographers* 16, 95–104

1992 'Corporate cultures in the modern landscape of New York City' in K. Anderson and F. Gale (eds.) *Inventing Places: Studies in Cultural Geography* (Melbourne) 72–86

1996 *Invented Cities: the Creation of Landscape in Nineteenth-Century New York and Boston* (New Haven, Conn.)

1997 'With "stout boots and a stout heart": historical methodology and feminist geography' in J. P. Jones, H. L. Nast and S. M. Roberts (eds.) *Thresholds in Feminist Geography: Difference, Methodology, Representation* (Lanham, Md) 225–37

Domosh, M. and Seager, J. 2001 *Putting Women in Place: Feminist Geographers Make Sense of the World* (New York)

Donkin, R. A. 1977 'Spanish Red: an ethnographical study of cochineal and the opuntia cactus' *Transactions of the American Philosophical Society* 67 Part 5

1985 'The peccary – with observations on the introduction of pigs to the New World' *Transactions of the American Philosophical Society* 75 Part 5

1989 *The Muscovy Duck: Carina Moschata: Origins, Dispersal and Associated Aspects of the Geography of Domestication* (Rotterdam)

1991 *Meleagrides: an Historical and Ethnographical Study of the Guinea Fowl* (London)

1997 'A "servant of two masters"?' *Journal of Historical Geography* 23, 247–66

1999 *Dragon's Brain Perfume: an Historical Geography of Camphor* (Leiden)

Dorling, D. 1992 'Visualising people in space and time' *Environment and Planning B: Planning and Design* 19, 613–37

1998 'Human geography – when it is good to map' *Environment and Planning A* 30, 277–88

Dovers, S. (ed.) 1994 *Australian Environmental History: Essays and Cases* (Melbourne)

Drabble, M. 1979 *A Writer's Britain* (London)

Drewett, P., Rudling, D. and Gardiner, M. 1988 *The South East to AD 1000* (London)

Driver, F. 1988a 'Moral geographies: social science and the urban environment in mid-nineteenth century England' *Transactions of the Institute of British Geographers* 13, 275–87

1988b 'The historicity of human geography' *Progress in Human Geography* 12, 497–506

1992a 'Geography and power: the work of Michel Foucault' in P. Burke (ed.) *Critical Essays on Michel Foucault* (Aldershot) 147–56

1992b 'Geography's empire: histories of geographical knowledge' *Environment and Planning D: Society and Space* 10, 23–40

1993 *Power and Pauperism: the Workhouse System, 1834–1884* (Cambridge)

1994a 'Bodies in space: Foucault's account of disciplinary power' in C. Jones and R. Porter (eds.) *Reassessing Foucault: Power, Medicine and the Body* (London) 113–31

1994b 'Making space' *Ecumene* 1, 386–90

Driver, F. and Gilbert, D. 1998 'Heart of empire? Landscape, space and performance in imperial London', *Environment and Planning D: Society and Space* 16, 11–28

1999 (eds.) *Imperial Cities: Landscape, Display and Identity* (Manchester)

Driver, F. and Samuel, R. 1995 'Spatial history: rethinking the idea of place' *History Workshop Journal* 39, vi–vii

Duby, G. 1985 'Ideologies in history' in J. Le Goff and P. Nora (eds.) *Constructing the Past: Essays in Historical Methodology* (Cambridge) 151–65

Dulau, R. and Pitte, J-R. (eds.) 1998 *Géographie des odeurs* (Paris)

Dunbar, G. 1974 'Geographical personality' in H. J. Walker and W. G. Haag (eds.) *Man and Cultural Heritage: Papers in Honor of Fred B. Kniffen* (Baton Rouge) 25–33

1980 'Geosophy, geohistory and historical geography: a study in terminology' *Historical Geography* 10 no. 2, 1–8

Duncan, J. 1980 'The superorganic in American cultural geography' *Annals of the Association of American Geographers* 70, 181–90

1990 *The City as Text: the Politics of Landscape Interpretation in the Kandyan Kingdom* (Cambridge)

1995 'Landscape geography, 1993–94' *Progress in Human Geography* 19, 414–22

Duncan, J. and Duncan, N. 1988 '(Re)reading the landscape' *Environment and Planning D: Society and Space* 6, 117–26

Duncan, J. and Ley, D. (eds.) 1993 *Place/Culture/Representation* (London)

Dunford, M. 1998 'Economies in space and time: economic geographies of development and under-development and historical geographies of modernisation' in B. Graham (ed.) *Modern Europe: Place, Culture, Identity* (London) 53–88

Dunford, M. and Perrons, D. 1983 *The Arena of Capital* (London)

Eagleton, T. 1986 *Against the Grain* (London)

Earle, C. 1978 'Comments' [on D. W. Meinig 1978] *American Historical Review* 83, 1206–9

    1992 *Geographical Inquiry and American Historical Problems* (Stanford, Calif.)

    1995 'Historical geography in extremis? Splitting personalities on the postmodern turn' *Journal of Historical Geography* 21, 455–9

    1999 'Continuity or discontinuity – that is the question: *The Shaping of America* in the gilded age and progressive era' *Journal of Historical Geography* 25, 12–16

Earle, C., Dilsaver, L. et alia 1989 'Historical geography' in G. L. Gaile and C. J. Willmott (eds.) *Geography in America* (Columbus, Ohio) 156–91

East, W. G. 1935 [revised edn 1965] *An Historical Geography of Europe* (London)

    1938 [revised edn 1965] *The Geography behind History* (London)

Ehrenberg, R. E. (ed.) 1975 *Pattern and Process: Research in Historical Geography* (Washington, D.C.)

Elkins, T. H. 1956 'An English traveller in the Siegerland' *Geographical Journal* 122, 306–16

Ellen, R. F. 1996 'Ecology' in A. Kuper and J. Kuper (eds.) *The Social Science Encyclopedia* 2nd edn (London)

Elton G. R. 1967 *The Practice of History* (Sydney)

Emery, F. V. 1958 'English regional studies from Aubrey to Defoe' *Geographical Journal* 124, 306–16

    1965 'Edward Lluyd and some of his Glamorgan correspondents: a view of the Gower in the 1690s' *Transactions of the Honorable Society of Cymmrodorion*, 59–114

    1974 *The Oxfordshire Landscape* (London)

Ennals, P. and Holdsworth, D. W. 1998 *Homeplace: the Making of the Canadian Dwelling over Three Centuries* (Toronto)

Entrikin, N. 1991 *The Betweenness of Places: Towards a Geography of Modernity* (Basingstoke)

    1994 'Place and region' *Progress in Human Geography* 18, 227–33

    1998 'Blurred boundaries: humanism and social science in historical geography' *Historical Geography* 26, 93–9

Evans, E. E. 1970 'The personality of Ulster' *Transactions of the Institute of British Geographers* 51, 1–20

    1973 *The Personality of Ireland: Habitat, History, Heritage* (London)

Evans, R. J. 1997 *In Defence of History* (London)

Everitt, A. M. 1966 *The Community of Kent and the Great Rebellion, 1640–1660* (Leicester)

    1977 'River and wold: reflections on the historical origins of regions and pays' *Journal of Historical Geography* 3, 1–20

    1979 'Country, county and town: patterns of regional evolution in England' *Transactions of the Royal Historical Society* 29, 79–108

    1985 *Landscape and Community in England* (London)

Farmer, B. H. 1973 'Geography, area studies and the study of area' *Transactions of the Institute of British Geographers* 60, 1–16

Farmer, S. B. 1995 'Oradour-sur-Glane: memory in a preserved landscape' *French Historical Studies* 19, 27–47

Faucher, D. 1927 *Plaines et bassins du Rhône Moyen entre Bas-Dauphiné et Provence: étude géographique* (Paris)

Febvre, L. 1922 *La terre et l'évolution humaine: introduction géographique à l'histoire* (Paris) [Translation published 1925 as *A Geographical Introduction to History* (London)]
 1950 'Histoire et géographie: Sisyphe et les géographes' *Annales économies sociétés civilisations* 5, 87–90
 1953 book review, *Annales économies sociétés civilisations* 8, 372–7
Fieguth, W. 1967 'Historical geography and the concept of the authentic past as a regional resource' *Ontario Geography* 1, 55–60
Fierro-Domenech, A. 1986 *Le pré-carré: géographie historique de la France* (Paris)
Finberg, H. P. R. 1952 *The Local Historian and his Theme* Department of English Local History, University of Leicester, Occasional Papers 1
 1962a (ed.) *Approaches to History* (London)
 1962b 'Local history' in H. P. R. Finberg (ed.) *Approaches to History* (London) 111–25
Firth, C. 1932 'Macaulay's third chapter' *History* 17, 201–19
Fleischer, H. 1973 *Marxism and History* (New York)
Fletcher, A. 1975 *A County Community in Peace and War: Sussex, 1600–1660* (London)
Fleure, H. J. 1921 'Countries as personalities' *Nature* 108, 573–5
Foncin, P. 1888 *Géographie historique* (Paris)
Foote, S. 2001 *Regional Fictions: Culture and Identity in Nineteenth-Century American Literature* (Madison, Wis.)
Ford, L. R. 1973 'The diffusion of the skyscraper as an urban symbol' *Yearbook of the Association of Pacific Coast Geographers* 35, 49–60
 1975 'Historic preservation and the stream of time: the role of the geographer' *Historical Geography Newsletter* 5 no. 1, 1–15
 1992 'Reading the skylines of American cities' *Geographical Review* 82, 180–200
Forman, R. T. T. and Godron, M. 1986 *Landscape Ecology* (New York)
Foucault, M. 1980 *Power/Knowledge: Selected Interviews and Other Writings* (Brighton)
Fowler, P. J. (ed.) 1972 *Archaeology and the Landscape* (London)
 1977 (ed.) *Approaches to Archaeology* (London)
Fox, C. 1932 *The Personality of Britain: Its Influence on Inhabitant and Invader in Prehistoric and Early Historic Times* (Cardiff)
Fox, E. 1971 *History in Geographic Perspective: the Other France* (New York)
Fox, H. 1989 'The people of the wolds in English settlement history' in M. Aston, D. Austin and C. Dyer (eds.) *The Rural Settlements of Medieval England: Studies Dedicated to Maurice Beresford and John Hurst* (Oxford) 77–101
Francaviglia, R. V. 1978 *The Mormon Landscape: Existence, Creation and Perception of a Unique Image of the American West* (New York)
Franklin, F. H. 2001 *The Historical Atlas of Christianity* (New York)
Freeman, E. A. 1881 *The Historical Geography of Europe* (London)
Freeman, M. 1984 'The industrial revolution and the regional geography of England: a comment' *Transactions of the Institute of British Geographers* 4, 507–12
Freeman-Grenville, G. S. P. 1993 *Historical Atlas of the Middle East* (New York)
French, R. A. 1964 'The reclamation of swamp in pre-revolutionary Russia' *Transactions of the Institute of British Geographers* 34, 175–88
Friedman, S. W. 1996 *Marc Bloch, Sociology and Geography: Encountering Changing Disciplines* (Cambridge)

Gachon, L. 1955 'Histoire, géographie et démographie' *Norois* 2, 281–316

Gaillabaud, L. 1999 'Réflexions sur la temporalité liée à l'étendu' in J-R. Pitte and A-L. Sanguin (eds.) *Géographie et liberté: mélanges en hommage à Paul Claval* (Paris) 157–61

Gandy, M. 1996 'Crumbling land: the postmodernity debate and the analysis of environmental problems' *Progress in Human Geography* 20, 23–40

Gaustad, E. S. and Barlow, P. L. 2001 *New Historical Atlas of Religion in America* (Oxford)

Gay, F. 1982 'Le temps en géographie' in *Géographie aujourd'hui: mélanges offerts en hommage à Jean Miège* (Nice) 71–8

Genovese, E. and Hochberg, L. (eds.) 1989 *Geographic Perspectives in History* (Oxford)

Gentilcore, L. (ed.) 1993 *Historical Atlas of Canada, Vol. II: The Nineteenth Century* (Toronto)

George, H. B. 1901 [5th edn 1924] *The Relations of Geography and History* (Oxford)
1904 [7th edn 1924] *A Historical Geography of the British Empire* (London)

George, P. 1935 *La région du Bas Rhône: étude de géographie régionale* (Paris)
1992 *La géographie à la poursuite de l'histoire* (Paris)

Geyer, M. and Bright, C. 1995 'World history in a global age' *American Historical Review* 100, 1034–60

Gibson, R. 1983 'French local and regional history' *Journal of Regional and Local Studies* 3 no. 2, 1–6

Giddens, A. 1984 *The Constitution of Society: Outline of the Theory of Structuration* (Cambridge)

Gilbert, E. W. 1932 'What is historical geography?' *Scottish Geographical Magazine* 48, 129–35
1960 'The idea of the region' *Geography* 45, 157–75
1972 'British regional novelists and geography' in E. W. Gilbert (ed.) *British Pioneers in Geography* (New York) 116–27

Glacken, C. J. 1967 *Traces on the Rhodian Shore: Nature and Culture in Western Thought from Ancient Times to the End of the Eighteenth Century* (Berkeley, Calif.)

Glasscock, R. E. 1975 *The Lay Subsidy of 1334* (London)
1992 (ed.) *Historic Landscapes of Britain from the Air* (Cambridge)

Godlewska, A. and Smith, N. (eds.) 1994 *Geography and Empire* (Oxford)

Goheen, P. 1992 'Parading: a lively tradition in early Victorian Toronto' in A. R. H. Baker and G. Biger (eds.) *Ideology and Landscape in Historical Perspective* (Cambridge) 330–51
1994 'Negotiating access to public space in mid-nineteenth century Toronto' *Journal of Historical Geography* 20, 430–49

Goldfield, D. R. 1984 'The new regionalism' *Journal of Urban History* 10, 171–86

Gombrich, E. 1953 'Renaissance artistic theory and the development of landscape painting', *Gazette des Beaux Arts* 6e période 41, 31–41; reprinted in E. Gombrich 1966 *Norm and Form: Studies in the Art of the Renaissance* (London) 107–21

Gorou, P. 1961 *The Tropical World* 3rd edn (London)

Goudie, A. 1973 *Duricrusts of Tropical and Sub-tropical Forests* (Oxford)
1983 'Dust storms in time and space' *Progress in Physical Geography* 7, 502–30
1993 *The Human Impact on the Natural Environment* 4th edn (Oxford)
2000 *The Human Impact on the Natural Environment* 5th edn (Oxford)

Gragson, T. 1998 'Potential versus actual vegetation: human behaviour in a landscape medium' in W. Balée (ed.) *Advances in Historical Ecology* (New York)

Graham, B. 1998 'The past in Europe's present: diversity, identity and the construction of place' in B. Graham (ed.) *Modern Europe: Place, Culture, Identity* (London) 19–49

2000 'The past in place: historical geographies of identity' in B. Graham and C. Nash (eds.) *Modern Historical Geographies* (Harlow) 70–99

Graham, B., Ashworth, G. J. and Tunbridge, J. E. 2000 *A Geography of Heritage* (London)

Graham, B. and Nash, C. (eds.) 2000 *Modern Historical Geographies* (Harlow)

Grataloup, C. (ed.) 1986 'Braudel dans tous ses états. La vie quotidienne des sciences sociales sous l'empire de l'histoire' *Espace temps* 34/35 [A special issue, a collection of articles on Braudel's impact on the social sciences]

1996 *Lieux d'histoire: essai de géohistoire systématique* (Montpellier)

Green, J. R. 1881 *The Making of England* (London)

Green, W. A. 1995 'Periodizing world history' *History and Theory* 34, 99–111

Gregory, D. 1976 'On rethinking historical geography' *Area* 8, 295–9

1982a 'Action and structure in historical geography' in A. R. H. Baker and M. Billinge (eds.) *Period and Place: Research Methods in Historical Geography* (Cambridge) 244–50

1982b *Regional Transformation and Industrial Revolution: a Geography of the Yorkshire Woollen Industry* (London)

1984 'Space, time and politics in social theory: an interview with Anthony Giddens' *Environment and Planning D: Society and Space* 2, 123–32

1985 *Space and Time in Social Life* (Worcester, Mass.)

1986 'Time-geography' in R. J. Johnston (ed.) *The Dictionary of Human Geography* 2nd edn (London) 485–7

1988 'The production of regions in England's Industrial Revolution' *Journal of Historical Geography* 14, 50–8

1989a 'Areal differentiation and post-modern human geography' in D. Gregory and R. Walford (eds.) *Horizons in Human Geography* (Basingstoke) 67–96

1989b 'Presences and absences: time-space relations and structuration theory' in D. Held and J. B. Thompson (eds.) *Social Theory of Modern Societies: Anthony Giddens and his Critics* (Cambridge) 185–214

1990a ' "A new and differing face in many places": three geographies of industrialisation' in R. A. Dodgshon and R. A. Butlin (eds.) *An Historical Geography of England and Wales* (London) 352–99

1990b ' "Grand maps of history": structuration theory and social change' in J. Clark, C. Modgil and S. Modgil (eds.) *Anthony Giddens: Consensus and Controversy* (Basingstoke) 217–33

1991 'Interventions in the historical geography of modernity: social theory, spatiality and the politics of representation' *Geografiska Annaler* B 73, 17–44

1994 *Geographical Imaginations* (Oxford)

1995 'Between the book and the lamp: imaginative geographies of Egypt, 1849–50' *Transactions of the Institute of British Geographers* 20, 29–57

Gregory, I. 2000 'Longitudinal analysis of age- and gender-specific migration patterns in England and Wales: a GIS-based approach' *Social Science History* 24, 471–503

2002 *A Place in History: a Guide to Using GIS in Historical Research* (Oxford)

Gregory, I. N., Dorling, D. and Southall, H. R. 2001 'A century of inequality in England and Wales using standardised geographical units' *Area* 33, 297–311

Gregory, I. N. and Southall, H. R. 1998 'Putting the past in its place: the Great Britain historical GIS' in S. Carver (ed.) *Innovations in GIS* (London) 210–21

2000 'Spatial frameworks for historical censuses – the Great Britain historical GIS' in P. K. Hall, R. McCaa and G. Thorvaldsen (eds.) *Handbook of Historical Microdata for Population Research* (Minneapolis) 319–33

Griffin, M. 1999 'The Great War photographs' in B. Brennen and H. Hardt (eds.) *Picturing the Past* (Urbana) 122–57

Griffiths, T. and Robin, L. 1997 *Ecology and Empire: Environmental History of Settler Societies* (Edinburgh)

Grigg, D. 1974 *The Agricultural Systems of the World: an Evolutionary Approach* (Cambridge)

Grim, R. E., Rumney, T. A. and McIlwraith, T. F. 2001 'Sources for recreating the North American past' in T. F. McIlwraith and E. K. Muller (eds.) *North America: the Historical Geography of a Changing Continent* 2nd edn (Lanham, Md) 471–82

Grove, A. T. and Rackham, O. 2001 *The Nature of Mediterranean Europe: an Ecological History* (New Haven, Conn.)

Grove, J. 1988 *The Little Ice Age* (London)

Grove, R. 1997 *Ecology, Climate and Empire: Colonialism and Global Environmental History* (Cambridge)

Grove, R., Damordaran, V. and Sangwan, S. (eds.) 1998 *Nature and the Orient: the Environmental History of South and Southeast Asia* (Delhi)

Guelke, L. 1974 'An idealist alternative in human geography' *Annals of the Association of American Geographers* 64, 193–202

1975 'On rethinking historical geography' *Area* 7, 135–8

1977 'Regional geography' *Professional Geographer* 29, 1–7

1982 *Historical Understanding in Geography: an Idealist Approach* (Cambridge)

1997 'The relations between geography and history reconsidered' *History and Theory* 36, 216–34

Guelke, L. and Katz, Y. 1999 'Ideas, ideologies and human landscapes: a proposal for the practice of historical geography' in Y. Ben-Artzi, I. Bartal and E. Reiner (eds.) *Studies in Geography and History in Honour of Yehoshua Ben-Arieh* (Jerusalem) 63–79

Guiomar, J-Y. 1997 'Vidal de la Blache's *Geography of France*' in P. Nora (ed.) *Realms of Memory: the Construction of the French Past, Vol. II: Traditions* (New York) 187–209

Guiraud, P. 1975 *Semiology* (London)

Gulley, J. L. M. 1959 'The Turnerian frontier: a study in the migration of ideas' *Tijdschrift voor Economische en Sociale Geografie* 50, 81–91

Hägerstrand, T. 1952 'The propagation of innovation waves' *Lund Studies in Geography Series B Human Geography* 4, 3–19

1953 *Innovation Diffusion as a Spatial Process* (Lund) [Translation by A. Pred published 1967 (Chicago)]

1970 'What about people in regional science?' *Papers of the Regional Science Association* 24, 7–21

1973 'The domain of human geography' in R. J. Chorley (ed.) *Directions in Geography* (London) 67–87

1975 'Space, time and human conditions' in A. Karlquist, L. Lundquist and F. Snickars (eds.) *Dynamic Allocation of Urban Space* (Farnborough) 3–14

Haggett, P. 1965 *Locational Analysis in Human Geography* (London)

1990 *The Geographer's Art* (Oxford)

Haigh, M. J. 1978 *Evolution of Slopes on Artificial Landforms – Blaenavon, UK*, Department of Geography, University of Chicago, Research Paper no. 183

Hall, D. 1982 *Medieval Fields* (Aylesbury)

Hall, P. 1998 *Cities in Civilization* (London)

Hannah, M. G. 2000 *Governmentality and the Mastery of Territory in Nineteenth-Century America* (Cambridge)

Hardy, D. 1988 'Historical geography and heritage studies' *Area* 20, 333–8

Harley, J. B. 1982 'Historical geography and its evidence: reflections on modelling sources' in A. R. H. Baker and M. Billinge (eds.) *Period and Place: Research Methods in Historical Geography* (Cambridge) 261–73

1988 'Maps, knowledge and power' in D. Cosgrove and S. Daniels (eds.) *The Iconography of Landscape: Essays on the Symbolic Representation, Design and Use of Past Environments* (Cambridge) 277–312

1989a 'Historical geography and the cartographic illusion' *Journal of Historical Geography* 15, 80–91

1989b 'Deconstructing the map' *Cartographica* 26, 1–20

2001 *The New Nature of Maps: Essays in the History of Cartography* (Baltimore)

Harley, J. B. and Woodward, D. (eds.) 1987 *The History of Cartography, Vol. I: Cartography in Prehistoric, Ancient and Medieval Europe and the Mediterranean* (Chicago)

Harris, R. 1993 'Industry and residence: the decentralisation of New York City, 1900–1940' *Journal of Historical Geography* 19, 169–90

1994 'Chicago's other suburbs' *Geographical Review* 84, 394–410

1996 *Unplanned Suburbs: Toronto's American Tragedy, 1900–1950* (Baltimore)

Harris, R. and Lewis, R. 1998 'Constructing a fault(y) zone: misrepresentations of American cities and suburbs 1900–1950' *Annals of the Association of American Geographers* 88, 622–39

Harris, R. C. 1967 'Historical geography in Canada' *Canadian Geographer* 11, 235–50

1971 'Theory and synthesis in historical geography' *Canadian Geographer* 15, 157–72

1977 'The simplification of Europe overseas' *Annals of the Association of American Geographers* 67, 469–83

1978a 'The historical mind and the practice of geography' in D. Ley and M. S. Samuels (eds.) *Humanistic Geography: Prospects and Problems* (London) 123–37

1978b 'The historical geography of North American regions' *American Behavioral Scientist* 22, 115–30

1987 (ed.) *Historical Atlas of Canada, Vol. I: Canada Before 1800* (Toronto)

1991 'Power, modernity and historical geography' *Annals of the Association of American Geographers* 81, 671–83

1995 'Maps as a morality play: Volume I of the *Historical Atlas of Canada*' in J. Winearls (ed.) *Editing Early and Historical Atlases* (Toronto) 163–79

1997 *The Resettlement of British Columbia: Essays on Colonialism and Geographical Change* (Vancouver)

1999 'Comments on *The Shaping of America' Journal of Historical Geography* 25, 9–11

Harris, R. C. and Warkentin, J. 1974 *Canada Before Confederation: a Study in Historical Geography* (New York)

Harsgor, M. 1978 'Total history: the Annales school' *Journal of Contemporary History* 13, 1–13

Hart, F. J. 1972 *Regions of the United States* (New York)

Hartshorne, R. 1939 *The Nature of Geography* (Lancaster, Pa.)

1959 *Perspective on the Nature of Geography* (Chicago)

Harvey, D. 1967 'Models of the evolution of spatial patterns in human geography' in R. J. Chorley and P. Haggett (eds.) *Models in Geography* (London) 549–607

1969 *Explanation in Geography* (London)

1973 *Social Justice and the City* (London)

1979 'Monument and myth: the building of the Basilica of the Sacred Heart' *Annals of the Association of American Geographers* 69, 362–81

1981 'The spatial fix – Hegel, von Thünen and Marx' *Antipode* 13, 1–12

1982a *The Limits to Capital* (Oxford)

1982b 'On the history and present condition of geography: an historical materialist manifesto' *Professional Geographer* 34, 1–11

1985 *Consciousness and the Urban Experience* (Oxford)

1989 *The Condition of Postmodernity* (Oxford)

1990 'Between space and time: reflections on the geographical imagination' *Annals of the Association of American Geographers* 80, 418–34

2000 *Spaces of Hope* (Edinburgh)

Hays, S. P. 1959 *Conservation and the Gospel of Efficiency: the Progressive Conservation Movement, 1890–1920* (Cambridge, Mass.)

1998 *Explorations in Environmental History* (Pittsburgh, Pa.)

Healey, R. G. 2000 'An historical GIS of nineteenth-century industrial development in the north eastern United States' *Historical GIS News* n.p.

Healey, R. G. and Stamp, T. R. 2000 'Historical GIS as a foundation for the analysis of regional economic growth – theoretical, methodological and practical issues' *Social Science History* 24, 575–612

Heathcote, R. L. 1965 *Back of Burke: a Study of Land Appraisal and Settlement in Semi-arid Australia* (Carlton, Victoria)

Heathcote, R. L. and McCaskill, M. 1972 'Historical geography in Australia and New Zealand' in A. R. H. Baker (ed.) *Progress in Historical Geography* (Newton Abbot) 144–67

Heffernan, M. 1995 'For ever England: the Western Front and the politics of remembrance in Britain' *Ecumene* 2, 293–324

1996 'Geography, cartography and military intelligence: the Royal Geographical Society and the First World War' *Transactions of the Institute of British Geographers* 21, 504–33

1998 *The Meaning of Europe* (London)

Helmfrid, S. 1972 'Historical geography in Scandinavia' in A. R. H. Baker (ed.) *Progress in Historical Geography* (Newton Abbot) 63–89

Helsinger, E. 1994 'Turner and the representation of England' in W. J. T. Mitchell (ed.) *Landscape and Power* (Chicago) 103–26

Henderson, G. 1999 *California and the Fictions of Capital* (Oxford)

Hewes, L. and Frandson, P. E. 1952 'Occupying the wet prairie: the role of artificial drainage in Store County, Iowa' *Annals of the Association of American Geographers* 42, 24–50

Heylyn, P. 1621 *Microcosmus, or a Little Description of the Great World* (Oxford)

Higounet, C. 1961 'La géohistoire' in C. Samaran (ed.) *L'histoire et ses méthodes* (Brussels) 68–91

Hill, D. 1981 *An Atlas of Anglo-Saxon England* (Oxford)

Hirsch, E. 1995 'Landscape: between place and space' in E. Hirsch and M. O'Handon (eds.) *The Anthropology of Landscape: Perspectives on Place and Space* (Oxford) 1–30

Hirsch, E. and O'Handon, M. (eds.) 1995 *The Anthropology of Landscape: Perspectives on Place and Space* (Oxford)

Hofmann, C. 2000 'The origins of the historical atlas in France (1630–1800): powers and limitations of maps as "eyes of history"' *Bibliothèque de l'Ecole des Chartes* 158, 97–128

Holdsworth, D. 1986 'Architectural expressions of the Canadian national state' *Canadian Geographer* 30, 167–71

1993 'Revaluing the house' in J. Duncan and D. Ley (eds.) *Place/Culture/Representation* (London) 95–109

1995 'The politics of editing a national historical atlas: a commentary' in J. Winearls (ed.) *Editing Early and Historical Atlases* (Toronto) 181–96

1997 'Landscape and archives as texts' in P. Groth and T. W. Bressi (eds.) *Understanding Ordinary Landscapes* (Newhaven, Conn.) 44–55

2002 'Historical geography: the ancients and the moderns – generational vitality' *Progress in Human Geography* 26, 671–8

Holmen, H. 1995 'What's new and what's regional in the "new regional geography"' *Geografiska Annaler* B 77, 47–63

Hooke, D. 1998 *The Landscape of Anglo-Saxon England* (London)

2001a (ed.) *Landscape: the Richest Historical Record* (Amesbury)

2001b 'The appreciation of landscape history' in D. Hooke (ed.) *Landscape: the Richest Historical Record* (Amesbury) 143–155

Hooke, J. M. and Kain, R. J. P. 1982 *Historical Change in the Physical Environment: a Guide to Sources and Techniques* (London)

Hopkins, A. G. 1999 'Back to the future: from national history to imperial history' *Past and Present* 164, 198–243

Hoppe, G. and Langton, J. 1994 *Peasantry to Capitalism: Western Östergötland in the Nineteenth Century* (Cambridge)

Hoskins, W. G. 1955 *The Making of the English Landscape* (London)

1957 *Leicestershire: an Illustrated Essay on the History of the Landscape* (London)

1959 *Local History in England* (London)

1963 *Provincial England: Essays in Social and Economic History* (London)

1966 *English Local History: the Past and the Future* (Leicester)

1967 *Fieldwork in Local History* (London)

Houston, C. J. and Smyth, W. J. 1980 *The Sash Canada Wore: a Historical Geography of the Orange Order in Canada* (Toronto)

1984 'Transferred loyalties: Orangeism in the United States and Canada' *American Review of Canadian Studies* 14, 193–212

1985 'The impact of fraternalism on the landscape of Newfoundland' *Canadian Geographer* 29, 59–65

Houston, J. M. 1953 *A Social Geography of Europe* (London)

Howard, P. 1991 *Landscapes: the Artists' Vision* (London)

Howell, P. 2001 'Prostitutional space in the nineteenth-century European city' in I. S. Black and R. A. Butlin (eds.) *Place, Culture and Identity: Essays in Historical Geography in Honour of Alan R. H. Baker* (Laval, Quebec) 181–202

Hudson, B. 1977 'The new geography and the new imperialism' *Antipode* 9, 12–19

Hudson, J. C. 1994 *Making the Corn Belt: a Geographical History of Middle-western Agriculture* (Bloomington)

Hudson, P. 1995 'A new history from below: computers and the maturing of local and regional history' *Local Historian* 25, 209–221

Hugill, P. 1993 *World Trade since 1431: Geography, Technology and Capitalism* (Baltimore)

1997 'World-system theory: where's the theory?' *Journal of Historical Geography* 23, 344–9

1999 *Global Communications since 1844: Geopolitics and Technology* (Baltimore)

Huntington, E. 1914 'The geographer and history' *Geographical Journal* 43, 19–32

1937 'Geography and history' *Canadian Journal of Economics and Political Science* 3, 565–72

Huppert, G. 1978 'The *Annales* school before the *Annales*' *Review* 1, 215–19

Hyams, E. 1977 *The Changing Face of Britain* (London)

Inglis, F. 1977 'Nation and community: a landscape and its morality' *Sociological Review* 25, 489–513

Innis, H. A. 1923 *A History of the Canadian Pacific Railway* (London)

1950 *Empire and Communications* (Oxford)

1951 *The Bias of Communications* (Toronto)

Jackson, J. B. 1972 *American Space: the Centennial Years, 1865–1876* (New York)

1979 'Landscape as theatre' *Landscape* 23, 3–7

1980 *The Necessity for Ruins and Other Topics* (Amherst, Mass.)

1984 *Discovering the Vernacular Landscape* (New Haven)

Jackson, P. 1988 '"Street life": the politics of carnival' *Environment and Planning D: Society and Space* 6, 191–212

1989 *Maps of Meaning* (1989)

Jacquart, J. 1990 'Histoire générale, histoire locale' in A. Croix and D. Guyvarc'h (eds.) *Guide de l'histoire locale* (Paris)

Jäger, H. 1969 *Historische Geographie* (Braunschweig)

Jakle, J. 1971 'Time, space and the geographic past: a prospectus for historical geography' *American Historical Review* 76, 1084–103

Jakle, J. and Sculle, K. A. 1994 *The Gas Station in America* (Baltimore)

Jakle, J. and Wilson, D. 1992 *Derelict Landscapes: the Wasting of America's Built Landscape* (Lanham, Md)

Janelle, D. G. 1968 'Central place development in a time-space framework' *Professional Geographer* 20, 5–10

Jarvis, P. J. 1979 'Plant introductions to England and their role in horticultural and sylvicultural innovation, 1500–1900' in H. S. A. Fox and R. A. Butlin (eds.) *Change in the Countryside* (London) 145–64

Jay, L. J. 1975 'The Black Country of Francis Brett Young' *Transactions of the Institute of British Geographers* 66, 57–72

Jeans, D. N. 1988 'Historical geography' *Australian Geographical Studies* 26, 105–11

Jelecek, L. 1999 'Environmentalism of historical geography, historiography, and historical land use' [in Czech] *Historicka Geografie* 30, 53–86

Jellicoe, G. and Jellicoe, S. 1975 *The Landscape of Man* (New York)

Jennings, J. N. 1952 *The Origin of the Broads* (London)

1966 'Man as a geological agent' *Australian Journal of Science* 28, 150–66

Johnson, N. C. 1996 'Where geography meets history: heritage tourism and the big house in Ireland' *Annals of the Association of American Geographers* 86, 551–66

1999 'The spectacle of memory: Ireland's remembrance of the Great War, 1919' *Journal of Historical Geography* 25, 36–56

2000 'Historical geographies of the present' in B. Graham and C. Nash (eds.) *Modern Historical Geographies* (Harlow) 251–72

Johnston, R., Allsopp, G., Baldwin, J. and Turner, H. 1990 *An Atlas of Bells* (Oxford)

Jones, Ll. R. 1925 'Geography and the university' *Economica* 5, 241–57

Jordan, T. G. 1978 *Texas Log Buildings: a Folk Architecture* (Austin, Tex.)

1982 *Texas Graveyards: a Cultural Legacy* (Austin, Tex.)

Journal of Biogeography 2002, vol. 29

Juillard, E. 1956 'Aux frontières de l'histoire et de la géographie' *Revue historique* 215, 267–73

1962 'La région: essai de définition' *Annales de géographie* 71, 483–99

Kain, R. J. P. 1986 *An Atlas and Index of the Tithe Files of Mid-Nineteenth Century England and Wales* (Cambridge)

Kain, R. J. P. and Ravenhill, W. (eds.) 1999 *Historical Atlas of South-West England* (Exeter)

Kark, R. (ed.) 1989 *The Land that Became Israel: Studies in Historical Geography* (London)

Kay, J. 1990 'The future of historical geography in the United States' *Annals of the Association of American Geographers* 80, 618–21

1991 'Landscapes of women and men: rethinking the regional historical geography of the United States' *Journal of Historical Geography* 17, 435–52

1997 'Sweet surrender but what's the gender? Nature and the body in the writings of nineteenth-century Mormon women' in J. P. Jones, H. L. Nast and S. M. Roberts (eds.) *Thresholds in Feminist Geography: Difference, Methodology, Representation* (Lanham, Md) 361–82

Kearns, G. 1988 'History, geography and world-systems theory' *Journal of Historical Geography* 14, 281–92

1997 'The imperial subject: geography and travel in the work of Mary Kingsley and Halford Mackinder' *Transactions of the Institute of British Geographers* 22, 450–72

Kellerman, A. 1987 'Time-space homology: a societal-geographical perspective' *Tijdschrift voor Economische en Sociale Geografie* 78, 251–64

1989 *Time, Space and Society: Geographical Societal Perspectives* (Dordrecht)

Kerr, D. G. and Holdsworth, D. W. (eds.) 1990 *Historical Atlas of Canada, Vol. III: Addressing the Twentieth Century, 1891–1961* (Toronto)

Keylor, W. R. 1975 *Academy and Community: the Foundation of the First Historical Profession* (London)

Kikuchi, T. 1977 [2nd edn 1987] *Method in Historical Geography* (Tokyo)

Kinda, A. 1997 'Some traditions and methodologies of Japanese historical geography' *Journal of Historical Geography* 23, 62–75

Kinser, S. 1981 '*Annaliste* paradigm? The geohistorical structuralism of Fernand Braudel' *American Historical Review* 86, 63–105

Kirk, W. 1951 'Historical geography and the concept of the behavioural environment' *Indian Geographical Journal* Silver Jubilee volume, 152–60

—— 1963 'Problems of geography' *Geography* 48, 357–72

Kleefeld, K. D. and Burggraaff, P. (eds.) 1997 *Perspektiven der Historische Geographie* (Bonn)

Kniffen, F. 1936 'Louisiana house types' *Annals of the Association of American Geographers* 26, 179–93

—— 1951 'The American covered bridge' *Geographical Review* 41, 114–23

—— 1965 'Folk housing: key to diffusion' *Annals of the Association of American Geographers* 55, 549–77

Knowles, A. K. 1997 *Capitalists Incorporated: Welsh Immigrants on Ohio's Industrial Frontier* (Chicago)

—— 2001 'Afterword: historical geography since 1987' in T. F. McIlwraith and E. K. Muller (eds.) *North America: the Historical Geography of a Changing Continent* 2nd edn (Lanham, Md) 465–70

—— 2002 (ed.) *Past Time, Past Place: GIS for History* (Redlands, Calif.)

Knowles, C. H. 1983 *Landscape History* (London)

Kobayashi, A. 1989 'A critique of dialectical landscape' in A. Kobayashi and S. Mackenzie (eds.) *Rethinking Human Geography* (Boston) 164–83

Konrad, V. 1986 'Recurrent symbols of nationalism in Canada' *Canadian Geographer* 30, 175–9

Kulikoff, A. 1973 'Historical geographers and social history: a review essay' *Historical Methods Newsletter* 6 no. 3, 122–8

Lacoste, Y. 1986 'Braudel géographe' *Hérodote* 40, 161–5

Lambert, J. H., Jennings, J. N., Smith, C. T., Green, C. and Hutchinson, J. N. 1970 *The Making of the Broads* (London)

Lamme, A. Jr III 1989 *America's Historic Landscapes: Community Power and the Preservation of Four National Historic Sites* (Knoxville, Tenn.)

Langton, J. 1979 *Geographical Change and Industrial Revolution: Coalmining in South-West Lancashire, 1590–1799* (Cambridge)

—— 1984 'The Industrial Revolution and the regional geography of England' *Transactions of the Institute of British Geographers* 9, 145–67

—— 1986 'Habitat, economy and society revisited: peasant ecotypes and economic development in Sweden' *Cambria* 13, 5–24

—— 1988a 'The two traditions of geography, historical geography and the study of landscapes' *Geografiska Annaler B* 70, 17–25

—— 1988b 'The production of regions in England's Industrial Revolution: a response' *Journal of Historical Geography* 14, 170–4

—— 1996 'The origins of the capitalist world economy' in I. Douglas, R. Huggett and M. Robinson (eds.) *Companion Encyclopedia of Geography: the Environment and Humankind* (London) 206–27

1998 'The continuity of regional culture: Lancashire Catholicism from the late-sixteenth to the early-nineteenth century' in E. Royle (ed.) *Issues of Regional Identity in Honour of John Marshall* (Manchester) 82–101

Langton, J. and Morris, R. J. (eds.) 1986 *Atlas of Industrialising Britain 1780–1914* (London)

Laverty, J. R. 1995 'The study of city and regional history in Australia' *Australian Journal of Politics and History* 41, 101–38

Lawton, R. 1983 'Space, place and time' *Geography* 68, 182–92

1987 'Peopling the past' *Transactions of the Institute of British Geographers* 12, 259–83

Le Goff, J., Chartier, R. and Revel, J. 1978 *La nouvelle histoire* (Paris)

Le Lannou, M. 1950 *Géographie de la Bretagne, tome I: Les conditions géographiques générales* (Rennes)

1952 *Géographie de la Bretagne, tome II: Economie et population* (Rennes)

Le Roy Ladurie, E. 1967 *Histoire du climat depuis l'an mil* (Paris) [Translation published 1971 as *Times of Feast, Times of Famine* (New York)]

1975 *Montaillou: village occitan de 1294 à 1324* (Paris) [translation published 1978 as *Montaillou: Cathars and Catholics in a French Village, 1294–1324* (London)]

Lefebvre, H. 1974 *La production de l'espace* (Paris) [Translation published 1991 as *The Production of Space* (Oxford)]

Lefebvre, T. 1933 *Les modes de vie dans les Pyrénées Atlantiques Orientales* (Paris)

Leighly, J. (ed.) 1963 *Land and Life: a Selection of the Writings of Carl Ortwin Sauer* (Berkeley)

1978 'Carl Ortwin Sauer, 1885–1975' in T. W. Freeman and P. Pinchemel (eds.) *Geographers: Bibliographical Studies* 2, 99–108

Lemon, J. T. 1972 *The Best Poor Man's Country: a Geographical Study of Early Southeastern Pennsylvania* (Baltimore)

1996 *Liberal Dreams and Nature's Limits: Great Cities of North America since 1600* (New York)

Lepetit, B. 1986a 'Espace et histoire, hommage à Fernand Braudel' *Annales économies sociétés civilisations* 41, 1187–91 [This is a theme issue, a collection of papers on space and history]

1986b 'Sur les dénivellations de l'espace économique en France, dans les années 1830' *Annales économies sociétés civilisations* 41, 1243–72

Lester, A. 1996 *From Decolonisation to Democracy: a New Historical Geography of South Africa* (London)

2000 'Historical geographies of imperialism' in B. Graham and C. Nash (eds.) *Modern Historical Geographies* (Harlow) 100–20

Levi, G. 1991 'On microhistory' in P. Burke (ed.) *New Perspectives on Historical Writing* (Cambridge) 93–113

Lewis, G. M. 1962 'Changing emphases in the descriptions of the natural environment of the American Great Plains region' *Transactions of the Institute of British Geographers* 30, 75–90

1966 'Regional ideas and reality in the Cis-Rocky Mountain West' *Transactions of the Institute of British Geographers* 38, 135–50

Lewis, P. F. 1979 'Axioms for reading the landscape: some guides to the American scene' in D. Meinig (ed.) *The Interpretation of Ordinary Landscapes* (New York)

Lewis, R. 1994 'Restructuring and the formation of an industrial district in Montreal's east end, 1850–1914' *Journal of Historical Geography* 20, 143–57

2000 *Manufacturing Montreal: the Making of an Industrial Landscape, 1850–1930* (Baltimore)

Ley, D. 1987 'Styles of the times: liberal and neo-conservative landscapes in inner Vancouver, 1968–86' *Journal of Historical Geography* 13, 40–56

Ley, D. and Olds, K. 1988 'Landscape as spectacle: world's fairs and a culture of heroic consumption' *Environment and Planning D: Society and Space* 6, 191–212

Leyshon, A. and Matless, D. 1998 *The Place of Music* (London)

Livingstone, D. N. 1992 *The Geographical Tradition: Episodes in the History of a Contested Enterprise* (Oxford)

1994 'Science and religion: foreword to the historical geography of an encounter' *Journal of Historical Geography* 20, 367–83

1995 'The spaces of knowledge: contributions towards a historical geography of science' *Environment and Planning D: Society and Space* 13, 5–34

Lobel, M. (ed.) 1969 *Historic Towns: Maps and Plans of Towns and Cities in the British Isles, with Historical Commentaries, from the Earliest Times to 1800, Vol. I* (London)

1975 *Historic Towns: Maps and Plans of Towns and Cities in the British Isles, with Historical Commentaries, from the Earliest Times to 1800, Vol. II* (London)

Lowenthal, D. 1958 *George Perkins Marsh: Versatile Vermonter* (New York)

1975 'Past time, present place: landscape and memory' *Geographical Review* 65, 1–36

1976 'The place of the past in the American landscape' in D. Lowenthal and M. J. Bowden (eds.) *Geographies of the Mind: Essays in Historical Geosophy in Honor of John Kirkland Wright* (New York) 89–117

1985 *The Past is a Foreign Country* (Cambridge)

1991 'British national identity and the English landscape' *Rural History* 2, 205–30

1994 'European and English landscapes as national symbols' in D. Hooson (ed.) *Geography and National Identity* (Oxford) 15–38

1998 *The Heritage Crusade and the Spoils of History* (Cambridge)

Lowenthal, D. and Bowden, M. J. (eds.) 1976 *Geographies of the Mind: Essays in Historical Geosophy in Honor of John Kirkland Wright* (New York)

Lowenthal, D. and Prince, H. C. 1964 'The English landscape' *Geographical Review* 54, 309–46

1965 'English landscape tastes' *Geographical Review* 55, 186–222

Lowther, G. R. 1959 'Idealist history and historical geography' *Canadian Geographer* 14, 30–6

Lucas, C. P. 1887 *Introduction to a Historical Geography of the British Colonies* (Oxford)

1888 *A Historical Geography of the British Colonies* (Oxford)

Macaulay, T. M. 1848 *The History of England from the Accession of James II* (London)

McCann, J. 1999 *Green Land, Brown Land, Black Land: an Environmental History of Africa, 1800–1990* (Portsmouth, N.H.)

McCord, N. 1979 *North-East England: an Economic and Social History* (London)

MacDonald, K. I. 1998 'Push and shove: spatial history and the construction of a portering economy in northern Pakistan' *Comparative Studies in Society and History* 40, 287–317

McDonald, T. J. (ed.) 1996 *The Historic Turn in the Human Sciences* (Michigan)

McEwan, C. 1994 'Encounters with West African women: textual representation of difference by white women abroad' in A. Blunt and G. Rose (eds.) *Writing Women and Space: Colonial and Postcolonial Geographies* (London) 73–100

McIlwraith, T. F. and Muller, E. K. (eds.) 2001 *North America: the Historical Geography of a Changing Continent* 2nd edn (Lanham, Md)

Mackie, J. D. 1952 *The Earlier Tudors, 1485–1558* (Oxford)

Mackinder, H. 1930 'The content of philosophical geography' *International Geographical Congress, Cambridge 1928: Report of Proceedings* (Cambridge) 305–11

McKinnon, M. (ed.) 1997 *Bateman New Zealand Historical Atlas/Ko Papatuanuku e Takoto Nei* (Auckland)

McManis, D. 1964 *The Initial Evaluation and Utilization of the Illinois Prairies, 1815–1840* University of Chicago Department of Geography Research Paper no. 94 (Chicago)

McNeill, J. 2000 *Something New Under the Sun: an Environmental History of the World* (New York)

McNeill, W. H. 1963 *The Rise of the West* (Chicago)

1967 *A World History* (New York)

1973 *The Ecumene: Story of Humanity* (New York)

1992 *The Global Condition: Conquerors, Catastrophes and Community* (Princeton)

1995 'The changing shape of world history' *History and Theory* 34, 8–26

McQuillan, D. A. 1982 'The interface of physical and historical geography: the analysis of farming decisions in response to drought hazards on the margins of the Great Plains' in A. R. H. Baker and M. Billinge (eds.) *Period and Place: Research Methods in Historical Geography* (Cambridge) 136–44

1993 'Historical geography and ethnic communities in North America' *Progress in Human Geography* 17, 355–66

1995 'New classics and diverse clusters in historical geography' *Progress in Human Geography* 19, 273–84

Maitland, F. W. 1897 *Domesday Book and Beyond* (Cambridge)

Malin, J. C. 1947 *The Grassland of North America: Prolegomena to its History* (Gloucester, Mass.)

1955 'Historians and geography' in J. C. Malin *On the Nature of History: Essays about History and Dissidence* (Lawrence, Kans.) 90–127

Mallory, W. E. and Simpson-Housley, P. (eds.) 1987 *Geography and Literature: a Meeting of the Disciplines* (Syracuse)

Mandrou, R. 1957 'Géographie humaine et histoire sociale' *Annales économies sociétés civilisations* 12, 619–27

Mann, W. A. 1993 *Landscape Architecture: an Illustrated History in Timelines, Site Plans and Biography* (New York)

Marconis, R. 1996 'Les relations entre la géographie et l'histoire' in P. Claval and A-L. Sanguin (eds.) *La géographie française à l'époque classique (1918–1968)* (Paris) 59–68

Marsh, G. P. 1864 *Man and Nature, or Physical Geography as Modified by Human Action* (New York)

Marshall, J. D. 1985 'Why study regions? (1)' *Journal of Regional and Local Studies* 5, 15–27

1986 'Why study regions? (2)' *Journal of Regional and Local Studies* 6, 1–12

Marshall, J. D. and Walton, J. K. 1981 *The Lake Counties from 1830 to the Mid-Twentieth Century* (Manchester)

Massey, D. 1995 'Places and their pasts' *History Workshop Journal* 39, 182–92

1999 'Space-time, "science" and the relationship between physical geography and human geography' *Transactions of the Institute of British Geographers* 24, 261–76

Matless, D. 1993 'One man's England: W. G. Hoskins and the English rural landscape' *Rural History* 4, 187–207

1994 'Moral geographies in Broadlands' *Ecumene* 1, 27–56

1995a '"The Art of Right Living": landscape and citizenship 1918–1939' in S. Pile and N. Thrift (eds.) *Mapping the Subject* (London) 93–122

1995b 'An occasion for geography: landscape representation and Foucault's corpus' *Environment and Planning D: Society and Space* 10, 41–56

1997 'Moral geographies of the English landscape' *Landscape Research* 22, 141–55

1998 *Landscape and Englishness* (London)

Mattingly, D. J. 1998 'Gender and the city in historical perspective: an introduction' *Historical Geography* 26, 1–4

Maxwell, G. S. 1983 *The Impact of Aerial Reconnaissance on Archaeology* (London)

May, J. and Thrift, N. (eds.) 2001 *TimeSpace: Geographies of Temporality* (London)

May, J. A. 1970 *Kant's Concept of Geography and its Relation to Recent Geographical Thought* University of Toronto, Department of Geography Research Publications 4

Mazlish, B. 1998 'Comparing global history to world history' *Journal of Interdisciplinary History* 28, 385–95

Mazlish, B. and Buultjen, R. (eds.) 1993 *Conceptualising Global History* (Boulder)

Mead, W. R. 1962 'Pehr Kalm in the Chilterns' *Acta Geographica* 17, 1–33

1963 'The adoption of other lands' *Geography* 48, 241–54

1980 'Regional geography' in E. H. Brown (ed.) *Geography: Yesterday and Tomorrow* (Oxford) 292–302

1981 *An Historical Geography of Scandinavia* (London)

Meade, R. and Trimble, S. 1974 'Effects of man on the interface of the hydrological cycle with the physical environment' *Publication 113 International Association of Scientific Hydrology* 99–104

Meinig, D. W. 1960 'Commentary on Walter Prescott Webb's geographical-historical concepts in American history' *Annals of the Association of American Geographers* 50, 95–96

1965 'The Mormon culture region: strategies and patterns in the American West, 1847–1964' *Annals of the Association of American Geographers* 55, 191–220

1968 *The Great Columbia Plain: a Historical Geography* (Washington, D.C.)

1969 *Imperial Texas: an Interpretive Essay in Cultural Geography* (Austin)

1971 *Southwest: Three Peoples in Geographical Change* (New York)

1978a 'The continuous shaping of America: a prospectus for geographers and historians' *American Historical Review* 83, 1186–1217

1978b 'Andrew Hill Clark, historical geographer' in J. R. Gibson (ed.) *European Settlement and Development in North America: Essays on Geographical Change in Honour and Memory of Andrew Hill Clark* (Toronto) 3–26

1979a (ed.) *The Interpretation of Ordinary Landscapes* (New York)

1979b 'The beholding eye: ten versions of the same scene' in D. W. Meinig (ed.) *The Interpretation of Ordinary Landscapes* (New York) 33–48

1979c 'Symbolic landscapes: some idealisations of American communities' in D. W. Meinig (ed.) *The Interpretation of Ordinary Landscapes* (New York) 164–92

1979d 'Reading the landscape: an appreciation of W. G. Hoskins and J. B. Jackson' in D. W. Meinig (ed.) *The Interpretation of Ordinary Landscapes* (New York) 195–244

1983 'Geography as an art' *Transactions of the Institute of British Geographers* 8, 314–28

1986 *The Shaping of America: a Geographical Perspective on 500 Years of History, Vol. I: Atlantic America, 1492–1800* (New Haven)

1989a 'The historical geography imperative' *Annals of the Association of American Geographers* 79, 79–87

1989b 'A geographical transect of the Atlantic world, *ca.* 1750' in E. Genovese and L. Hochberg (eds.) *Geographic Perspectives in History* (Oxford) 185–204

1993 *The Shaping of America: a Geographical Perspective on 500 Years of History, Vol. II: Continental America, 1800–1867* (New Haven)

1997 'Commentary: a response' *Historical Geography* 25, 1–9

1998 *The Shaping of America: a Geographical Perspective on 500 Years of History, Vol. III: Transcontinental America, 1850–1915* (New Haven)

1999a 'National historical geographies: necessities, opportunities, cautions' in Y. Ben-Artzi, I. Bartal and E. Reiner (eds.) *Studies in Geography and History in Honour of Yehoshua Ben-Arieh* (Jerusalem) 80–8

1999b 'The shaping of America, 1850–1915' *Journal of Historical Geography* 25, 1–16

Meinig, D. W. et al. 1982–8 *The Making of America: a Series of Seventeen Maps* (Washington, D.C.)

Merrens, H. R. 1964 *Colonial North Carolina in the Eighteenth Century: a Study in Historical Geography* (Chapel Hill)

1965 'Historical geography and early American history' *William and Mary Quarterly* 22, 529–48

1969 'The physical environment of early America: images and image-makers in colonial South Carolina' *Geographical Review* 59, 530–56

Michelet, J. 1833–44 and 1855 *Histoire de France* (19 vols., Paris)

Mieczkowski, Y. 2001 *The Routledge Historical Atlas of Presidential Elections* (New York)

Mikesell, M. 1960 'Comparative studies in frontier history' *Annals of the Association of American Geographers* 50, 62–74

1976 'The rise and decline of "sequent occupance": a chapter in the history of American geography' in D. Lowenthal and M. J. Bowden (eds.) *Geographies of the Mind: Essays in Historical Geosophy in Honor of John Kirkland Wright* (New York) 149–69

Miller, C. and Rothman, H. (eds.) 1997 *Out of the Woods: Essays in Environmental History* (Pittsburg, Pa.)

Miller, D. W. 1990 'Social history update: spatial analysis and social history' *Journal of Social History* 24, 213–20

Miller, E. 1915 'La géographie au service de l'histoire' *Revue trimestrielle canadienne* 1, 45–53

Miller, J. 1998 *An Environmental History of Northeast Florida* (Gainesville, Fla)

Mills, S. F. 1997 *The American Landscape* (Edinburgh)

Millward, R. 1955 *The Making of the English Landscape: Lancashire* (London)

Mirot, L. and Mirot, A. 1929 [2nd edn 1947] *Manuel de géographie historique de la France* (Paris)

Mitchell, D. 2000 *Cultural Geography* (Oxford)

2001 'Culture is not what it used to be: the transformation of Anglo-American cultural geography' *The Human Geography: Jimbun-Chiri* 53, 36–53

2002 'On Cole Harris' *Historical Geography* 30, 93–7

Mitchell, J. B. 1954 *Historical Geography* (London)

Mitchell, R. D. 1987 'The North American past: retrospect and prospect' in R. D. Mitchell and P. A. Groves (eds.) *North America: the Historical Geography of a Changing Continent* (Totowa, N.J.) 3–21

Mitchell, R. D. and Groves, P. A. (eds.) 1987 *North America: the Historical Geography of a Changing Continent* (Totowa, N.J.)

Mitchell, W. J. T. 1994a 'Imperial landscape' in W. J. T. Mitchell (ed.) *Landscape and Power* (Chicago) 5–34

1994b (ed.) *Landscape and Power* (Chicago)

Monk, J. 1992 'Gender in the landscape: expressions of power and meaning' in K. Anderson and F. Gale (eds.) *Inventing Places: Studies in Cultural Geography* (Melbourne) 123–38

Monkman, M. H. 1997 'Landscapes in music: an overview' (www.coastnet.com/-monkman/music/geomus1.htm)

Moodie, D. W. 1976 'The Hudson's Bay Company and its geographical impress, 1670–1870' *International Geography '76, section 9, Historical Geography* (Moscow) 71–4

Moodie, D. W. and Lehr, J. C. 1981 'Macro-historical geography and the great chartered companies: the case of the Hudson's Bay Company' *Canadian Geographer* 25, 267–71

Moran, E. F. (ed.) 1990 *The Ecosystem Approach in Anthropology: From Concept to Practice* (Ann Arbor)

Morgan, M. 1979 *Historical Sources in Geography* (London)

Morgan, W. T. W. 1983 *The World's Landscapes: Nigeria* (London)

Morin, K. M. 1999 'Peak practices: Englishwomen's "heroic" adventures in the nineteenth-century American West' *Annals of the Association of American Geographers* 89, 489–514

Morris, M. S. 1997 'Gardens "for ever England": landscape identity and the First World War British cemeteries on the Western Front' *Ecumene* 4, 410–34

Muir, R. 1999 *Approaches to Landscape* (London)

Naipaul, V. S. 1987 *The Enigma of Arrival* (London)

Nash, C. 2000 'Historical geographies of modernity' in B. Graham and C. Nash (eds.) *Modern Historical Geographies* (Harlow) 13–40

Nash, P. H. and Carney, G. O. 1996 'The seven themes of music geography' *Canadian Geographer* 40, 69–74

Nash. R. 1967 *Wilderness and the American Mind* (New Haven, Conn.)

National Geographic Society 1988 *Historical Atlas of the United States* (Washington, D.C.)

Naveh, Z. and Lieberman, A. S. 1990 *Landscape Ecology: Theory and Application* (New York)

Newcomb, R. M. 1979 *Planning the Past: Historical Landscape Resources and Recreation* (Folkestone)

Newton, N. T. 1971 *Design on the Land: the Development of Landscape Architecture* (Cambridge, Mass.)

Nir, D. 1983 *Man, a Geomorphological Agent: an Introduction to Anthropic Geomorphology* (Jerusalem)

Nitz, H. J. (ed.) 1987 *The Medieval and Early-Modern Rural Landscape of Europe under the Impact of the Commercial Economy* (Göttingen)

Noble, A. G. 1984 *Wood, Brick and Stone: the North American Settlement Landscape* (Amherst, Mass.)

Noble, A. G. and Dhussa, R. 1990 'Image and substance: a review of literary geography' *Journal of Cultural Geography* 10, 49–65

Nora, P. (ed) 1996 *Realms of Memory: the Construction of the French Past, Vol. I: Conflicts and Divisions* (New York)

1997 (ed.) *Realms of Memory: the Construction of the French Past, Vol. II: Traditions* (New York)

1998 (ed.) *Realms of Memory: the Construction of the French Past, Vol. III: Symbols* (New York)

Norton, W. 1984 *Historical Analysis in Geography* (London)

Odum, E. P. 1969 'The strategy of ecosystem development' *Science* 164, 262–70

Ogborn, M. 1998 *Spaces of Modernity: London's Geographies 1680–1780* (London)

1999 'Modernity and modernization' in P. Cloke, P. Crang and M. Godwin (eds.) *Introducing Human Geography* (London) 153–61

2000 'Historical geographies of globalisation, *c.* 1500–1800' in B. Graham and C. Nash (eds.) *Modern Historical Geographies* (Harlow) 43–69

Ogborn, M. and Philo, C. 1994 'Soldiers, sailors and moral locations in nineteenth-century Portsmouth' *Area* 26, 221–31

Ogden, P. E. 1973 *Marriage Patterns and Population Mobility: a Study in Rural France* University of Oxford School of Geography Research Papers 7

Ogilvie, A. G. 1952 'The time-element in geography' *Transactions and Papers of the Institute of British Geographers* 18, 1–16

Ophir, A. and Shapin, S. 1991 'The place of knowledge: a methodological survey' *Science in Context* 4, 3–21

O'Riordan, T. 1996 'Environment' in A. Kuper and J. Kuper (eds.) *The Social Sciences Encyclopedia* 2nd edn (London) 250–2

Orme, A. R. 1970 *The World's Landscapes: Ireland* (London)

Osborne, B. S. 1988 'The iconography of nationhood in Canadian art' in D. Cosgrove and S. Daniels (eds.) *The Iconography of Landscape: Essays on the Symbolic Design and Use of Past Environments* (Cambridge) 162–78

1992 'Interpreting a nation's identity: artists as creators of national consciousness' in A. R. H. Baker and G. Biger (eds.) *Ideology and Landscape in Historical Perspective* (Cambridge) 230–54

2001 'Warscapes, landscapes, inscapes: France, war, and the Canadian national identity' in I. S. Black and R. A. Butlin (eds.) *Place, Culture and Identity: Essays in Historical Geography in Honour of Alan R. H. Baker* (Laval, Quebec) 311–33

Overton, M. 1977 'Computer analysis of an inconsistent data source: the case of the probate inventories' *Journal of Historical Geography* 4, 317–26

1979 'Estimating crop yields from probate inventories: an example from East Anglia, 1585–1735' *Journal of Economic History* 39, 363–78

1985 'The diffusion of agricultural innovations in early modern England: turnips and clover in Norfolk and Suffolk 1580–1740' *Transactions of the Institute of British Geographers* 10, 205–21

1996 *Agricultural Revolution in England: the Transformation of the Agrarian Economy 1500–1850* (Cambridge)

Ozouf-Marignier, M-V. 1995 'Géographie et histoire' in A. Bailly, R. Ferras and D. Pumain (eds.) *Encyclopédie de géographie* 2nd edn (Paris) 75–89

Pacione, M. (ed.) 1987 *Historical Geography: Progress and Prospect* (London)

Palmer, J. 1986 'Computerising Domesday Book' *Transactions of the Institute of British Geographers* 11, 279–89

2000 'Mapping Domesday' *Historical GIS News* n.p.

Palmer, M. 1994 *Industry in the Landscape, 1700–1900* (London)

Parker, I. 1993 'Innis and the geography of communications and empire' *Canadian Geographer* 37, 353–5

Parker, W. H. 1968 *An Historical Geography of Russia* (London)

Parkes, D. N. and Thrift, N. J. 1980 *Times, Spaces and Places: a Chronographic Perspective* (Chichester)

Parr, H. and Philo, C. 1996 '"A forbidding fortress of locks, bars and padded cells": the locational history of mental health care in Nottingham' *Historical Geography Research Series* 32

Parry, M. 1978 *Climatic Change, Agriculture and Settlement* (Folkestone)

Paterson, J. H. 1974 'Writing regional geography' *Progress in Geography* 6, 1–26

Paullin, C. O. 1932 *Atlas of the Historical Geography of the United States* (New York)

Pawson E. and Brooking, T. (eds.) 2002 *Environmental Histories of New Zealand* (Oxford)

Pergameni, C. 1942 'Géographie humaine et géographie de l'histoire' *Scientia* 71, 24–30

Perry, P. J. 1977 'Mariage et distance dans le canton du Bleymard (Lozère) 1811–20 et 1891–1900' *Etudes rurales* 67, 61–70

Phillips, A. D. M. 1989 *The Underdraining of Farmland in England during the Nineteenth Century* (Cambridge)

Philo, C. 1992a 'Foucault's geography' *Environment and Planning D: Society and Space* 10, 137–61

1992b 'The space reserved for insanity: studies in the historical geography of the mad-business in England and Wales' (unpublished PhD dissertation, University of Cambridge)

1994 'History, geography and the "still greater mystery" of historical geography' in D. Gregory, R. Martin and G. Smith (eds.) *Human Geography: Society, Space and Social Science* (London) 252–81

1995 'Journey to asylum: a medical-geographical idea in historical context' *Journal of Historical Geography* 21, 148–68

2001 'The "total environment" and other byways of historical geography' in I. S. Black and R. A. Butlin (eds.) *Place, Culture and Identity: Essays in Historical Geography in Honour of Alan R. H. Baker* (Laval, Quebec) 45–67

(n.d.) 'The space reserved for insanity: an historical geography of the mad-business in England and Wales to the 1860s' (unpublished manuscript)

Phythian-Adams, C. 1987 *Re-thinking English Local History* (Leicester)

1991 'Local history and national history: the quest for the peoples of England' *Rural History* 2, 1–23

1992 'Hoskins's England: a local historian of genius and the realisation of his theme' *Local Historian* 22, 170–83

Pinchemel, G. and Pinchemel, P. 1981 'Réflexions sur l'histoire de la géographie: histoire de la géographie, histoire des géographes' *Comité des Travaux Historiques et Scientifiques, Bulletin de la Section de Géographie* 84 for 1979, 221–31

Pinol, J-L.1996 *Atlas historique des villes de France* (Barcelona)

Pitte, J-R. 1983 *Histoire du paysage français* (2 vols., Paris)

1989 'Enjeux: le retour de la géographie' *Vingtième siècle* 23, 83–90

1994 'De la géographie historique' *Hérodote* 74/75, 14–21

1995 (ed.) *Géographie historique et culturelle de l'Europe: hommage au Professeur Xavier de Planhol* (Paris)

Piveteau, J-L. 1995 *Les temps du territoire* (Geneva)

Planhol, X. de. 1972 'Historical geography in France' in A. R. H. Baker (ed.) *Progress in Historical Geography* (Newton Abbot) 29–44

1988 *Géographie historique de la France* (Paris) [Translation published 1994 as *An Historical Geography of France* (Cambridge)]

Ploszajska, T. 1994 'Moral landscapes and manipulated spaces: gender, class and space in Victorian reformatory schools' *Journal of Historical Geography* 20, 413–29

2000 'Historiographies of geography and empire' in G. Graham and C. Nash (eds.) *Modern Historical Geographies* (Harlow) 121–45

Pocock, D. C. D. (ed.) 1981a 'Place and the novelist' *Transactions of the Institute of British Geographers* 6, 337–47

1981b *Humanistic Geography and Literature* (London)

1987 *A Sound Portrait of a Cathedral City* [sound recording; cassette] (Durham)

1988 'Geography and literature' *Progress in Human Geography* 12, 87–102

1989 'Sound and the geographer', *Geography* 74, 193–200

Pomper, P. 1995 'World history and its critics' *History and Theory* 34, 1–7

Poole, R. L. (ed.) 1902 *Historical Atlas of Modern Europe from the Decline of the Roman Empire* (Oxford)

Pounds, N. J. G. 1947 *An Historical and Political Geography of Europe* (London)

1979 *An Historical Geography of Europe, 1500–1840* (Cambridge)

1985 *An Historical Geography of Europe, 1800–1914* (Cambridge)

Poussou, J-P. 1997 'Dialogues et rapports de la géographie et de l'histoire en France' in J-R. Pitte (ed.) *Apologie pour la géographie* (Paris) 167–83

Powell, J. M. 1970 *The Public Lands of Australia Felix* (Oxford)

1977 *Mirrors of the New World: Images and Image-makers in the Settlement Process* (Folkestone)

1988 *An Historical Geography of Modern Australia* (Cambridge)

1989 *Watering the Garden State: Water, Land and Community in Victoria, 1834–1988* (Sydney)

1991 *Plains of Promise, Rivers of Destiny: Water Management and the Development of Queensland, 1824–1990* (Brisbane)

1993 *The Emergence of Bioregionalism in the Murray-Darling Basin* (Canberra)

1996 'Historical geography and environmental history: an Australian interface' *Journal of Historical Geography* 22, 253–73

1998 *Watering the Western Third: Water, Land and Community in Western Australia, 1836–1998* (Perth)

1999 'Environment, culture and modern historical geography: recent Anglophone contributions' *The Human Geography: Jimbun-Chiri* 51, 477–93

2000 'Historical geographies of the environment' in B. Graham and C. Nash (eds.) *Modern Historical Geographies* (Harlow) 169–92

Pratt, M. L. 1992 *Imperial Eyes: Travel Writing and Transculturation* (New Haven)

Pred, A. R. 1966 *The Spatial Dynamics of US Urban-Industrial Growth, 1800–1914* (Cambridge, Mass.)

1973 *Urban Growth and the Circulation of Information: the United States' System of Cities, 1790–1840* (Cambridge, Mass.)

1984 'Place as historically contingent process: structuration and the time-geography of becoming places' *Annals of the Association of American Geographers* 74, 279–97

1986 *Place, Practice and Structure: Social and Spatial Transformation in Southern Sweden 1750–1850* (Cambridge)

1990 *Making Histories and Constructing Human Geographies* (Boulder)

Pregill, P. and Volkman, N. 1999 *Landscapes in History: Design and Planning in the Eastern and Western Traditions* (New York)

Preston, P. and Simpson-Housley, P. (eds.) 1994 *Writing the City: Eden, Babylon and the New Jerusalem* (London)

Prince, H. C. 1962 'Pits and ponds in Norfolk' *Erdkunde* 16, 10–31

1964 'The origin of pits and depressions in Norfolk' *Geography* 49, 15–32

1969 'Progress in historical geography' in R. U. Cooke and J. H. Johnson (eds.) *Trends in Geography: an Introductory Survey* (London)

1978 'Time and historical geography' in T. Carlstein, D. Parkes and N. Thrift (eds.) *Making Sense of Time* (London) 17–37

1979 'Marl pits or dolines of the Dorset chalklands?' *Transactions of the Institute of British Geographers* 4, 116–17

1988 'Art and agrarian change, 1710–1815' in D. Cosgrove and S. Daniels (eds.) *The Iconography of Landscape: Essays on the Symbolic Design and Use of Past Environments* (Cambridge) 98–118

1997 *The Wetlands of the American Midwest: a Historical Geography of Changing Attitudes* (Chicago)

Pringle, T. 1988 'The privation of history: Landseer, Victoria and the Highland myth' in D. Cosgrove and S. Daniels (eds.) *The Iconography of Landscape: Essays on the Symbolic Design and Use of Past Environments* (Cambridge) 142–61

Pryce, W. T. R. (ed.) 1994 *From Family History to Community History* (Cambridge)

Pugh, S. (ed.) 1990 *Reading Landscape: Country–City–Capital* (Manchester)

Ramsay, W. M. 1890 *The Historical Geography of Asia Minor* (London)

Randle, P. 1966 *Geografía Historica y Planeamiento* (Buenos Aires)

Reed, M. 1990 *The Landscape of Britain from the Beginnings to 1914* (London)

Ren-Zhi Hou 1979 *Theory and Practice in Historical Geography* (Beijing)

1985 *Historical Atlas of Beijing City* (Beijing)

Revill, G. 1991 '*The Lark Ascending*: monument to a radical pastoral' *Landscape Research* 16, 25–30

2000a 'English pastoral: music, landscape, history and politics' in I. Cook, D. Crouch, S. Naylor and J. R. Ryan (eds.) *Cultural Turns/Geographical Turns* (Harlow) 140–58

2000b 'Music and the politics of sound: nationalism, citizenship, and auditory space' *Environment and Planning D: Society and Space* 18, 597–613

Reynaud, A. 1981 'Les différentes utilisations de l'histoire par la géographie' *Comité des Travaux Historiques et Scientifiques, Bulletin de la Section Géographique* 84 for 1979, 9–26

Richards, J. F. 1990 'Land transformation' in B. L. Turner and W. C. Clarke (eds.) *The Earth as Transformed by Human Action* (Cambridge) 163–78

Roberts, B. K. 1987 'Landscape archaeology' in J. M. Wagstaff (ed.) *Landscape and Culture: Geographical and Archaeological Perspectives* (Oxford)

Roberts, N. 1998 *The Holocene: an Environmental History* 2nd edn (Oxford)

Robic, M-C. (ed.) 2000 *Le 'Tableau de la géographie de la France' de Paul Vidal de la Blache: dans le labyrinthe des formes* (Paris)

Robson, B. T. 1973 *Urban Growth: an Approach* (London)

Roche, M. M. 1987 *Forest Policy in New Zealand: an Historical Geography, 1840–1919* (Palmerston North)

Rogers, A. 1977 *This Was Their World: Approaches to Local History* (London)

Rogers, J. D. 1911 *A Historical Geography of the British Colonies* (Oxford)

Roncayolo, M. 1989 'Histoire et géographie: les fondements d'une complémentarité' *Annales économies sociétés civilisations* 44, 1427–34

Rose, G. 1993 *Feminism and Geography: the Limits of Geographical Knowledge* (Cambridge)

1997 'Engendering the slum: photography in east London in the 1930s' *Gender, Place and Culture* 4, 277–300

2000 'Practising photography: an archive, a study, some photographs and a researcher' *Journal of Historical Geography* 26, 555–71

Rose, G. and Ogborn, M. 1988 'Feminism and historical geography' *Journal of Historical Geography* 14, 405–9

Ross, E. 1970 *Beyond the River and the Bay. Some Observations on the State of the Canadian Northwest in 1811* (Toronto)

Roupnel, G. 1932 *Histoire de la campagne française* (Paris)

Rowley, T. 1972 *The Shropshire Landscape* (London)

1978 *Villages in the Landscape* (Gloucester)

Rowley, T. and Breakell, M. (eds.) 1975 *Planning and the Historic Environment* (Oxford)

Rowse, A. L. 1941 *Tudor Cornwall* (London)

1950 *The England of Elizabeth* (London)

Roxby, P. M. 1930 'The scope and aims of human geography' *Scottish Geographical Magazine* 46, 276–90

Rühl, A. 1929 'Das Standortsproblem in der Landwirtschafts-Geographie. Das Neuland Ost-Australien' *Institut für Meereskunde, Neue serie B, Historisch Volkwirtschaftliche Reich* 6 (Berlin)

Ryan, J. R. 1997 *Picturing Empire: Photography and the Visualisation of the British Empire* (London)

Rycroft, S. and Cosgrove, D. 1995 'Mapping the modern nation: Dudley Stamp and the Land Utilisation Survey' *History Workshop Journal* 40, 91–105

Said, E. 1978 *Orientalism: Western Conceptions of the Orient* (London)

Samuel, R. 1994 *Theatres of Memory, Vol. I: Past and Present in Contemporary Culture* (London)

1998 *Theatres of Memory, Vol. II: Island Stories: Unravelling Britain* (London)
Samuels, M. S. 1979 'The biography of landscape: cause and culpability' in D. W. Meinig
   (ed.) *The Interpretation of Ordinary Landscapes* (New York) 51–88
Sanguin, A-L. 1993 *Vidal de la Blache. Un génie de la géographie* (Paris)
Sauer, C. O. 1920 *The Geography of the Ozark Highland of Missouri* (Chicago)
   1925 *The Morphology of Landscape*, University of California Publications in Geography
   2, 19–54; reprinted in J. Leighly (ed.) 1963 *Land and Life: a Selection of the Writings
   of Carl Ortwin Sauer* (Berkeley, Calif.) 315–30
   1938a 'Theme of plant and animal destruction in economic history' *Journal of Farm
   Economics* 20, 765–75
   1938b 'Destructive exploitation in modern colonial expansion' *International Geographical Congress* Vol. III Section IIIc (Amsterdam) 494–9
   1941a 'Foreword to historical geography' *Annals of the Association of American Geographers* 31, 1–24; reprinted in J. Leighly (ed.) 1963 *Land and Life: a Selection of the
   Writings of Carl Ortwin Sauer* (Berkeley, Calif.) 351–79
   1941b 'The personality of Mexico' *Geographical Review* 31, 353–64
   1947 'Early relations of man to plants' *Geographical Review* 37, 1–25
   1952 *Agricultural Origins and Dispersals* (New York)
   1966 *The Early Spanish Main* (Berkeley, Calif.)
   1969 *Seeds, Spades, Hearths and Herds* (Cambridge, Mass.)
   1974 'The fourth dimension of geography' *Annals of the Association of American
   Geographers* 64, 189–92
Sax, B. 1992 'Jacob Burkhardt and national history' *History of European Ideas* 15, 845–50
Sayer, A. 1989 'The "new" regional geography and the problems of narrative' *Environment
   and Planning D: Society and Space* 7, 253–76
Scarpino, P. V. 1985 *Great River: an Environmental History of the Upper Mississippi 1890–
   1950* (Columbia, Miss.)
Schama, S. 1995 *Landscape and Memory* (London)
Schein, R. H. 1997 'The place of landscape: a conceptual framework for interpreting an
   American scene' *Annals of the Association of American Geographers* 87, 66–80
   2001 'Practicing historical geography: re-placing the past' *Historical Geography* 29,
   7–13
Schivelbusch, W. 1986 *The Railway Journey: Trains and Travel in the Nineteenth Century*
   (Oxford)
Schmid, D. 1995 'Imagining safe urban spaces: the contribution of detective fiction to
   radical geography' *Antipode* 27, 242–69
Schofield, R. S. 1965 'The geographical distribution of wealth in England 1334–1649'
   Economic History Review 18, 483–510
Schwartz, J. M. 1996 '*The Geography Lesson*: photographs and the construction of imagi-
   native geographies' *Journal of Historical Geography* 22, 16–45
   2000 '"Records of simple truth and precision": photography, archives, and the illusion
   of control' *Archivaria: Journal of the Association of Canadian Archivists* 50, 1–40
Schwartzberg, J. E. 1978 [2nd edn 1992] *Historical Atlas of South Asia* (New York)
Seddon, G. 1997 *Landprints: Reflections on Space and Place* (Cambridge)
Semple, E. C. 1903 [revised edn 1933] *American History and its Geographic Conditions*
   (Boston, Mass.)

1909 'The operation of geographic factors in history' *Report of the Ohio Valley Historical Association* 2, 26–41

Seymour, S. 2000 'Historical geographies of landscape' in B. Graham and C. Nash (eds.) *Modern Historical Geographies* (Harlow) 193–217

Sheail, J. 1971 *Rabbits and their History* (Newton Abbot)

1972 'The distribution of taxable population and wealth in England during the early sixteenth century' *Transactions of the Institute of British Geographers* 55, 111–20

1980 *Historical Ecology: the Documentary Evidence* (Cambridge)

1997 'Environmental history: a challenge for the local historian' *Archives* 22, 157–69

Sheeran, G. and Sheeran, Y. 1998 'Discourses in local history' *Rethinking History* 2, 63–85

Sherlock, R. L. 1922 *Man as a Geological Agent: an Account of His Action on Inanimate Nature* (London)

Shils, E. 1968 'The concept and function of ideology' in D. L. Sills (ed.) *International Encyclopedia of the Social Sciences, Vol. VII* (New York) 66–76

Siebert, L. 2000 'Using GIS to document, visualise and interpret Tokyo's spatial history' *Social Science History* 24, 537–74

Simmons, I. G. 1993 *Environmental History: a Concise Introduction* (Oxford)

1996 *Changing the Face of the Earth: Culture, Environment, History* 2nd edn (Oxford)

Sinnhuber, K. A. 1954 'Central Europe-Mitteleuropa-Europe Centrale' *Transactions of the Institute of British Geographers* 20, 15–39

Sion, J. 1908 *Les paysans de la Normandie orientale: étude géographique sur les populations rurales du Caux et du Bray, du Vexin Normand et de la vallée de la Seine* (Paris)

Skipp, V. 1981 'Local history: a new definition and its implications' *Local Historian* 21, 325–91

Smith, C. A. 1987 'Regional analysis in world-system perspective: a critique of three structural theories of uneven development' *Review* 10, 597–648

Smith, C. T. 1965 'Historical geography: current trends and prospects' in R. J. Chorley and P. Haggett (eds.) *Frontiers in Geographical Teaching* (London) 118–43

1967 *An Historical Geography of Western Europe before 1800* (London)

1969 'The drainage basin as an historical basis for human activity' in R. J. Chorley (ed.) *Water, Earth and Man: a Synthesis of Hydrology, Geomorphology and Socio-economic Geography* (London) 101–10

Smith, D. 2000 *Moral Geographies: Ethics in a World of Difference* (Edinburgh)

Smith, J. 1993 'The lie that binds: destabilising the text of landscape' in J. Duncan and D. Ley (eds.) *Place/Culture/Representation* (London) 78–92

Smith, N. 1984 [2nd edn 1990] *Uneven Development: Nature, Capital and the Production of Space* (Oxford)

1986 'On the necessity of uneven development' *Journal of Urban and Regional Development* 10, 87–104

Snyder, T. 1994 'Territorial photography' in W. J. T. Mitchell (eds.) *Landscape and Power* (Chicago) 175–202

Soja, E. W. 1985 'Regions in context: spatiality, periodicity and the historical geography of the regional question' *Environment and Planning D: Society and Space* 2, 175–90

1989 *Postmodern Geographies: the Reassertion of Space in Critical Social Theory* (London)

Sorre, M. 1943–52 *Les fondements de la géographie humaine* (3 vols., Paris)

Soulet, J-F. 1988 'Une nouvelle approche de la France rurale au XIXe siècle?' *Revue historique* 279, 381–92

Southall, H. 2002 'National Lottery funding for Great Britain Historical GIS' *Historical GIS News* Spring, n.p.

Sparks, E. E. 1909 'Report on the conference on the relations of geography and history' *American Historical Association, Annual Report 1908* (Washington, D.C.) 57–61

Spate, O. H. K. 1979 *The Pacific since Magellan, Vol. I: The Spanish Lake* (London)
1983 *The Pacific since Magellan, Vol. II: Monopolists and Freebooters* (London)

Sperling, C. H. B., Goudie, A. S., Stoddart, D. R. and Poole, G. C. 1979 'Origin of the Dorset dolines' *Transactions of the Institute of British Geographers* 4, 121–4

St Joseph, J. K. (ed.) 1977 *The Uses of Air Photography* (London)
1979 *Medieval England: an Aerial Survey* (Cambridge)

Stanislawski, D. 1946 'The origin and spread of the grid-pattern town' *Geographical Review* 36, 105–20
1959 *The Individuality of Portugal* (Austin, Tex.)
1963 *Portugal's Other Kingdom: the Algarve* (Austin, Tex.)

Starrs, P. E. 1998 *Let the Cowboy Ride: Cattle Ranching in the American West* (Baltimore)

Stilgoe, J. R. 1982 *Common Landscapes of America, 1580 to 1845* (Newhaven, Conn.)

Stoddart, D. R. 1965 'Geography and the ecological approach: the ecosystem as a geographic principle and method' *Geography* 50, 242–51

Stover. J. 1999 *The Routledge Historical Atlas of American Railroads* (New York)

Subbarao, B. 1958 *The Personality of India* (Baroda)

Summers, R. 1960 'Environment and culture in southern Rhodesia: a study in the "personality" of a landlocked country' *American Philosophical Society, Proceedings* 104, 266–92

Tate, T. W. 1981 'Problems of definition in environmental history' *American Historical Association Newsletter*, 8–10

Taylor, C. C. 1973 *The Cambridgeshire Landscape* (London)
1974 *Fieldwork in Medieval Archaeology* (London)
1975 *Fields in the Landscape* (Gloucester)
1983a *The Archaeology of Gardens* (Aylesbury)
1983b *Village and Farmstead* (London)
2001 'The plus fours in the wardrobe: a personal view of landscape history' in D. Hooke (ed.) *Landscape: the Richest Historical Record* (Amesbury) 157–62

Taylor, E. G. R. 1936 'Leland's England' and 'Camden's England' in H. C. Darby (ed.) *An Historical Geography of England before AD 1800* (Cambridge) 330–53 and 354–86

Taylor, P. J. 1985 *Political Geography: World Economy, Nation-State and Locality* (London)
1999a 'A geohistorical interpretation of the modern world' in P. Cloke, P. Crang and M. Goodwin (eds.) *Introducing Human Geographies* (London) 162–9
1999b *Modernities: a Geohistorical Interpretation* (Cambridge)

Terrie, P. G. 1989 'Recent work in environmental history' *American Studies International* 27, 42–63

Thirsk, J. (ed.) 2000 *The English Rural Landscape* (Oxford)

Thomas, D. 1954 *Under Milk Wood* (London)

Thomas, K. 1983 *Man and the Natural World: Changing Attitudes in England 1500–1800* (London)

Thomas, W. L. (ed.) 1956 *Man's Role in Changing the Face of the Earth* (Chicago)

Thompson, J. M. 1929 *An Historical Geography of Europe, 800–1789* (Oxford)

Thrift, N. 1983 'On the determination of social action in space and time' *Environment and Planning D Society and Space* 1, 23–57

1988 'Vivos voco: ringing the changes in the historical geography of time consciousness' in T. Schuller and M. Young (eds.) *The Rhythms of Society* (London) 53–94

1990 'For a new regional geography 1' *Progress in Human Geography* 14, 272–7

1991 'For a new regional geography 2' *Progress in Human Geography* 15, 456–65

1993 'For a new regional geography 3' *Progress in Human Geography* 17, 92–100

1996 *Spatial Formations* (London)

Thrift, N. and Pred, A. 1981 'Time-geography: a new beginning' *Progress in Human Geography* 5, 277–86

Thuillier, G. and Tulard, J. 1992 *Histoire locale et régionale* (Paris)

Tindall, G. 1991 *Countries of the Mind: the Meaning of Places to Writers* (London)

Tobey, G. B. 1973 *A History of Landscape Architecture: the Relationship of People to Environment* (New York)

Trevelyan, G. M. 1930 *England under Queen Anne* (London)

Trimble, S. W. 1974 *Man-induced Soil Erosion on the Southern Piedmont, 1700–1970* (Ackeny, Iowa)

1988 'Environmental impacts in the American past' in C. Earle and L. Dilsaver (eds.) *Foreword to Historical Geography: Accomplishments and Agenda of its North American Practitioners*, Working Papers in Historical Geography, Association of American Geographers' Historical Geography Specialty Group 2, 49–51; reprinted in G. L. Gaile and C. J. Willmott (eds.) 1989 *Geography in America* (Columbus, Ohio) 179–80

1990 'Nature's continent' in M. P. Conzen (ed.) *The Making of the American Landscape* (London) 9–26

1992 'Preface' in L. M. Dilsaver and C. E. Colten (eds.) *The American Environment: Interpretations of Past Geographies* (Lanham, Md)

Trimble, S. W. and Cooke, R. U. 1991 'Historical sources for geomorphological research in the United States' *Professional Geographer* 43, 212–28

Trimble, S. W. and Crosson, P. 2000 'US soil erosion rates – myth and reality' *Science* 289, 248–50

Trochet, J-R. 1997 *La géographie historique de la France* (Paris)

1998 *La géographie historique: hommes et territoires dans les sociétés traditionelles* (Paris)

Tunbridge, J. E. 1998 'The question of heritage in European cultural conflict' in B. Graham (ed.) *Modern Europe: Place, Culture and Identity* (London) 236–60

Tupling, G. H. 1926 *The Economic History of Rossendale* (Manchester)

Turner, B. L. and Clarke, W. C. (eds.) 1990 *The Earth as Transformed by Human Action* (Cambridge)

Turner, F. J. 1891 *The Character and Influence of the Indian Trade in Wisconsin* (Baltimore)

1894 'The significance of the frontier in American history' *American Historical Association, Annual Report 1893* (Washington, D.C.); reprinted in F. J. Turner 1920 *The Frontier in American History* (New York) 1–38

1908 'Report on the conference on the relations of geography and history' *American Historical Association, Annual Report 1907* vol. 1 (Washington, D.C.) 45–8

1914 'Geographical influences in American political history' *Bulletin of the American Geographical Society* 46, 591–5

Turnock, D. 1967 'The region in modern geography' *Geography* 52, 374–83

1982 *The Historical Geography of Scotland since 1707: Geographical Aspects of Modernisation* (Cambridge)

Unstead, J. F. 1907 'The meaning of geography' *Geographical Teacher* 4, 19–28

Vallaux, C. 1925 *Les sciences géographiques* (Paris)

Vance, J. E. Jr 1995 *The North American Railroad: Its Origins, Evolution and Geography* (Baltimore)

Veyret, P. 1944 *Les pays de la moyenne Durance alpestre: étude géographique* (Grenoble)

Vidal de la Blache, P. 1903 *Tableau de la géographie de la France* in E. Lavisse (ed.) *Histoire de France*, vol. I part 1 (Paris) [Translation published 1928 as *The Personality of France* (London)]

1922 *Principes de géographie humaine* (Paris) [Translation published 1926 as *Principles of Human Geography* (London)]

Vigier, P. 1963 *Essai sur la répartition de la propriété foncière dans la région alpine* (Paris)

Wade-Martins, P. 1993 *An Historical Atlas of Norfolk* (Norwich)

Waller, P. (ed.) 2000 *The English Urban Landscape* (Oxford)

Wallerstein, I. 1974 *The Modern World-System, Vol. I: Capitalist Agriculture and the Origins of the European World-Economy in the Sixteenth Century* (London)

1979 *The Capitalist World-Economy* (Cambridge)

1980 *The Modern World-System, Vol. II: Mercantilism and the Consolidation of the European World-Economy, 1730–1840s* (London)

1983 *Historical Capitalism* (London)

1984 'Long waves as capitalist process' *Review* 7, 559–76

Walter, F. 1990 *Les suisses et l'environnement: une histoire du rapport à la nature du 18e siècle à nos jours* (Geneva)

Walton, J. K. 1987 *Lancashire: a Social History, 1558–1939* (Manchester)

Ward, D. (ed.) 1979 *Geographic Perspectives on America's Past: Readings on the Historical Geography of the United States* (New York)

Watson, J. W. 1965 'Canadian regionalism in life and letters' *Geographical Journal* 131, 21–33

1969 'Role of illusion in North American geography: a note on the geography of North American settlement' *Canadian Geographer* 13, 10–27

1983 'The soul of geography' *Transactions of the Institute of British Geographers* 8, 385–99

Watts, D. 1987 *The West Indies: Patterns of Development, Culture and Environmental Change since 1492* (Cambridge)

Webb, W. P. 1931 *The Great Plains* (Boston)

1960 'Geographical-historical concepts in American history' *Annals of the Association of American Geographers* 50, 85–93

Weber, E. 1977 *Peasants into Frenchmen: the Modernisation of Rural France 1870–1914* (London)

Weimin Que 1995 'Historical geography in China' *Journal of Historical Geography* 21, 361–70

2000 *Ideas of Historical Geography: Representation, Reconstruction, Imagination* (Hangzhou)

Westcoat, J. L. Jr 1994 'The scale(s) of dynastic representation: monumental tomb-gardens in Mughal Lahore' *Ecumene* 1, 324–48

Wheatley, P. 1971 *The Pivot of the Four Quarters: a Preliminary Enquiry into the Origins and Character of the Ancient Chinese City* (Edinburgh)

White, P. 1984 'Simenon, Maigret and the social geography of Paris' *Don* 22, 8–14

White, R. 1985 'American environmental history: the development of a new historical field' *Pacific Historical Review* 54, 297–335

Whitehead, N. L. 1998 'Ecological history and historical ecology: diachronic modelling versus historical explanation' in W. Balée (ed.) *Advances in Historical Ecology* (New York) 30–41

Whitney, G. G. 1994 *From Coastal Wilderness to Forested Plain: a History of Environmental Change in Temperate North America, 1500 to the Present* (Cambridge)

Whittlesey, D. 1929 'Sequent occupance' *Annals of the Association of American Geographers* 19, 162–5

1945 'The horizon of geography' *Annals of the Association of American Geographers* 35, 1–36

1954 'The regional concept and the regional method' in P. James and C. F. Jones (eds.) *American Geography: Inventory and Prospect* (Syracuse) 19–68

Whyte, I. D. and Whyte, K. 1991 *The Changing Scottish Landscape 1500–1800* (London)

Williams, M. 1970 *The Draining of the Somerset Levels* (Cambridge)

1974 *The Making of the South Australian Landscape: a Study in the Historical Geography of Australia* (London)

1983 '"The apple of my eye": Carl Sauer and historical geography' *Journal of Historical Geography* 9, 1–28

1987 'Sauer and "Man's Role in Changing the Face of the Earth"' *Geographical Review* 77, 218–31

1989a 'Deforestation: past and present' *Progress in Human Geography* 13, 176–208

1989b *Americans and their Forests: a Historical Geography* (Cambridge)

1989c 'Historical geography and the concept of landscape' *Journal of Historical Geography* 15, 92–104

1994 'The relations of environmental history and historical geography' *Journal of Historical Geography* 20, 3–21

1998 '"The end of modern history"?' *Geographical Review* 88, 275–300

Williams, R. 1973 *The Country and the City* (Cambridge)

Winearls, J. (ed.) 1995 *Editing Early and Historical Atlases* (Toronto)

Withers, C. W. J. 2001 *Geography, Science and National Identity: Scotland since 1520* (Cambridge)

Woodell, S. R. J. (ed.) 1985 *The English Landscape: Past, Present and Future* (Oxford)

Wooldridge, S. W. 1936 'The Anglo-Saxon settlement' in H. C. Darby (ed.) *An Historical Geography of England before AD 1800* (Cambridge) 88–132

Worster, D. 1977 *Nature's Economy: a History of Ecological Ideas* (Cambridge)

1979 *Dust Bowl: the Southern Plains in the 1930s* (New York)

1984 'History as natural history: an essay on theory and method' *Pacific Historical Review* 53, 1–19

1985 *Rivers of Empire: Water, Aridity and the Growth of the American West* (New York)

1988a 'Doing environmental history' in D. Worster (ed.) *The Ends of the Earth: Perspectives on Modern Environmental History* (Cambridge) 289–307

1988b (ed.) *The Ends of the Earth: Perspectives on Modern Environmental History* (Cambridge)

Wright, J. B. 1993 *Rocky Mountain Divide: Selling and Saving the West* (Austin, Tex.)

Wright, J. K. 1943 'Where history and geography meet' *Proceedings of the Eighth American Scientific Congress* 9, 17–23; reprinted in J. K. Wright 1966 *Human Nature in Geography* (Cambridge, Mass.) 24–32

1947 *Terrae incognitae:* the place of the imagination in geography' *Annals of the Association of American Geographers* 37, 1–15

Wright, P. 1985 *On Living in an Old Country: the National Past in Contemporary Britain* (London)

Wrigley, E. A. 1965 'Changes in the philosophy of geography' in R. J. Chorley and P. Haggett (eds.) *Frontiers in Geographical Teaching* (London) 3–20

Wrigley, E. A. and Schofield, R. S. 1981 *The Population History of England 1541–1871: a Reconstruction* (Cambridge)

Wyckoff, W. and Dilsaver, L. M. (eds.) 1995 *The Mountainous West: Explorations in Historical Geography* (Lincoln, Nebr.)

Wynn, G. 1981 *Timber Colony: a Historical Geography of Early Nineteenth Century New Brunswick* (Toronto)

1990 (ed.) *People, Places, Patterns, Processes: Geographical Perspectives on the Canadian Past* (Toronto)

1993 'Geographical writing on the Canadian past' in M. Conzen, T. A. Rumney and G. Wynn (eds.) *A Scholar's Guide to Geographical Writing on the American and Canadian Past*, University of Chicago Geography Research Paper no. 235 (Chicago) 91–124

1998 *Remaking the Land God Gave to Cain: a Brief Environmental History of Canada*, Canada House Lecture Series 62 (London)

Xiaofeng Tang 2000 *From Dynastic Geography to Historical Geography* (Beijing)

Yeoh, B. 2000 'Historical geographies of the colonised world' in B. Graham and C. Nash (eds.) *Modern Historical Geographies* (Harlow) 146–66

Zelinsky, W. 1973 *The Cultural Geography of the United States* (Englewood Cliffs, N.J.)

1986 'The changing face of nationalism in the American landscape' *Canadian Geographer* 30, 171–5

1988 *Nation into State: the Shifting Symbolic Foundations of American Nationalism* (Chapel Hill, N.C.)

1990 'The imprint of central authority' in M. Conzen (ed.) *The Making of the American Landscape* (London) 310–34

Zhang Butian 1993 *An Introduction to Historical Geography* (Henan)

Index

Cambridge Studies in Historical Geography

*Titles marked with an asterisk * are available in paperback.*